Experimental Behaviour

*a basis for the
study of mental disturbance*

Experimental Behaviour

A Basis for the Study of Mental Disturbance

Papers presented at a symposium in Ireland
at Galway April 1972
edited by
JOHN H. CULLEN

A HALSTED PRESS BOOK

John Wiley & Sons

NEW YORK — TORONTO

First published 1974 by Irish University Press
81 Merrion Square Dublin Ireland

Published in the U.S.A. and Canada by Halsted Press,
a Division of John Wiley & Sons, Inc., New York

Library of Congress catalog no. 73–8497

ISBN 0 470–18932–0

Printed in the Republic of Ireland

CONTENTS

LIST OF PARTICIPANTS

* Professor Albert Bandura, Stanford University, California

Dr. Nigel Bark, St. Patrick's Hospital, Dublin

** Professor Peter G. S. Beckett, St. Patrick's Hospital, Dublin

* Professor Henry B. Biller, University of Rhode Island

* Professor Joseph V. Brady, Johns Hopkins University School of Medicine

Dr. Thomas Brennan, Eastern Health Board, Dublin

** Professor Ivor W. Browne, Chief Psychiatrist, Eastern Health Board, Dublin

** Dr. Fergus Campbell, Department of Health, Dublin

* Dr. Ron Carino, State University of New York

* Professor Colin Cherry, Imperial College of Science and Technology, London

Dr. Henry Crawley, St. Brendan's Hospital, Dublin

** Dr. John Cullen, Department of Psychiatry, University College, Dublin

Dr. Patrick Cullen, St. John of God Hospital, Dublin

Dr. Liam Daly, Central Mental Hospital, Dublin

Professor Robert Daly, Department of Psychiatry, University College, Cork

* Mr. Roger Ewbank, University of Liverpool

* Professor Kenneth D. Feigenbaum, Antioch College, Columbia

Dr. Joseph A. Fernandez, St. Brendan's Hospital, Dublin

Professor Derek Forrest, Department of Psychology, Trinity College, Dublin

* Professor M. W. Fox, Washington University

Dr. Vincent T. Greene, St. Brendan's Hospital, Dublin

Professor John N. R. Grainger, Department of Zoology, Trinity College, Dublin

* Professor Harry F. Harlow, University of Wisconsin

* Dr. David Hathway, Huntingdon Research Centre, England

Dr. Nuala Healy, Mater Misericordiae Hospital, Dublin

Professor W. J. E. Jessop, Honorary Secretary, Medical Research Council of Ireland

 * Dr. Aubrey Kagan, World Health Organisation, Geneva
 * Dr. Eileen Kane, University of Pittsburg
 * Dr. Augustus F. Kinzel, New York State Psychiatric Institute
 * Professor Bibb Latané, Ohio State University
** Professor Sean M. Lavelle, Department of Experimental Medicine, University College, Galway
 * Professor Seymour Levine, Stanford University Medical Centre
 * Dr. Stuart A. Lewis, University of Edinburgh
 * Professor Robert J. Lifton, Yale University
** Professor Thomas Lynch, St. Brendan's Hospital, Dublin
 * Dr. Jules H. Masserman, President, International Association of Social Psychiatry
 * Dr. Richard P. Michael, Bethlem Royal Hospital, Kent
 * Professor G. Mitchell, University of California
    Dr. Patrick Murray, Lota Hospital, Cork
** Dr. Sean D. McGrath, St. John of God Hospital, Dublin
 * Professor Martin McHugh, Department of Psychology, University College, Galway
    Professor John McKenna, St. John of God Hospital, Dublin
    Mr. James McLoone, Woodlands Psychological Service, Galway
    Dr. Paul McQuaid, Mater Misericordiae Hospital, Dublin
 * Dr. Grant Noble, University of Leicester
    Rev. Professor E. F. O'Doherty, Department of Psychology, University College, Dublin
    Professor Eoin O'Malley, Chairman, Medical Research Council of Ireland
    Dr. Carl O'Sullivan, St. Patrick's Hospital, Dublin
 * Dr. Richard H. Porter, University of Leicester
 * Professor David Premack, University of California
    Dr. B. McN Ramsey, Department of Health, Dublin
 * Professor Derek Russell Davis, University of Bristol
 * Professor Gene P. Sackett, University of Washington
 * Dr. George D. Scott, Institute of Psychotherapy, Kingston, Ontario
** Dr. John J. Stack, Child Guidance Clinic, Dublin
    Dr. Noel Walsh, St. Vincent's Hospital, Dublin
    Dr. Marcus Webb, St. Patrick's Hospital, Dublin

       * Invited speakers
      ** Members of the Mental Health Committee

PREFACE

Over the past two decades or so there has been a vast expansion of research and theory-formation in the behavioural sciences. The literature is daunting in its volume, its increasing precision, and in its neologisms. Nevertheless, the experimental analysis of behaviour has generated new concepts in psychopathology which are displacing or, perhaps in some instances, refining, the theoretical constructs of the 'depth psychologists'. Most of this work has been with animals either in the field or in the laboratory. It has looked at a range of living creatures extending from protozoa to primates. It has grown in stature as a science, refining its methods and its self-critique. Above all, it has shown the immense complexities of the determinants of behaviour even in the lowest forms of life. Extrapolations to man have been few enough and frequently the attempt has been naïve and imprecise. The difficulties are formidable. Ethical considerations, cross-cultural variation and the extended duration of development and dependency in the human present the researcher into human behaviour with problems which will only be solved by multi-disciplinary teams, patient longitudinal or prospective studies, and humble beginnings. Humility is, perhaps, the greatest contribution the scientist studying man's behaviour and its aberrations can draw from the work of the ethologists and behavioural scientists.

Studies of human behaviour at a scientific level frequently rely on hypotheses derived from studies of animal behaviour. The study of the behaviour of animals from the ontogenetic and phylogenetic points of view has now become a well established science in its own right. While it is true that extrapolations from these studies to the human must remain hypothetical until the usual scientific criteria are met, they are none the less valid and useful within these limits. It is also a fact that the scientific bases of many of the growing points of psychiatry are to be found in animal studies. For example, in psychopharmacology, chemical and biological methods are now almost invariably linked with behavioural ones using measures of alteration in instinctive patterns of behaviour or in behaviours induced in animal subjects under precisely controlled learning situations. Higher integrative functions in the central nervous system and cortico-hypothalamic links with the endocrine control systems are being worked out, in collaborative studies on animals, between physiologists and behavioural scientists. These often involve complex analyses of behaviour as correlates in the experimental situation. Aerospace medicine, too, has used animal behaviour studies. It is obvious that ethical considerations demand long and painstaking animal studies of this kind which could not be undertaken with humans. Extrapolations to the human clinical situation are, of course, subject to the necessary strictures but they are inevitable for this has been the historical pattern in all of modern medicine.

A major area where animal studies by behavioural scientists are proving of immense value is in the elucidation of the interweavings of heredity, maturation and learning in the developing organism, where a mass of insights and hypothesis await validation for the human, both in the clinic and in the experimental laboratory. Many other examples could be given as animal studies have at least the advantage of providing an outline framework in which the parameters for study of human behaviour can be conceived, e.g., the interplay of instinct, drive and learned behaviour. Animal studies can provide the most appropriate basic concepts about elementary social groupings, e.g., the biological drive influences in sexual behaviour. Researches with animals allow of more ethically acceptable and experimentally manageable studies in ecology and in organism–environment interaction, e.g., the psychobiological effects of crowding or population density. This book discusses many facets of these problems.

All in all, the behavioural scientists in these fields are at least asking many of the important questions in a more precise way, and the future clinician or medical scientist will have to be equipped to assess critically the merits of these studies. It is certain that, whatever his special field, more and more he will need these studies as the present technological fragmentation of medicine evolves towards a true holistic human biology based on experiment and clinical study. The clinician in psychiatry, in particular, has a grave difficulty in deriving precise and quantifiable descriptions of the behaviours of his patients. His traditional nosology is a mixture of terms and concepts derived from sources widely distributed in their origins and in their intent. Experimental psychology is providing access to some degree of precision for measuring changes in some of the relevant processes in cognition, emotion and other parameters, but we are still, for instance, far from anything like a true scientific base in psychopharmacology or psychoendocrinology in man. When descriptions of the whole human in his environment are required we are in an even worse situation. It is, perhaps, from the students of animal behaviour and the ethologists that the most immediate help will come in answer to these problems.

The symposium, sponsored by the Medical Research Council of Ireland, was designed to contribute towards a number of aims. It was felt that the bringing together of eminent representatives of work in different fields with a request to address themselves to topics almost eccentric in their novelty or intent but with a bias towards real-life problems, could provide a fresh opportunity for them to suspend territorial behaviour for a short period of useful interaction. It was hoped that the participation of Irish clinicians and scientists would provide for the former an increased awareness of the theoretical and biological underpinnings of their approach to patients and for the latter an opportunity to consider the scant provision for formal representation of these studies in institutes of higher education in Ireland. Lastly, it was hoped that it would inspire a serious sense of challenge which would help to generate an interest in research in these and related mental health fields in this country.

It is far too early for any judgement to be made as to how well our aims and hopes have been realized. Many years of work will be required before even a small number of the creative ideas which were expressed at the symposium can be explored and validated experimentally. Clinicians, too, have a long and difficult task before them. Firstly, there is the need to assimilate these insights into the intricacies of the genesis of behaviour in man and in animals. Secondly, there is the challenge to increase their precision in describing behaviour and behavioural change. However, we feel that if the enthusiasm and unselfish effort shown by all who came is maintained then a good beginning has been made. For this we are most grateful to those who read papers or otherwise participated in the proceedings. My own thanks are especially due to my colleagues on the Editorial Committee, Prof. Jessop, Prof. Lavelle and Commander Furniss.

JOHN H. CULLEN

ACKNOWLEDGEMENTS

The Medical Research Council of Ireland has very great pleasure in recording its gratitude to the then Tánaiste and Minister for Health, Mr Erskine Childers, now President of Ireland, for his encouragement and financial help. We are sincerely grateful to Mr Bernard McDonagh of West Virginia, U.S.A., for his most generous donation of the major portion of the funds for the Symposium. Our thanks are also due to Hygeia Ltd., Galway and to Bord Fáilte for their contributions to the hospitality enjoyed by the participants. Finally, on behalf of all the participants we thank the President and Governing Body of University College, Galway for their hospitality, the help of their efficient and courteous staff members and for the use of College equipment.

Effects of impoverished early environment

Maternal influences on adaptive function[1]

SEYMOUR LEVINE[2]

Department of Psychiatry, Stanford University
School of Medicine, California

In 1956 two papers were published (Levine; Levine, Chevalier and Korchin) which demonstrated a very profound influence of manipulation of the neonatal environment on the adult behaviour of the rat. Although there had been an extensive literature (Bowlby, 1951) indicating that manipulations of mother/infant environment lead to profound and permanent changes in the behaviour of the newborn, these data were mostly based on clinical observations. The experimental investigations of the influence of a multitude of environmental parameters on a multitude of functions are approximately fifteen years old. Yet during that fifteen years there has been an explosion of information so that it is impossible to review comprehensively. At least four major volumes have appeared containing information related to the influence of the neonatal environment on growth, development and behaviour (Ambrose, 1969; Bliss, 1962; Denenberg, 1972; Newton and Levine, 1968).

The task assigned to me in this symposium is to discuss the effects of impoverished early environments. Impoverished early environ-

[1]This study was supported by research grant NICH&HD 02881 from the National Institute of Health and the Leslie Fund, Chicago.
[2]Supported by USPHS Research Scientist Award L–K05–MH–19936 from the National Institute of Mental Health.

17

B

ments involve both object deprivation and maternal deprivation. For the most part the major variable which has been examined extensively has been maternal deprivation, for obvious reasons. There are members of this symposium who have had far more extensive experience and whose own research is clearly directed toward this problem. Thus, I have chosen to pursue this subject in a different way; namely, what is the influence of the mother and what alterations in the mother/infant interactional system lead to changes in both the developing and the adult organism? We will focus predominantly on our own research which has used the rat and the mouse as primary experimental subjects and has utilized both behavioural and physiological responses as indices of the effects of variations in both prenatal and postnatal environments.

Although the early experimental research in these fields has been concentrated on various kinds of extra-stimulation procedures to which the newborn were subjected, there has been an increasing attention focused upon the hypothesis that the influence of all of these parameters may not be directly on the offspring but mediated via some alteration in the mother/infant interactions.

Denenberg and Whimbey (1963) reported that in rats, the offspring of mothers that had been handled in infancy were heavier at weaning as compared to young rats of mothers that had not been handled. Further, the experience of the mother during her infancy resulted in differential open field behaviour of the infant rats when they reached adulthood. It has been reported (Levine, 1967) that the offspring of mothers which had been handled in infancy show a reduced plasma steroid response to novel stimuli when compared to weanling rats of nonhandled mothers. However, if the offspring themselves are handled, these differences are abolished (Table 1). The procedure for exposing the rat to novelty used in this and other studies to be discussed on weanling rats involved placing the animals in small compartments 3·8 cm high, 6·82 cm wide, and 13·64 cm long. The animals were retained for fifteen minutes, at which time they were decapitated and a blood sample was obtained. Control blood samples were obtained by rapidly decapitating animals quickly removed from their home cage.

These data can be interpreted in either of two ways: first, direct stimulation of the infant rat is so profound that it overrides the maternal influence; or second, handling the infant alters maternal physiological and behavioural responses, and disturbance of the

TABLE 1

Plasma corticosterone concentration (mean and standard error of the mean) for the different groups. The number of animals per mean is given in parentheses

Abbreviations: M, mother; P, pups; N, nonhandled; H, handled

Infant experience		Plasma corticosterone (μg/100 ml)	
M	P	Control	Experimental
N	N	$21 \cdot 1 \pm 2 \cdot 28$ (8)	$45 \cdot 67 \pm 2 \cdot 32$ (8)
N	H	$11 \cdot 39 \pm 0 \cdot 96$ (8)	$34 \cdot 34 \pm 3 \cdot 27$ (8)
H	N	$12 \cdot 84 \pm 1 \cdot 22$ (9)	$25 \cdot 31 \pm 3 \cdot 24$ (9)
H	H	$19 \cdot 23 \pm 1 \cdot 88$ (9)	$28 \cdot 68 \pm 3 \cdot 29$ (9)

mother, as a function of handling, tends to counteract the influence of the experience of the mother during her infancy. For the present we favour the second of these interpretations. This is not to indicate that handling per se cannot have a direct effect on the offspring at the time of handling. We do suggest, however, that one of the major effects of infantile handling results from some alteration in the maternal/infant relationship.

In view of the data which has implicated maternal influences on subsequent adrenocortical activity, it was decided to investigate whether directly exposing the lactating female to a stressful experience also resulted in modification of the response to stress of the offspring at weaning. In this experiment, lactating females were subjected to ether exposure at three, six or nine days postpartum. An additional group of females was subjected to electric shock at three days following birth. The offspring of these females were not disturbed during this period. Figure 1 presents the steroid data for the twenty-four-day old offspring of females stressed while nursing. It can be seen that all of the offspring of stressed females showed significantly higher levels of corticosterone following exposure to novel stimuli when compared to nontreated controls. In addition, the basal levels of offspring treated at the age of three days, either with ether or with electric shock, were also significantly higher that the basal values of control offspring (Levine & Thoman, 1969).

The endocrinological literature (Zarrow, 1961) has claimed that adrenalectomizing the mother during pregnancy results in the failure to carry offspring. Further, that offspring of adrenalectomized lactating females fail to survive principally because lactation is disrupted.

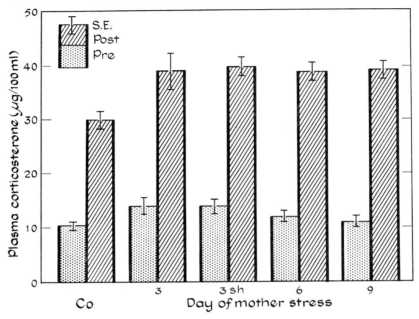

Fig. 1. Mean basal and stress plasma corticosterone levels of 24-day offspring of stressed and nonstressed mothers. Bars represent the mean of the group; vertical line bars represent the standard error of the mean. Sh=shock; all other experimental groups were ether-stressed. N in each group=14 or greater.

The present experiments were initiated in an attempt to demonstrate the effects of adrenalectomy on both the disruption of pregnancy and lactation. However, much to our surprise, the females that had been adrenalectomized prior to mating, both carried their offspring to term and maintained them through weaning (Thoman, Sproul, Seeler and Levine, 1970).

The principal difference between the procedure used in these studies and the procedure used in prior experiments involving maternal adrenalectomy is that the mother was adrenalectomized prior to mating, whereas in other studies the adrenalectomy occurred either during the pregnancy or postnatally. Inasmuch as the offspring were carried to term, successfully delivered, and survived through weaning, these offspring of adrenalectomized mothers were studied at weaning, at which time they were exposed to novelty. Infant rats aged twenty-one days and thirty-one days were exposed to novel stimuli as previously described. The results (Fig. 2) indicate that the offspring of adrenalectomized mothers have significantly higher concentrations of plasma corticosterone following exposure to novelty. In addition, these animals also tend to have significantly

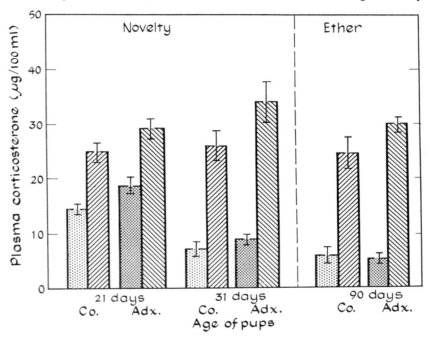

Fig. 2. Basal and stress plasma corticosterone concentrations of offspring of control and adrenalectomized mothers at the ages of 21, 31 and 90 days. Bars represent the mean of the group; vertical line bars represent the standard error of the mean. N=at least 12 in each group.

higher basal levels than the appropriate controls. Although the off-spring of adrenalectomized mothers, both at weaning and at the age of thirty-one days, tend to be significantly lighter than control animals (Table 2), no significant correlation was obtained both at weaning and in adulthood between body weight and plasma corticosteroids.

TABLE 2

Weights of male and female offspring (mean and standard error of the mean) for the two groups

Number of animals per mean is given in parentheses

	21 days of age	
	Male S.E.	Female S.E.
Adrenalectomized	29·8 ± 1·44 (26)	25·6 − 0·67 (21)
Control	43·0 ± 1·57 (25)	41·0 − 1·38 (23)
	31 days of age	
	Male S.E.	Female S.E.
Adrenalectomized	67·5 ± 3·83 (13)	63·0 ± 2·85 (16)
Control	93·5 ± 2·02 (29)	85·9 ± 2·29 (22)

The results of these studies on basal and stress levels of plasma corticosterone bear a striking similarity to those presented for weanling rats of mothers which were stressed during the period of nursing.

It has been observed that the adrenal weights of offspring of adrenalectomized mothers are significantly heavier than those seen in control newborns (Knobil and Briggs, 1955). In contrast, if steroids are elevated by a variety of techniques (Milkovic and Milkovic, 1966), the adrenal weights of these offspring are significantly reduced. Although, in the studies reported in this paper on maternal adrenalectomy the adrenal function of the newborn was not observed, it can be assumed on the basis of other literature that adrenal activity in the newborn rat deprived of maternal steroids is significantly greater than that seen in normal newborn rats. It thus appears that if adrenal steroids are elevated during the early postnatal period this results in a differential setting of the regulatory mechanisms for neuroendocrine activity in both the weanling and the adult organism, leading to a subsequently greater release and perhaps synthesis of ACTH and a subsequent increase in the concentrations of plasma corticosterone. This is in contrast to that which had been postulated previously by Levine and Mullins (1966) and Zarrow and colleagues (1966), which states that increases in adrenal activity during infancy lead to a reduced steroid response later in life.

As an extension of the previous studies on offspring of females which were adrenalectomized prior to mating, additional observations were made on adult rats (ninety days) exposed to ether. The technique used in these studies was to take both basal and stress samples from the same animal; thus, the animals were rapidly anesthetized with ether and a sample withdrawn from the jugular vein. Fifteen minutes following the initial exposure to ether and venipuncture a second sample was taken, again under ether anesthesia. It has been demonstrated (Davidson, Jones and Levine, 1968) that the initial sample represents true basal levels. Fifteen minutes later the peak of plasma corticosterone concentrations occurs to this type of stress (see Fig. 2). The adult rats of adrenalectomized mothers showed a significantly higher concentration of plasma corticosterone following ether stress than controls. Again the prenatal and postnatal effects of maternal adrenalectomy have not been segregated in these studies. The use of maternal adrenalectomy, however, appears to be a most promising technique for investigating both the prenatal and postnatal role of maternal steroids on many aspects of the psychophysiological development of the offspring.

Recently a technique has been developed for the handrearing of newborn rats. Thus, rats can be separated immediately after birth and reared successfully through weaning by the use of a specific set of techniques which have been described in detail elsewhere (Thoman and Arnold, 1968). The technique involves rearing the animals in an incubator in which there is a warm, moist, pulsating tube which serves as a surrogate to provide warmth and stimulate defecation in the newborn rat. The animals are tube fed at four-hour intervals until they are capable of eating solid food. A group of these handreared animals was tested in adulthood for their adrenocortical response to ether stress as previously described.

It can be seen (Fig. 3) that handreared animals show a slight but significant elevation in basal levels and a significantly greater increase in plasma corticosterone concentrations following stress than do mother-reared animals. Although these data tend to implicate a maternal factor, it should be noted that this procedure is indeed a complicated one involving: (a) a large amount of stimulation through the process of hand feeding; and (b) different dietary

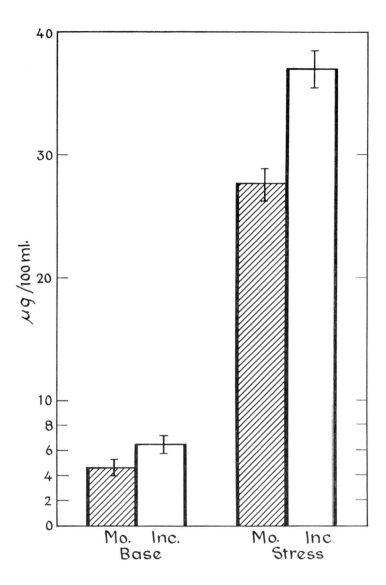

Fig. 3. Basal and stress plasma corticosterone levels of mother-reared and incubator-reared animals. Bars represent the mean of the group; vertical line bars represent the standard error of the mean. N=19 in each group.

conditions, in addition to many other conditions which differ from the normal rearing. Thus, it would be difficult at this time to specify that only removal from the mother leads to the differences observed in this experiment (Thoman, Levine and Arnold, 1968).

Levine and Treiman (1964), measuring circulating plasma corticosteroids following a brief exposure to electric shock, reported striking differences between four inbred strains of mice. The differences observed were both quantitative, in terms of the amount of circulating steroids following stress, and qualitative, in terms of the different time course of the stress response between different inbred strains. Following these initial observations, a subsequent study was performed to investigate the interaction between genotype and maternal environment as modifiers of the temporal pattern of plasma corticosteroid response to stress in two inbred strains of mice and their reciprocal crosses. The two strains, C57BL/10 and DBA/2, which had been shown to differ in their steroid response to electric shock, were crossed in all four possible combinations to provide a two-by-two diallel cross allowing genetic and maternal effects to be assessed.

The temporal pattern of steroid response to electric shock was determined using the procedure reported by Levine and Treiman (1964). Animals were tested under two conditions, control and electric shock. Control animals were removed from their cages and rapidly decapitated. Shocked animals were placed in a shock box and given 0·5 ma to the feet for one minute. They were then placed in a holding compartment and decapitated at one of three time intervals, following termination of shock, one minute, fifteen minutes and sixty minutes. Analysis of the data (Fig. 4) indicated that the maternal environment is clearly important as a modifier of the qualitative and quantitative aspects of the steroid response to electric shock. Thus, it can be seen from Fig. 4 that the C57BL/10 and C × D crosses showed identical patterns of steroidogenesis following stress and the DBA/2 and D × C crosses also showed identical patterns of elevations of plasma corticoids. Within this experiment, however, all animals were raised by their own parents so that one cannot isolate whether or not the effects are prenatal, postnatal, or an interaction of prenatal and postnatal events (Treiman, Fulker and Levine, 1970).

Although a number of hypotheses have been offered to account for the effects of infantile stimulation on later emotional behaviour

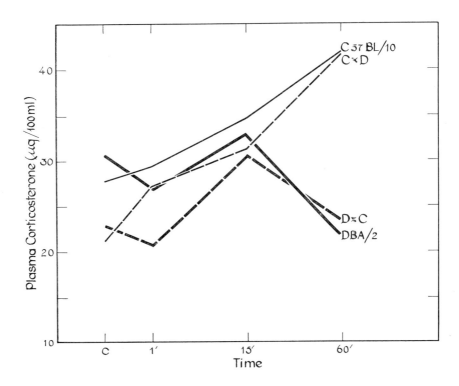

Fig. 4. Time course of plasma corticosterone concentrations following electric shock in two inbred strains of adult male mice and their reciprocal crosses. Each point represents mean value for four animals.

and physiological responses to stress (Bovard, 1958; Levine, Chevalier and Korchin, 1956; Levine and Mullins, 1966), thus far the most conclusive evidence implicating any single factor as a possible mediator of the effects of infantile stimulation has been reported by Schaefer and his associates.

Schaefer (1963) reports a number of experiments performed over several preceding years. Observing that most young mammals, especially rats, cannot regulate body temperature, Schaefer suggested that the infant rat rapidly loses body heat unless it is regulated by the mother. He hypothesized, therefore, that a drop in body temperature was the critical factor in mediating the effects of infantile stimulation. The crucial experiment reported by Schaefer to support his supposition consisted of handling young rats under conditions designed to maintain the normal body temperature. Rats handled under these conditions did not differ from nonhandled controls as measured by adrenal ascorbic acid depletion response to cold stress at the age of fourteen days. Infant rats handled at room temperature, however, did differ significantly from both the incubator handled heat controlled, and control animals. Although Schaefer does emphasise body temperature as the critical factor, his results could also be interpreted as indicating that cold offspring alter the behaviour of the mother and, thus, it is the disturbance in maternal-infant relationship which results in these differences, rather than any specific effect of body temperature. In order to test this latter hypothesis, the following experiment was conducted. Six groups of animals were treated differentially in infancy from days two to seven. The first group of animals was removed from the mother and placed on a warm surface designed to maintain their body temperature at the same level as that observed in the nest (between 34° and 36°C). The pups were maintained at this temperature for ten minutes. A second group was removed from the nest, maintained on the warm surface for five minutes, and for the remaining five minutes was permitted to cool. A third group of subjects was removed from the nest and handled in the usual procedure which does involve cooling for a five-minute period; however, for the remaining five minutes, these animals were placed on a warm surface and thus returned to the mother warm rather than cool. The fourth group of animals was handled by the usual method involving cooling for the full ten minutes. An additional group involved removing the mother and leaving the pups in the nest. All of these animals were compared with untreated controls. At the age of ninety days all subjects, male and female, were run on an open field test for four days. Fifteen minutes following the onset of the fourth open field session the animals were decapitated and plasma corticosteroids were determined by the method of Glick, von Redlich and Levine (1964). All plasma concentrations of corticosterone used throughout this experiment were determined by this method.

Although there were no apparent differences observed in the open field behaviour between any of the groups, there was a highly significant effect on concentrations of plasma corticosterone between the various groups (Fig. 5). All of the treated groups differed significantly from the untreated group and had significantly lower plasma corticosterone concentrations than the untreated group following the exposure to the open field. These data, therefore, implicate the mother as one of the determinants regulating the neuroendocrine activity concerning ACTH release following exposure to novel stimuli (Thoman and Levine, 1969).

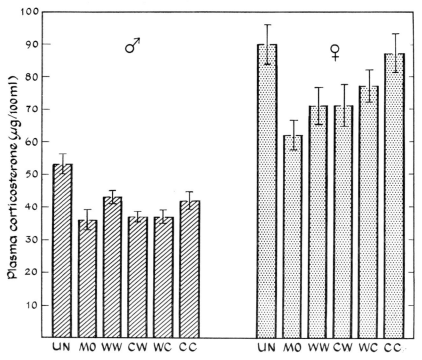

Fig. 5. Plasma corticosterone levels of all experimental groups 15 min. following the onset of the fourth open field session. Bars represent the mean of the group. Vertical line bars represent the standard error of the mean. W=warm; C=cool; UN=untreated; MO=mother removal; N=at least 12 in each group.

The data presented in this paper indicate that the nature of the mother/infant environment is an important determinant of subsequent neuroendocrine regulation of ACTH. The data presented, along with the extensive literature on maternal variables affecting behaviour, emphasize the total organismic effects of those events occurring during critical periods in development. In the mammal this critical period is intimately shared with the mother and it is not surprising, therefore, that maternal variables should affect many aspects of the total system's function. It is surprising, however, in view of the importance which has been placed on the maternal figure, that so little is known about maternal influences on the developing organism's subsequent physiological processes.

Although we have focused on the physiological events related to stress and on the neuroendocrine regulation of ACTH, it is important to point out that there is indeed a variety of behavioural effects which have been clearly demonstrated as a consequence of maternal factors. Further, the investigations of neuroendocrine activity also have important behavioural implications. Numerous studies have been reported which clearly indicate that alterations in those hormones emanating from the pituitary-adrenal system have profound effects on adaptive behaviour (Levine, 1971).

References

Ambrose, A., ed. 1969. *Stimulation in Early Infancy*. London: Academic Press.

Bliss, E. I., ed. 1962. *Roots of Behavior*. New York: Harper & Brothers.

Bovard, E. W. 1958. *Psychol. Rev.*, 65: 257-71.

Bowlby, J. 1951. *Maternal Care and Mental Health*. Geneva: World Health Organization, Monograph Series No. 2.

Davidson, J. M.; Jones, L. E.; and Levine, S. 1968. *Endocrinology*, 82: 655-63.

Denenberg, V. H., ed. 1972. *The Development of Behavior*. Stamford, Conn.: Sinauer Assoc.

Denenberg, V. H., and Whimbey, A. E. 1963. *Science*, 142: 1192-93.

Glick, D.; von Redlich, D.; and Levine, S. 1964. *Endocrinology*, 74: 653-55.

Knobil, E., and Briggs, F. N. 1955. *Endocrinology*, 57: 147-52.

Levine, S. 1956. *J. Personality*, 25: 70-80.

Levine, S. 1967. *Science*, 156: 258-60.

Levine, S. 1971. *Sci. Amer.*, 224: 26-31.

Levine, S.; Chevalier, J. A.; and Korchin, S. J. 1956. *J. Personality*, 24: 475-93.

Levine, S., and Mullins, R. F., Jr. 1966. *Science*, 152: 1585-92.

Levine, S., and Thoman, E. B. 1969. *Physiol. Behav.*, 4: 139-42.

Levine, S., and Treiman, D. M. 1964. *Endocrinology*, 75: 142-44.

Milkovic, K., and Milkovic, S. 1966. In *Neuroendocrinology*, eds. L. Martini and W. F. Ganong, pp. 371-405. New York: Academic.

Newton, G., and Levine, S., eds. 1968. *Early Experience and Behavior, The Psychobiology of Development*. Springfield: C. C. Thomas.

Schaefer, T., Jr. 1963. *Trans. N.Y. Acad. Sci.*, 25: 871-89.

Thoman, E. B., and Arnold, W. J. 1968. *J. comp. physiol. Psychol.,* 65: 441-46.

Thoman, E. B., and Levine, S. 1969. *Physiol. Behav.,* 4: 143-45.

Thoman, E. B.; Levine, S.; and Arnold, W. J. 1968. *Developmental Psychobiol.,* 1: 21-23.

Thoman, E. B.; Sproul, M.; Seeler, B.; and Levine, S. 1970. *J Endocrinology,* 46: 297-303.

Treiman, D. M.; Fulker, D. W.; and Levine, S. 1970. *Developmental Psychobiol.,* 3: 131-40.

Zarrow, M. X. 1961. In *Sex and Internal Secretions,* ed. W. C. Young, pp. 958-1031. Baltimore: Williams & Wilkins.

Zarrow, M. X.; Haltmeyer, G. C.; Denenberg, V. H.; and Thatcher, J. 1966. *Endocrinology,* 79: 631-34.

Discussion

after the opening paper entitled — Effects of impoverished early environment by S. Levine

Prof. Sackett : The thing that has always puzzled me is the assumption that for rats a laboratory is by definition an impoverished environment and therefore must produce a deprived rat. When these rats escape, which they do every once in a while, they manage to survive fantastically well. I have seen situations where they escape out into the neighbourhood. You have got to get exterminators to exterminate them and you are lucky if you can ever exterminate them. They live in the walls of university buildings for years, they find things to eat and they reproduce. If you use a basic survival criterion, then laboratory rats are certainly apt animals, whether they are branded normal or abnormal by some person.

Prof. Levine : But I can argue that your animals that escape are a biased population. It might not be true but I can say it. I really do not have any systematic data. It would indeed be rather interesting to see if one could in fact provide a behavioural model. The only experiment I have seen was by Denenberg. What he did was take these animals and put them in an enriched environment and found that a handled animal tended to interact to its environment, whereas a non-handled animal tended to show avoidance.

Prof. Sackett : I wonder what would happen if handled or non-handled animals were placed with a cat?

Prof. Levine: I can tell you what would happen based on very good predictions. The chances are that the handled animal would survive and one of the characteristics of the handled animal is that it is apparently capable of making more relevant discriminations about its environment and could avoid much better what it had to avoid. There is a very nice experiment which I have just read in which what they did was this—provided the handled and non-handled animals with choices. They had a maze in which one end was an open field and at the other end was food. If the handled animal was non-deprived, he spent more time in the open field than the non-handled animal, but when he was deprived he would spend more time with the food than the non-handled animal did. We have other data which indicates that if you have the handled animal in a novel environment it responds less, but if you give the handled an acute stress it actually responds more, that is what is meant by adaptation—the capacity to respond to the relevant aspects of the environment with the relevant responses. This may be a question you will want to address yourself to with the preparation of the kind of animal you are dealing with—its capacity to respond less or more to any environmental change.

Prof. Fox: You did not mention anything about the handled or stress phenomenon being time limited or restricted to a sensitive period?

Prof. Levine: No, I have not. There are sensitive periods very clearly. As far as we can best determine the sensitive period of the rat is about the first seven days; pre-natally I do not know. If you look at the development of the adrenal, prenatally what you see in the rat is a long period of quiescence during which the glands are not active. At seventeen days it starts kicking off very actively. Until one or two days postnatally it is very active, then it drops off very rapidly. During that time you get a very active endocrinological system working. It is the same in the gonads which first gave us the hypothesis that the adrenals were acting to programme the central nervous system much in the same way as the gonads were. We have yet been unable to prove this experimentally.

Dr. Porter: One typically finds induced abortion as a function of prenatal stress administered early in pregnancy. I would be interested in any behavioural syndromes in later life resulting from such early prenatal stress in those offspring that survive such traumata.

Prof. Levine : I do not know. We tried this in another way but unfortunately all we did was terminate pregnancy. We tried to block adrenal cortical hormones by placing hormones directly into the brain. Unfortunately, at any point during pregrancy this produced spontaneous abortion. Most stresses occur late in pregnancy and I should not think that the early stress would have much effect because foetal development is so primitive.

Prof. Biller : You mentioned some studies where mothers had the adrenal cortex removed—

Prof. Levine : Prior to conception.

Prof. Biller : But they are still able to have normal sexual functioning?

Prof. Levine : They are able to conceive, they are able to deliver, they are able to maintain their young. They are not able to lactate very well, so we cross-foster them as a general rule. What happens to the foetus is what is important. In some recent work we have found that the foetus of adrenalectomized mothers not only produces more of its own endogenous hormone but the system seems to become active earlier in development. What does appear to be reliable is that the adrenalectomized mother causes behavioural changes in the offspring when they reach adulthood. They learn an avoidance response better and appear to be emotionally stable in the open field.

Prof. Latane : I am interested in your experiments on the offspring of reciprocal cross-matings of two strains of mice and your conclusions that differences in the offspring are due to maternal influences rather than being genetic in nature. Is it not possible that the effects are indeed genetic, but are transmitted through sex-linked genes?

Prof. Levine : The data on reciprocal processes appears predominantly to indicate a pre-natal maternal factor. Ginsburg has produced data which has shown pre-natal effects by transplanting ova of a pure bred mouse into a hybrid mother which changes the phenotype towards the maternal host.

Syndromes resulting from object deprivation — 1

Environmental restrictions on chickens

RICHARD H. PORTER

Department of Psychology, University of Leicester

INTRODUCTION

A number of recent studies have been concerned with the effects of early stimulus deprivation or isolation upon the behavioural development of precocial birds. Precocial avian species (e.g. ducks, chicks, and quail) are ideally suited for deprivation experiments of various kinds since they can be raised singly with no maternal care necessary for their survival and physiological development. Also, simple behavioural responses can be measured in such species beginning at several days prior to hatching (cf. Gottlieb, 1971).

The present paper is a brief review of some of the behavioural syndromes resulting from rearing in a restricted environment shown by the domestic chicken (Gallus domesticus) and its wild relative the Red Junglefowl (Gallus gallus spadiceus).

1. Attachment Behaviour

Various manifestations of attachment behaviour have been the most common dependant variables in studies investigating the effects of early social and stimulus deprivation upon chicks.

C

A frequently reported syndrome resulting from rearing in a restricted environment is prolonged responsiveness to novel moving stimuli (see Sluckin, 1964 or Smith, 1969 for reviews. Sluckin and Salzen (1961), for example, found that while some isolate chicks would actively follow a moving box at five days of age, no socially reared chicks displayed such positive responsiveness to this novel stimulus. Further, three chicks that had been isolated for six days showed strong following within the first three minutes of exposure to a moving box. Bateson (1964a) reports that when tested for twenty minutes on the third day of life, the majority of isolated chicks displayed an initial avoidance of a novel moving object. A number of chicks eventually ceased avoiding the model, however, and of these, the majority subsequently began to follow the previously avoided model. Even when isolated from the first day of life and given only several hours of exposure to a moving object on days fifteen and twenty-two, three out of four chicks were found to prefer the training stimulus to a novel stimulus during a discrimination test on day twenty-two (Sluckin, 1962).

According to Guiton (1958, 1959) although the following responses of isolated chicks does eventually decline with age, such socially deprived chicks will continue to be responsive towards a novel moving object at a later age than will socially reared chicks. When first presented with a novel moving stimulus in tests on days four and five of age, socially reared chicks displayed persistent 'searching' behaviour and distress calling, which was assumed to be due to separation from their companions rather than to the presence of the novel moving stimulus. Isolate chicks, on the other hand, were much more reactive to the novel stimulus, either showing strong avoidance responses or approaching and following the object. These behavioural differences between the isolate versus socially reared chicks appear to have been a result of the socially reared birds having become imprinted onto one-another (Guiton, 1959).

In a related study, Salzen (1962) found that the fear responses normally shown by socially housed chicks when put into a strange environment could be alleviated by introducing other chicks into the test situation. Chicks that had been reared in isolation prior to testing did not display comparably reduced fear responses when tested with conspecifics present in the strange environment. Salzen concluded that whilst the presence of the other chicks would have conformed to the previous experience of the socially reared chicks, neither the strange environment *nor* the stimulus chicks conformed to the previously established 'neuronal model' of the isolates. Thus, the unfamiliarity of the test situation, as reflected in the behavioural results, would have been greater for the chicks reared in isolation.

Baron and Kish (1960) compared the behaviour of isolates, paired and flock reared chicks at four weeks of age. Their results indicate that chicks from the two social rearing conditions spent more time near stimulus chicks of the same age than did the isolates. Despite this difference between the rearing conditions, during the second hour in the test situation, the isolate chicks spent about 50% of their time near the stimulus birds. When subsequently tested at ten weeks of age, after five weeks of social rearing, no significant differences were found to exist between the groups. Thus, social experiences beginning as late as five weeks of age were found to obliterate the retarding influence of early social isolation upon flocking behaviour.

The activity level of chicks reared in isolation over the first seven days post-hatch has been investigated by Bateson (1964b). Throughout the seven day isolation period, chicks that were individually housed in *grey* painted boxes were found to be more active than chicks isolated in boxes painted with vertical black-and-white stripes. It was concluded (Bateson, 1969) that the chicks reared in the relatively conspicuous black-and-white environment were more likely to have become imprinted onto the static features of their cages than were the chicks reared in the less conspicuous grey cages. Although these data are open to alternative interpretations, it was suggested that the heightened level of activity in the grey reared chicks reflected an active searching for conspicuous stimuli by birds that had not yet been effectively imprinted.

My co-workers and I (Porter, Fullerton and Berryman, 1972) have recently completed a series of experiments in which a modified version of the visual cliff was used to test attachment strength in chicks. Since preliminary study indicated that chicks would not be harmed by a fall from the eighteen-inch high cliff, the deep side of the apparatus was not covered with glass—thereby being an actual cliff rather than a 'visual' cliff. This procedure was used because behaviour on a visual cliff might be influenced by visual or auditory reflections off the glass covering the cliff. A section of the wall at the far side of the cliff was cut out to allow for the insertion of a moving stimulus (i.e. a knotted piece of red yarn which pivoted up and down in a vertical plane).

Two groups of newly hatched chicks were tested for their responsiveness to the moving stimulus across the precipice of the cliff. One group of chicks had been removed from an unlit incubator and exposed to the stimulus in a runway for thirty minutes—one hour before the cliff test. Chicks in the second group had been removed from the incubator and isolated in a lighted unpainted cardboard box for one to two hours prior to testing. During individual five-minute tests, a large proportion of the chicks from both conditions descended the cliff, apparently in an attempt to reach the stimulus object.

TABLE 1

Responses of chicks tested on the Cliff

	Day 1			Day 2		
	Prior Exposure Stimulus present over Cliff	No Exposure Stimulus present over Cliff	No Exposure No Stimulus (Control)	Prior Exposure Stimulus present over Cliff	No Exposure Stimulus present over Cliff	No Exposure No Stimulus (Control)
Deep ..	19	14	2	13	2	0
Shallow ..	2	3	18	6	12	21
No Response	3	7	4	5	10	3
Totals ..	24	24	24	24	24	24

(Based upon Porter, Fullerton and Berryman—1972.)

This experiment was replicated with chicks that were removed from the incubator several hours after hatching, but tested on the cliff on the *second* day of life. All chicks were housed in individual unpainted cardboard boxes, with one group being individually exposed to the stimulus for thirty minutes on days one and two post-hatch, and the second receiving no such training exposure. When tested on the cliff in the presence of the stimulus, slightly more than half of the exposure trained chicks descended the cliff, while only two of the twenty-four isolates descended the cliff to approach the stimulus.

Most relevant for the present discussion was the finding that a large number of the naïve chicks tested on day one descended the cliff in an attempt to approach a moving stimulus to which they had *not* been previously exposed—and thereby had no opportunity to become imprinted onto it. In fact, there was no significant difference in the frequencies of cliff descents by chicks with previous exposure to the stimulus as compared to naïve chicks. This somewhat unexpected behaviour tends to emphasise the degree to which chicks housed in a restricted environment will seek the proximity of the first moving stimulus to which they are exposed during the sensitive period for the development of social attachments. Since individual chicks will expose themselves to great potential danger in an attempt to approach the first moving object with which they are confronted, the survival value to the species of such approach and proximity seeking behaviour must be very great indeed.

The reduced number of naïve isolate chicks descending the cliff to approach the stimulus on day two could possibly be a function of their having become attached to static features of their environment (as discussed below), or may simply reflect reduced responsiveness to novel stimuli as a function of maturational processes. Since only two of twenty-four control chicks went over the cliff in the absence of the stimulus on day one, and none of twenty-four on day two, it is unlikely that maturation of perceptual capacities or of a 'cliff-avoidance response' could account for the reduced cliff descents in the presence of the stimulus on day two.

As I have briefly mentioned above, isolate chicks appear to become attached to various features of their inanimate environment. At one day of age, isolates which are placed into a different box 'of exactly the same design' as their rearing box show more distress peeps than do chicks which are simply lifted up and replaced into their home cage (Fullerton, Berryman and Sluckin, 1970). Socially reared chicks, however, displayed a similar high rate of distress peeping when placed alone in a box of the same design as their rearing box, or when left in their home pen after the removal of the other chicks with which they had been housed. Andrew (1964) considers such vocalizations to be a function of persistent contrast between past and present sensory input. Therefore, even at one day of age, isolate chicks appear to be able to discriminate subtle differences between their home cage and a similar cage, and show behavioural indications of distress when their environmental attachments are disrupted. Salzen (1966) has reported that isolate chicks may become attached to the galvanized cans from which they drink. These chicks were frequently seen resting beside the drinking can and would retreat to it when disturbed and otherwise behave in a social manner towards it. Removal of the can would be followed by distress peeps until it was returned.

Several authors have investigated the effects of similarity between rearing environment and test stimulus upon subsequent responsiveness to that stimulus. In simultaneous choice tests, chicks are more likely to approach an object coloured the same as their isolation cage rather than a differentially coloured object (Taylor et al., 1969). Likewise, at three days of age, isolated chicks that were tested with a model patterned the same as their home pen avoided this model for a shorter period and showed positive responses towards it sooner than did chicks tested with a model dissimilar to their rearing pen (Bateson, 1964c).

2. Sexual and Aggressive Behaviour

Chicks as young as forty-eight hours have been observed to copulate with a moving object when exposed to rapid thrusts of that object before being allowed to mount (Andrew, 1966). Chicks that had been housed with other chicks over the first two days of life showed a higher percentage of copulations with such objects than did isolates when tested at two, four or eight days of life—especially on the first test with the object. However, although social experiences during the first two days of life did facilitate copulation over the next two weeks, the behaviour of the isolates indicated that experience with a moving object is 'not necessary for the later evocation of copulation' (Andrew, 1966).

In daily tests of sexual responsiveness towards chick models beginning on the second day of life, isolate male chicks reacted with flight or avoidance during the initial introductions of the model (Vidal, 1971). The first copulatory behaviour by these isolate males was observed at eleven days of age and was subsequently found on every later test. In comparison to chicks reared in various social conditions, the early sexual behaviour of the isolated males showed a delayed appearance. All of their copulatory attempts were found to be normal, however, in that the body was oriented along the same axis as the model and the head-feathers of the model were pecked during the attempts.

Wood-Gush (1958) reports data based upon four male chicks that were raised in isolation for the first six-and-a-half months of life. At that time, the behaviour of these males towards females was compared to that of socially reared males of the same age that had been isolated just two weeks prior to testing. The two groups of males were not found to differ consistently in their behaviour towards the stimulus females. While some individuals of each condition were found to show normal courtship of the females at the beginning of the test, others initially directed aggressive responses towards the females. In such instances, the latency for courtship following initial aggression varied between the males within each group.

Fisher and Hale (1957) found that one out of six cockerels that had been isolated for their first eight months displayed sexually to a live female during their first encounter. Isolate females were not observed to crouch in the sexual posture when housed with a group of previously isolated males. These females, however, did crouch to humans entering the pen (i.e. they probably had become imprinted onto their human caretaker).

The previously isolated males were given a series of tests with normal females after being housed for one week with the 'non-reactive' isolate females. On the second test, all six of the males 'waltzed' (a courtship display), two mounted and one displayed a complete mating sequence. The sexual behaviour of these males was unique in the following ways, however: (1) Although all the isolate males waltzed to the hens, they stopped waltzing and walked away if the hen responded by crouching. (2) None of these males was observed to mount, or attempt to mount, a squatting hen. All of the matings were 'forced' onto a standing or retreating hen, rather than being directed onto a behaviourally receptive hen.

As part of his extensive study of the development of social behaviour in the Burmese Red Junglefowl, Kruijt (1962, 1964) raised a number of males in visual isolation (but allowed to see beyond their cages) from the day of hatching until testing at six to sixteen months of age. Within the first few months of life, most of these isolate males displayed prolonged escape behaviour, apparently in response to 'innocuous environmental disturbances', or even to their own body movements (Kruijt, 1964). These males also displayed abnormally directed aggressiveness after about three months; some even attacking their own tail so frequently that most of the tail feathers were missing. In general, the isolates appeared to be either too afraid or overly aggressive, 'and the normal ambivalence of the two is often absent' (Kruijt, 1962).

Although three males that were isolated for six to nine months all showed successful copulations within seven ten-minute test encounters with females, their sexual behaviour differed greatly from that of controls. Courtship displays were rare or missing, aggression was common, and they often mounted the females in the reverse direction. Of the eight males tested after ten to fourteen months of isolation, only two performed copulatory behaviour. Three males that were isolated for fifteen to sixteen months continually attacked the test females and never displayed copulatory behaviour—despite a long series of tests. Even after living with receptive females for one to six weeks, the unsuccessful males were not observed to copulate. One male was observed to copulate with feathers during the isolation period—possibly due to self-imprinting.

Unsuccessful male isolates did appear to possess normal sexual physiology and were observed to court females. When the females crouched, however, the isolate males would typically respond by ignoring the females, walking away (as reported by Fisher and Hale, 1957, for domestic chicks), persisted with their courting, or attacked the females. Such behaviours may also appear in socially reared males, but *not* in the persistent manner displayed by the isolates.

Kruijt (1962) concluded that, in general, the isolate birds appeared to have less difficulty in copulatory patterns when tested at an early as compared to a later age. This agrees with the studies of domestic chicks referred to above.

Junglefowl in a second experiment were raised in isolation in cages which did *not* allow the birds to see out of the confines of their rearing cage. At five months of age, these severely restricted birds showed no social behaviours and would not even move away when attacked by male conspecifics (Kruijt, 1964).

CONCLUSION

Social and stimulus deprivation have been shown to influence various manifestations of attachment and sexual behaviour in chicks. Such behavioural disruption resulting from deprivation during the first few days or weeks after hatching can generally be alleviated by subsequent social experiences. This does not necessarily imply that the effects of all early experiences are readily reversible—one has only to look at the literature concerning the lasting influences of early atypical imprinting to realize that certain brief experiences early in life may have lasting effects upon adult behaviours.

Chicks that are subjected to social and stimulus deprivation lasting several months generally display long-term, or possibly permanent, bizarre sexual and aggressive behaviours as a function of such treatments.

ACKNOWLEDGEMENTS

I am indebted to Dr. Uli Weidmann for his valuable comments on this manuscript and to Professor W. Sluckin for his frequent advice and encouragement. I would also like to express my appreciation to Clare Fullerton and Julia C. Berryman who assisted in numerous ways.

References

Andrew, R. J. 1964. Vocalization in chicks, and the concept of 'stimulus content'. *Anim. Behav.*, 12: 64-76.

Andrew, R. J. 1966. Precocious adult behaviour in the young chick. *Anim. Behav.*, 14: 485-500.

Baron, A., and Kish, G. B. 1960. Early social isolation as a determinant of aggregative behaviour in the domestic chicken. *J. comp. physiol. Psychol.*, 53: 459-63.

Bateson, P. P. G. 1964a. Changes in chicks' responses to novel moving objects over the sensitive period for imprinting. *Anim. Behav.*, 12: 479-89.

Bateson, P. P. G. 1964b. Changes in the activity of isolated chicks over the first week after hatching. *Anim. Behav.*, 12: 490-92.

Bateson, P. P. G. 1964c. Effect of similarity between rearing and testing conditions on chicks' following and avoidance responses. *J. comp. physiol. Psychol.*, 57: 100-3.

Bateson, P. P. G. 1969. Imprinting and the development of preferences. In *Stimulation in early infancy*, ed. A. Ambrose, 109-25. London: Academic Press.

Fisher, A. E., and Hale, E. B. 1957. Stimulus determinants of sexual and aggressive behavior in male domestic fowl. *Behaviour*, 10: 309-23.

Fullerton, C.; Berryman, J. C.; and Sluckin, W. 1970. Peeping in chicks as a function of environmental change. *Psychon. Sci.*, 21: 39-40.

Gottlieb, G. 1971. *Development of Species Identification in Birds*. Chicago: University of Chicago Press.

Guiton, P. 1958. The effect of isolation on the following-response of Brown Leghorn chicks. *Proc. royal phys. soc. Edinburgh,* 27: 9-14.

Guiton, P. 1959. Socialisation and imprinting in Brown Leghorn chicks. *Anim. Behav.,* 7: 26-34.

Kruijt, J. P. 1962. Imprinting in relation to drive interactions in Burmese Red Junglefowl. *Symp. zool. soc. London,* No. 8: 219-26.

Kruijt, J. P. 1964. Ontogeny of social behaviour in Burmese Red Junglefowl (Gallus gallus spadiceus). *Behaviour,* Suppl. 12.

Porter, R. H.; Fullerton, C.; and Berryman, J. C. 1972. Cliff descent as a measure of attachment strength in chicks. *Anim. Behav.,* 20: in press.

Salzen, E. A. 1962. Imprinting and fear. *Symp. zool. soc. London,* No. 8: 199-217.

Salzen, E. A. 1966. The interaction of experience, stimulus characteristics and exogenous androgen in the behaviour of domestic chicks. *Behaviour,* 26: 286-322.

Sluckin, W. 1962. Perceptual and associative learning. *Symp. zool. soc. London,* No. 8: 193-98.

Sluckin, W. 1964. *Imprinting and Early Learning.* London: Methuen.

Sluckin, W., and Salzen, E. A. 1961. Imprinting and perceptual learning. *Quart. J. exp. Psychol.,* 13: 65-77.

Smith, F. V. 1969. *Attachment of the Young.* Edinburgh: Oliver & Boyd.

Taylor, A.; Sluckin, W.; and Hewitt, R. 1969. Changing colour preferences of chicks. *Anim. Behav.,* 17: 3-8.

Vidal, J. M. 1971. Precocial sexual behaviour ontogeny of sexual behaviour in the domestic cock (Gallus domesticus). *Behaviour,* 39: 20-38.

Wood-Gush, D. G. M. 1958. The effect of experience on the mating behaviour of the domestic cock. *Anim. Behav.,* 6: 68-71.

Syndromes resulting from object deprivation — 2

Effects on development of rhesus monkeys

Gene P. Sackett

University of Washington Psychology Department,

Regional Primate Research Center,

Child Development and Mental Retardation Center

Rhesus monkey (*Macaca mulatta*) infants deprived of socal inter-actions and varied sensory experiences exhibit a wide variety of anomalous behaviours throughout their life span. Major abnormali-ties occur in sexual, maternal, and exploratory behaviour, as well as bizarre personal and interpersonal responses. The latter category includes high levels of stereotyped motor activities, self-clutching and self-directed orality, body rocking, hyperaggression directed toward other monkeys and toward parts of the monkey's own body, and 'floating limb' reactions in which the monkey's arm or leg floats upward in movements that are incompatible with and in-appropriate for ongoing behaviour. The types of rearing experiences producing this behavioural syndrome involve situations in which the infant lives alone, having no physical interaction with other animals during the first nine to twelve months of life (see Harlow and Harlow, 1965 or Sackett, 1970 for comprehensive reviews of this material).

43

The purpose of this paper is to describe some of the specific effects of rearing in total deprivation from social experience with varied conditions of deprivation from nonsocial object experiences. The two general types of deprivation rearing experiences to be discussed include *total* and *partial* isolation. In partial isolation (Fig. 1a) the infant monkey lives alone in a wire mesh cage. It receives hand feeding by humans until it becomes self-feeding at two to three weeks after birth. From then until the end of the rearing treatment, the partial isolate receives visual, auditory, and olfactory stimulation from other monkeys, but it has no opportunity to physically contact other monkeys.

In total isolation (Fig. 1b) the infant lives in a completely enclosed cage. It receives minimal contact with humans during hand feeding, and has no physical or distance receptor stimulation from other monkeys. The sole sources of varied input for total isolates come from scanning the lighted cage interior, from feeding, and from self-produced stimulation while moving about the cage or making responses directed toward its own body.

Control treatments involve rearing in the laboratory with mother and peer experience (mother-peer), or with no mother but receiving daily peer interaction (peer-only). In some experiments feral, wild-born, controls are compared with total and partial isolate subjects.

In many early experience experiments effects are assessed during rearing and shortly after its termination. Although the effects of early experiences on early behaviours are of interest, such effects seem relatively unimportant unless they persist into later juvenile and adult stages of life. Therefore, this paper will be restricted to describing effects of rearing experiences that lead to long-term deviations from general control group norms.

SOME GENERAL EFFECTS OF SOCIAL-SENSORY DEPRIVATION

Object Deprivation and Exploratory Behaviour

Two studies compared feral-born rhesus monkeys with laboratory-raised animals. The laboratory group included mother-peer, surrogate mother, partial isolation, and six to twelve months total isolation groups. The experiments assessed response to a novel environment and to complex visual stimuli. The complete study was conducted in two independent replications, performed three

Fig. 1. Partial isolation cages (left) from which infants can see and hear, but not touch, other animals; and one type of total isolation cage (right) in which infants live in an enclosed metal chamber deprived of all social stimulation and of most temporally varying nonsocial stimulus changes.

years apart (Sackett, 1972a). The subjects were 3·5-5 years old when tested, so effects upon exploration were assessed 2·5-4 years after the termination of the original rearing treatments.

TABLE 1

Sample sizes for each group, sex, and replication in the studies of response in a novel environment and preference for patterned visual stimuli varying in complexity

Replication 1			Replication 2		
Rearing Group	Males	Females	Rearing Group	Males	Females
Feral	2	2	Feral	2	2
Mother-Peer	6	5	Mother-Peer	3	3
Surrogate and Wire Cage	9	3	Wire Cage	4	3
6 Month Isolate	3	3	6 Month Isolate	2	2
1 Year Isolate	2	2	9 Month Isolate	4	4

The apparatus used in these tests is shown in Fig. 2, and subject characteristics are given in Table 1. In experiment I, each subject was given seven daily trials spaced over a twelve day period. On each trial the monkey was placed in the start cage with the guillotine door closed. After five minutes the door was raised and ten minutes were allowed for exploration of the test cage. On alternate days a dark or light gray square was projected on the screen. Three measures are shown in Fig. 3 for each group and sex, averaged over replications and trials. Statistical tests had indicated no effects of trials or replications on these measures.

Latency to enter the test cage when the guillotine door opened had reliable effects between groups, but the groups effect interacted with sex. This measure is assumed to index the subject's sex willingness to expose itself to a novel environment, as the test cage was that part of the situation to which the subject was least adapted. The results show that feral animals were quickest to enter the test cage, followed closely by mother-peer monkeys. Surrogate, partial isolate, and six-month isolate subjects took much longer to enter.

TWO CAGE TEST UNIT

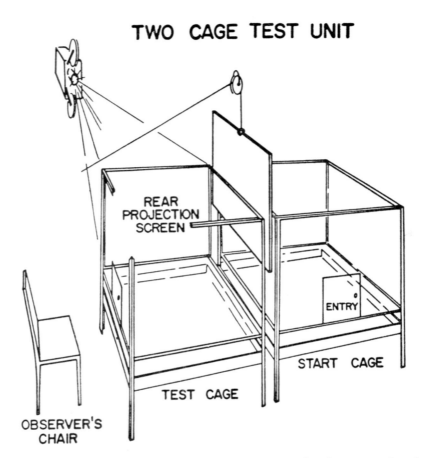

Fig. 2. Dual cage test unit used to study response to a novel environment and preference for visual complexity. In the novelty experiment the observer sat opposite the rear projection screen; in the complexity study the observer's position was as shown in the drawing.

Animals raised in total isolation for nine to twelve months from birth took the longest. However, sex differences in the deprived groups revealed that males had much longer latencies to enter the novel cage than did females.

Group and sex effects also appeared in time spent exploring the projection screen. Groups were ordered on this measure from feral to nine to twelve month isolate. However, sex interactions almost

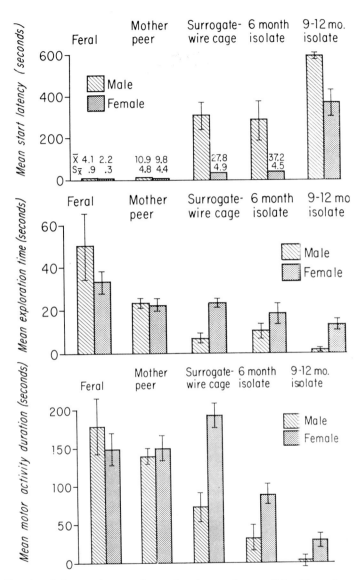

Fig. 3. Results of the novelty experiment showing rearing condition X *sex* interactions for (top) the latency to leave the start cage when the guillotine door was opened, (middle) amount of time spent exploring the screen and (bottom) amount of time spent moving. Lines show standard error of the mean.

completely offset rearing effects. Feral males explored significantly more than did feral females, with no sex differences appearing in the mothered group. In all deprived groups, females explored more than males. A similar effect appeared in the amount of locomotor activity, measured by time spent during the 600 second trials changing location rather than staying in one place. Again feral males were more active than feral females, with no sex difference in the mothered group. In the peer deprived groups, females were reliably more active than males.

This experiment shows that infancy rearing conditions have important effects on later behaviour in a novel situation. However, the extent of detrimental effects of object deprivation rearing experiences depend on sex. Females in all deprivation groups except nine to twelve month total isolates show almost no differences from feral or mothered control females, while even nine to twelve months of isolation produces females that explore more than counterpart males.

A similar effect was found comparing juvenile 2-2·5 year old rhesus monkeys raised with mothers and peers, peers alone, or in isolation for the first nine months of life (Sackett, 1972b). Males raised with mothers and peers or with peers alone were more active and explored somewhat more than females. For total isolates the sex relationship was reversed. Thus any deprivation from peer experiences coupled with object deprivation produced juvenile males who were deficient in exploratory behaviour; while deprived juvenile females showed only minor deficiencies compared with female controls.

The adult subjects tested in the dual-cage situation for response in a novel environment were also tested for response to visual complexity (Sackett, 1972a). In this five day study each subject was placed directly into the test cage side of the dual cage (Fig. 2). On each test day the stimuli shown in Fig. 4 were projected individually onto the screen for two one-minute periods. An observer recorded duration of stimulus exploration during each one-minute presentation. The primary effects, which appeared on all five test days, are shown in Fig. 4.

Feral and mothered groups, those reared during infancy under the most complex conditions, spent more time exploring the most complex stimulus (small checkerboard) than exploring the other stimuli. They spent the least amount of their time exploring the

D

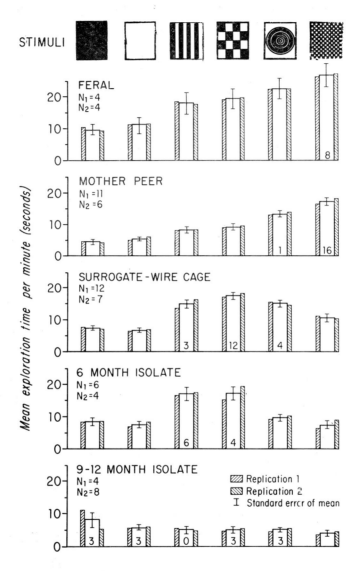

Fig. 4. The six visual stimuli used to test preference for visual complexity and the amount of time spent exploring each stimulus by animals in each rearing condition on each of the two replications of the study.

unpatterned stimuli. Surrogate and partial isolate subjects, who were reared in a less complex setting, exhibited maximal exploration with the intermediate complexity stimuli. Six month isolates preferred the simplest patterns, decreasing in exploration time when shown more complex stimuli. Nine and twelve month total isolates had no pattern stimulus preferences, and had the lowest overall amount of exploration time.

These results suggest that preadult monkeys raised under progressively greater degrees of object deprivation during infancy, when given a free choice, prefer to interact with progressively lower degrees of complex perceptual input. This seems to be the case even when the dimensions of complexity relevant to the task are not directly related to the stimulus dimensions present early in the animal's life. Thus, such data suggest that object deprivation produces a less 'psychologically complex' individual, who chooses not to attend to stimuli that are very complex regardless of their specific dimensions and input modality.

This conclusion finds support in a study involving preference for movement stimuli (Sackett, 1965). In this experiment juvenile feral monkeys, partial isolates, and one-year total isolates were allowed to interact with a swinging chain, a stationary T-Bar that could be pulled downward, and a T-Bar that did not move. Feral animals spent a great deal of time climbing on the chain, and had little time contacting the other two objects. Partial isolates contacted only the objects that had little or no movement potential. Total isolates showed no interest in either of the moveable objects, touching only the nonmoving T-Bar for one minute out of sixteen total rest hours. Thus, object deprivation produced a general aversion to stimuli containing any amount of complex movement. This could be a specific aversion to moving objects, or it could be simply part of a general aversion to complex stimulus inputs regardless of their modality.

Reactions to Noxious Stimulation

A major effect of object deprivation rearing in dogs and rats is deficient pain responses (e.g., Melzack and Scott, 1957). One effect of deprivation in monkeys is self-directed aggression, with biting sometimes resulting in injury or maiming. Such self-directed attacks become more probable and intense as the isolate matures to adulthood, indicating that pain from these attacks does not decrease their frequency or intensity.

Lichstein and Sackett (1971) assessed pain reactions in six to eight year old isolates. The procedure involved competition between self-paced thirst and avoidance of electric shock. The subject had a choice between tolerating two-seconds of mouth shock on a drinking tube to get water versus going twenty-four hours without water to avoid shock. The five male experimental subjects were reared in total isolation for six months during infancy, while the five male controls were reared during infancy with mother and peer experience.

The results showed that isolates were more reactive to very low, presumably nonpainful, levels of shock than controls. Conversely, isolates tolerated much higher shock than controls. Controls stopped touching the electrified tube at 1.2 ma, while isolates did not stop up to the highest, 2.5 ma, current levels delivered. Surprisingly, even though isolates tolerated higher shock levels, they exhibited more generalized aversive behaviour than did controls when shock was not on the drinking tube.

Thus, isolate monkeys as well as dogs and rats appear to have a major deficit in either perceiving noxious stimuli as potentially harmful, or in learning to react appropriately to noxious stimuli. However, a second experiment showed that shock is not a preferred stimulus by isolates. In this study isolates and controls were given a choice between drinking from a shocked or from a nonshocked tube. Both groups preferred the nonshocked tube, indicating that shock was an aversive stimulus for each type of subject.

Hyperphagia and Polydipsia

Studies by Miller, Caul, and Mirsky (1971) revealed another serious biological anomaly produced by object deprivation rearing. These investigators studied eating and drinking patterns by adult isolate and feral raised rhesus monkeys tested under *ad libitum* ingestion conditions. Initially, all subjects were under a scheduled feeding regimen, receiving food only once each day. No differences were apparent in body weight under these conditions. After free access to food and water for several months, isolates consumed much more of both substances than controls. In fact, isolates consumed up to three times as much water and 50% more calories daily. Surprisingly, isolates showed *no greater weight gain* than controls under these conditions. Also, observations of motor activity revealed no group differences during each twenty-four hour day. This suggests that isolation rearing produces adults with markedly atypical basic metabolic processes, although the exact mechanism involved is not yet known.

Similar polydipsic effects were found by Gluck (1971), studying operant learning under various reinforcement schedules. In this study total isolates consumed more water in the test chamber and in their home cages than did mother-peer raised controls. In the test situation water was available on a free access basis, and was unrelated to the operant task, which was lever pressing for food. As greater demands were placed on the monkey by increases in the duration of fixed interval schedules and in the reward ratio of fixed ratio schedules, isolates consumed even greater amounts of water in both the test and home cage situations. Thus, 'stress induction' produced by stringent operant schedules appears to be one type of situation leading to polydipsia, and presumably to induction of extreme metabolic needs for water or to extreme psychological needs to perform a task-irrelevant repetitive response.

SOME EFFECTS OF SPECIFIC TYPES OF OBJECT STIMULATING DURING INFANCY

The first study described in this section was performed in a free choice situation for assessing social preferences, the Self-Selection Circus (Fig. 5). Hexagonally shaped and constructed of metal channels, the Circus contains a central *start* compartment, bounded by six *choice* compartments. Clear Plexiglas or opaque Masonite walls slide in the channels. Behaviour of the subject is viewed over closed circuit TV, with movement of the animal from compartment to compartment measured by activation of switches in the floors.

In testing social preferences stimulus animals are placed in cages attached to the outside of choice compartments. A standard trial consists of an *exposure* period, with the subject in the start area and the inner Plexiglas doors between start and choice compartments closed. During this time the monkey can look through the choice compartments and see the stimulus monkeys, but it cannot

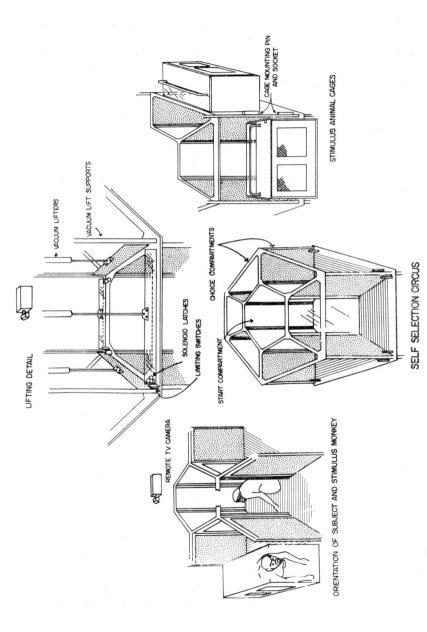

Fig. 5. THE CIRCUS APPARATUS. Lower: centre view showing centre start compartment and choice compartments. The stippled walls are opaque Masonite, the front and inner walls indicated by slashed lines are Plexiglas. Upper: centre vacuum cylinders which lift inner walls, TV camera for viewing subject during test and solenoid latches which lock walls so they cannot be raised by the subject during a trial. Right mounting: brackets for the stimulus animal cages which have Plexiglas front and top sections. Left: relative position of social stimulus object and subject monkey during the exposure period of a test trial.

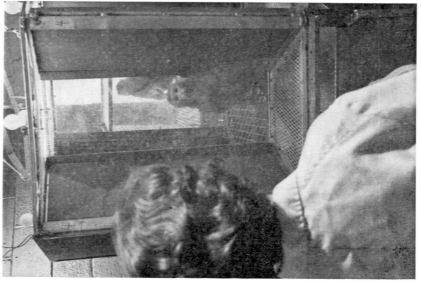

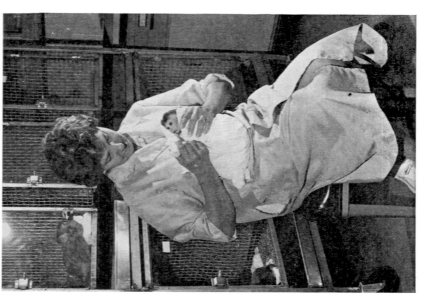

Fig. 6. (Left) nursery situation showing intimate contact between human and neonate monkey. (Right) stimulus situation used in the human versus monkey preference experiment.

enter the choice areas. After exposure, the Plexiglas doors are raised and the subject receives a *choice* period when it is free to enter and reenter any choice area, or to remain in the centre. Preferences are indexed by time spent in choice compartments near each of the stimulus monkeys attached to the outside.

Effects of Specific 'Object' Experience during the Neonatal Period

This study was designed to attack the question of how early in life effects of specific rearing stimuli could affect later preference

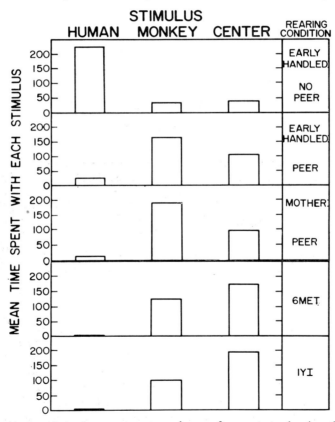

Fig. 7. Results of the human versus monkey preference test, showing that partial isolates prefer the human, mother-peer and peer-only subjects prefer the monkey, and six or twelve month total isolates spend most of their time in the centre start area.

behaviours (Sackett, Porter, and Holmes, 1965). Subjects were allowed Circus choices between an agemate monkey and an adult female human (Fig. 6). The human was one of the people that feed and care for neonates during the first thirty days of life before they are placed into partial isolation or peer-only rearing cages. The five test groups included (a) partial isolates who received early human handling and no physical contact with peers during infancy, although they did receive distance receptor stimulation from other monkeys; (b) peer-only monkeys who received human handling followed by group living with agemates during year one of life; (c) mother-peer infants who lived with their mothers and received daily peer interaction; and (d and e) six and twelve month total isolates who spent part or all of infancy in totally enclosed cages receiving no social or object contact and only minimal handling by humans during the first two weeks of life. When tested in this study all subjects were between 3·5-4·5 years old and had extensive social experiences after year one.

The average time spent near the human, near the monkey, and in the centre start area during five-minute Circus choice trials is shown in Fig. 7. Partial isolates preferred the human, peer and mother-peer subjects preferred the monkey, and total isolates spent significantly more time in the centre—a position maximally distant from either social object—than proximal to either stimulus. However, when isolates left the centre they did approach the monkey, not the human.

These data show that neonatal experiences with a particular stimulus can affect preadult choice behaviour. However, stimulus contacts with a new social object after this time, but still during the first several months of life, can alter this early learning effect. This process appears to be similar to the concept of imprinting, but either the imprinting experience can be reversed by subsequent infancy experiences, or the critical period for such early learning in monkeys lasts for many months after birth.

The isolate data show the total lack of contact with social objects for even the first six months of infancy produces a permanent decrement in the value of social stimuli as positive objects. It is conceivable that a similar process would occur with inanimate objects. Thus, object deprivation, as suggested by the data on exploratory behaviour presented previously may induce a general lack of preference for, and attention to, any objects that are not present in some form in the rearing environment.

Effects of Visual Stimulation during Isolation Rearing

The experimental group in the study presented next was composed of *Picture Isolates*, rhesus monkeys reared from birth through the first nine months of life in completely enclosed cages (Sackett, 1966). During this time each picture isolate received visual stimulation from coloured slides and motion pictures projected on one cage wall added to the object deprived environment. The stimuli included pictures of threatening, playing, fearful, withdrawing, and sexing monkeys, as well as infants, mothers and infants, and monkeys doing 'nothing'. Control pictures included humans, landscapes, and geometric patterns. Behaviour during experimenter-controlled picture presentations was coded by an observer through a nonreflective one-way viewing window. The subjects also had opportunities to turn on the stimuli themselves by touching a small lever mounted below the projection screen. Examples of the types of pictures used are shown in Fig. 8. These picture types were chosen to represent a sample of what laboratory raised monkeys would ordinarily see during rearing and during postrearing social behaviour tests.

Two general effects characterized response to the pictures by all eight subjects. (a) After the first month of life pictures of monkeys elicited more exploration and play than nonmonkey pictures. Pictures of infants and of monkeys displaying threat patterns produced more of all measured reactions, except fear responses, than any other type of picture. (b) No pictures produced fear behaviours until about day eighty. From days 80-120 fear, withdrawal, and disturbance occurred frequently for all infants when threat pictures were shown, even though these pictures had not previously elicited such reactions.

These data suggest that species-appropriate, socially meaningful, visual stimuli depicting infants and threatening monkeys have unlearned, prepotent, activating properties for socially naive infant monkeys. Also, visual components of threat displays appear to function as an inborn releaser of fear, but this releaser requires postnatal maturation before becoming operative. Thus, these picture isolates were presented with functionally effective visual 'objects',

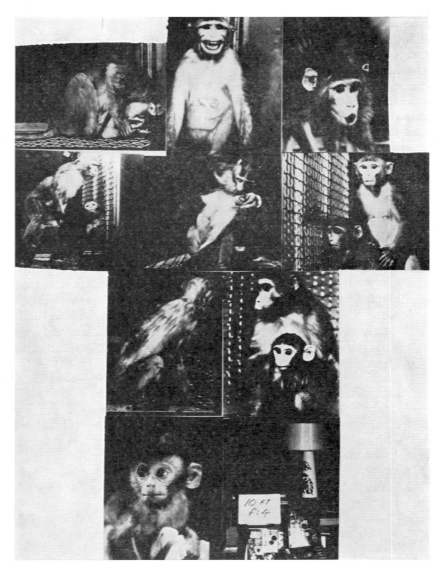

Fig. 8. Examples of the ten types of pictures used in the Picture Isolate study. (Row 1, left-right) Fear-withdrawal, fear grimace, and threat; (Row 2, left-right) sex, play, and exploration; (Row 3, left-right) 'nothing', and mother with infant; (Row 4, left-right) infant, control nonmonkey picture.

which elicited at least some species-typical and appropriate responses.

During months nine to fifteen each picture isolate was paired with a same-age and sex partial isolate who received an identical, gradual schedule of introduction to new nonsocial objects, a new wire mesh living cage, and exposure to a live animal for the first time. In addition, a control group of nine-month total isolates was reared under identical conditions as the picture isolates, but did not receive any picture stimulation. These control isolates were also matched with partial isolates and exposed to the paced schedule of postrearing experiences.

On tests of response to novelty and exploratory behaviour during months nine to fifteen, total, picture, and partial isolate subjects did not differ in any important respects. All groups showed moderate levels of motor activity, approached novel stimuli, and exhibited minimal disturbance behaviour. This suggested that the gradual pacing procedure was effective in eliminating any major traumatic effect of separation from the isolation rearing cage, which might produce negative emotional responses in any novel situation, thereby debilitating exploratory tendencies. However, during these exploratory behaviour tests, female total and picture isolates had significantly more motor activity and exploration, and less disturbance and self-directed rocking and clutching reactions than did males (Pratt, 1969). This reconfirmed the interaction of sex with object deprivation for older infants, which was reported above for juvenile and adult isolates.

When paired in a social situation with their matched partial isolate partners total and picture isolates showed the typical isolate behaviour syndrome of withdrawal, stereotyped motor reactions, and almost complete absence of positive social responding. Thus, isolation rearing with or without the addition of appropriate visual stimuli did not materially reduce anomalous reactions to initial encounters with live monkeys.

From months fifteen to twenty-four the total, picture, and partial isolates and peer-only controls received social interaction experiences in a playroom. Data representative of behaviour throughout this series of tests is shown in Fig. 9. The picture and total isolates were complete and equally debilitated in social and nonsocial behaviour throughout this eleven-month period of playroom social experiences. The only reliable differences between these total isolate

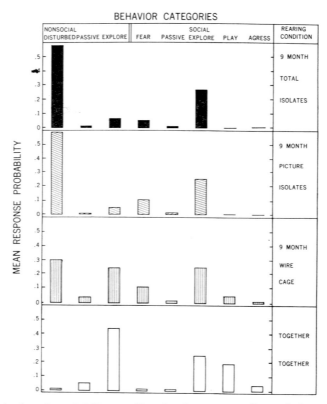

Fig. 9. Behavioural probability profiles showing a mutually exclusive, exhaustive categorization of the social behaviour of total and picture isolates, partial isolates and peer-only monkeys tested in a playroom from months fifteen to twenty-four of age.

groups occurred in socially elicited fear. The probability of this behaviour was higher for the picture isolate monkeys. Partial isolates were less adversely affected than the total isolate groups, but were inferior to the peer raised animals in nonsocial exploratory behaviour, had a higher probability of disturbance, and much lower probabilities of positive social reactions.

These results suggest several conclusions. (a) Adding visual stimulation to an object deprivation situation, stimulation that is effective in producing some species normal responses during isolation rearing, in no way offsets isolation induced social behaviour deficits. (b) Gradually pacing the introduction to novel and complex postrearing stimuli does offset some exploratory behaviour deficits of isolates, but does not offset social deficits.

An important effect found in this study was a sex difference

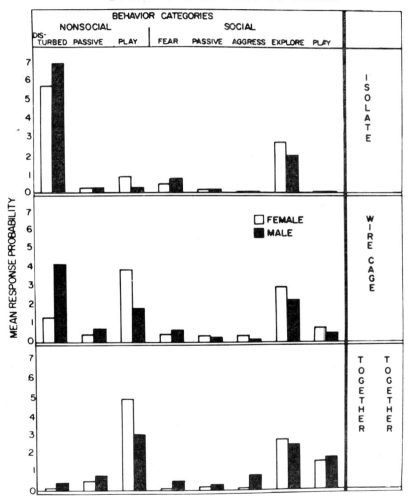

Fig. 10. Interaction of sex with rearing conditions in the social and nonsocial behaviour of total and picture isolates (pooled together in the total isolate grouping), partial isolates and peer-only controls tested in a playroom between fifteen to twenty-four months of age.

determining the degree of social behaviour deficits in deprived subjects. This sex effect is shown in Fig. 10. Female total isolates were significantly less disturbed and fearful than males, and had more nonsocial exploratory behaviour than males. This sex difference was extreme in partial isolates, where females were the only subjects showing positive social behaviour, and females had lower probabilities of nonsocial disturbance reactions and much higher probabilities of nonsocial exploration than males.

Harlow (1965) has shown a similar effect in adult sexual responding. When studied in mating tests with sexually sophisticated partners, adult males who were raised in partial isolation were uniformly incompetent. However, some partial isolate females showed adequate sexual behaviour on initial sex tests, and many of these females who were inadequate on their initial sex pairings developed adequate sexual reactions with experience. Thus, as in the case of exploratory behaviour and social development of juveniles, male sexual respondings appear to be much more susceptible to social-sensory deprivation effects than sex reactions of females.

Peer-Only Rearing under Object Deprivation Conditions

The study reported next concerns a 'pure' case of object deprivation rearing with added social stimulation (Sackett, Tripp, and Grady, 1972). Rhesus newborns were raised together during the first nine months of life in same-sex pairs. The rearing environment was a completely enclosed, sound-attenuating chamber containing no moveable objects and no stimulus variations other than opportunities for visually scanning the unchanging cage interior. Control subjects were raised in pairs in wire mesh cages, where they could also see and hear other monkeys and humans. From months nine to twenty-four the subjects were housed in new cages and received daily social interaction experiences with other peer raised monkeys and with monkeys reared under several total isolation conditions described below. Data representative of the behaviour of peer-only isolates and their controls are presented in the top two rows of Fig. 11).

On postrearing tests no social behaviour differences occurred between peer-only isolates and their nonisolated peer raised controls. Behavioural profiles revealed almost no fear, disturbance,

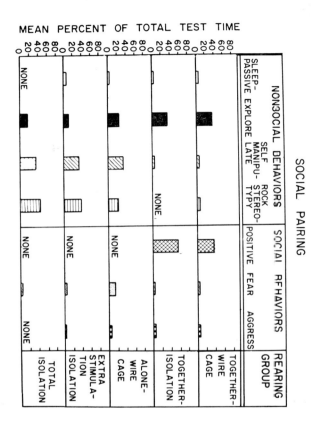

Fig. 11. Behavioural probability profiles for monkeys tested in home cage paired social situations between nine to twenty-four months of age. The top two rows present results for peer-only controls reared together in a wire cage compared with animals raised in pairs in a total isolation environment. The last three rows give data for partial isolates and for total isolates reared with object stimuli added to the situation or reared without any varied environmental input.

self-directed, or stereotypic reactions for either group. The most probable behaviour in both groups included nonsocial exploration and positive social reactions. Thus, the addition of peer contact to an environment void of object stimulation appears to completely offset the appearance of abnormal behaviours characteristic of social-sensory deprivation rearing.

Object 'Enrichment' during Social Isolation Rearing

The following groups of total social isolates were reared in sound-attenuating chambers as part of the previous study. (a) *Total Isolate* controls included monkeys placed into isolation at birth, receiving no object stimulus variations. (b) *Extra stimulation* subjects lived in total social isolation from birth. However, they received a variety of nonsocial object stimuli including pictures projected onto a screen, tape recorded sounds, a chain hanging from the ceiling available for climbing and swinging, and novel objects varying in tactile and movement qualities. A partial isolate control group was also reared for comparisons with these total isolates and with the two peer raised groups described in the preceding experiment.

Data representative of social responding during postrearing social behaviour tests from months nine to twenty-four are shown in the bottom three rows of Fig. 11. The behaviour of total isolates and extra stimulation isolates did not differ on these tests. Their response profiles were characterized by no positive social responding, little environmental exploration, and high probabilities of self-directed clutching and body rocking, and stereotyped motor activities. Thus, the presence of added object stimulation failed to offset the typical isolation syndrome in any way. This was surprising, as results reported by Mason (1968), who studied isolated monkeys reared with a nonmoving or with a moving surrogate 'mother', suggest that movement stimulation offsets self-directed and stereotyped reactions—at least in tests conducted in the isolation rearing environment.

At face value, Mason's swinging surrogate, which moved randomly about the cage interior, is a similar condition to the swinging chain situation in our study. However, a major difference between Mason's situation and the swinging chain extra stimulation situation lies in the types of responses elicited by the two conditions. Mason's swinging surrogate subjects had to clutch the surrogate and maintain contact with it, or they would fall off onto the cage floor. Further, the cage interior was quite small, and the animals apparently could not avoid being hit by the randomly moving surrogate if they were sitting on the floor. Thus, typical isolate self-directed clutching, rocking, and stereotyped behaviours were incompatible with surrogate-clinging reactions. Therefore,

E

isolate-type behaviours were largely precluded from the repertoire of responses learned by these animals, who were forced to spend a large portion of each day clinging to their surrogates.

Utilizing Mason's results, Prescott (1971) had suggested that vestibular system movement stimulation, acting on cerebellar mechanisms, is critical for normal infant development in primates. This theory predicts that isolation rearing conditions that include movement stimulation should result in some decrease in isolated-type personal behaviours. In our study, the swinging chain extra stimulation monkeys spent up to eight hours each day climbing and swinging on their chains. Although they received a great deal of movement stimulation, they showed no improvement on post-rearing tests over the abnormal behaviour levels of total isolates receiving no object stimulation. Thus, it is not evident that movement stimulation, *per se*, is a necessary condition for eliminating symptoms of object deprivation rearing. It seems equally likely that the development of *competing responses*—reactions which interfere with the development of typical isolate behaviour patterns —does not ameliorate isolate-type behaviour.

CONCLUSIONS

The selected studies reviewed in this paper point to several conclusions about the role of object stimulation in monkey development. First, rearing environments lacking physical interaction with other monkeys produce long-term deficits in both social and nonsocial behaviour. These deficits include anomalies in basic behaviour such as pain reactions and ingestion responses. Such deficits are less extreme, and show some remission, if monkeys receive partial isolation experiences involving distance receptor contact with other animals. If totally isolated infant monkeys receive visual object experience or a variety of nonsocial experiences involving vision, movement, audition, and touch there is no evidence of modification of the basic isolate rearing anomalies.

An exception to this last statement is found in monkeys raised with swinging surrogates. However, this exception suggests that the role of object stimulation is to produce response alternatives for the developing individual which compete with self-stimulated behaviours such as rocking, self-clutching, and motor stereotypes.

Such competition might lead to development of a response repertoire during isolation that precludes self-directed behaviours.

This viewpoint suggests that there may be two roles for object stimulation during monkey development. One role might be to produce responses that can be used directly and successfully in adapting to novel postrearing experiences. A second role might be to simply inhibit the development of responses that will compete with the behaviours that the monkey must develop during postrearing experiences to be successful as a social individual. This implies that the responses learned during object interaction in infancy need not directly transfer to postrearing situations. Rather, even the production of a behaviourally neutral individual—one who is ready to learn new behaviours because it does not have a large set of unlearned behaviours that compete with the response demands of new experiences—may be a satisfactory product of rearing experiences for adequate later behavioural adjustment.

Some support for this notion is found in studies of learning by isolation raised monkeys. Work by Harlow, Schiltz, and Harlow (1969) and by Gluck (1971) suggest that isolates can learn both complex discriminations, simple operant tasks, and complex reinforcement schedules with the same facility as mother-peer raised control monkeys. However, major differences occur between isolates and controls in time taken to adapt to test situations. It may take control monkeys only one to two weeks before they are ready to perform on learning trials in standard monkey learning situations. Isolates, however, may take as long as six to nine months to adapt to the new situation. One interpretation of such data is that isolates have a major deficit in their ability to inhibit responses that compete with the response demands of learning situations, but, once they are willing or able to stop making such interfering reactions, their learning performance is no different from nonisolated monkeys.

A second conclusion about object deprivation during rearing concerns the critical finding of sex interactions with rearing conditions. Females were found to be much less detrimentally affected by deprivation rearing than males. The source of this difference must be biological—lying in neural, sensory, and/or biochemical differences between males and females. In most studies of human behaviour, sex differences are hopelessly confounded by sex-role cultural-familial factors. In these nonhuman primate studies, however, such factors are eliminated because social stimulation is not available during infancy. Sex effects appearing under such conditions must, therefore, have a basic biological cause.

One hypothesis to explain these effects is that reduced female susceptibility may occur because females have a larger complement of unlearned, adaptive, mechanisms that do not require environmental stimulation for their maturation. In terms of the inhibition and competing response notions outlined above, it is conceivable that in females, mechanisms for inhibition of competing responses are largely unlearned. Male inhibitory processes, on the other hand, may require much more postnatal experience in order to operate in an adaptive fashion. Regardless of the specific mechanism involved, the finding of differential vulnerability poses serious problems for developmental theories that propose identical early life experiences as being critical for later behaviour regardless of the maturing individual's biologically based sex-correlated characteristics.

ACKNOWLEDGEMENTS

Preparation of this paper and some of the studies reported in it were supported by grant RR-00166 from the National Institutes of Health to the Washington Regional Primate Research Centre. Other work reported in the paper was supported by National Institutes of Health grants MH-4528 to the Wisconsin Regional Primate Laboratory and RR-0167 to the Wisconsin Regional Primate Research Centre.

References

Gluck, J. P. 1971. 'An operant analysis of the effects of differential rearing experiences in rhesus monkeys.' Unpublished doctoral dssertations. University of Wisconsin.

Harlow, H. F. 1965. Sexual behavior in the rhesus monkey. *Sex and behavior.* ed. F. A. Beach, New York: Wiley.

Harlow, H. F., and Harlow, M. K. 1965. The effectional systems. In *Behavior of nonhuman primates,* ed. A. M. Schrier, New York: Academic Press.

Harlow, H. F.; Schiltz, K. A.; and Harlow, M. K. 1969. Effects of social isolation on the learning performance of rhesus monkeys. In *Proc. 2nd. Inter. Cong. Primatology,* Basel: Karger.

Lichstein, L., and Sackett, G. P. 1971. Reactions by differentially raised rhesus monkeys to noxious stimulation. *Develop. Psychobiol.,* 4: 339-52.

Mason, W. A. 1968. Early social deprivation in the nonhuman primate: Implications for human behavior. In *Biology and Behavior: Enviornmental influences,* ed. D. C. Glass, New York: Rockefeller University Press.

Melzack, R., and Scott, T. H. 1957. The effects of early experience on the response to pain. *J. comp. physiol. Psychol.,* 50: 155-61.

Miller, R. E.; Caul, W. R.; and Mirsky, I. A. 1971. Patterns of eating and drinking in socially-isolated rhesus monkeys. *Physiology and Behavior,* 7: 128-34.

Pratt, C. L. 'The developmental consequences of variations in early social stimulation.' Unpublished doctoral dissertation, University of Wisconsin, 1969.

Prescott, J. W. 1971. Early somatosensory deprivation as an ontogenetic process in the abnormal development of the brain and behaviour. In *Medical Primatology,* ed. I. E. Goldsmith, Basel: Karger.

Sackett, G. P. 1965. Manipulatory behavior in monkeys reared under different levels of early stimulus variation. *Percept. motor Skills,* 20: 1027-28.

Sackett, G. P. 1966. Monkeys reared in isolation with pictures as visual input: Evidence for an innate releasing mechanism. *Science,* 154: 1486-72.

Sackett, G. P. 1970. Innate mechanisms, rearing conditions, and a theory of early experience effects in primates. In *Miami symposium on prediction of behavior: Early experience,* ed. M. R. Jonas, Coral Gables: University of Miami Press.

Sackett, G. P. 1972a. Exploratory behavior of rhesus monkeys as a function of rearing experiences and sex. *Develop. Psychol.,* 6: 260-70.

Sackett, G. P. 1972b. Sex interactions with rearing experiences in the exploratory behavior of juvenile rhesus monkeys. In preparation.

Sackett, G. P.; Porter, M.; and Holmes, H. 1965. Choice behavior in rhesus monkeys: Effect of stimulation during the first month of life. *Science,* 147: 304-6.

Sacket, G. P.; Tripp, R.; and Brady, S. 1972. Effects of peer interaction and varied nonsocial stimulation added to isolation rearing in monkeys. In preparation.

Syndromes resulting from object deprivation — 3

Analogues in human behaviour

GEORGE D. SCOTT,
Institute of Psychotherapy
Kingston, Ontario,
Canada

An object can be medically classified as any material body which can, under special circumstances, develop emotional significances. The dimensions of the object include size, shape, colour and texture, each again with concurrent emotional significances.

The good-luck rabbit paw differs from the paw of the aged rabbit lying on the roadside. Size, shape, colour and texture apply to similar objects with emotional conditioning.

We will exclude the paradoxical emotional object with secondary object features, the mother and the father, real or surrogate.

Professor Sackett's work[1] at Wisconsin and Dr. Harry Harlow's work at the Primate Laboratory,[2] by reducing stimulation—visual, auditory, and kinaesthetic, produced macaca mulattas who spent hours in rhythmic rocking, crouching in the schizophrenic and autistic positions with eventual pathological behaviour, ineffective social behaviour, little interest in toys and climbing, a lack of aggressiveness, with eventual depression and withdrawn behaviour. These abnormalities were reversible between six and twelve months but after that date, social maladaption occurred. Sackett concludes, that inexperienced, inconsistent and inadequate mothers show defective offspring in terms of the above symptoms in varying degrees from self-biting, self-clasping, fear grimacing, rocking, huddling, vocalization to the more dramatic schizoid and autistic mannerisms.

Children deprived of a major sensor organ, such as bilateral blindness, develop with an object awareness conditioned, not by sight and colour, but by consistency, texture, size, weight and the various inter-relations—an air balloon has the size, texture and consistency of a plastic mass except for the one variable of weight.[3]

Freedman reported that a significant percentage of congenitally blind children developed symptoms similar to infantile autism.[4] Spitz[5] calls the eye and ear input of the infant child 'co-enesthetic non-specific modalities' and stated that early co-enesthetic deprivation may be more devastating than either congenital blindness, thalidomide or rubella effects.[6] This differs from Sackett's views on the mulatta monkeys.

Freedman again points out that at five months of age, there develops the ability to discriminate objects through vision and to co-ordinate hand and eye. He also re-inforces Harlow's views that handling, by the mother, stimulates the proprioceptive kinaesthetic and labrythine mechanism which result in early physical mobility in the wiggling and crawling phase of development.

The thirteenth century saw Frederick the Great determining the most ancient language—Hebrew, Greek, Latin, or Arabic 'so he bade foster-mother and nurses to suckle children, bath and wash them, but not to prattle and speak to them'—but he laboured in vain because all the children died, for they could not live without the petting and joyful faces and loving words of their foster-mothers.[7]

Altshuler's paper of 1970, discusses this same sound element 'loving words' in terms of the deaf child.[8] A child without audition and without language cannot help but realize his difference from his silent world and expresses them in frustration tantrums. Hospital admissions of the deaf include such items as impulsive, aggressive behaviour, generally egocentric. The deaf child wants to do what he wants, has a low frustration tolerance and may act impulsively or explosively as tension mounts. Concomitantly, an object without a name, a sound, or movement which has no psychological echo greatly alters the individual's relationship with the object identification.

The absence of perceptual modes may preclude adaptive options, thus, without sight, impulsivity is not possible while head banging is!

A last clinical point involves the recently blind adults who develop receding depressions, hallucinatory visual experiences during sleeping and wakefulness, concurrent affective responses, and long hours of day dreaming.[9] These people stubbornly resist their blindness and reflect turmoil, fear, and depression, well portrayed by R. B. Lamb in his book 'Fire Blind'.

Kerr, Chamove and Harlow observe that children reared without social stimulation may fail to grow despite a reportedly normal dietary intake.[10] However, the article concludes that inadequate nutrition should be re-evaluated as a probable cause and postulates that the phenylalanine diet may have a relationship to learning ability in the primate rhesus.

Analogues in human behaviour may be transient, repressive or fixed. Behavioural disorders have to be considered as a four-sided box with nominates of neuroses, psychoses, character disorders and normal behaviour which is a blend of acceptable amounts of mental variables, emotional reactions and identification pathology.

Object deprivation is seen in its clearest form in controlled institutional life of the antisocial character disorder.[11] This world has been a world of the immediate reward, the criminals anagram; he lives in quest of object acquisition and reward principle. When he is imprisoned, his acquisitiveness is eliminated to the point of a loss of personal identification. As a result, immense and powerful mechanisms of repression force him into a fog and coasting state, where object acquisition is unimportant. After some six months, the dynamic mechanism awakes and object acquisition becomes a hungry appetite to alleviate the deprivation caused by forced loss of objects, cars, watches, old friends, old streets, music halls and even a filthy old boarding house. Acquisitiveness in a prison is a compulsiveness beyond the normal acquisitiveness. A different object is a special award—a hand made belt, a different uniform, a rubber-soled pair of shoes. The criminal, with few exceptions, is tired of being without and wants to increase his objects without the avenue of work (see appendix).

Deprivation of these objects produces anger, retaliation and a feeling of deranking much similar to the mother, whose object affluence is reduced by death until there is actual object deprivation, when the mother-object dies, leaving the children angry at the loss of the object, which has nothing to do with their emotional relationship with their mother.

The prisoner, although in total less than 1% of our population, is an example of the glory of civilized existence wherein penuriousness was a virtue, cash was an asset and bills were as unaccountable as sin! Object deprivation produces tremendous contemporary anxiety in civilized man who has been brain-washed through the advertising media to have certain object attributes in his home; freezer, hair dryer, bicycle, ski-doo, skis, two cars, etc.—and a consequent physical-status life devoid of humanistic realism or religious compassion.

Object deprivation in childhood is a comparative process as to the child's contemporaries. It has no real significance unless the social status impinges on the relationship and produces feelings of inferiority and a fear of further psychological castration by loss of one's own singular possession, as in a young girl with only one change of dress attending a school where the other girls have many.

The obsessive child who hoards his possessions is setting his picture puzzle on an unrelenting course of psychological obsessiveness as an antidote to criticism and the pursuit of material consistency. Oftimes, the obsessive boy grown into a jealous paranoid man, may remember the important object of his early life—a wooden boat, a broken wheel, a fancy hubcap and onto this he has attached numerous human emotions of possessiveness, defensiveness and a peculiar feeling of total hostility to the world.

Infant children develop a sight and sound reality long before their useful sensualities. The infant brain, with its millions of neuronal connections and with its eager Reticulo–Activating System is overready to pick up any sensory input.

The wiggling of the infant, the cooing sounds, which stimulate the child's own receiving system may be his built-in radar tract.[12] His body supplies him with kinaesthetic impulses. His developing hearing is attacked by myriads of threatening and confusing sounds —a bang will cause a startle reaction, a mother's voice will produce an upward smile. The visual object while static is important, but visual object movement, gives the infant visual stimulation, head-arm kinaesthetic stimulation, auditory stimulation—either through his own sound apparatus or his attendant's voice—a perfect practice to keep the developing brain cells in an active participation with reality.

Work in the field of child study reinforces the concept that early acceptable object movement is an apparent stimulation to the receptor and memory cells, and actually the child becomes more aware, more active, more self-participatory and less aware of immediate personal physical discomforts. The addition of a changing sound element (music box) adds to the child's object input and consequently he, like his congeners, the animals, begins to associate mental, physical and emotional satisfaction as a composite factor—the real basis of intellectual man who co-relates his mental, emotional and physical attributes in a flowing and continuous reflection of his changing environment.

ANALOGUES IN HUMAN BEHAVIOUR

Syndrome one—	Parental Emotional Indifference or Object identification: selfishness
Syndrome two—	Parental Emotional Rejection or Object regression: inadequacy
Syndrome three—	Object acquisitiveness or Anti-social behaviour
Syndrome four—	Neuronal hunger or Pseudo-Retardation
Syndrome five—	Homing Deprivation or Familiar object deprivation
Syndrome six—	Nihilistic absolutism or Religious object rejection
Syndrome seven—	Planetary absolutism or Object competition

Syndromes resulting from object deprivation have been generally discussed in terms of developmental pathology. Let us now move to a contentious area of qualitative study.

Syndrome One:

Object Identification (Parental Emotional Indifference). In this area are the children who have been treated in the growing years as objects and possessions. As a result, they have an inanimate granite-like defence with no emotional values. Such a child has a materialistic identification, has no knowledge of affection, the counterparts of holding, kissing or hugging—with the general development of feelings of isolation inadequacy, an inability to compete, a desire to be handled as a possession and a complete indifference to ambition and a subconscious desire to be used to the best advantage for himself—which can be interpreted as the ultimate in selfishness. They identify themselves as objects, not individuals. They do not love because they know not love.

Syndrome Two:

Acceptance; then regression; then inadequacy (Parental Emotional Rejection). In this state, early emotional deprivation is related empirically to emotional blindness and deafness where the child does not develop through lack of handling, visual and auditory stimulation, and grows almost as an obedient animal without warmth and its related loyalties to parents in terms of judgement, reasoning and respect. Because of lack in accepting significant emotion, defensiveness, hostility, self-stimulating movements, all similar to the rejected maternal dependency, leave the infant in the object identification group with Levine's category of:

a) high level of anxiety, screaming, incessant talking, criticism of environment;
b) restriction of normal fondling, exploratory and manipulative efforts;
c) fears unlimited of height, dark, strangers etc.; rejection of social objects, material or emotional factors such as attitudes to neighbours, and aggressive feelings towards the paternal-maternal possessions;
d) neurotic-like, repetitive conversations, e.g., 'do you like my dress' × 100 times, self-stimulating movements to the intensity of masturbation, and sleeping in the clutching and rocking position.

Syndrome Three:

Object Acquisitiveness. In this condition the personality is formalized with a one channel homing emotional receptor, a conscience free type who acquires other peoples' objects as a means of compensatory expression to get back at the dispassionate parent. The sneak thief who steals for the emotional satisfaction always has a fractured emotional balance in the pre-adolescent years. He acquires objects which have a negative emotional complex, hence are materially valueless but are valuable because they deprive others of the emotional satisfactions.

Syndrome Four:

Neuronal Hunger. This syndrome can be called sensory-seeking deprivation which affords the infant a genetic right to use his adaptable sensory organs to their fullest. The sound, sight and movement deprived child has been considered as a secondary retardate who is ignorant, not because of neuronal equipment but because of neuronal mal-usage. The study of mental defectives reveals that many clinical defectives, in terms of performance, have a normal mental acquisitive appetite which if whetted can be sharpened to normal efficiency. In effect, the degree of mental defect is due to lack of sensory experience not due to lack of cerebral ability.

Syndrome Five:

Familiar object deprivation or homing deprivation is actually a sensory starvation, based upon a previous history of adequate sensory object impact. The territorial areas of the biologists reveal that animals, including man, revert to familiar objects when they are under pressure or conversely they function more efficiently with familiar objects around them, which objects may even take on human characteristics (idols and symbols). Michelangelo, after years of work, attributed to his marble Moses the characteristics of man when he angrily struck the left leg and shouted 'speak to me'.

In social and criminal behaviour, each human animal has his social habitat—his objects with their colours, their odours and their physical characteristics. Many criminals are tied in emotionally and object-deprived environments, and consequently feel more at home there than in the resplendency of good times; they prefer a nice jail. On attaining freedom they will, against all professional advice, return to their boyhood haunts and objects, only to replay in elephantine fashion the emotional death previously suffered, and return to the conforming safe environment of the jail world.

Syndrome Six:

Object deprivation can be carried to the matured point of renouncing all worldly possessions and this may be identified as 'nihilistic absolutism'. It is a condition seen in religious contexts and is reflected in Lenten ceremonies, pagan rites and in neo-god cultist movements. The originators of these faiths or beliefs have to be raised by object-positive, sensory active parents to assure them the maturity by which they can turn upon their parents and deny themselves their emotional birth-rights. These psychological pilgrimages reduce all objects to substance of eternal matter, are ions of the gods and have no reality in time; hence they are not material objects in the psychological sense. Such conditions are usually transient with the believer developing less arduous beliefs as his audience disappears and his hunger, emotional and physical, becomes over-powering.

Syndrome Seven:

Once the language barrier is broken between man and animal, the human race may well profit from the wisdom of the animals. Objects are the centre of man's destiny, it appears, whether in jewellery, art, architecture or land. The world economics are conducted on object requirements, social function is computed on object efficiency and one cannot help but wonder 'what fools we mortals be' when our heritage ought to be thought, judgement, wisdom and a compassion for all living matter, while we participate in the dynamics of planet Earth.

APPENDIX

Objects forfeited through prison life

Money:

When walking along the street I always keep my hand in my pocket and jingle the change.

Books:

I am allowed to have books in my possession but I can't buy them and keep them only for me.

Pens:

Until recently, I was not allowed to buy a ball point pen—I can now, but only a very small selection. On the street I always carried a good gold pen in my breast pocket.

Pets:

I always had an aquarium at home stocked with various kinds of fish and spent many hours watching them and caring for them. Also I used to trade species with friends.

Telephone:

Wherever I live I have always had a telephone—not that I used it that much—but I didn't feel cut off from everything when I had it.

Sports equipment:

At home I play a lot of ball, just as I do here. But, here I am not allowed to buy my own ball spikes, nor am I allowed to wear the same pair from one game to another—first come first served.

Rings:

I have always worn a ring on my little finger left hand. Many times I find myself turning an imaginary ring.

Razor:

I have always used an electric razor but am not allowed to have one here.

Eye glasses:

I have to take the type of glasses offered here—I am not allowed more than one pair.

Drinking glass:

It gives me the worst feeling to drink milk or water out of a cup. I always use a glass at home but I am not allowed to have a glass here.

Grooming aids:

Some of these I am allowed to purchase from my canteen but not the brand I would buy on the street. I miss most, good after shave lotion and I always touched up my hair but am not allowed to do it here.

Keys:

I would like to be able to lock my own place when I am away, besides I like the feel of having a case of keys in my pocket—everything I own is safe.

Stuffed animals:

I have a collection of stuffed animals at home. I particularly like the French Poodle I have but am not allowed to have anything like that here.

Lighter:

I detest using matches and always carried a lighter on my person on the street.

Car:

I spent many hours polishing and shining my car and was proud of it.

Watches:

We can get watches now, but they still aren't the kind I would normally wear.

Scarves—Cravats:

I always wore a scarf on the street—it made me feel as I was dressed up.

Shoes:

I am only given one pair of shoes. The type of shoe I wear is nothing like the ones given me here.

Furniture:

I would like to be able to own my own furniture. I do not like having something everyone else does.

References

1. Sackett, G. 1968. *Abnormal Behaviour in Animals,* ed. M. Fox, Philadelphia: W. B. Saunders. 1968.
2. Harlow, H., and Woolsey, C. 1958. *Biological and Biochemical Bases of Behaviour.* University of Wisconsin Press.
3. Scott, G. D, Unpublished results.
4. Freedman, D. A., 1971. Some studies in early development. *Amer. J. Psychiat.,* 1539-45.
5. Spitz, R. 1945. Diacritic and co-enesthetic organization, Psychanal. Review, 32: 146-61.
6. Decarie, T. 1969. A study of mental and emotional development in the thalidomide child. In *Determinants of Human Behaviour,* ed. B. M. Foss, vol. 4. London: Methuen.
7. Solomon, and Kleeman. 1971. Sensory deprivation. *Am. J. Psychiat.,* 1546-47.
8. Altshuler, K. Z. 1971. Studies of the deaf. *Amer. J. Psychiat.,* 1521-26.
9. Fitzgerald, R. G. 1971. Visual phenomenology in recently blinded adults, *Amer. J. Psychiat.,* 1533-39.
10. Kerr, Chamove, and Harlow, H. 1969. Development cf infant monkeys fed low phenyl-alanine diets. *Paed. Res.,* 3: 305-12.
11. Scott, G. D. Person as a prisoner, Queen's Printer, chapter 12, Personality and Captivity.
12. Scott, J. P. Early experience and the organization of behaviour, Brooks and Cole, chapter 6.

Discussion

after papers

by PORTER, SACKETT and SCOTT

Prof. Sackett: I was asked by Professor Levine to speculate about the nature of the sex differences found in our studies.

I have a speculation that is based on my theory of what isolation rearing produces. The theory is a simple idea, probably wrong, that isolation rearing produces individuals whose responses are incompatible with the demands of post rearing environments. For example, if a monkey spends 90% of its time clutching itself, rocking, huddling it cannot be spending very much of its time learning to do new things. First it must stop huddling, clutching and making stereotyped movements, those behaviours that compete with the behaviours that are demanded by the situation. In other words, you have to stop doing the bad stuff before you start doing the good stuff. With respect to sex differences this theory suggests that somehow female behaviours are a) either based more on built-in mechanisms of response inhibition than males or b) female inhibitory mechanisms are less dependent for development on environmental input during infancy. Now that is probably not very satisfying but it is where I would begin in speculating on why we are finding that males seem to be more vulnerable to deprivations during infancy.

Prof. Levine: I am not talking about sexually related differences, I am talking about sex differences in non-sexual behaviour. What I am referring to are differences in performance factors, differences in exploratory behaviour, differences in positive responding etc.

Prof. Brady: You promised to summarize briefly the brain stimulation studies.

Prof. Sackett: We cannot find any beneficial effects on post rearing behaviour of the simple object stimulation 'enrichment' conditions that we have studied. However, we have reared several animals in total isolation that had brain stimulation electrodes implanted when they were twenty days old. They were raised in isolation from birth, receiving experimenter-controlled brain stimulation through nine months of age. The brain stimulated monkeys do explore and so show some positive social behaviour in these situations, isolates raised with or without object stimulation do not explore, show no positive social behaviours and spend 90 to 95% of their time in self-directed activities. The brain stimulation animals spend only 10% of their time in such behaviours. In the initial brain stimulated animals we attempted to put the four electrodes away in the mesencephalic reticular nucleus, superior colliculus, medial fore-brain bundles and diffuse sensory thalamus.

Prof. Mitchell: Do the experiments that you have done involving brain stimulation change exploration during the isolation treatment? Is there some practice in exploring things that are there because of the stimulation?

F

Prof. Sackett: In the initial studies the stimulation was all experimenter-controlled—the animal could not turn it on or off. What happens is that the infant shows more sleep during the twenty-four hours, which is not surprising because it is getting four hours a day with the brain 'juiced up'. There were very few specific behaviours that were elicited by these particular electrode implacements which was not surprising. There was some head turning and eye rolling with superior colliculus stimulation which makes some sense. Medial forebrain bundle stimulation had some tendency to produce drinking at stimulus onset. The only trouble is the other electrodes tended to do that too after a while. There were no really bizarre behaviours that seemed to be any different than usual for isolates. During isolation the brain stimulation animals, although they were more inactive than non-brain stimulation isolates, did make isolate type behaviours, they looked like isolates. It was after they came out of isolation that they did not look like isolates.

Dr. Kinzel: Could Dr. Scott elaborate on what led him to think that the inmates were treating their mothers as inanimate objects?

Dr. Scott: This particular observation is deduced from clinical experience rather than one area of prison experience. Where the child is treated like an object by the mother who rejects the child, the child becomes an object, begins to have no emotional contact, so that the child may then feel negligent of the other's emotions, so therefore he can do what he wants with it, regard it as an object. The person does not exist. It is a mobile object actually in the child's experience.

Prof. Fox: I wonder if I can come back to what Professor Levine was saying. He implied in some of the work that he was doing, particularly on prenatal influence stuff, that he had to hunt around for a variety of stress procedures and so on that would in fact influence the behaviour of the offspring. I am wondering whether it is not equally important for us to know about the stresses that do not produce any effect, to demonstrate the range of adaptability if you like of the animals?

Prof. Levine: I could not argue with the proposition. Really what I think is important is to find the common elements among environmental conditions. One introduces stress at the onset of pregnancy, during mid-pregnancy and in late pregnancy, so you have the problem of timing, that is one of the issues, the issue also has to do with chronicity, and intensity. The problem with most laboratory sets of conditions in which the situations are imposed is that they are terribly unlifelike and that they are usually a brief and transient experience which usually leads to rapid elevations in hormone levels which eventually get shut off. In most life situations, in the sense that we are talking about the kinds of life situations, you get the chronicity of events in which stimuli are there repeatedly and response to stimuli are not a matter of rapid onset and rapid offset, and I think if we are going to try to get models, what kinds of situations which do or do not cause this and that may have to do with parameters of intensity, parameters of duration and parameters of individual differences in response to this or that particular stress and we have to get all three of these in some way related.

Prof. Lavelle: I would like to ask Dr. Porter who is making by implication the case for the necessity of objects in the environment for the maturation of ordinary physical responses, is there any work on the children affected by thalidomide and deprived of their limbs as to mental deficits as a result of the inability to manipulate?

Dr. Porter: I know nothing at all about that.

Prof. Sackett: I know one study in which human thalidomide babies showed the same social and intellectual development by standard tests as a control group of non-thalidomide babies raised in the same institution, although thalidomide babies generally lack normal ability to manipulate objects, this is a relative thing because if the thalidomide baby even has a little stump it turns out that it can do amazing things with this little stump. Not having normal manipulative abilities did not eliminate intellectual development or formation of social attachments.

Prof. Mitchell: I have done some work with Lindburg and Davis on thalidomide monkeys. The animals had been raised having no upper limbs at all and the mothers compensate for this. The play behaviour and the social behaviour of these monkeys are normal. They explore using the mouth, their feet and so forth, and whatever they have for limbs.

Syndromes resulting from maternal deprivation — 1

Maternal and peer affectional deprivation in primates[1]

HARRY F. HARLOW,
University of Wisconsin

Maternal deprivation in primate infants is devastating because it involves destruction of the intimate love bonds existing between primate mothers and their infants. The basis for these beauteous bonds lies in the fact that the mother, even an inanimate one, gives the baby intimate bodily contact, as shown in Fig. 1. This is the primary variable tying infant to mother and mother to infant. There are a host of secondary variables including rocking motion, nursing and other activities associated with the breast, warmth, and maternal protection. Through these gifts, given by Gods, or rather Godesses, the mother imparts to the infant basic security and trust which are essential to all subsequent social and sexual development. For reasons mysterious and magnificent, basic trust may be imparted effectively by human mothers, monkey mothers, and even by inanimate mothers, a fact which suggests that intelligence is not a prime requisite for motherhood. However, no detraction from the meaning of motherhood is implied since monkeys raised by inanimate mothers have social shortcomings endowing them with socially moronic motivation.

[1]This research was supported by UPHS grant no. MH–11894 from the National Institutes of Mental Health to the University of Wisconsin Primate Laboratory.

85

Fig. 1. Mother giving bodily contact to frightened infant.

If a monkey infant is placed in a strange environment it will cling closely to the maternal body until replete with mother love. Subsequently it responds to the charms of the outside world and even leaves its mother to explore them. At the slightest disturbance or distress the baby flees back to the mother's body (see Fig. 2), and maternal contact deconditions, reconditions or extinguishes the 'Thing' of fear. After this process has been repeated a dozen or a hundred times the object or situation, awful or awesome,

Fig. 2. Frightened infants return to mother.

becomes subject to desensitization, leaving the infant free to investigate and contact the fearful objects. We have even had cases (as illustrated in Fig. 3) where desensitized infants went out later and chewed frightful fear stimuli to shreds, at no cost to themselves but frightful cost to the experimenter.

If a normal monkey or human infant is separated from its mother and placed alone in a strange or unfamiliar setting, the infant falls prostrate in piteous panic which does not end until maternal contact is reestablished. At this time infant faith immediately triumphs over infant fear. When the infant of an unloving mother, such as a wire surrogate mother, is placed in a strange room with

Fig. 3. Infant attacking previously feared monster.

the unloving mother present, the infant does not even attempt to gain maternal contact. Instead, as is shown in Fig. 4, it assumes an autistic posture, rocking back and forth and crying piteously. No animal can love a wire mother, or even worse, a wire wife!

If human or monkey infants are separated from their loving mothers for a period of hours or days they develop depression, given the term by Spitz of anaclitic or infant depression. According to Bowlby anaclitic depression proceeds through the three stages of protest, despair and detachment. By detachment Bowlby and Robertson referred to the fact that many human children actively resisted maternal attempts to reattach after separation. Instead of a state of detachment, almost all monkeys exhibit a third stage of reattachment or reunion in which they quickly accept and return the maternal advances. Bowlby has recently indicated that this may hold true with many human children. Obviously, immediate reattachment or detachment is dependent upon many personal and experiential variables.

Fig. 4. Infant in strange environment with its wire mother.

A series of formal studies at the University of Wisconsin were conducted using the apparatus shown in Fig. 5. The apparatus consisted of two living cages for mother-infant pairs and an interconnecting playpen unit. The apparatus was so constructed that the monkey mothers were confined to their cages, but the infants were free to go back and forth and play together. We wanted to study the effect of infant-mother separation on play behaviour, since play is the highest and most complex form of infant interaction. Using the described apparatus, two monkey infants, each one hundred and eighty days of age, were separated simultaneously from their mothers for a three week period. They exhibited a stage of protest followed by a state of despair until the period of reunion. Protest was characterized by an extremely high series of vocalizations and by random and unavailing maternally directed behaviour. Protest was followed by despair where the pattern of depression fully flared. Each infant assumed prone postures with body clasping and was frozen in fear, catastrophically crushed and

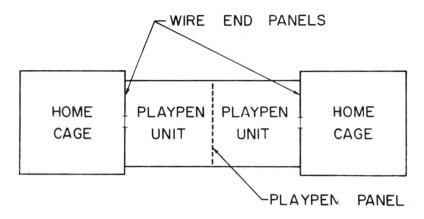

DEPRIVATION APPARATUS

Fig. 5. Mother-infant deprivation apparatus.

heartrendingly hopeless. As depicted in Fig. 6, play behaviour was almost totally eradicated throughout the period of separation. All of these behaviours persisted in spite of the fact that the infant pairs had access to each other. Upon reattachment, the infants clung closely to the mothers but subsequently demonstrated all normal social behaviours, including play.

In the first formal separation study infants and mothers were separated by transparent screens. A second, comparable investigation was conducted using opaque screens. Again, all of the behaviours found in the first study occurred in the second, although distress and despair were somewhat less intense, proving apparently the old adage 'Out of sight—out of mind'. The original Wisconsin studies have served as models for other investigators using varying experimental situations and species of monkey subjects. Although the maternal and infant attachments between monkeys of different species and genera differ, all of the basic findings have been confirmed.

We have long presented the iconoclastic position that the love between infant peers or playmates was stronger and of greater subsequent sexual and social importance than the deep affectional bonds between mother and child. Suomi demonstrated this concept by measuring the effects of multiple separations

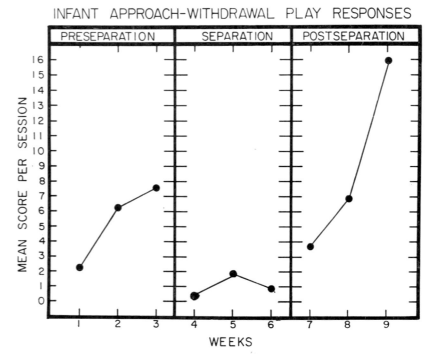

Fig. 6. Effects of maternal deprivation upon infant play behaviour.

between age-mate monkey friends rather than separations between mother and child. The study was spectacularly successful in that the monkeys proceeded through the three stages on each and every separation during the half year in which twenty successive separations were achieved. The protest stage encompassed in the first separation days was characterized by high levels of locomotion and vocalization as shown in Fig. 7. Despair, progressing throughout the next three separation days, was exemplified by persistent self-clasp and rock-and-huddle. Following these manifestations the separated peer was returned to his playmate friends and rapidly went into the pattern of close ventral cling. These data round out the obvious conclusion that anaclitic depression is caused by any deep affectional loss by the infant monkey. A dramatic and hitherto non-reported pattern of infantalization occurred in all of the peers of this particular study and is illustrated in Fig. 8. Ventral cling

EFFECT OF 12 SEPARATION SECTIONS
ON BEHAVIOR OF MONKEYS

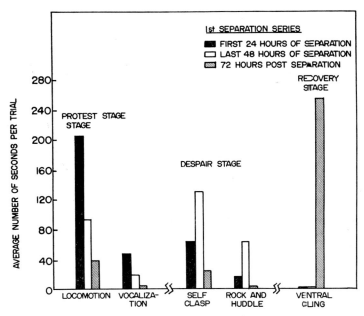

Fig. 7. Behaviour of peer separated monkeys during three separation stages.

and self-mouth are normal neonatal and infant patterns, but they are non-existent in normal monkeys after ninety days of age. In the case of the multiply separated infants these responses had not decreased at even six or nine months of age. It was as if all of these infants had walked through Ponce de Leon's Fountain of Youth and were cast and condemned to babyhood forever. Even more dramatic data are shown for the relatively late maturing variable of social play. Play normally begins at three months of age, flares forward at six months and dominates monkey behaviour three months later. It is perfectly obvious from the figure that infant play is minimal at ninety days with these separated monkeys but this is normal and natural. The multiply separated infants, however, showed no increase in play at six months and even at nine months, and this persisted even though they were allowed six weeks of continuous interaction between the twelfth and thirteenth

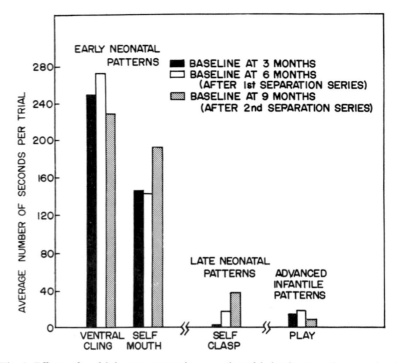

Fig. 8. Effects of multiple peer separation on selected behaviours at three age levels.

separation. The loss of play behaviour shows the most drastic and prolonged example of affectional behavioural obliteration ever reported in separation studies.

We have preliminary data on the attempted production of juvenile or nonanaclitic depression in rhesus monkeys, to be produced either by multiple separation of these juvenile three-year-old monkeys or by confinement in vertical chambers which will be subsequently described. The depression behaviour exhibited by these juvenile monkeys is not nearly as striking as that demonstrated by the infant monkey, either after the multiple separations or after release from the vertical chamber. In both cases, however, the juvenile monkeys do show an abnormal pattern of maintained bodily proximity which appeared and persisted after the separations and release from the chamber. Spontaneous locomotion also diminished. Further experimentation is needed to assess the effect of social deprivation on juvenile monkeys previously provided a rich social experience with effective mothers and agemates. If the juvenile monkey presently remains a recalcitrant subject for social separation studies this is not surprising. All adolescent primates have always been recalcitrant subjects and they will always be recalcitrant subjects.

> Standing with reluctant feet,
> Between the certain and the sweet,
> Imposes problems never ended,
> Which still with time can be transcended.

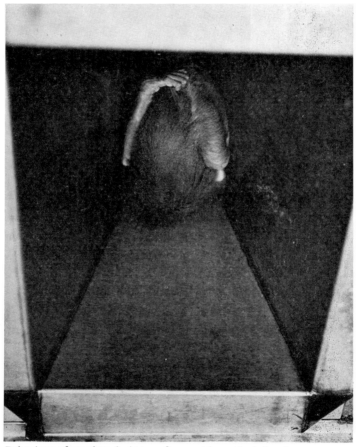

Fig. 9. Behaviour of monkey during confinement in vertical chamber.

Early depression commonly involves loss of social bonds. However, we created the vertical chamber, an apparatus already mentioned, which rapidly produced and prolonged depression in the infant monkey. This chamber, illustrated in Fig. 9, is adjusted to the size of the subjects and has sloping steel walls descending to a four inch wide wire base three inches above the rounded bottom. Here the animal is protected against contact with feces and urine. The apparatus thus allows freedom of movement in all three planes even though the top is screened to prevent egress. The restrained monkeys showed normal appetite and thirst, normal weight gain and no abnormal susceptibility to disease. They are apparently physiologically normal but became behaviourally depressed as illustrated in Fig. 9.

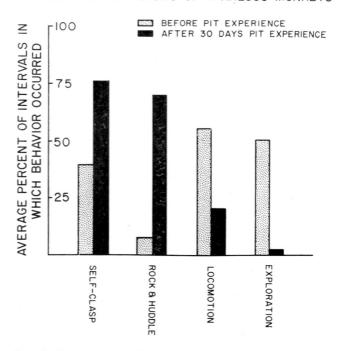

Fig. 10. Effect of thirty antecedent chamber days on selected monkey behaviours.

In a preliminary study a group of monkeys approximately one year of age were confined in vertical chambers thirty days, and the frequency of selected behaviours was measured before and after containment (Fig. 10). Abnormal behaviours of self-clasp and rock-and-huddle were significantly increased whereas complex behaviours of locomotion and particularly exploration were significantly decreased or almost obliterated. Furthermore the great increase in deviant behaviours and the great increase in complex behaviours persisted throughout eight weeks of constant testing after chambering had ceased.

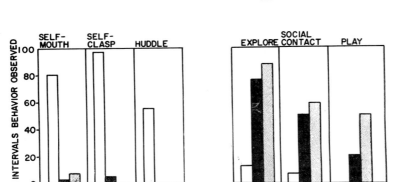

Fig. 11. Effect of forty-five antecedent chamber days on behaviour after six to eight months removal.

In a second experiment, the behaviours of four macaques that had been chambered for forty-five days antecedent to ninety days of age were compared to the behaviours of two equal-age control groups; a normal group, raised with playmates and an intermediate group individually raised from birth in the partial isolation of bare wire cages. The chambering effects were both profound and prolonged.

The depressive measures of self-mouth, self-clasp and huddle were extremely high in the chambered monkeys and almost nonexistent in the control groups six to eight months after release from the chambers. Contrariwise, normal behaviours such as explore, social contact and play were nonexistent or near nonexistent in the chambered monkeys and were very high in both control groups with the exception of play where the partially isolated control group measures half-way between the normal and the chambered monkeys (as graphed in Fig. 11).

At present the vertical chamber remains a room of mystery and a chamber of challenge, adding its unknown factor to the known effects of maternal and peer deprivation in primates. The devastating social depression achieved by relatively brief confinement in the vertical chambers raised theoretical problems which we are investigating. Chambering involves social separation and deprivation, but a relatively short period of separation, thirty to forty-five days, produces deep and lasting effects that have not been demonstrated by any other method for a near equal separation time.

From a practical point of view this precipitously produced social paralysis is an inestimable psychopathological research gain Techniques for unfailing production of depression by rapid and rampant means enormously expedite research on variables that facilitate depression, such as separation age, separation duration and previous or present social bonds. Of equal importance, rapid and unrelenting depression offers unparalleled opportunities to measure the magnitude of depression-alleviating conditions ranging from bilateral and unilateral EST to such chemical agents as selected tricyclic drugs, MAO inhibitors, lithium carbonate and others as they may appear. Theoretically, the effect of chemical controls on depressive syndromes might be removed from the hazy realms of guesswork and consigned to the holy realm of fact.

When we have shattered the monkey ego by maternal separation, peer or agemate separation or both plus the interposition of the vertical chamber, we have destroyed affectional bonds formed in the past while substituting merely attitudes of helplessness and hopelessness, and we have come less than halfway to our research goals.

Anyone can destroy. Only the gifted can create or recreate. There is the biblical injunction, 'What God hath joined together let no man put asunder'. Or, at a nursery rhyme level.

G

> Some monkeys were placed on a therapist's wall,
> Their bodies and minds took a maddening fall,
> The therapist's task was obvious then
> To put broken monkeys together again.

We have already embarked on a mission of macaque monkey rehabilitation. We have completed three experiments involving rehabilitation of monkeys socially separated from birth from all living forms for six or twelve months. Our previous prediction that such monkeys could not be rehabilitated is false. Successful behaviour rehabilitation has already been achieved in monkeys so abnormal that we previously thought they were doomed to social extinction. We are starting 'psychotherapy' with monkeys emotionally 'eradicated' by confinement in the vertical chambers. We await the results since we have a large emotional stake in them. So do the monkeys. We believe they have nothing to fear, not even fear itself.

Syndromes resulting from maternal deprivation — 2

Analogues in human behaviour

K. Feigenbaum,
Antioch College, Columbia

The term maternal deprivation has been associated with a plethora of pathological syndromes including such behaviour as language and sensori-motor retardation; deficits in concept formation; affective blandness and psychopathic personalities to name but a few. For some psychologists and psychiatrists maternal deprivation appears to be their 'root of all evil'.

To present a comprehensive critical review of the literature employing the concept of maternal deprivation would exceed the time I have for presentation today. Therefore, I intend mainly to concentrate upon what I believe to be the 'logical' inadequacies of the concept and in doing so review some of the major findings and conclusions.

A review of the literature quickly indicates that the term maternal deprivation is a conglomerate one, and appears to be used in a number of different ways. Sometimes it is employed as synonym for maternal separation; sometimes for multiple mothering; sometimes for 'distortions' in maternal care; sometimes for sensory-deprivation; or as being a covariant of separation anxiety. It can also refer to post-natal or pre-natal conditions.

Given the variety of definitions, one can ask whether different investigators of 'maternal deprivation' are analyzing the same phenomena or different ones, either with the same or different consequences. Clarity of definition is a functional pre-requisite before any valid conclusions can be drawn from the 'jabberwocky' of concepts hiding under the wings of maternal deprivation.

Let us at least begin here by providing some definitions that I hope to use in a consistent fashion. In my discussion of the maternal-deprivation literature, by sensory-deprivation I mean a quantitative lack of tactile, kinesthetic, auditory, of perceptual stimulation. Here, I assume a norm necessary to allow the development of functional behaviour. In other words, enough stimulation to provide 'an average expectable environment'. When I say maternal deprivation I mean distortions in maternal care which may or may not include sensory-deprivation but certainly includes a lack of sensitive individualized adaptation to the child's needs. Multiple mothering means that there is more than one caretaker responsible for the 'caring' of the child. Here, however, one should distinguish between the conditions where there are a large number of changing caretakers such as is reported in some orphanages and hospitals of 'dubious' quality and the condition where there are a few permanent caretakers such as on the Kibbutz-im or in polymatric families. By maternal separation, I mean a break in continuity with a mother figure after a meaningful focused, relationship has been established. There are obviously various permutations of separation that may produce psychologically different experiences, separations can be of short or long lived duration. It can be repeated with a variety of degrees of external stress (a trip, short hospitalization, death of a parent, war time emergency separation, foster placement, etc.)

In defining separation anxiety, I plead 'fuzziness' but the definition has clear meaning for me: fear of loss, of being without the presence of another person or persons to interact with. Finally, by pre-natal maternal deprivation, I refer to either the psychological condition (anxiety) or physical condition (lack of adequate protein, heroin use in pregnancy) that may be injurious to the child's physical and mental well-being after birth. So much for definitions!

Besides lacking precision in definition, maternal deprivation cannot be viewed as a simple causal antecedent variable. To pose this symposium's question in the form: 'what are the syndromes associated with maternal deprivation' will lead us into confusion. It is like asking the question 'what is the effect of a right hand punch on the jaw'. From Joe Frazier to Joe O'Leary, or from

Joe O'Leary to Joe Frazier? Who punches and whose jaw? The effect cannot be separated from an understanding of the history (genetic-environmental interaction) of the organism to which the treatment is applied; for how long; for how many times. And at what period in their lives. The question of the 'long-term' or lasting effects of the treatment be it a 'poison' can only be answered by observations of conditions where an 'antidote' is given ideally in Newtonian principle form: equal-opposite to the supposed negative treatment (sensory-deprivation followed by sensory-stimulation etc.). At a cultural level this means looking at whether the culture in which 'maternal deprivation', or what you will, occurs, is continuous or discontinuous in its cultural conditions. Dennis in his study of the Crèche in Lebanon has indicated that intellectual retardation seen in infants who had been subjected to sensory-deprivation and perhaps maternal deprivation was not irreversible. Could this be a result of a discontinuity in the conditioning process?

I will now briefly interpret the major research findings:

1) PRE-NATAL DEPRIVATION—Most of the work in this area is epidemiological and retrospective in nature. Prolonged malnutrition of the mother can bring about fetal death and mental retardation (Hopner 1958; Pasmanick and Knoblock 1958). Fetal infection such as caused by Syphilis or Rubella can also produce congenital abnormalities. Drug addiction, especially heroin can bring about deleterious effects as well as many drugs that cross the placental barrier, the most insidious being Thalidomide.

Psychological stress in pregnancy may also effect fetal development and has been associated with colicky babies (Stewart et al. 1954). Sontag (1941) reported marked increases in fetal movement when the mother was under stress. Infants born to 'disturbed mothers' are reported to have high activity levels after birth. The problem of relating disturbances in infancy and childhood to the mother's psychological state during pregnancy is extremely difficult since the stress and anxiety usually continues after birth.

2) MATERNAL DEPRIVATION: INSTITUTIONALISM AND SENSORY-DEPRIVATION—Most of the early studies attributing physical and mental retardation to the effect of 'maternal deprivation' have been strongly criticized for poor experimental design; invalid and un-

reliable instruments of measurement; lack of adequate control groups (Pinneau 1950). Therefore the findings and interpretations of Spitz, Ribble and the long term effects attributed to maternal deprivation by Goldfarb, (1947) have been seriously questioned. Furthermore in the cases of Spitz and Goldfarb we have the situation of a confounded variable: conditions in which sensory-deprivation; multiple mothering; maternal separation and possible maternal deprivation took place. In fact, multiple mothering, under conditions when there are a large number of caretakers should be highly associated with lack of sensitive individualized care (maternal deprivation).

The intervention studies of Castler (1965), White and Castle (1964) seem definitely to implicate sensory-deprivation as one of the major causes of intellectual and sensori-motor retardation. In both cases additional stimulation, the first through rocking and the second through tactile stimulation reduced retardation. Dennis and Sayegh (1965) provided opportunities to sit in an upright position, watch and manipulate objects to institutionalized infants for fifteen days. This experience also seems to have resulted in improved performances on developmental test. Regardless of the specific variable or variables involved, however, the 'deprived' environment and restricted opportunities for learning in institutions have been clearly documented if not by Bowlby (1952) then certainly by Provence and Lipton (1962).

Multiple Mothering

Here again one has to distinguish between effects of a few caretakers such as in the Kibbutz or polymatric family where sensitive individualized care is possible and the case where there may be many caretakers involving more separations and the greater possibility of lack of sensitive care. In the former case Rabin (1958) reported 'developmental retardation' among infants in the Kibbutz which do not persist in later life. Other investigators have not reported this, and it has been suggested that Rabin's population was not a representative Kibbutz one, if such exists, since there appears to be a good deal of variability in social organization among them.

In a recent study by Parakevopoulous and McV. Hunt (1971) the development of object constancy and vocal imitation was compared in children reared at home or in an orphanage with a three to one caretaker ratio and one where there was a ten to one ratio. For object construction, the children living in the orphanage with the ten to one ratio achieved the upper levels of object permanence about a year later than did those in the orphanage with a three to one ratio, and the latter orphanage averaged older, but not significantly older, than home-reared children. For vocal imitation, the children living under the high infant-caretaker ratio averaged older, but not significantly older than those living under the low infant caretaker ratio, and both averaged from nine months to one year older than home-reared children. In describing the two different institutions it must be added that the high caretaker ratio was more bland in physical surroundings. Reports that institutionalized children showed no preference for one toy rather than another (Provence and Lipton, 1962), retardation in the time when the smile appears, indiscriminative smiling and lack of fear of strangers may be related therefore to delay in the formation of object constancy accompanied by the consequent inability to form a strong social attachment to a single caretaker. Delay or diminished imitation reports should if one extrapolates from Piaget (1950) affect both the course of sensori-motor development; language development and concept formation. Delay or diminished imitation also limits the interaction possibilities with a maternal figure or surrogate. Lack of response on the part of the infant can in turn bring lack of response from the adult: in turn bringing affect blandness in the child and lack of desire to seek contact with the mother and expectation of need gratification for the child or mother.

Separation Anxiety

It may be that I have a form of separation anxiety about imparting my conclusions about the work which goes under the aegis of maternal separation and separation anxiety; does to give to you mean fear of loss for me somewhere in my pre-conscious?

It follows not only at a personal level but at an interpersonal one that separation from mother or others is not always a negative event for the well-being of the child. A single example would be the case of an unloved or battered baby placed into 'loving hands'.

There is no question however, that there is such an entity as attachment behaviour; Ainsworth (1963); Ainsworth and Bell

(1970); Schaeffer (1964). To summarize one study by Coates et al. (1972) 'Attachment behaviour in the presence and absence of the mother was investigated among ten, fourteen and eighteen month infants. Visual regard, touching and proximity to the mother were more frequent following separation than before. Patterning in infant behaviour is sufficiently extensive to warrant the use of the attachment concept'. Infants seem to react differently both toward their general environment and to their caretaker before and after separation but just how differently they react depends upon their pre-separation relationship with the environment and caretaker; their age at separation and the kind, number and degree of separation. Thompson and Casler have each intimated that many of the ill effects attributed to either maternal deprivation or maternal separation during the first six months may be due to perceptual deprivation. Whereas those after six months are due both to perceptual deprivation and the affective problems due to breaking an established emotional bond or never forming an attachment. The cutoff age of six or seven months is not arbitrary. Bowlby and Schaeffer and Callender report different reactions from infants separated before or after six months. Bowlby claims that children who are separated from their mothers after six months fret but those who are separated before do not. Schaeffer and Callender (1959) found that infants under six months accepted mother substitutes without protest. Schaeffer also reports that babies under six months when they return from a hospital are unresponsive to people and explore the environment whereas after six months they cling to the maternal figure and are fearful of strangers.

I know both experientially and clinically that separation anxiety is a powerful variable affecting behaviour. It may be as Freud has postulated that once we have been in contact with a drive satisfying object or person we refuse to let it go and fear separation. What conditions promote separation anxiety or the intenseness of separation anxiety? How does the age related cognitive structure of the child intervene? How does the permanent separation (death) of the maternal figure contribute to separation anxiety? What relationship is there between 'over-dependence' and separation anxiety? Between lack of feelings of acceptance and separation anxiety? Between the socialization condition where the mother intimates or says directly to the child that if you do not behave in a certain way she is going to leave? Between feelings of omnipotence and aggression projection (I wish to kill you: you wish to kill me) and separation anxiety? Experimental empirical evidence is either non-existent or too scanty to provide any cogent answers to the above questions. All one can say with assurance, is the cliche that investigations of an empirical order, are in order.

A Selected Bibliography follows

Bibliography

Ainsworth, M. D. 1963. The development of infant-mother interaction among the Ganda. In *Determinants of infant behavior,* ed. B. M. Foss, vol. 2: 67-112, New York: Wiley.

Ainsworth, M. D. & Bell, S. M. 1970. Attachment exploration and separation. *Child Dev.,* 41: 49-67.

Ainsworth, M. D. and Wittig, B. A. 1969. Attachment and exploratory behavior of one-year-olds in a strange situation. In *Determinants of infant behavior,* ed. B. M. Foss, vol. 4, New York: Wiley.

Ambrose, J. A. 1961. The development of the smiling response in early infancy. In *Determinants of infant behavior,* ed. B. M. Foss, vol. 1: 179-96. New York: Wiley.

Antonov, A. N. 1947. Children born during the siege of Leningrad in 1942. *J. Pediat.,* 30: 250-59.

Bakwin, H. 1949. Emotional deprivation in infants. *J. Pediat.,* 35: 512-21.

Bateson, P. P. G. 1966. The characteristics and context of imprinting. *Biol. Rev.,* 41: 177-220.

Bender, L. 1947. Psychopathic behavior disorders in children. In *Handbook of correctional psychology,* eds. R. M. Lindner and R. V. Seliger, New York: Philosophical Library.

Bender, L. 1950. Anxiety in disturbed children. In *Anxiety,* eds. P. H. Hoch and J. Zubin, 119-39. New York: Grune and Stratton.

Bender, L., and Yarnell, H. 1941. An observation nursery: a study of 250 children in the psychiatric division of Bellevue Hospital. *Am. J. Psychiat.,* 97: 1158-74.

Benedict, Ruth. *Continuities and Discontinuities in Cultural Conditioning.*

Benjamin, J. D. 1963. Further comments on some developmental aspects of anxiety. In *Counterpoint,* ed. H. S. Gaskill, 121-53, New York: International Universities Press.

Bernstein, B. 1961. Social class and linguistic development: a theory of social learning. In *Education, economy and society,* eds. A. H. Halsey, J. Flovot and C. A. Anderson, Glencoe, Ill.: Free Press.

Bernstein, L. 1952. A note on Christie's 'Experimental naivete and experiential naivete.' *Psychol. Bull.,* 49: 38-40.

Birch, H. G. and Belmont, L. 1961. The problem of comparing home rearing versus foster-home rearing in defective children. *Pediatrics,* 1: 813-15.

Bostock, J. 1961. Thieving in childhood. *Med. J. Aust.,* 1: 813-15.

Bowlby, J. 1940. The influence of early environment. *Int. J. Psycho-Analysis,* 21: 154-78.

Bowlby, J. 1944. Forty-four juvenile thieves. *Int. J. Psychol.-Analysis,* 25: 1-57.

Bowlby, J. 1952. Maternal care and mental health. *WHO Monogr.* No. 2.

Bowlby, J. 1957. An ethological approach to research in child development. *Br. J. med. Psychol.,* 30: 230-40.

Bowlby, J. 1958. The nature of the child's tie to his mother. *Int. J. Psycho-Analysis,* 39: 350-73.

Bowlby, J.; Ainsworth, M.; Moston, M.; and Rosenbluth, D. 1956. The effects of mother-child separation: a follow-up study. *Br. J. med. Psychol.,* 29: 211-47.

Bowlby, J. 1969. *Attachment and loss*: Volume I Attachment, London: Hogarth Press.

Burlingham, D., and Freud, A. 1944. *Infants without families.* London: Allen and Unwin.

Caldwell, B. M. 1962. The usefulness of the critical period hypothesis in the study of filiative behavior. Merrill-Palmer *Q. behav. Devel.,* 8: 229-42.

Caldwell, B. M.; Hersher, L.; Lipton, E. L.; Richmond, J. B.; Stern, G. A.; Eddy, E.; Drachman, R.; and Rothman A. 1693. Mother infant interaction in monomatric and polymatric families. *Am. J. Orthopsychiat.,* 33: 653-64.

Campbell, B. A. 1967. Development studies of learning and motivation in infraprimate mammals. In *Early behavior,* eds. H. W. Stevenson, E. H. Hess and H. L. Rheingold. New York: Wiley.

Campbell, B. A. and Jaynes, J. 1966. Reinstatement. *Psychol. Rev.* 73: 478-80.

Campbell, B. A., and Pickleman, J. R. 1961. The imprinting object as a reinforcing stimulus, *J. comp. physiol. Psychol.,* 54: 592-96.

Campbell, D., and Thompson, W. R. 1968. Development. *Ann. Rev. Psychol.,* 19: 251-92.

Carlson, P. V. 1961. 'The development of emotional behavior as a function of diadic mother-young relationships.' Unpublished doctoral dissertation, Purdue University.

Carmichael, L. 1954. The onset and early development of behavior. In *Manual of child psychology,* ed. L. Carmichael, 2nd ed. New York: Wiley.

Castler, L. 1961. Maternal deprivation: a critical review of the literature. *Monogr. Soc. Res. Child Dev.,* 26: No. 2.

Castler, L. 1965. The effects of extra tactile stimulation on a group of institutionalized infants. *Genet. psychol. Monogr.,* 71: 137-75.

Centerwall, S. A., and Centerwall, W. R. 1960. A study of children with mongolism reared in the home compared to those reared away from the home. *Pediatrics,* 25: 678-85.

Clarke, A. D. B., and Clarke, A. M. 1954. Cognitive changes in the feebleminded. *Br. J. Psychol.,* 45: 197-99.

Coates, B., Anderson and Hartup, 1972. Interrelations in the attachment behavior of human infants, *Devel. Psychol.,* vol. 6, No. 2: 218-30.

Coleman, R. W., and Provence, S. 1957. Environmental retardation (hospitalism) in infants living in families. *Pediatrics,* 19: 285-92.

David, M., and Appell, G. A study of nursing care and nurse-infant interaction. In *Determinants of infant behavior,* ed. B. M. Foss, vol. 1: 121-41. New York: Wiley. 1961.

Denenberg, V. H. 1962. The effects of early experience. In *The behavior of domestic animals,* ed. E. S. E. Hofez. Baltimore, Md.: Williams and Wilkins. (a)

Denenberg, V. H. 1962. An attempt to isolate critical periods of development in the rat. *J. comp. physiol. Psychol.,* 55: 813-15. (b)

Denenberg, V. H. 1964. Critical periods, stimulus input, and emotional reactivity. *Psychol. Rev.,* 71: 335-51.

Denenberg, V. H. 1966. Animal studies on developmental determinants of behavioral adaptability. In *Experience structure and adaptability,* ed. O. J. Harvey. New York: Springer.

Dennis, W. 1960. Causes of retardation among institutional children: in Iran. *J. genet. Psychol.,* 96: 47-59.

Dennis, W., and Najarian, P. 1957. Infant development under environmental handicap. *Psychol. Monogr.,* 71: No. 7.

Dennis, W., and Sayegh, Y. 1965. The effect of supplementary experiences upon the behavioral development of infants in institutions. *Child Dev.,* 36: 81-90.

Deutsch, M. 1962. The disadvantaged child and the learning process: Some social, psychological and development considerations. Columbia University, New York: Paper prepared for the Ford Foundation *Work Conference on Curriculum and Teaching in Depressed Areas.*

Dispensa, J., and Hornbeck, R. T. 1941. Can intelligence be improved by prenatal endocrine therapy. *J. Psychol.,* 12: 209-24.

Dolittle, R. F., and Meade, R. The effect of gentling on some psychological and physiological phenomena. Paper read at the meetings of the Easter Psychological Association, New York, April, 1957.

Ebbs, J. H.; Tisdall, F. F.; and Scott, W. A. 1942. The influence of prenatal diet on the mother and child. *Millbank mem. Fund Q. Bull.,* 20: 35-36.

Freud, A., and Burlingham, D. T. 1944. *Infants without families.* New York: International universities Press.

Freud, A., and Dann, S. 1951. An experiment in group upbringing. *Psychoanal. Study Child,* 6: 127-68.

Gardner, D. B.; Hawkes, G. R.; and Burchinal, L. G. 1961. Noncontinuous mothering in infancy and development in later childhood. *Child Dev.,* 32: 225-34.

Gardner, D. B.; Pease, D.; and Hawkes, G. R. 1961. Responses of two-year old children to controlled stress situations. *J. genet. Psychol.,* 98: 23-35.

Geber, M. 1958. The psychomotor development of African children in the first year and the influence of maternal behavior. *J. Soc. Psychol.,* 47: 185-95.

Geber, M. and Dean, R. F. A. 1957. Gesell tests on African children. *Pediatrics,* 20: 1055-65.

Gebhard, P. H.; Pomeroy, W. B.; Martin, C. E.; and Christerson, C. V. 1958. *Pregnancy,* birth, and abortion. New York: Harper anc Row.

Gesell, A. The ontogenesis of infant behavior. 1946. In *Manual of child psychology,* ed. L. Carmichael. New York: Wiley.

Gewirtz, J. L. 1961. A learning analysis of the effects of normal stimulation, privation and deprivation on the acquisition of social motivation and attachment. In *Determinants of infant behavior,* ed. B. M. Foss, vol. I. New York: Wiley.

Glass, H. B. 1954. The genetic aspects of adaptability. *Proc Ass. Res. nerv. ment. Dis.,* 23: 367-77.

Glass, N. 1949. Eating, sleeping, and elimination habits in children attending day nurseries and children cared for at home by mothers. *Am. J. Orthopsychiat.,* 19: 697-711.

Goldfarb, W. 1945. Effects of psychological deprivation in infancy and subsequent stimulation. *Am. J. Psychiat.,* 102: 18-33. (a)

Goldfarb, W. 1945. Psychological privation in infancy and subsequent adjustment. *Am. J. Orthopsychiat.,* 15: 247-55. (b)

Goldfarb, W. 1947. Variations in adolescent adjustment cf institutionally reared children. *Am. J. Orthopsychiat.,* 17: 449-57.

Goldfarb, W. 1949. Rorschach test differences between family-reared institution-reared, and schizophrenic children. *Am. J. Orthopsychiat.,* 19: 625-33.

Goodenough, F. L. 1939. A critique of experiments on raising the I.Q. *Educ. Meth.,* 19: 73-79.

Goodenough, F. L., and Mauer, K. M. 1940. The mental development of nursery school children compared with that of non-nursery school children. *Yearbook of the National Society for Studies in Education,* vol. 39, part II: 161-78.

Goodpasture, E. W. 1942. Virus infection of the mammalian fetus. *Science,* 95: 391-96.

Gray, P. H. 1958. Theory and evidence of imprinting in human infants. *J. Psychol.,* 46: 155-66.

Gray, S. W., and Klaus, R. A. 1965. An experimental preschool program for culturally deprived children. *Child Dev.,* 36: 887-98

Green, C., and Zigler, E. 1962. Social deprivation and the performance of feeble-minded and normal children on a satiation type task. *Child Dev.,* 499-508.

Gregg, N. McA. 1941. Congenital cataract following German measles in the mother. *Trans. opth. Soc. Aust.,* 3: 35-46.

Halverson, H. M. 1931. An experimental study of prehension in infants by means of systematic cinema records. *Genet. psychol, Monogr.,* 10: 107-286.

Hamburger, V. Ontogeny of behaviour and its structural basis. *Compar. Neurochem. Proc. Int.* Neurochem. Sympos., 1962.

Harlow, H. F.; Harlow, M. K.; and Hansen, E. W. 1963. The maternal affectional system of rhesus monkey. In *Maternal behavior in mammals,* ed. H. Rheingold. New York: Wiley.

Hattwick, B. W. 1936. The influence of nursery school attendance upon the behavior and personality of the preschool child. *J. exp. Educ.,* 5: 180-90.

Haynes, H., White, B. L., and Held, R. 1965. Visual accommodation in human infants. *Science,* 148: 528-30.

Hebb, D. O. 1942. The effect of early and late brain injury upon test scores, and the nature of normal adult intelligence. *Proc. Am. Phil. Soc.,* 85: 275-92.

Heinicke, C. M. 1956. Some effects of separating two-year-old children from their parents: a comparative study. *Hum. Relat.,* 9: 105-76.

Held, R., and Bossom, J. 1961. Neonatal deprivation and adult rearrangement: complementary techniques for analyzing plastic sensory-motor coordinations. *J. comp. physiol.,* 54: 33-37.

Held, R., and Heim. A. 1963. Movement-produced stimulation in the development of visually guided behavior. *J. comp. physiol. Psychol.,* 56: 872-76.

Held, R., and Schlank, M. 1959. Adaptation to disarranged eye-hand coordination in the distance-dimension. *Am. J. Psychol.,* 72: 603-5.

Hopner, R. 1958. Maternal nutrition and the fetus. *J. Am. Med. Ass.* 168: 1774-77.

Hess, R. D., and Shipman, V. C. 1965. Early experience and the socialization of cognitive modes in children. *Child Dev.,* 36: 869-86.

Hetzer, H., and Wolf, K. 1928. Baby tests. *Z. Psychol.,* 107: 62-104.

Hodges, W. L.; McCandless, B. R.; and Spicker, H. H. The development and application of a diagnostically-based curriculum for culturally deprived preschool children. Washington, D.C. U.S. *Office of Education Research Proposals,* 1964-66.

Hopper, H. E., and Pinneau, S. R. 1957. Frequency of regurgitation in infancy as related to the amount of stimulation received from the mother. *Child Dev.,* 28: 229-35.

Hooker, D. 1952. *The prenatal origins of behavior.* Lawrence: University of Kansas Press.

Hunt, J. McV. 1961. Intelligence and experience. New York: Ronald Press.

Jersild, A. T., and Fite, M. D. 1939. The influence of nursery school experience on children's social adjustments. *Monogr. Soc. Res. Child Develop.,* no. 2.

Jones, H. E., and Jorgensen, A. P. 1940. Mental growth as related to nursery school attendance. *Yearbook of the National Society for Studies in Education,* vol. 39, part II: 207-22.

Kaufman, I. C., and Rosenblum, L. A. 1968. The reaction to separation in infant monkeys: anaclitic depression and conservation-withdrawal. *Psychosomat. Med.*

Kessen, W. *The Child.* 1965. New York: Wiley.

McNemar, Q. 1940. A critical examination of the University of Iowa studies of environmental influences upon the I.Q. *Psychol. Bull.,* 37: 63-92.

Meehl, P. E. 1962. Shizotaxia, schizotypy and schizophrenia. *Am. Psychol.,* 17: 827-38.

Melzack, R. 1962. Effects of early perceptual restriction on simple visual discrimination. *Science,* 137: 987-97.

Melzack, R. 1965. Effects of early experience on behavior: experiments and conceptual considerations. In *Psychopathology of perception,* eds. P. H. Hoch and J. Zubin. New York: Grune and Stratton.

Melzack, R., and Burns, S. K. 1965. Neurophysiological effects of early sensory restriction. *Exper. Neurol.,* 13: 163-75.

Melzack, R., and Scott, T. H. 1957. The effects of early experience on the response to pain. *J. comp. physiol. Psychol.,* 50: 155-6 .

Melzack, R., and Thompson, W. R. 1956. Effects of early experience on social behavior. *Can. J. Psychol.,* 10: 82-90.

Menlove, F. L. 1965. Aggressive symptoms in emotionally disturbed adopted children. *Child Dev.,* 36: 519-32.

Montague, M. F. A. 1950. Constitutional and prenatal factors in infant and child health. In *Symposium on the healthy personality,* ed. M. J. E. Senn, pp. 148-75. New York: Josiah Macy, Jr., Foundation.

Montague, M. F. A. 1962. *Prenatal influences,* Urbana, Ill.: Thomas.

Nalbandov, A. V. 1958. *Reproductive physiology.* San Francisco: Freeman.

Kessen, W. Sucking and looking: two organized congenital patterns of behavior in the human newborn. In *Early behavior,* eds. H. W. Stevenson, E. H. Hess, and H. L. Rheingold. New York: Wiley, 1967.

Krech, D., Rosenzweig, M. R., and Bennett, E. L. 1966. Environmental impoverishment, social isolation and changes in brain chemistry and anatomy. *Physiol. Behav.,* 1: 99-109.

Lakin, M. 1957. Personality factors in mothers of excessively crying (colicky) infants. *Monogr. Soc. Res. Child Devel.,* 22: no. 64.

Landauer, T. K., and Whiting, J. N. M. 1963. Infantile stimulation and adult stature of human males. *Am. Anthrop.,* 66: 1007-28.

Lewis, H. 1954. *Deprived children.* New York: Oxford University Press.

Lieberman, M. W. 1963. Early development stress and later behavior. *Science,* 141: 824-25.

Lilienfeld, A. M.; Pasamanick, B.; and Rogers, M. E. 1955 The relationship between pregnancy experience and the development of certain neuro-psychiatric disorders in childhood. *Am. J. Publ. Hlth ,* 45: 637.

Lowrey, L. G. 1940. Personality distortion and early institut onal care. *Am. J. Orthopsychiat.,* 10: 576-86.

Lynn, R. 1966. *Attention, arousal and the orientation reaction.* Oxford: Pergamon Press.

Maas, H. 1963. Long-term effects of early childhood separation and group care. *Vita hum.,* 6: 34-56. (a)

Maas, H. 1963. The young adult adjustment of twenty wartime residual nursery children. *Child Welfare,* 57-62. (b)

Neel, J. V. 1953. The effect of exposure to the atomic bombs on pregnancy termination in Hiroshima and Nagasaki: preliminary report. *Science,* 118: 537-41.

Newton, G., and Levine, S. 1968. *Early experience and behavior:* psychological and physiological effects of early environmental variation. Urbana, Ill.: Thomas.

Orlansky, H. 1949. Infant care and personality. *Psychol. Bull.,* 46: 1-48.

Ottinger, D. R.; Denenberg, V. H.; and Stephens, M. W. 1963. Maternal emotionality, multiple mothering and emotionality at maturity. *J. comp. physiol. Psychol.*, 56: 313-17.

Ourth, L., and Brown, K. B. 1961. Inadequate mothering and disturbance the neonatal period. *Child Dev.*, 32: 287-95.

Page, E. W. 1957. Transfer of materials across the human placenta. *Am. J. Obstet. Gynec.*, 74: 705-18.

Pasamanick, B., and Knoblock, H. 1961. Epidemiologic studies on the complications of pregnancy and the birth process. In *Prevention of mental disorders in children*, ed. C. Caplan. New York: Basic Books.

Penner, L. R., Jr. 1966. The effect of pre- and early postnatal protein deficiency on maturation and intelligence of the albino rat. *Diss. Abstr.*, 27: 988.

Piaget, J. 1950. *The psychology of intelligence*. London: Routledge and Kegan Paul.

Pinneau, S. A. 1950. A critique on the articles by Margaret Ribble. *Child Dev.*, 21: 203-228.

Parakevopoulous, J., and Mc V. Hunt, D. 1971. Object construction and imitation under differing conditions of rearing. *T. Genet. Psychol.*, 119: 301-22.

Pinneau, S., 1955. The infantile disorders of hospitalism and anaclitic depression. *Psychol. Bull.*, 52: 429-52.

Provence, S., and Lipton, R. C. 1962. *Infants in institutions*. New York: International Universities Press.

Rabin, A. I. 1958. Some psychosexual differences between kibbutz and non-kibbutz Israeli boys. *J. Project. Tech.*, 22: 328-32.

Ressler, R. H. 1966. Inherited environmental influences on the operant behavior of mice. *J. Comp. physiol. Psychol.*, 26-267. (a)

Ressler, R. H. 1966. Avoidance conditioning in mice: prenatal influence of mother's treatment before mating. *Am. Zool.*, 6: 7. (b)

Rheingold, H. L. 1956. The modification of social responsiveness in institutional babies. *Monogr. Soc. Res. Child develop.* 21, No. 2.

Rheingold, H. L. 1961. The effect of environmental stimulation upon social and exploratory behavior in the human infant. In *Determinants of infant behavior,* ed. B. M. Foss, vol. 1: 143-77. New York: Wiley.

Rheingold, H. L., and Bayley, N. 1959. The later effects of an experimental modification of mothering. *Child Dev.*

Rheingold, H. L.; Gewirtz, J.; and Ross, H. 1959. Social conditioning of vocalizations in the infant. *J. comp. physiol. Psychol.*, 52: 58-73.

Rheingold, H. L. and Keene, G. C. 1963. Transport of the human young. *Determinants of infant behavior,* ed. B. M. Foss, vol. 3: 87-110. New York: Wiley.

Ribble, M. 1939. Significance of infantile sucking for psychic development. *J. nerv. ment. Dis.*, 90: 455-63.

Ribble, M. A. 1944. Infantile experience in relation to personality development. In *Personality and the behavior disorders,* ed. J. McV. Hunt, pp. 621-51. New York: Ronald Press.

Riccio, D. C., and Campbell, B. A. 1966. Adaptation and persistence of adaptation to a cold stressor in weanling and adult rats *J. comp. physiol. Psychol.,* 61: 408-10.

Roudinesco, J.; David, M.; and Nicolas, J. Responses of young children to separation from their mothers. 1. Observation of children ages 12 to 17 months recently separated from their families and living in an institution. *Courr. Cent. int. Enf.,* 2: 66-78.

Rudolf, G. de M. 1950. The treatment of mental defectives with aneuria for one year. *J. Ment. Sci.,* 96: 265-71.

Sackett, G. F. 1967. Some persistent effects of different rearing conditions on preadult social behavior of monkeys. *J. comp. physiol. Psychol.,* 64: 363-65.

Sackett, G. P.; Porter, M.; and Holmes, H. 1965. Choice behavior in Rhesus monkeys: effect of stimulation during the first month of life. *Science,* 147: 304-6.

Schaefer, T. 1963. Early 'experience' and its effects on later behavioral processes in rats: II. A critical factor in the early handling phenomena. *Trans. N.Y. Acad. Sci.,* 25: 871-89.

Schaffer, H. R. 1958. Objective observations of personality development in early infancy. *Br. J. med. Psychol.,* 31: 174-83.

Schaffer, H. R. 1963. Some issues for research in the study of attachment behavior. In *Determinants of infant behavior,* ed. B. M. Foss, vol. 2: 179-99. New York: Wiley.

Schaffer, H. R., and Callender, W. M. 1959. Psychological effects of hospitalization in infancy. *Pediatrics,* 24: 528-39.

Schaffer, H. R., and Emerson, P. E. 1964. Patterns of response to physical contact in early human development. *J. Child. Psychol. Psychiat.,* 5: 1-13. (a)

Schaffer, H. R., and Emerson, P. E. 1964. The development of social attachments in infancy. *Monogr. Soc. Res., Child Develop.* 29: No. 1. (b)

Schneirla, T. C., and Rosenblatt, J. 1963. 'Critical periods' in the development of behavior. *Science,* 139: 1110-15.

Schwartz, S. 1964. Effect of neonatal cortical lesions and early environmental factors on adult rat behavior. *J. comp. physiol. Psychol.,* 57: 72-77.

Schwartz, S. 1964. Effect of neonatal cortical lesions and early environing environments on later behavior in the rat. *J. Genet. Psychol.,* 109: 255-63.

Scott, J. P. 1962. Critical periods in behavioral development. *Science,* 138: 949-58.

Scott, J. P. 1963. The process of primary socialization in canine and human infants. *Monogr. Soc. Res. Child Develop.,* 28: No. 1. (b)

Scott, J. P., and Fuller, J. L. 1965. *Genetics and the social behavior of the dog.* Chicago: University of Chicago Press.

Sears, R. R.; Maccoby, E. E.; and Levin, H. 1957. *Patterns of child rearing.* Evanston, Ill.: Row, Peterson.

Seay, B.; Hansen, E.; and Harlow, H. F. 1962. Mother-infant separation in monkeys. *J. Child Psychol., Psychiat.,* 3: 123-32.

Shock, N. W. 1951. Growth curves. In *Handbook of experimental psychology,* ed. S. S. Stevens, pp. 330-46. New York: Wiley.

Skeels, H. M., and Dye, H. A. 1939. A study of the effects of differential stimulation in mentally retarded children. *Proc. Am. Ass. Ment. Def.,* 44: 114-36.

Skeels, H. M.; Updegraff, R.; Wellman, B. L.; and Williams, H. M. 1938. A study of environmental stimulation: an orphanage preschool project. *University of Iowa Studies in Child Welfare,* 15: 7-191.

Skodak, M. 1939. Children in foster homes: a study of mental development. *University of Iowa. Studies in Child Welfare,* 16, No. 1.

Sluckin, W. 1964. *Imprinting and early learning.* London: Methuen.

Smith, C. A. 1947. Effects of maternal undernutrition upon the newborn infant in Holland (1944-1945). *J. Pediat.,* 30: 229-43.

Sontag, L. W. 1941. The significance of fetal environmental differences. *Am. J. Obstet. Gynec.,* 42: 996, 1003.

Spitz, R. A. 1945. Hospitalism: an inquiry into the genesis of psychiatric conditions in early childhood. *Psychoanal. study Child,* 1: 53-74.

Spitz, R. A. 1946. Hospitalism: an inquiry into the genesis of psychiatric conditions in early childhood: a follow-up report. *Psychoanal. study Child,* 2: 113-17.

Spitz, R. A., and Wolf, K. 1946. Anaclitic depression. *Psychoanal. study Child,* 2: 313-42.

Starkweather, E. K., and Roberts, K. E. 1940. I.Q. changes occurring during nursery school attendance at the Merrill-Palmer School. *Yearbook of the National Society for Studies in Education,* vol 39, part II: 315-35.

Stearns, G. 1958. Nutritional state of the mother prior to conception. *J. Am. med. Ass.,* 168: 1655-59.

Stevenson, H. W.; Hess, E. H.; and Rheingold, H. L. 1967. *Early behavior: comparative and developmental approaches.* New York: Wiley.

Stewart, A. H.; Weiland, I. H.; Leider, A. R.; Mangham, C. A.; Holmes, T. H.; and Sipley H. S. 1954. Excessive infant crying (colic) in relation to parent behavior. *Am. J. Psychiat.,* 110: 687-94.

Stott, D. H. 1957. Physical and mental handicaps following a disturbed pregnancy. *Lancet,* 1006-12.

Swift, J. W. 1964. Effects of early group experience: the nursery school and day nursery. In *Review of Child Development Research,* eds. M. L. Hoffman and L. W. Hoffman, vol. 1: 249-88. New York: Russell Sage.

Tennes, K. H., and Lampl, E. E. 1964. Stranger and separation anxiety in infancy. *J. nerv. ment. Dis.,* 139: 247-54.

Thompson, W. R. 1955. Early environment—its importance for later behavior. In *Psychopathology of childhood, eds.* P. H. Hoch and J. Zubin. New York: Grune and Stratton.

Thompson, W. R. 1966. Early experiential and genetic influences on flexibility. In *Experience structure and adaptability,* ed. O. J. Harvey. New York: Springer.

Thompson, W. R. 1968. Development and the biophysical bases of personality. In *Handbook of personality,* eds. E. Borgatta and W. Lambert. Chicago: Rand McNally.

Thompson, W. R., and Goldenberg, L. 1962. Some physiological effects of

H

maternal adrenalin injections during pregnancy on rat offspring. *Psychol. Rep.,* 10: 759-74.

Thompson, W. R., and Schaefer, T. 1961. Early environmental stimulation. Function of varied experience, ed. D. W. Fiske and S. Maddi. Chicago: Dorsey Press.

Tizard, J. 1960. Residential care of mentally handicapped children. *Br. med. J.,* 1: 1041-46.

Wallin, R., and Riley, R. 1950. Reactions of mothers to pregnancy and adjustment of offspring in infancy. *Am. J. Orthopsychiat.,* 20: 616-22.

Walters, R. H., and Parke, R. D. 1956. The role of the distance receptors in the development of social responsiveness. *Advances in child development and behavior,* eds. L. P. Lipsitt and C. C. Spiker, vol. 2. New York: Academic Press.

Wellman, B. L. 1932. The effect of preschool attendance upon the I.Q. *J. exp. Educ.,* 1: 48-69.

Wellman, B. L. 1945. I.Q. changes of preschool and nonpreschool groups during the preschool years: a summary of the literature. *J. Psychol.* 20: 327-68.

Wellman, B. L., and Pegram, E. L. 1944. Binet I.Q. changes of orphanage preschool children: a reanalysis. *J. genet. Psychol.,* 65: 239-63.

Werner, H. 1957. The concept of development from a comparative and organismic point of view. In *The concept of development,* ed. D. Harris. Minneapolis: University of Minnesota Press.

Whalen, R. E., and Nadler, R. D. 1965. Modification of spontaneous and hormone-induced sexual behavior by estrogen administered to neonatal female rats. *J. comp. physiol. Psychol.,* 60: 150-52.

Whimbey, A. E., and Denenberg, V. H. 1966. Programming life histories: creating individual differences by the experimental control of early experiences. *Multiv. Behav. Res.,* 1: 279-86.

White, B. L., and Castle, P. W. 1964. Visual exploratory behavior following postnatal handling of human infants. *Percept. Mot. Skills,* 18: 497-502.

Whiting, J. W. M. 1965. Menarcheal age and infant stress in humans. *Sex and behavior,* ed. F. A. Beach. New York: Wiley.

Whiting, J. W. M., and Landauer, T. K. 1963. 'Some effects of infant stress upon human stature.' Unpublished manuscript, Harvard University.

Discussion

After papers

by HARLOW and FEIGENBAUM

Prof. Fox : Professor Harlow, can you elaborate a little bit more on the vertical pit and also what behaviours do occur in the pit isolation apparatus?

Prof. Harlow : I shudder at the term vertical pit. May we say vertical chamber? The animal can locomote freely in all three directions. It eats and drinks normally and shows no abnormal susceptibility to disease. In other words, the animal is physiologically normal but psychologically damaged. At first the monkey tries to escape, attempting to climb up the steel sides. After variable periods of time, escape behaviour subsides and the animals assume depressive attitudes. As a matter of fact prolonged depression can be produced in a relatively short period. We do not know exactly but certainly within thirty to forty-five days which is a very short time compared to the months required to produce less severe depression by separation or total social isolation.

Dr. Murray : Professor Harlow: I am interested in the induction of acute juvenile depression in your monkeys. One of the problems we find in developmental work in depression in children is that we seldom see an anaclitic type depression now. I believe that Bowlby's three stages describe a mourning reaction which may progress to clinical depression later because children who go through these three stages in a paediatric hospital do not appear to become depressed in such a fashion as children of the same age who develop depression outside of hospital. The type of depression that one sees in a three year old differs much from that found in a seven or a twelve year old. My two questions are a) Can one correlate the developmental age of these monkeys with children and b) how do you know that this is a clinical depression?

Prof. Harlow : Monkeys mature four or five times as fast as human infants. Thus, four years of monkey age is about sixteen to eighteen years of human age and half a year of monkey age is about two to two-and-a-half years of human childhood. Depression in human beings may be measured by either verbal report or bodily posture. In monkeys our measures of depression are, of course, limited to bodily postures, but these are thoroughly comparable to the poses and postures of human beings. Exploration and social behaviour such as play are totally absent. Activity is enormously reduced and the monkeys frequently wrap their heads and bodies in their arms and legs. They retreat personally and perceptually from the world about them. When people behave this way they are hospitalized.

Dr. Michael : May I ask you Harry you have once or twice referred to the biochemical variables which you propose to study. Could you tell us a little bit about this and perhaps give us an indication of the preliminary results?

Prof. Harlow : We are measuring the biochemical effects of induction and, hopefully, the alleviation of depressive states, particularly the concentration of the catecholamines and the indolamines. These biochemical assays are being made under the direction of Dr. William McKinney at the University of Wisconsin and also at a number of other institutions co-operating with us in this project, particularly the National Institutes of Health, the University of North Carolina, University of Pittsburg and the University of Washington. Chlorapromazine, even though not a specific anti-depressant, reduces the intensity of many depression signs. Reserpine stimulates some but by no means all of the depressive signs.

Dr. Biller : Dr. Harlow, any mention of the father was peculiarly absent from your lecture and I wonder if you have ever considered using him during periods of separation and if he might have a therapeutic value?

Prof. Harlow : It is hard to find an unlearned basis for paternal behaviour but the adult males do take over basic social roles. The primary role is protection of the group from aggression both from without and within the group. The adult male will not allow any female to abuse its own or any other children, or a larger child to abuse an infant. The adult male's primary role is protection, but the males engage in limited play, primarily with male infants and show an enormous tolerance for the behaviour of the infants which may tweek their ears and pull their fur. Not infrequently the male will adopt a baby who has been separated from its mother, usually by the advent of the next child.

Dr. Lifton : The specificity of sex related responses has come up today and it appears to me from hearing Professor Sackett's discussion and from informal discussions with others that the males in the lower animals appear to be more vulnerable. In many ways it almost suggests that males are more dependent upon stimuli and upon some sort of social support for reinforcement and of course that carries true in many ways in human experience. It may be that it is another mal-effect of man being the symbolic animal. I do not know but I would like to ask Professor Harlow more about his impression on that issue.

My second question is one I have talked about with Dr. John Bowlby. My impression is even though the evidence is very clear that separation in extreme ways, certainly deprivation of the kind that Dr. Spitz and in a lesser way also Dr. Bowlby have recorded, is harmful to the infant and creates things like depressive syndromes. But I also believe that many outstanding people have in early life experienced separations and yet have outstanding achievements. Perfect experience may not be the ideal experience for outstanding individuals. I would like to ask any of the speakers to comment on that as well.

Prof. Harlow : In our large amount of data on monkeys which were socially isolated at birth for various fixed periods of time and also data on monkeys which were raised normally for six months and then socially isolated for equal periods of time, the results show that a limited period of normal social existence greatly ameliorates the effects of subsequent isolation. In so far as sex is concerned, the females are more resistant to the effects of social isolation than are the males.

Prof. Forrest : I really want to make an observation which perhaps Professor Feigenbaum would comment upon and that is to stress the importance of field studies of human mothers and infants. I came across, very recently, a study by Anderson, who has observed mothers and children in London parks and he has noticed that there is not a linear relationship between the age of the child and the amount of locomation away from the mother in which the child indulged. He compared infants of from about one year to eighteen months with two year olds and three year olds and found that the very young children (one year to eighteen months) tended to move further away from the mother than the two year old children. In fact the two year old children stayed very close to the mother for long periods of time, while the three year old children were typically distracted by other children and engaged in play at a distance from the mother. He also noticed, and this is relevant to the point made by Dr. Lifton about sex differences, that girls remained much more frequently with the mother than did the boys, and that one reason for this was that the mothers engaged in grooming behaviour much more with their girl infants than they did with their boy infants; therefore it was possibly the differences in maternal behaviour which led to the distinction observed between the locomotory patterns of the two sexes of infant.

Prof. Levine: I wonder if I may comment on squirrel monkeys.

The female squirrel monkey attains independence much earlier than the male.

Prof. Feigenbaum: Well very simply 'hurrah' for field studies, which have for the last five or ten years been increasing in number. There are ongoing programmes at Brown, Yale and Harvard among others. So that the realization of the problem you raise certainly exists.

I would be interested in knowing in your biographical studies, Dr. Lifton, as to what you mean by separation. There is the phenomena of being separated from an environment and coming back into that same environment or into a different environment. But the question of effect appears to me based upon the factors involved in who is being separated; at what time of their life; into what; and for how long. As far as I know no large-scale population studies have been completed concerning the phenomena you speak about. I am sure that Professor Lifton knows the study by Aronoff—the one that was done on death in the family and choice of occupation. There it would indicate that at least where there is death in the early years, that the choice later on would be for a secure occupational position. For example, they would rather be cane cutters than fishermen, which required a degree of risk which they refused to take. Your hypothesis seems to run counter to the notion that security needs satisfaction before higher needs operate.

Prof. Browne: All the papers this morning seem to be about the damaging effect of separation except that of Seymour Levine at the beginning, where he was stressing the improved adaptability of handled rats. Now we seem to be going back a little to that with the possible beneficial effect that stimulation and separation might have with helping mother and infant to disengage so that the child can achieve autonomy.

Prof. Levine: We are talking about the consequences of separating mothers and children. If you separate for a long time it will have a much different effect than if you separate for a brief time. The nature of the problem is so terribly important and involves age at separation, duration of separations as well as genetic considerations.

Prof. Fox: May I make a comment here. We are talking about the various species of animals used in research and we are already getting into the bind of different biological (animal) models and of the difficulties in making comparisons. Similarly for man, we must consider cultural differences in mothering practices for example and how far can animal models take us. I think one major question is the problem of the symbiotic relationship between parent and child and the importance of growth to independence and individuation of the child. Many psychotherapists, especially the Gestalt Therapy group, believe that most human disorders are based on one form of dependancy disorder or another. When in fact we do not have complete individuation, dependency needs and manipulative games or strategies can influence later relationships. The main point of therapy is not to assume too much responsibility for the dependent patient but to encourage him to individuate, to become independent and responsible for himself.

A propos of optimal early stimulation, Dr. Levine has shown in rat studies that part of the effect is due to repeated short term deprivation from the mother. Now is there an optimal rearing condition for developing individuation in the human infant? We might entertain the possibility that the 'optimal' programme would be to give short term repeated separations. The infant would develop its own autonomy and internal resources so that it can handle such separations and knowing that it is going to go back to mother, separation anxiety would be reduced.

Prof. Sackett: I have good examples for some of these problems and I think at least two more issues are involved. Dr. Harlow began this study, we followed up the animals when they were three to four years old. One infant group received multiple mothering, they were separated from their current 'mother' every two weeks and given to a new adult female. Another group was separated from its own mother for two hours every two weeks and was then put back with its own mother. A third group was never separated during rearing until final separation when they were eight months old. On criterion tests when the animals were one year old, the end of the so-called infancy period, there were only minor differences between the groups, except the multiple mothered offspring seemed to be a little more aggressive. When these animals were three years old, two years after the final separation, we found enormous differences. In leadership it turned out that the multiple mothered animals were the most dominant regardless of sex and the separation controls were the least dominant. The separation controls were also least aggressive, least exploratory and had the least play behaviour. This suggests that repeated separations from a single 'mother' have different effects than repeated separations from many mothers, these effects are toward the biologically maladaptive extreme for this species, and these effects do not appear until much later in life than the time at which treatment differences ceased.

Dr. Scott: Is there a difference between the killing mother and the true mother and between that and the good mother? Are you able to define perhaps by some genetic code the kind of mother that is consistent, does not totally reject perhaps or behave like a custodian mother in a cold way.

Prof. Harlow: I do not think we have enough data on individual differences in normal mothers. I think most normal mothers are good and it would take quite a bit of skill and quite a number of animals to get any factual information.

Prof. Mitchell: I think that you are asking whether or not they were mothers who were not brutal, yet not normal. Approximately half of these mothers which were raised in isolation were indifferent mothers, some were arbitrary in their behaviour, not brutal, and these did not produce the most aggressive infants. I wonder if it would follow from what Professor Harlow said, that possibly mothers when infants learned how to do their mothering, and that when they became mothers they behaved appropriately. Is that how he imagines it happens?

Prof. Harlow: We have studies comparing primiparous and multiparous mothers and so far as the initial maternal loving stage goes, there was no difference but in the second loving stage the experienced mothers rejected their infants sooner but it is a good rejection. The inexperienced mothers did not know when to help to get the infant away from maternal love. Experienced mothers were much better at that.

Dr. Crawley: In this question maybe there is a case for defining the distinction between what the observer would call a separation and what the subject would call a perceived loss, because obviously in this case with the monkeys you have an analogue perhaps of the human situation as regards the possible favourable reaction to separation that sometimes arises. Another point I would like to ask, because nobody has mentioned it, is in relation to aggression—has anybody observed self-destructive behaviour in experimental animals?

Prof. Levine: There will be a paper on this later.

I want to emphasize that you cannot discuss the mother without bringing in the infant—she is still part of an ongoing system and in fact the infant is going to make a very big difference to the type of response this infant elicits from the mother. The one thing that Professor Harlow did show is that even though you get the brutal mothering, the infant takes a very active role in its mothering, so where the mother is not responding appropriately, the infant initiates maternal behaviour. We have been concentrating enormously on the role of the mother, placing the mother as the great spectre, the good and evil doer at the same time without regarding the characteristics of the infant.

Prof. Mitchell: This point just made about the infant became very clear to me in some studies I have done where males are raising babies by themselves—these are rhesus monkeys who are not supposed to do this at all but they do in artificial situations. The infant is one who establishes all the contact, the male scrapes the infant off him repeatedly, it is a great attraction for almost any animate object on the part of the infant, the males do adopt because as Dr. Harlow pointed out they are very patient.

Dr. Cullen: One of the points which struck me about Chairman Levine's last remarks is that he had not really made the links between his work and Professor Harlow's work although the species are different. It seems to me that some of the characteristics of the infant arising from under-stimulation in the neonatal period could determine the effects of separation situations and so on in the later stages of development. I was also wondering why he had not any descriptions of the effects on the mother of separation, and further whether mother might not be described under some kind of mothering index and whether they contributed to the recovering of an infant after separation and how effective they were in inducing restitution of normal security patterns of behaviour or whatever base line behaviour we are using in measuring change.

Prof. Sackett: I can tell you about an experiment that we have just finished on that topic. This was not on rhesus monkeys, but on pigtail monkeys. We gave monkeys mothering before they were isolated. Either they had two weeks of mothering, a month of mothering, two months of mothering or six months of mothering, before total isolation was begun, so that meant that at all these different intervals of course we had to separate the mother from a baby. After we separated the mother from the baby we gave the mother a choice, in a multiple choice test situation, between an unfamiliar adult female, juvenile and a neonate, so we are looking at preference for a neonate, a juvenile or an adult as a function of the age at which the monkey baby is taken away. We did this within an hour of separation, a day later and a week later. Basically if the mother had the baby for two months or more, she did not like babies. If the mother had it for a month or for two weeks she showed initial high maternal motivation for the neonate, but the only mother that this persisted in for a week after separation was the two week group females. Of course, if the females were separated from their babies at birth they showed no difference from controls that did not have babies at all. It seems that pigtail monkey females must have baby experience, recent baby experience, to show a baby preference, and if the female rears its baby for more than one month she does not seem to care much for babies after separation from her own child.

Dr. Cullen: There is a rather poignant human situation in the separations that occur due to puerperal psychotic conditions in the mother regardless of the antecedent personalities involved. There are differences that mothers experience in relationship to their children due to intercurrent life situations where they may be more welcoming towards one infant arrival than another, and for some they may say that they feel very little affection for them at all. You get these sorts of intermediate effects and I am just wondering about the effect on the mothers of these separations.

Prof. Lavelle: There was a paper in the New England Journal of Medicine a few weeks ago in which a group in Boston left the babies with the mother after delivery in hospital for four extra hours each day and then measured the bond between the mother and the infant for some months afterwards and compared them with controls for the degree to which the mother tended to intervene when the doctor examined the baby. The bond was much stronger in the test children.

Prof. Lifton: I would like to make a point both philosophical and psychological at the same time—one that comes out from the spirit of what was presented this morning. We are pretty humble in what we can claim in terms of variables predicting good or bad as resulting processes from things we observe about separation and other matters and that really means that as scientists investigating these matters we do not really see a provincial vision of ourselves as really evolving a point of view around say child rearing that is applied to culture as the scientific truth. Rather we see ourselves as coming close to a certain understanding of these issues that are so complex and that there will not be evolved any single scientific truth. They will depend eventually on certain ethical preferences. I would prefer for instance, sharing with another commentator a Ghandian view, that children grow up with a non-violent bias at the expenses of aggression but others might prefer other kinds of children or adults. Finally, I would make a plea that those involved in ethological work, perhaps especially with animals, look upon the self as an instrument in the scientific investigation in which at least the point of view about what one is finding is to be influenced by one's ethical position and one's own preferences.

Dr. McQuaid : In responding to some earlier comments on the response on the mother's part to the infant, I was wondering are there any studies coming out of animal laboratories on the effect on mothering behaviour of neurologically and or physically damaged animals, infants, neonates and how does this correlate with mother's handling and measurements of anxiety?

Prof. Sackett : The only work that I know is being carried out in a systematic way is by a man named Gershon Berkson. He is using blindness as a model type of handicap and looking not only at the effect of blind babies on mother's behaviour but the effects on social groups. He is doing this work in laboratories and in a free environment. Unfortunately I cannot tell you too much about it. But there are protective behaviours that are developed by the mother and the group particularly in free ranging rhesus monkeys. The baby seems to get a lot more attention from individuals that he would not usually get attention from and is even tended to by adult males.

Dr. McQuaid : There is a good deal of evidence to show that children may be born with minimal forms of neurological impairment that are only detectable in the first few months of life, and that they disappear, and may not then emerge again until later on as brain syndromes, learning disorders, etc. which are very accurate predictors of behaviour disorders in late infancy, early childhood and later on in adolescence. I am wondering how does this connect up with handling, mothering and so on.

Prof. Fox : I would like to broaden this talk a little with a couple of references. I remember first of all some works by Sade who showed that the rank of the rhesus monkey mother determines the later social rank of the infant. We must therefore consider more than the mere relationship between mother and infant. Kaufman has shown that mother Bonnet Macaque are very open with the infant to strangers and so when she is removed, the infant does not show much depression at all since it is buffered and accepted by others. With the Pigtail Macaque the mother is very aggressive and threatens any other member of the group that comes near her infant. When she is taken out the infant is of course not buffered by social milieu and goes into depression.

Prof. Mitchell : I just want to add to what Professor Fox has said— the rhesus monkey is more like the pigtail monkey, being more aggressive, less open and so should probably put those separation studies into this context. It may be that with a rather loving atmosphere, separation would not be anywhere near as damaging and may be even beneficial in some places.

Prof. Fox : The critical thing in the two Macaque species studied by Kaufman is of course cross fostering.

Dr. McKenna : I would like to comment on the implications of this morning's findings for early compensatory education programmes especially in the U.S.A. When one visits some of the early com-pensatory programmes in the States, one gets the impression that most psychologists and educationalists know what they are talk-ing about, but today's proceedings would throw a great deal of doubt on this. I am saying this constructively. What they seem to be doing mainly in the early compensatory programmes, is varying and redistributing favourable environmental effects such as books, toys, talking, conversation, more educated people round about children, more teachers per disadvantaged child and a whole series of presumably favourable conditions which have been found in association with a middle class environment. This seems to be what is being done, just varying environmental con-ditions, when in fact this morning's work has shown that probably there are more significant changes taking place as a result of earlier interactive processes in mother child relationships. Your paper, Professor Levine, especially showed the strong interactive effects of early environmental handling in infancy. Probably it is because early compensatory education programmes are generally started round about the age of three, that this may be one of the reasons for their relative failure to do so well as it was hoped they would do initially. And when you finished up an excellent paper this morning by knocking heritability, I was a bit disappointed because I thought your paper was one of the best examples of how the heredity environment debate was now a lost case, a non-argument.

Prof. Levine : Yes. You are right in the sense that I always find the heredity—environment question a non-question, unanswerable because of the totality of the system.

Factors in family relationships — 1

Hormonal factors

RICHARD MICHAEL,
Bethlem Royal Hospital,
Kent

If one looks at a group of the anubis baboon moving across country, the important thing is the structure of this group. It is highly organized and in a sense it is a family. There is a special order of the march and all relationships between these animals in the group are determined ones, they are not casual, they are not random. The centre of the group is occupied by females that have either young suspended underneath their bellies or young sitting on their backs. The juveniles of both sexes are in a peripheral position. The group is led by certain dominant males and a dominant mature male brings up the rere. What is actually determining these interrelations is the sexual status of the animals, whether they are male or whether they are female, whether they are pregnant or have young, whether they have sexual swelling. This determines the relationships of the male of this particular species so that the whole thing is really bound together in biometrics which are determined by maturational, gender and formational factors.

I want to deal with four things. They are not terribly well related. This first is the influence of the menstrual cycle on relationships between adults. I want to deal with aggression. I want to deal a little bit with bi-sexuality, and I have to deal also a little bit with

126

olfaction, because that's a subject about which I am very interested at the moment.

If you take an adult male and an adult female rhesus monkey in a laboratory and pair them together under standard observation conditions and look for instance at the number of mounts that the male makes on the female and relate these mounts to the stage of the cycle, you don't get a constant pattern. The situation depends upon the identity of the pair. Depending upon the individual pair, the number of mounts that the male makes varies, there may be very low levels of sexual interaction throughout. There may be rather high levels of interaction throughout, but there may be a cycle of activity, and the cycle of activity falls into two main kinds. Those with a peak of activity around about mid-cycle and secondary rises immediately before menstruation. Or there may be generally high levels of activity in the first half of the cycle, in the follucular phase of the cycle, with low levels in the second half of the cycle after ovulation has occurred. These animals are rhythmic ovulators just like the human, they have a twenty-eight day cycle as the human female does also. One sees here a rhythm of behaviour between the male and the female that is in fact determined in part by the stage of the female cycle. One could demonstrate that very easily by ovariectomising the female of the pair, showing that these rhythms disappear, and then reinstating behaviour by hormone replacement treatments. There is no one pattern in this primate species that characterizes the behaviour of the species. There are variations and it depends upon who makes up the pair, the identity of the pair of partners. But if one takes a lot of group data, what one wants to know is the behavioural characteristic of the species. We have data taken from some seventy-five rhesus monkeys. If one looks at the frequency of ejaculation, in relationship to the cycle, not simply the number of mounts and if one takes all these animals and all their cycles, including the types that were flat and showed no rhythmic changes and pool the whole thing together there is indeed a rhythm of behaviour with fluctuating decline through the luteal phase of the cycle. What one has here is a situation where the relationship between the pair is being influenced by the endocrine status of the female partner and I cannot elaborate on that any further.

But I want to talk now about my second topic namely—aggression. And I'm not talking here about tremendously destructive aggression when one animal kills or destroys another or maims it severely. I'm talking about the incidence of threat behaviour, the open-mouthed threat that was illustrated I think by Dr. Sackett in his talk. The lunging forward, slapping, hitting and superficial biting. The kind of aggressive behaviour that does happen between the male and female in the course of their normal caged behaviour. The fact is that the amount that the male aggresses the female also depends upon her hormonal state. Aggressive episodes are very low by the male directed towards the female and by the female directed towards the male. Some of the females' aggression is reactive aggression as initiated by the male. If you are a female and if you are ovariecto-mised the amount of aggression that goes on between you and your male partner is dramatically increased. The female rhesus monkey is much more likely to be aggressed by the male if she doesn't have ovaries than if she does. As you treat the ovariectomised female with a combination of estrogen and progesterone her aggressivity towards the male is increased. Now this is again a thumbnail sketch, but I do think this kind of data may have a bearing on the aggression irritability and the interactions that go on in the human species in relation to the menstrual cycle.

Now I do want very briefly to diverge here onto the theme of bi-sexuality because this is the subject that occasions quite a lot of divided opinion. Our experience is that in every mammalian species where this has been studied, bi-sexual patterns of behaviour are seen in normal animals, that is, in animals that are caged and housed under normal conditions. This condition is also true of the rhesus monkeys, animals that have been newly caught in the jungles of India and have maybe three months of the experience of cage life. What we see in a certain percentage of our animals is mounting behaviour by the female towards the male. The male is about twice the size of the female. There is a big somatic sexual dimorphism in this species. This kind of behaviour where the female clasps the male is seen spontaneously in quite a large percentage of our animals studied. One third shows this behaviour spontaneously. This be-haviour is not just random. Our data seems to show that there may be a cyclical mounting activity that is shown by the female towards the male. In some pairs this is at the time, in the middle part of the cycle, when the male is most frequent in also mounting the female. Bi-sexual behaviour is seen in primates, it is seen quite regularly, is under some sort of endocrine control, and it can be influenced by the dominant relationships between the members of the pair.

Many people in the course of today's papers have referred to perceptual factors that may influence behaviour extra to the vision cues, to emotive patterns of behaviour, even to, of course, the climatic factors that might influence behaviour through the endocrine system. But let me mention olfaction to-day. It is thought this is a form of distance communication that we do not feel exists. I want to change your views about that. Now the reason why olfaction perhaps is not so interesting to us is that we as human beings are regarded as a microsmatic species. In a pro-simian brain, the kind you find in a lemur, one of those species that have a lot of olfaction, there is a great mass of olfactory structures. In the brain of a typical monkey, monkeys like the rhesus monkey and the anubis baboon, one sees that its relative size is between the pro-simian and the old world monkeys. The olfactory brain in these animals much more nearly resembles that of ourselves than it does the pro-simian. Nevertheless they are quite interested in matters olfactory. In a test situation for olfactory behaviour, an ordinary rhesus monkey shows a kind of wry face which is partly the way his mouth wrinkles when he is sniffing and he is not just looking. We have been doing a series of studies that have involved collecting vaginal secretion from rhesus monkeys and transferring those secretions to the rear ends of the females but not introducing them to the vagina. Just put them on the rear end of the ovariectomised rhesus monkeys and then one can test the recipient animal and the behavioural effect the secretion has by the effect it produces on the male. We found as one of several positive results in different experiments that if we put secretions that are aspirated from the vagina of estrogen treated females on to the rear-end of an ovariectomized animal we can stimulate very dramatically male behaviour. The male partner will then show a lot of sexual interest in the female. One can fractionate these secretions by means of gas-chromatography and get certain peaks. This again is a very shortened presentation but if you chromatograph the vaginal secretions from an ovariesctomized animal you don't get a series of peaks. Now you can track these peaks out on the gas-chromatograph and you can actually collect this fraction. But you haven't shown anything until you show that the fraction has behavioural activity. We have taken these fractions from the gas-chromatograph, and put very tiny amounts on to the rear-end of the test female and find the behaviour of the male with these females is greatly stimulated. Mounting activity appears and

I

ejaculation has occurred. Then with the withdrawal of secretions in some cases you get an immediate drop down to base line, in some cases you don't. Activity in these latter males goes on for some time, they are acting on some kind of memory. Well now, this is quite interesting because it illustrates that we have got behaviourally active material in these trapped fractions.

These particular chemical substances turn out to be a series of straight chained fatty acids. Now is this just a quirk of fate? Or is this situation widely represented in primates generally? If you look at the vaginal secretions of a series of different primates, you find that these substances, these acids are present in a very wide range of species and we can show by cross transfer experiments that the secretions, for instance of the anubis baboon, can drive the behaviour of the male rhesus. These substances are also present in the human female. We have no idea of what their function is, if indeed they have any, but they are present, and furthermore they are active in the monkey test situation. You can show that human secretions are active in driving the behaviour of the monkey male. Now whether this has any bearing on what was it?—Factors in Family Relationships, I don't know!

Factors in family relationships —2

Adult male parental behaviour in feral- and isolation-reared rhesus monkeys (Macaca Mulatta)*

WILLIAM K. REDICAN, JODY GOMBER and G. MITCHELL, UNIVERSITY OF CALIFORNIA

As a step toward clarifying the role of the adult male in socializing immature conspecifics (cf. Mitchell, 1969), we have set up a controlled laboratory situation in which infant rhesus monkeys transfer their attachment or identification at a premature developmental stage from their own mother to an adult male. Thus far, one isolation-reared and three feral-born adult male rhesus monkeys have accepted one-month-old infants and have been rearing them in individual laboratory cages in the absence of the infants' mothers.

The present paper will emphasize the development of an infant male who was paired with a feral-born adult male, and of an infant female who was paired with an isolation-reared adult male. In some instances, comparisons will be made with a completed study of four mother-infant pairs conducted in our laboratory under similar circumstances (Baysinger, Brandt and Mitchell, in press). In all studies,

*This presentation was made possible by the Medical Research Council of Ireland and by USPHS grant numbers HD04335, MH17425, MH19760, and RR00169, as well as a National Science Foundation Traineeship. Parts of this report were taken from a paper read at the fifty-second annual meeting of the Western Psychological Association, April 28, 1972, Portland, Oregan, by W. K. R. and G. M.

131

contact with peers was prohibited to rule out any interactive effects of peer rearing.

Because reports of infanticide by adult macaque males, Thompson, 1967) have not been clear as to whether the male responded to an unfamiliar mother, infant, or dyad, our pairing procedure included methods of familiarizing the male with both the mother and infant as well as some means of protecting the infant from unexpected and possibly fatal aggression. Basically, the procedure involved three phases. In the first, a multiparous mother and infant were separated from a fully adult male by a thick clear Plexiglas barrier placed in the center of a 3 x 3 x 6 foot indoor cage. When the infant was approximately one month old, the mother was removed from her half of the cage and the infant was trained to feed from a bottle mounted on the cage wall.

The second phase was initiated after the infant had learned to reliably feed from the bottle. The infant was placed in a small stainless steel cage within the larger cage and the clear Plexiglas barrier was withdrawn. The adult male's behaviour was watched for signs of aggression and after approximately ten minutes the barrier was once again replaced, with the animals on their respective sides.

In the third and final phase, initiated shortly after the infant was taken from the smaller cage, the barrier was slowly removed and the male was allowed actual physical contact with the infant.

Throughout data collection, a time-sampling technique was used to measure frequency and duration of behaviours, and detailed written records were also taken.

Feral-male rearing

The first infant, a male, has completed his seven-month period of rearing with an adult male. Seven months was the same length of time that control infants were reared with their mothers. This first male-infant pair has been the most compatible in the study, both in terms of degree of attachment and absence of aggression.

The adult male ('Mellow') bit himself repeatedly and inflicted superficial wounds during the separation of the mother-infant pair. The separation was conducted in an adjacent room so that he could not actually see the separation but could hear the distress vocalizations of the mother and infant. During the second phase of the pairing procedure he exhibited no aggression and, to the contrary, occasionally sat with the infant's cage close to his ventrum.

In the final phase, brief contact followed mutual approach, and after less than a minute, prolonged contact was established when the male groomed the infant ('Pierre') very carefully. Although at first Mellow tolerantly, albeit somewhat anxiously, allowed Pierre to climb all over him, he later (almost thirteen minutes after pairing) began to threaten the infant as he climbed on his back. At this point, the infant fled. The infant's assumption of a depressed posture seemed to be a crucial variable in eliciting grooming from the male, which was instrumental in their re-establishing contact. Grooming persisted throughout the infant's development, with Mellow grooming Pierre far more frequently and for longer durations than the converse.

Generally speaking, over a period of seven months the control infants became progressively more independent of their mothers. Frequency of physical contact increased but duration of contact declined (see also Hansen, 1966). For Pierre, however, there was a constant frequency of contact with a steadily increasing duration over seven months. (Ventral-ventral contact between Mellow and Pierre was extremely rare.) We consider these data as one line of evidence which suggests an *increasingly* intense attachment between Mellow and Pierre over time.

In this pair, Pierre was unquestionably the active member of the dyad, and he consistently established contact more frequently than he broke it, whereas the reverse held true for Mellow. The control infants terminated contact with their mothers as often as they initiated it.

In terms of visual orientation, Pierre showed a generally increasing duration in the middle months, which tapered off in the later months. Most interesting were Mellow's scores for visual orientations toward Pierre, which were remarkably high in the final months. They were approximately six times the scores for any of the infants. We suggest that this is indicative of a rather intense attachment on the part of Mellow, but one which was very much delayed in development. (Generally, looks of long duration may be indicative of more affiliative behaviours, whereas quick and repeated looks are related to more fearful ones.)

Prior to the pairing Pierre began to suck his penis, but over the seven months this behaviour declined, suggesting a progressive

Fig. 1. Shortly after pairing, Pierre climbed up Mellow's ventrum and hung from his ears and fur. Mellow tried to induce him to let go by carefully lowering his own head to the cage floor, but Pierre continued to climb and to cling.

Fig. 2. Mellow experienced considerable difficulty in assuming the correct posture when Pierre clung to his ventrum. Mellow is holding a piece of shredded towel in his hand.

Fig. 3. After a certain amount of threatening by Mellow, Pierre screeched and fled. Moments after Pierre assumed a depressed posture (sucking his penis) Mellow approached and groomed him carefully.

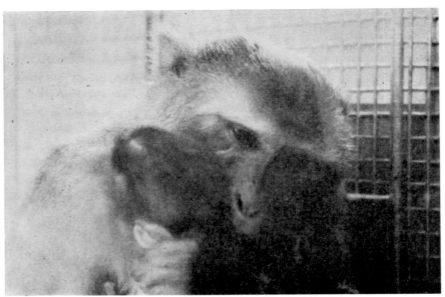

Fig. 4. Mellow administering a play-bite to Pierre. Their play was of an extraordinary intensity and was much more vigorous than that seen among mother-infant pairs.

Fig. 5. Mellow and Pierre were separated for a two-day period and then reunited to assess their degree of attachment. Pierre resumed penis-sucking for prolonged periods and in a sense regressed to an earlier developmental stage.

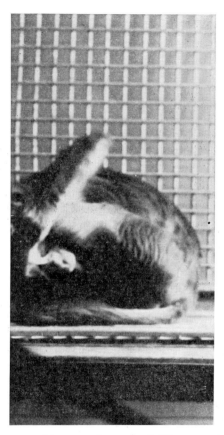

Fig. 6. Postures became more bizarre as time passed. (Pierre eventually bit himself on the arms and legs, a behaviour which he had never exhibited except in milder form during play. Mellow's response to separation was extremely violent. Close to a minute after separation he bit his leg with his canines and severed several major blood vessels within approximately ten seconds. He would have literally killed himself if he had not received veterinary attention.)

Fig. 7. Mellow and Pierre assumed ventral-ventral contact shortly after reunion, a posture common for mother-infant pairs but very rare for this dyad.

Fig. 8. Mellow attempting to mount Pierre after reunion. He was previously seen to do so after the latter had a rectal prolapse and when they were introduced into a new cage.

recovery from a partial deprivation syndrome which followed his separation from his mother.

The developmental sequence observed for aggression seemed to fall into three stages: in the first, aggressive outbursts by Mellow were relatively frequent and would often occur because of simple proximity or for seemingly inexplicable reasons. In the second phase, rather than aggress the infant when Pierre approached or made contact, Mellow often merely got up and moved away. Aggressive interactions in the third phase were much less frequent and often took place for very straightforward reasons. A relationship often mentioned in the literature is one in which play becomes too intense and leads to agonism, but we almost exclusively found the converse: brief aggressive outbursts by the adult male often merged directly into play sessions. The play itself was one of the most extraordinary aspects of this dyad's social behaviour. In the control pairs infants principally used their mothers as objects to bounce or jump on, and when the mothers did respond it was usually with a mild cuff. Mellow and Pierre's play, in contrast, was of extreme intensity. It, along with grooming, appeared in the very first week after pairing, and steadily increased in intensity. These two behaviours seemed to be the principal regulators of the attachment between the male and his infant. In particular, Pierre's enhanced capacity for rough-and-tumble play apparently helped to account for the increasingly intense bond between himself and Mellow. This attachment was so strong that during separation Mellow bit himself so severely that had he not received veterinary care he would have died.

Isolate-male rearing

In this section we will report on the progress of our first pairing of an isolation-reared adult male with an infant female. This particular fully mature isolate ('Clyde') was chosen to be the first 'motherless-father' mainly because he displayed, among other bizarre behaviours, a wide-eyed expressionless gazing. Although Clyde's wide-eyed stares seemed to be interpreted by control adult males as atypical stare threats—which may explain why he was successful in many interactions with these males (Mitchell, 1970; Brandt, Stevens, and Mitchell, 1971)—we felt this looking behaviour might be helpful in enhancing attachment between himself and the infant ('Bonnie').

During the second phase of the pairing procedure, Clyde exhibited much less interest in the infant in her small cage than had the feral-born males. After observing the infant quite intensely, he spent most of this period either exploring the cage or lying down. Although this appeared promising in terms of lack of aggression, one of the most predictable things about isolate-reared animals is their unpredictability. In an effort to test his reactions while Bonnie was still safely in her small cage, we directed threatening behaviours towards both the male and the infant. This elicited an unusual response from Clyde which still persists: he immediately turned from his antagonist to threaten and slap at the infant in the small cage. This was in marked contrast to the feral adult males and to adult females, who were quick to protect their infants by directing threats toward any potential aggressors.

The third phase of the pairing procedure was initiated, much to our surprise, by the male himself who, discovering that we had left the barrier unlocked, pushed it aside and entered Bonnie's half of the cage. Brief gentle contact was soon established when the infant approached the male. In the course of the next few hours, although the isolate male punished the infant twice and observed the infant intensely whenever he found himself in close proximity with her, prolonged contact was not observed until three days had passed.

As this isolate-infant pair has only entered its second month of cohabitation, no rigorous comparisons can be made with the data from the Mellow-Pierre or mother-infant pairs. However, we will discuss the general trend of their interactions up to this point.

Throughout the first month that they have been together, there has been much incidental contact (e.g., when they brushed past each other) which has seemed to cause little or no anxiety. Prolonged contact was first seen in the form of grooming and during sleep. Initially the male groomed the infant very intensely when she assumed a depressed posture, but with time the infant began to groom Clyde more, and the male has begun to groom Bonnie less. This is perhaps because she showed the depressed posture less frequently and because they began to sleep in close physical contact after the first few days. Often a nap was preceded by Bonnie sucking Clyde's ear, finger, toe, or penis. This elicited no annoyance reactions from the male. In fact, the male's rate of punishing the infant declined precipitously after the first few days of the pairing, until it occurred only rarely and in a form quite different from the way it was initially. Clyde still punishes Bonnie severely when a threat is initiated toward him by an observer, but ceases this behaviour as soon as the stimulation ceases. At other times he has been seen to punish her only when she played or quite actively used his body as a play-object for an extended period of time. In these cases he either gently cuffed her or pulled her hair, and this produced no protest vocalizations from Bonnie and no cessation of contact.

This decrease in punishment seemed to be related to two factors. First, the infant began to respond to the gross body cues of the male and retreated when the male jerked his upper body. More important, the male became more tolerant of the infant, allowing interactions which he would not have endured initially. In fact, it might be said that Clyde has exhibited an increasing 'awareness' of the infant's

Fig. 9. Second phase of the pairing procedure. Clyde, upon instigation by *E*, directs a stare-threat at Bonnie in her small cage.

Fig. 10. Second phase of the pairing procedure. Clyde threatens Bonnie and pushes at her cage.

Fig. 11. Second phase of the pairing procedure. When *E* pushes a pole towards Clyde, he directs a threat only at Bonnie.

Fig. 12. Shortly after the actual pairing, the two examine each other.

Fig. 13. Still in the pairing cage, Clyde watches Bonnie as she apprehensively walks past him.

presence. He still displays a high frequency of self-directed be-haviours such as stereotypic swaying, saluting, self-mounting, and self-biting. But whereas at the beginning of the study he swayed in spite of the fact that he was stepping on the infant with each return motion, he has recently been seen to gently push the infant out of the way before beginning a bout of swaying.

The infant has recently been observed to exhibit some behaviours that might be considered similar to those shown by isolation-reared infants. These include a 'floating' hind limb, clasping the foot with the hand, pulling hair from her head, and sucking her knee. How-ever, since these behaviours occurred during an observation session which was marked by the unusually great amount of play behaviour in the infant it is unclear whether she was actually exhibiting bizarre behaviours, or simply playing with herself.

To conclude and summarize, we have demonstrated: 1) that it is possible for an adult male rhesus macaque—either feral-born or isolation-reared—raise a young infant in the absence of a mother without inflicting severe trauma on the former; 2) that the infants

K

so reared do not exhibit marked behavioural pathology; 3) that the attachment appears to increase in strength over time, particularly in the adult male; and 4) that for the male infant the form of play exhibited was of a frequency and intensity not at all characteristic of mother-infant pairs. In future research with these dyads we intend to explore the effects of the shift in 'identification' models from adult female to adult male on sexual, aggressive, parental, play, and attachment behaviours in infancy and adulthood. The personality and hormonal characteristics of males displaying high and low degrees of paternal attachment will also be examined as well as the possible therapeutic effects of close interaction with infants on the behaviour of isolation-reared males.

References

Baysinger, C.; Brandt, E. M.; and Mitchell, G. Development of Infant rhesus monkeys (*Macaca mulatta*) in their isolation cages. *Primates,* in press.

Brandt, E. M.; Stevens, C. W.; and Mitchell, G. 1971. Visual socialcommunication in adult male isolate-reared monkeys (*Macaca mulatta*). *Primates,* 12: 105-112.

Hansen, E. W. 1966. The development of maternal and infant behavior in the rhesus monkey. *Behaviour,* 27: 107-149.

Mitchell, G. 1969. Paternalistic behavior in primates. *Psychological Bulletin,* 71: 399-417.

Mitchell, G. 3 May 1970. The development of abnormal behavior in monkeys. Paper presented at the *Behavior Modificction Workshop,* Stockton, California.

Thompson, H. S. 1967. Primate infanticide: A note and a request for information. *Laboratory Primate Newsletter,* 6: 18-19.

Factors in family relationships
—3

Syndromes of paternal deprivation in man

Henry B. Biller,
University of Rhode Island,
Emma Pendleton Bradley Hospital

Paternal deprivation can be considered to be a deficiency in fathering which often has negative consequences on the individual's development. Paternal deprivation can be in the context of father absence or separation from the father for some period of time. But the father does not necessarily have to be living away from his family for there to be paternal deprivation. For example, a man who has an extensive work schedule may be a very unavailable father. There can also be paternal deprivation when the father is available but there is not a meaningful father-child attachment. In such cases, there needs to be an examination of the quality of the father's behaviour when he is available and interacting with his child. In addition, a child's attachment to an inadequate father can be conceived of as a particular form of paternal deprivation. A child can be attached to a father who is ineffectual, emotionally disturbed.

A child does not suffer from paternal deprivation in a vacuum. To fully understand the effects of paternal deprivation one must take into account the reason for paternal deprivation, its duration, the sex and developmental status of the child, the quality of the mother-child and mother-father relationship, the family's structure and sibling composition, the socio-cultural background of the family, and the availability of surrogate models. We are just beginning to understand the role that paternal factors play in both adequate and inappropriate development. This presentation is by necessity brief and incomplete.

Father absence. There is a growing concern with the psychological, social and economic disadvantages often suffered by fatherless children. However, father absence *per se* does not necessarily lead to developmental deficits, or render the father-absent child inferior in psychological functioning relative to the father-present child. Fatherless children are far from a homogeneous group. An almost infinite variety of patterns of father absence can be specified. The father-absent child may not be paternally deprived if he has a very adequate father-surrogate or he may be less paternally deprived than many father-present children.

Nevertheless, the child who has both an involved and competent mother *and* father is less likely to suffer from developmental deficits and psychopathology, than is the child who is reared in a one-parent family (Biller, 1971a, 1972). Children with competent mothers are less likely to have certain types of developmental deficits than are children who have a dominating mother and a passive-ineffectual father. The father-absent child may develop a more flexible image of adult men, and at least be seeking out some type of father surrogate, whereas the child with a passive-ineffectual or rejecting father may have a very negative image of adult males and avoid interacting with them (Biller, 1971a).

Early paternal deprivation

The age at which paternal deprivation occur appears to be a very important factor. Infants often form strong attachments to their fathers as well as their mothers (Ban and Lewis, 1971; Biller, 1971a; Pederson and Rabson, 1969). A positive attachment to a competent father can facilitate the infant and young child's development. Our observations have suggested that children who are able to form strong attachments to both their mothers and fathers during infancy have more positive self-concepts and success in interpersonal relations than children who have only an attachment to their mothers (Biller, 1971a; 1972).

We have consistently found that boys who become father absent before the age of four or five have less masculine sex role orientations (self-concepts) and more sex-role conflicts than either father-present boys or boys who became father-absent at a later time (Biller, 1968b; 1969b; Biller and Bahm, 1971). Early father absence is more often associated with a low level of independence and assertiveness in peer relations (Hetherington, 1967), feelings of inferiority and mistrust of others (Santrock, 1970b), academic underachievement (Blanchard and Biller, 1971) and antisocial behaviour (Siegman, 1966).

Close and exclusive relationships with mothers in the first two or three years of life, and the relative unavailability of fathers, are related to sex role conflicts and sexual anxiety in adolescence and adulthood (Burton, 1972; Burton and Whiting, 1961; Stephens, 1962). There is a particularly high frequency of early father absence (before age four) among emotionally disturbed children (Holman, 1953) and adults (Beck, Sehti, and Tuthill, 1963). It may be that father absence at different age periods affects different dimensions of personality development (Biller, 1970; 1971a; Herzog and Sudia, 1970; Nash, 1965).

Cognitive deficits

The father-absent child often suffers from intellectual deficits (Blanchard and Biller, 1971; Deutsch and Brown, 1964; Landy, Rosenberg, and Sutton-Smith, 1969). Father absence appears to be particularly inhibiting for the interpersonal and cognitive development of lower-class children (Bronfenbrenner, 1967; Pettigrew, 1964). Paternal inadequacy and poor father-child relationships have also been reported to be associated with academic underachievement (Biller and Winebrenner, 1972; Grunebaum et al, 1962; Kimball, 1952).

Blanchard and I attempted to specify different levels of father availability and to ascertain their relationship to academic functioning among third grade boys (Blanchard and Biller, 1971). The boys were of average intelligence and were from working class and lower middle class backgrounds. Four groups of boys were studied; early father-absent (beginning before age three), late father-absent (beginning after age five), low father-present (less than six hours per week), and high father-present (more than two hours per day). Each boy from the early father-absent group was matched with a boy from each of the other three groups in terms of age, intelligence, socio-economic status, and presence or absence of male siblings.

Academic performance was assessed in terms of Stanford Achievement Test Scores and teachers' grades. With respect to achievement test scores, the high father-present group performed consistently above grade level, the low-father-present and late father-absent boys usually functioned somewhat below grade level, and the early father-absent boys were generally underachievers. Compared to the high father-present group, the early father-absent group scored significantly lower on every achievement test index as well as on teachers' grades. The early father-absent group functioned below grade level in terms of both language and mathematical skills.

The early father-absent boy, especially if he is from a lower-class background, often enters school with much uncertainty about his ability to succeed. Boys with high paternal availability and nurturance seem much more likely to actualize their intellectual potential than do children with unavailable or inadequate fathers. Active involved fathers seem to afford their children models of perseverance and achievement motivation. Frequent opportunity to observe and imitate his father seems to facilitate the development of the child's overall instrumental competence and problem-solving skill. The consistent availability of an active and nurturant father is positively related to the child's intellectual functioning and problem-solving skill even before he enters school (Biller and Winebrenner, 1972; Radin, 1972).

Differential abilities. Carlsmith (1964) found that upper-middle-class high school boys who were father-absent before the age of five were more likely than boys who were father-present to have a feminine pattering of aptitude test scores and to have, in contrast to the usual male pattern, a verbal score higher than their math score. The likelihood was positively related to the length of father-absence and negatively related to the child's age at the onset of father absence. Carlsmith reasoned that such a score pattern was a reflection of a feminine-global conceptual style. Boys who are father-absent and those who have passive or neglecting fathers are likely to be relatively low in analytical ability (Barclay and Cusumano, 1967; Biller and Winebrenner, 1972).

Although Carlsmith (1964) did not specifically report such analyses it appears that the father-absent group tended to be equal or superior in verbal aptitude but inferior in mathematical aptitude. Since adequate performance in most classroom endeavours is so heavily dependent on verbal ability, paternally deprived *middle class* children may not be very handicapped in their academic achievement (Gregory, 1965; Hilgard, Newman and Fisk, 1960; Lessing, Zagorin and Nelson, 1970; Levy, 1943).

When the father is absent or relatively unavailable, the mother usually assumes an especially salient role in socializing the child (Biller, 1971a, b). A paternally deprived boy with an overprotective but intellectually-focused mother would seem to be at an advantage in many facets of school adjustment. He might find the transition from home to the typically feminized classroom quite comfortable and do particularly well in tasks where verbal skills and conformity were rewarded. The expectations of the mother and the peer group are extremely important. Among children in the lower class, paternal deprivation usually intensifies lack of exposure to certain cognitive experiences. In addition, the school situation which presents women as authority figures and with strong demands for obedience and conformity, is often antithetical to many lower class boys' peer group values (Biller and Winebrenner, 1972).

Problems in self-control

Inadequate conscience development is frequently associated with paternal deprivation (Hoffman, 1971). Weak father identification among father-present boys was related to relatively inadequate conscience development. The boy was asked whom he felt most similar to, most admired, and most wanted to resemble when he grew up. Boys with weak father identifications scored lower on internal moral judgment, moral values, and conformity to rules than did boys with strong father identifications. Father-absent boys scored lower than father-present boys on measures of internal moral judgment, guilt following transgressions, acceptance of blame, moral values and rule conformity. There is a linkage between father absence and the child's inability to delay gratification (Mischel, 1958, 1961).

Delinquency. Juvenile delinquency can have many different etiologies but paternal deprivation is frequently a contributing factor, particularly among lower class children (Miller, 1958). Father absence is more common among delinquent boys than among non-delinquent boys (Andersen, 1968; Glueck and Glueck, 1950; Gregory, 1965a). Father-present juvenile delinquents generally have very poor relationships with their fathers, who are often un-affectionate, uncommunicative, and generally inadequate (Andry, 1962; Bandura and Walters, 1959; McCord, McCord and Thurber, 1962). Societies which have a low level of paternal availability during the child's first few years of life may have a large amount of theft and personal crime (Bacon, Child and Barry, 1963).

A boy who has experienced paternal deprivation may have par-ticular difficulty in respecting and communicating with adult males in positions of authority. The child whose father has nurturantly and realistically set limits for him is better able to set limits for himself (Biller, 1971a). Boys who receive appropriate and consistent discipline from their fathers are less likely to commit delinquent acts even if they are gang members (Glueck and Glueck, 1950; Stan-field, 1966).

Interpersonal difficulties

Father-absent boys have more difficulty in forming satisfying peer relationships than do father-present boys (Mitchell and Wilson, 1967; Stolz et al., 1954; Tiller, 1958). They may be less popular with their peers because they more often lack a masculine orientation (Biller, 1968b, 1969b; Biller and Bahm, 1971). Paternal warmth and perceived similarity to the father are associated with self-confidence and positive peer relationships (Gray, 1959; L. Hoffman, 1961; Mussen et al., 1963).

I found a strong relationship between kindergarten-age boys' masculinity, particularly in relation to their self-concepts, and perceived paternal involvement including paternal nurturance, and decision-making (Biller, 1969a). Furthermore, paternal influence in father-mother interaction was positively related to the degree to which the boys perceived their fathers to actively participate in their families. Families in which the mother dominated the father were very inhibiting of boys' masculine development.

Mothers in father-absent homes are more likely to overprotect their children and encourage over-dependency (Biller, 1969b; Stend-ler, 1954; Stolz et al., 1954). In homes in which the father plays a very submissive or ineffectual role, there is frequently maternal over-protection and children are often extremely dependent on their mothers (Levy, 1943; Sears, 1953). Mothers in father-absent homes,

as compared to those in father-present homes, give less encouragement to their sons to behave in a masculine manner or to enter
into masculine peer group activities (Biller, 1969b; Stolz et al., 1954;
Tiller, 1958).

Reactive maternal overprotection is found less often among lower
class children than among middle class children. The lower class
paternally-deprived boy more frequently rebels against his unmasculine family environment and engages in overcompensatory gang
behaviour. He is more likely to be maternally neglected or rejected
than is the middle class paternally deprived boy. He appears to be
more influenced by his peers and often develops a very negative
attitude toward many endeavours that he perceives as feminine
(Biller, 1971a).

In contrast, the boy who experiences positive fathering is particularly well-suited to both learn and effectively influence his peer
group. He is secure in interacting with other males and he is also
assertive and independent enough to resist submissive conformity.
He is likely to have considerable skill in communicating with his
peers and to be a leader, and less likely to attempt to prove himself
through overcompensatory behaviour (Biller, 1971a).

Sexual Inadequacies. Although no systematic studies have been
made concerning the rates of homosexuality among father-absent
males, some results have suggested that father-absent males are
more prone than are father-present males to become homosexual
(O'Connor, 1964; West, 1959). Males who have ineffectual fathers,
together with being involved in an intense relationship with their
mothers, seem particularly likely to develop homosexual or a
sexually inverted pattern of behaviour (Bieber, et al., 1962);
Gundlach, 1969; Stoller, 1968; West, 1967).

A close-binding mother-son relationship, more common in father-
absent homes, may lessen the probability of the boy entering into
meaningful heterosexual relationships (Biller, 1971a; Hilgard,
Neuman and Fisk, 1960; Jacobson and Ryder, 1969; Pettigrew,
1964).

Maladjustment and psychopathology

A paternally deprived child may be very insecure in his interpersonal relationships and this can contribute to feelings of anxiety
and low self-esteem. The father-absent child, in particular, is likely
to encounter economic insecurity and, depending on the reason for

father absence, may be concerned with his father's well-being. Feelings of being different from other children may also increase his anxiety and perception of being inadequate (Biller, 1971a).

A principal role of the father is to help the family actively deal with environmental problems, and it could be expected that the paternally-deprived child would encounter many seemingly unsolvable crises. Some investigators have reported an association between father absence and high anxiety (e.g., Koch, 1961; Stolz et al., 1954). Similarly, poor father-child relationships in the intact home may entail a high level of anxiety and poor sex-role adjustment (Biller, 1971a; Beier and Ratzeburg, 1953; Lazowick, 1955).

Children with serious behaviour problems generally lack a close and nurturant relationship with their fathers (Biller, 1971a). There may be a connection between particular types of paternal inadequacy and specific behaviour problems. Antisocial behaviour is often found among children with uninvolved fathers who are not consistently concerned with setting realistic limits. Domineering and hostile fathers, on the other hand, frequently have shy and emotionally immature children (Becker et al., 1962; Petersen et al., 1959; Rosenthal et al., 1962). Father-absent children have also been reported to have a high rate of problems in adjustment to school, both academic and interpersonal (Holman, 1953; Risen, 1939; Rouman, 1956; Russell, 1947). Unfortunately, studies linking paternal deprivation with maladjustment in children have usually lacked adequate comparison groups and analyses relating to such variables as socio-economic background and sex of child (Biller, 1971a).

Children with adequate and available fathers profit from exposure to a model who can realistically deal with some of the problems that a mother may not have the experience or the time to solve. Frequent opportunities for observing a competent adult male in a variety of situations are important in the development of the child's maturity and responsibility. Bronfenbrenner (1961) indicated that the amount of time adolescent boys spent with their fathers was positively related to the amount of leadership and responsibility that the boys displayed in school. Mussen et al., (1963) found that instrumental achievement striving was more frequent among adolescent boys with affectionate father-son relationships than among those with inadequate father-son relationships.

Reuter and I studied the relationship between various combinations of perceived paternal nurturance-availability and college males' personality adjustment (Reuter and Biller, 1972). High paternal nurturance combined with at least moderate paternal availability, and high paternal availability combined with at least moderate paternal nurturance, were related to high scores on the personality adjustment measures. A male who has adequate opportunities to observe a nurturant father can imitate his behaviour and develop positive personality characteristics. The father who is both relatively nurturant and relatively available may have a particularly adequate personality adjustment.

In contrast, high paternal availability combined with low paternal nurturance, and high paternal nurturance combined with low paternal availability were associated with relatively poor scores on the personality adjustment measures. Males who reported that their fathers had been home much of the time but gave them little attention perceived themselves as undependable and insecure. The unnurturant father is an inadequate model and his consistent presence is a detriment to the boy's personality functioning. The boy with an unnurturant father may be better off if his father is not very available. Males who were high in paternal nurturance but low in paternal availability also seemed to be quite handicapped in their psychological functioning. The boy with a highly nurturant but seldom-home father may feel quite frustrated that his father is not home more often or may find it difficult to imitate such an elusive figure.

Vocational failure. Males who have had absent fathers tend to have lower achievement motivation and to experience less career success than do males who have been father-present (McClelland, 1961; Terman and Oden, 1947). They often have much difficulty in learning how to delay gratification of needs and to control impulses. One might therefore predict that males who have been father-absent would find it very frustrating to persist in arduous situations and in meeting certain long-term responsibilities. An investigation with Peace Corps volunteers, revealed that those who were father-absent during childhood were less likely to complete their scheduled overseas tours than were those who had not been father-absent (Suedfield, 1967). Reasons for premature termination were associated with problems of adjustments and conduct, and included some psychiatrically-based decisions.

The father who is involved in his family and is viewed as a salient family decision maker can do much to facilitate his son's personality development and cognitive functioning. However, the father must allow his child to function in an independent and assertive manner. Paternal interference and pressure can hamper the child's ability to think flexibly and independently (Busse, 1969; Rosen and D'Andrade, 1959). Paternal domination as well as maternal domination can undermine the child's competency by not allowing sufficient opportunity to solve his own problems. Rigid paternal subordination of the mother and child stifles the boy's achievement strivings (Strodbeck, 1958).

Severe mental disturbance. Adults who have been father-absent are more likely to become depressed than are adults who have been father present (Beck, Sehti, and Tuthill, 1963; Haworth, 1964). Beck, Sehti, and Tuthill (1963) found that paternal absence before the age of four was highly associated with depression. It may be that loss of father due to death is more strongly related to chronically depressed behaviour than is loss of father due to other factors.

However, Brill and Liston (1966) reported that loss of father due to death in childhood was not unusually high among mental patients. Loss of father due to divorce or separation in childhood was much higher for individuals suffering from neurosis, psychosis, or personality disorders than for a number of different comparison groups. Other investigations have also revealed that rates of childhood father absence are higher among adult patients classified as neurotic or schizophrenic than among the general population (Madow and Hardy, 1947; Norton, 1952; Oltman, McGarry and Friedman, 1952; Wahl, 1954, 1956).

Paternal passivity combined with maternal domination appears to be particularly common in the development of severe psychopathology (Biller, 1971a). High paternal involvement and decision making are uncommon in families in which there is a severely disturbed son (Mishler and Waxler, 1968; Schuham, 1970). Males having inadequate fathering seem much more likely to develop severe behaviour disturbances or schizophrenia (Farina, 1960; Kayton and Biller, 1971; Lidz, Parker and Cornelison, 1956; Warren and Cameron, 1950).

Adequate personality development seems facilitated in families in which the father clearly represents a positive masculine role, and the mother a positive feminine role. Kayton and I (1971) studied matched groups of non-disturbed, neurotic, paranoid schizophrenic and non-paranoid schizophrenic adult males. We found that the non-disturbed subjects perceived their parents as exhibiting sex-appropriate behaviours to a greater extent than did the disturbed subjects. A smaller proportion of individuals in the disturbed groups viewed their fathers as possessing masculine-instrumental traits, and particularly among the schizophrenic groups, their mothers as having feminine-expressive characteristics. Schizophrenic behaviour is frequently associated with disturbances in the sex role development process (Biller and Poey, 1969; Kayton and Biller, 1972; Lidz, Fleck and Cornelison, 1965; McClelland and Watt, 1968).

The female's development

Most of the research concerning paternal influence and the child's personality development has focused on the father-son relationship, or has failed to take into account sex differences. However, the quantity and quality of fathering can affect females as well as males (Biller, 1971a; Biller and Weiss, 1970; Johnson, 1963).

Although males and females are both influenced, paternal deprivation has a somewhat more negative effect on the personality development of males (Biller, 1971a; Bach, 1946; Helson, 1967; Hoffman, 1971; Lessing, Zagorin and Nelson, 1970; Lynn and Sawrey, 1959). Nevertheless, the degree and direction of sex differences probably varies with respect to which components of personality functioning are considered.

The behaviour of fathers can do much to motivate girls' intellectual attainment. High paternal expectations coupled with a warm father-daughter relationship are conducive to the development of autonomy, high achievement and creativity among girls (Biller and Winebrenner, 1972; Crandall et al., 1964; Helson, 1969; Nakamura and Rogers, 1969). Bing (1963) found a positive association between the amount of reading fathers did at home and their daughters' verbal ability. On the other hand, paternal indifference or rejection seems related to deficits in females' functioning in certain types of cognitive tasks (Heilbrun et al., 1967).

Fathers appear to be more concerned with the sex role development of their children than are mothers (Biller, 1971a). The father may play a major role in the girl's development of a positive view of her femininity (Biller, 1969a; 1971a; Biller and Weis, 1970; Johnson, 1963). Strong paternal expectations for feminine behaviour seem to be particularly conducive to the girl's participation in culturally defined sex-appropriate activities (Fling and Mansosevitz, 1972; Mussen and Rutherford, 1963; Sears, Rau and Alpert, 1965). The father who reinforces passivity, timidity and dependency rather than intellectual and interpersonal competence can greatly restrict his daughter's potential for self-actualization (Biller, 1971a, 1972).

Girls with highly active and decisive fathers are likely to be self-confident and well accepted by other children whereas girls from maternally dominated homes more often have interpersonal difficulties (Hoffman, 1961). Perceptions of excessive maternal control and intrusiveness are associated with high anxiety and sex role conflict among elementary school girls (Biller and Zung, 1972).

The quality of the father-daughter relationship is a significant factor in the girl's personality development (Fish and Biller, 1972). College girls' perceptions of their relationships with their fathers during childhood were assessed by means of an extensive family background questionnaire. Girls who perceived their fathers as having been highly rejecting scored extremely low on the measure of personality adjustment. In contrast, girls who perceived their fathers as having been very nurturant and positively involved scored high on the measure of personality adjustment. A positive father-daughter relationship may facilitate the girl's ability to have successful heterosexual relationships (Biller, 1971a).

Inadequate development. Overdependency on the mother appears to be a common problem for the father-absent girl (Lynn and Sawrey, 1959). Because of a relatively exclusive and intense relationship with her mother, the father-absent girl may also have problems in handling her aggressive impulses (Sears, Pintler and Sears, 1946). A higher incidence of delinquent behaviour has been reported for father-absent girls (Monahan, 1957; Toby, 1957). Females who have been father-absent more often have negative attitudes towards being wives and mothers than do those who have been father-present (Seward, 1945). The father-absent female is likely to have sex role conflicts and difficulties in attaining a satisfactory heterosexual adjustment (Leonard, 1966; Neubauer, 1960).

Paternal inadequacy and overrestrictiveness are sometimes associated with sexual acting out among adolescent females (Kaufman et al., 1954; Robey et al., 1964). A variety of negative paternal behaviour patterns (including uninvolvement, passivity, rejection, extreme possessiveness, and hostile manipulativeness) have been found to be prominent in the family backgrounds of female homosexuals (Bené, 1965; Kaye et al., 1967; West, 1967).

Perceived similarity to the father, in terms of adaptive personality characteristics, appears to be positively associated with the female's personality development whereas feelings of marked father-daughter dissimilarity seem to be related to psychopathology among females (Fish and Biller, 1972; Lazowick, 1951; Sopchak, 1952). Investigators examining the family background of hospitalized schizophrenic women reported that almost seventy-five percent had experienced some inadequacy of fathering in childhood (Hamilton and Wahl, 1948). Prolonged father-absence, paternal rejection and paternal abuse were very common.

There is a high incidence of inadequate fathering among both male and female schizophrenics (e.g., Lidz, Fleck and Cornelison, 1965; Lidz, Parker and Cornelison, 1956). The fathers of schizophrenic females were in severe conflict with their wives, and frequently degraded their wives in front of their daughters. They made rigid and unrealistic demands on their wives, and were insensitive to their daughters' needs to develop an independent self-concept. They made attempts to manipulate and mould their daughters in terms of their own unrealistic needs. Females who formed an allegiance with a disturbed father, frequently in reaction to rejection by an unloving mother, seemed most likely to become psychotic.

Constitutional factors

The child's constitutionally predisposed traits can affect the father-child relationship and the probability of paternal deprivation (Bell, 1968, Biller, 1971a). The following are a few over-simplified examples. A child who is temperamentally unresponsive may not respond to the father's attempts to form a positive relationship with him. A father may be much more available and nurturant to a bright child than one who appears to be handicapped in his intellectual ability. He may be more interested in interacting with a son who has excellent physical development than one who is weak and frail.

The child's constitutional predispositions can also be very important. Biller (1968a, 1969b) has indicated that among father-absent boys those who were highly mesomorphic and intelligent were less likely to suffer personality deficits and interpersonal difficulties than were those with unmasculine physiques and average intelligence. A boy's physique has an important stimulus value in terms of the responses that it elicits from others and it may, along with cor-related congenital factors, predispose him toward success or failure in terms of certain types of activities.

Most children are handicapped if they have experienced paternal deprivation, but it is also important to emphasize that extremely severe psychopathology (such as infantile autism or childhood schizophrenia) does not usually develop simply as a function of inadequate parent-child relationships. The severity of the indi-vidual's psychopathology may be much associated with his genetic or constitutional predispositions. In most cases, insufficient or inappropriate fathering (or mothering) per se does not account for individuals who are completely unable to develop basic communica-tion skills and to form even immature interpersonal attachments. In fact, constitutionally atypical children can contribute to the develop-ment of psychopathology in their parents (Biller, 1971a, 1972).

Further research considerations

There is a great need for more direct observation of father-child interactions (Biller, 1971a; Rebelsky and Hanks, 1971); it would be very helpful for more specific criteria for paternal adequacy, and for reference points for defining paternal deprivation. Important questions include what type and amount of paternal nurturance is most effective and what paternal behaviour and skills are essential.

Older brothers may facilitate the father-absent boy's personality development (Santrock, 1970; Sutton-Smith, Rosenberg and Landy, 1968; Wohlford et al., 1971). Stepfathers or father surrogates can positively influence the boy who has been father-absent (Anderson, 1968; Nash, 1965; Lessing, Zagorin and Nelson, 1970, and a close relationship with a father surrogate can be very therapeutic for delinquent males (Glueck and Glueck, 1950; Trenaman, 1952).

A mother who is emotionally disturbed or interpersonally handi-capped can have a very negative effect on the father-absent child's self-concept and ability to relate to others (e.g., Pedersen, 1966; McCord, McCord and Thurber, 1962). On the other hand, mothers who are self-accepting, have high ego strength, and are inter-personally mature can do much to facilitate positive personality functioning among paternally deprived children (Biller, 1971a, b).

Investigations comparing paternally deprived individuals having different types of adjustments with respect to their relationships with their mothers might be quite revealing. There is a great need for more investigations exploring potential relationships between individual differences in mothering in various types of paternally deprived families and the child's personality development (Biller, 1971a, b). Much more attention also needs to be focused upon socio-economic factors, including the family's income level (Herzog and Sudia, 1970).

Some practical implications

There are many relevant descriptions of how psychotherapists have attempted to help emotionally disturbed individuals who are paternally deprived (Forrest, 1967; Meerloo, 1956; Neubauer, 1960; Stoller, 1968; Wiley and Delgado, 1959). Nevertheless, the emphasis on the mother-child relationship in most child psychotherapy has usually obscured the father's role in terms of both etiology and treatment (Biller, 1971a; Rubenstein and Levitt, 1957).

Therapists could strengthen their impact on the paternally deprived child by also working with the child's father or potential father surrogate. They could accomplish this by consultation, but engaging the father (surrogate) and child in joint sessions (or in groups with other children and father surrogates) might be even more beneficial. The use of modelling and related behaviour modification techniques such as those described by Bandura (1969) seems to be an especially worthwhile course to explore in individual, family and group therapy with paternally deprived individuals. In many cases, the probability of successful treatment could be greatly increased if knowledge concerning the basics of positive fathering were integrated into the therapy process, especially in the context of family therapy (Biller, 1971a).

Community mental health. Many organizations (e.g., Big Brother, YMCA, Boy Scouts, athletic teams, churches, settlement houses) provide children with father surrogates. An extremely significant implication from available research is that even in the first few years of life, the child's personality development can be very much influenced by positive involvement with his father or a father surrogate. Day care centers and group settings such as Head Start

L

can be used as vehicles to provide adequate father surrogates for very young children (both boys and girls).

Nursery schools, kindergartens, and elementary schools could have a much greater positive influence on children if more competent male teachers were available (Biller and Winebrenner, 1972). Male teachers can facilitate certain types of cognitive functioning in paternally deprived children as well as contributing to their interpersonal development. Institutionalized children including those who are orphaned or emotionally disturbed could also benefit from a larger proportion of interaction with effective adult males.

An essential function of community mental health efforts, both in terms of prevention and treatment, should be making available father surrogates to groups of paternally deprived children. Education and the mass media can be powerful influences in helping potential fathers and father surrogates become more aware of the significance of men in child development and, along with other programmes, can lessen the number of families which become paternally deprived.

Assistance, in terms of financial support and counselling, to help fathers have an active role in their families would be a progressive step away from the current rewarding of father absence by many welfare departments.

Preventive programmes can be created especially for families which have a high risk of being paternally deprived; individuals from certain sociocultural backgrounds and with particular personality patterns are highly vulnerable to separation and divorce (Loeb, 1966; Loeb and Price, 1966; Pettigrew, 1964). Methods should be developed to determine the potential consequences of father absence for a family in which the parents are contemplating separation or divorce. When the divorce process is taking place, more consideration should be given to whether some or all of the children might benefit from remaining with their fathers rather than with their mothers.

The mother in the paternally deprived family must not be neglected; her reaction to the ineffectiveness or absence of her husband may greatly influence the extent to which paternal deprivation affects her children. Mothers in paternally-deprived families are often in need of psychological as well as social and economic support (e.g. Glasser and Navarre, 1965; Kriesberg, 1967; Schlesinger, 1966). Educational and therapeutic groups such as 'Parents without Partners' (Freudenthal, 1959; Schlesinger, 1966) can be very helpful to mothers in paternally deprived families. Smith and I worked with a welfare mothers group in which one of the central goals was to help husbandless mothers constructively deal with their social and familial problems (Biller and Smith, 1972). Other suggestions concerning ways to help the paternally-deprived family are available (Biller, 1971a; Biller and Winebrenner, 1972; Despert, 1957; Kriesberg, 1967; Lerner, 1954; McDermott, 1968; Wylie and Delgado, 1959).

References

Anderson, R. E. 1968. Where's Dad? Paternal deprivation and delinquency. *Archives of General Psychiatry,* 18: 641-49.

Andry, R. G. 1962. Paternal and maternal roles in delinquency. In *Deprivation of maternal care.* Public Health Paper No. 14. Geneva: World Health Organization, 31-43.

Bach, G. R. 1946. Father-fantasies and father typing in father-separated children. *Child Development,* 17: 63-80.

Bacon, M. K.; Child, I. L.; and Barry, H. III. 1963. A cross-cultural study of correlates of crime. *Journal of Abnormal and Social Psychology,* 66: 291-300.

Ban, P. L., and Lewis, M. Mothers and fathers, girls and boys: Attachment behavior in the one-year-old. Paper presented at the meeting of the Eastern Psychological Association, New York, April, 1971.

Bandura, A. 1969. *Principles of behavior modification.* New York: Holt, Rinehart, and Winston.

Bandura, A., and Walters, R. H. 1958. Dependency conflicts in aggressive delinquents. *Journal of Social Issues,* 14: 52-65.

Bandura, A., and Walters, R. H. 1963. *Social learning and personality development,* New York: Holt, Rinehart, and Winston.

Barclay, A. G., and Cusumano, D. 1967. Father-absence, cross-sex identity, and field dependent behavior in male adolescents. *Child Development,* 38: 243-50.

Bartemeir, L. 1953. The contribution of the father to the mental health of the family. *American Journal of Psychiatry,* 110: 277-80.

Beck, A. T.; Sehti, B. B.; and Tuthill, R. W. 1963. Childhood bereavement and adult depression. *Archives of General Psychiatry,* 9: 295-302.

Becker, W. C.; Peterson, D. R.; Luria, Z.; Shoemaker, D. S.; and Hellmer, L. A. 1962. Relations of factors derived from parent interview ratings to behavior problems of five-year-olds. *Child Development,* 33: 509-35.

Beier, E. C. and Ratzeburg, F. 1953. The parental identifications of male and female college students. *Journal of Abnormal and Social Psychology,* 48: 569-72.

Bell, R. Q. 1968. A reinterpretation of the direction of effects of studies of socialization. *Psychological Review,* 75: 81-95.

Bené, E. 1965. On the genesis of female homosexuality. *British Journal of Psychiatry,* 3: 815-21.

Bieber, I., et al. 1962. *Homosexuality: A psychoanalytic study.* New York: Basic Books.

Biller, H. B. 1968. A multiaspect investigation of masculine development in kindergarten age boys. *Genetic Psychology Monographs,* 76: 89-139. (a)

Biller, H. B. 1968. A note on father-absence and masculine development in young lower-class Negro and white boys. *Child Development,* 39: 1003-1006. (b)

Biller, H. B. 1969. Father dominance and sex role development in kindergarten age boys. *Developmental Psychology,* 1: 87-94. (a)

Biller, H. B. 1969. Father-absence, maternal encouragement and sex-role development in kindergarten age boys. *Child Development,* 40: 539-46. (b)

Biller, H. B. 1970. Father-absence and the personality development of the male child. *Developmental Psychology,* 2: 181-201. (a)

Biller, H. B. 1971. *Father, child, and sex role.* Lexington, Mass.: Heath Lexington Books, D.C. Heath. (a)

Biller, H. B. 1971. The mother-child relationship and the father-absent boy's personality development. *Merrill-Palmer Quarterly,* 16: 227-41. (b)

Biller, H. B. 1972. *Sex role development.* Monterey, California: Brooks/Cole, Wadsworth, in preparation.

Biller, H. B., and Bahm, R. M. 1971. Father-absence, perceived maternal behavior, and masculinity of self-concept among junior high school boys. *Developmental Psychology,* 4: 78-181.

Biller, H. B., and Barry, W. 1971. Sex role patterns, paternal similarity, and personality adjustments in college males. *Developmental Psychology,* 4: 107.

Biller, H. B., and Poey, K. 1969. An exploratory comparison of sex role related behavior in schizophrenics and non-schizophrenics. *Developmental Psychology,* 1: 629.

Biller, H. B., and Smith, A. E. 1972. An AFDC mothers group: An exploratory effort in community mental health. *Family Coordinator,* 21, in press.

Biller, H. B., and Weiss, S. 1970. The father-daughter relationship and the personality development of the female. *Journal of Genetic Psychology,* 114: 79-93.

Biller, H. B., and Winebrenner, R. 1972. *Paternal influence, father absence, classroom adjustment, and reading ability.* Newark, Delaware: The International Reading Association—ERIC/CRIER, in press.

Biller, H. B. and Zung, B. 1972. Perceived maternal control, anxiety, and opposite sex role preference among elementary school girls. *Journal of Psychology,* in press.

Bing, E, 1963. Effect of child-rearing practices on development of differential cognitive abilities, *Child Development,* 34: 631-48.

Blanchard, R. W., and Biller, H. B. 1971. Father availability and academic performance among third grade boys. *Developmental Psychology,* 4: 301-5.

Brill, N. Q., and Liston, E. H., Jr. 1966. Parental loss in adults with emotional disorders. *Archives of General Psychiatry,* 14: 307-14.

Bronfenbrenner, U. 1961. Some familial antecedents of responsibility and leadership in adolescents. In *Leadership and interpersonal behavior,* eds. L. Petrullo and B. M. Bass, 239-72. New York: Holt, Rinehart, and Winston.

Bronfenbrenner, U. 1967. The psychological costs of quality and equality in education. *Child Development,* 38: 909-25.

Burton, R. V. 1972. Cross-sex identity in Barbados. *Developmental Psychology,* in press.

Burton, R. V., and Whiting, J. W. M. 1961. The absent father and cross-sex identity. *Merrill-Palmer Quarterly,* 7: 85-95.

Busse, T. W. 1969. Child-rearing antecedents of flexible thinking. *Developmental Psychology,* 1: 585-91.

Carlsmith, L. 1964. Effect of early father-absence on scholastic aptitude. *Harvard Educational Review,* 34: 3-21.

Crandall, V.; Dewey, R.; Katkovsky, W.; and Preston, A. 1964. Parents' attitudes and behaviors and grade-school children's academic achievements. *Journal of Genetic Psychology,* 104: 53-56.

Despert, L. J. 1957. The fatherless family. *Child Study,* 34: 22-28.

Deutsch, M. 1960. Minority group and class status as related to social and personality factors in scholastic achievement. *Monograph of the Society for Applied Anthropology,* 2: 1-32.

Deutsch, M., and Brown, B. 1964. Social influences in Negro-white intelligence differences. *Journal of Social Issues,* 20: 24-35.

Eisenberg, L. 1957. The fathers of autistic children. *American Journal of Orthopsychiatry,* 27: 715-25.

Farina, A. 1960. Patterns of role dominance and conflict in parents of schizophrenic patients. *Journal of Abnormal and Social Psychology,* 61: 31-38.

Fish, K. D., and Biller, H. B. 1972. Perceived childhood paternal relationships and college females' personal adjustment. *Adolescence,* in press.

Fleck, S., Lidz, T., and Cornelison, A. 1963. A comparison of parent-child relationships of male and female schizophrenic patients. *Archives of General Psychiatry,* 8: 1-7.

Fling, S. and Manosevitz, M. 1972. Sex typing in nursery school children's play interests, *Developmental* Psychology, in press.

Forrest, T. 1967. The paternal roots of male character development. *The Psychoanalytic Review,* 54: 81-99.

Freudenthal, K. 1959. Problems of the one-parent family. *Social Work,* 4: 44-48.

Garbower, C. 1959. *Behavior problems of children in Navy officers' families: As related to social conditions of Navy family life.* Washington, D.C.: Catholic University Press.

Gardiner, G. E. 1959. Separation of the parents and the emotional life of the child. In *The problems of delinquency,* ed. S. Glueck, 138-43. Boston: Houghton-Mifflin.

Gray, S. W. 1959. Perceived similarity to parents and adjustment. *Child Development,* 30: 91-107.

Gerard, D. L., and Siegal, J. 1950. The family background of schizophrenia. *Psychiatric Quarterly,* 24: 47-73.

Glasser, P., and Navarre, E. 1965. Structural problems of the one-parent family. *Journal of Social Issues,* 21: 98-109.

Glueck, S., and Glueck, E. 1950. *Unravelling juvenile de'inquency.* New York: Commonwealth Fund.

Gregory, I. 1965. Anterospective data following childhood loss of a parent: II. Pathology, performance, and potential among college students. *Archives of General Psychiatry,* 13: 110-20.

Gundlach, R. H. 1969. Childhood parental relationships and the establishment of gender roles of homosexuals. *Journal of Consulting and Clinical Psychology,* 33: 136-39.

Grunebaum, M. G.; Hurwitz, I.; Prentice, N. M.; and Sperry, B. M. 1962. Fathers of sons with primary neurotic learning inhibition. *American Journal of Orthopsychiatry,* 32: 462-73.

Hamilton, D. M. and Wahl, J. G. 1948. The hospital treatment of dementia praecox. *American Journal of Psychiatry,* 105: 346-52

Haworth, M. R. 1964. Parental loss in children as reflected in projective responses. *Journal of Projective Techniques,* 28: 31-35.

Heckel, R. V. 1963. The effects of fatherlessness on the pre-adolescent female. *Mental Hygiene,* 47: 69-73.

Heilbrun, A. B.; Harrell, S. N.; and Gillard, B. J. 1967. Perceived child rearing attitudes of fathers and cognitive control in daughters. *Journal of Genetic Psychology,* 111: 29-40.

Helson, R. 1967. Personality characteristics and developmental history of creative college women. *Genetic Psychology Monographs,* 76: 205-56.

Herzog, E., and Sudia, C. E. 1970. *Boys in fatherless families.* Washington: Office of Child Development.

Hetherington, E. M. 1967. Effects of paternal absence on sex-typed behaviors in Negro and white pre-adolescent males. *Journal of Personality and Social Psychology,* 6: 119-25.

Hilgard, J. R.; Neuman, M. F.; and Fisk, F. 1960. Strength of adult ego following bereavement. *American Journal of Orthopsychiatry,* 39: 788-98.

Hoffman, L. W. 1961. The father's role in the family and the child's peer-group adjustment. *Merrill-Palmer Quarterly,* 7: 97-105.

Hoffman, M. L. 1971. Father absence and conscience development. *Developmental Psychology,* 4: 400-406.

Holman, P. 1953. Some factors in the etiology of maladjustment in children. *Journal of Mental Science,* 99, 654-88.

Jacobson, G., and Ryder, R. G. 1969. Parental loss and some characteristics of the early marriage relationship. *American Journal of Orthopsychiatry,* 39: 779-87.

Johnson, M. M. 1963. Sex-role learning in the nuclear family. *Child Development,* 34: 319-33.

Kaye, H. E., et al. 1967. Homosexuality in women. *Archives of General Psychiatry,* 17: 626-34.

Kayton, R., and Biller, H. B. 1971. Perception of parental sex-role behavior and psychopathology in adult males. *Journal of Consulting and Clinical Psychology,* 36: 235-37.

Kayton, R., and Biller, H. B. 1972. Sex role development and psychopathology in adult males. *Journal of Consulting and Clinical Psychology,* in press.

Kaufman, I.; Peck, A. I.; and Tagiuri, C. K. 1954. The family constellation and overt incestuous relations between father and daughter. *American Journal of Orthopsychiatry,* 24: 266-77.

Kimball, B. 1952. The Sentence Completion Technique in a study of scholastic underachievement. *Journal of Consulting Psychology,* 16: 353-58.

Koch, M. B. 1961. Anxiety in pre-school children from broken homes. *Merrill-Palmer Quarterly,* 1: 225-31.

Kriesberg, L. 1967. Rearing children for educational achievement in fatherless families. *Journal of Marriage and the Family,* 29: 288-301.

Landy, F.; Rosenberg, B. G.; and Sutton-Smith, B. 1969. The effect of limited father-absence on cognitive development. *Child Development,* 40: 941-44.

Lazowick, L. M. 1955. On the nature of identification. *Journal of Abnormal and Social Psychology,* 51: 175-83.

Leonard, M. R. 1966. Fathers and daughters. *International Journal of Psychoanalysis,* 7: 325-33.

Lerner, S. H. 1954. Effect of desertion on family life. *Social Casework,* 35: 3-8.

Lessing, E. E.; Zagorin, S. W.; and Nelson, D. 1970. WISC subtest and IQ score correlates of father absence. *Journal of Genetic Psychology,* 67: 181-95.

Levy, D. M. *Maternal overprotection.* 1943. New York: Columbia University Press.

Lidz, R. W., and Lidz, T. 1949. The family environment of schizophrenic patients. *American Journal of Psychiatry,* 106: 332.

Lidz, T.; Fleck, S.; and Cornelison, A. R. 1965. *Schizophrenia and the human family.* New York: International Universities Press.

Lidz, T.; Parker, N.; and Cornelison, A. R. 1956. The role of the father in the family environment of the schizophrenic patient. *American Journal of Psychiatry,* 13: 126-32.

Loeb, J. 1966. The personality factor in divorce. *Journal of Consulting Psychology,* 30: 562.

Loeb, J., and Price, J. R. 1966. Mother and child personality characteristics related to parental marital status in child guidance cases. *Journal of Consulting Psychology,* 30: 112-17.

Lynn, D. B., and Sawrey, W. L. 1959. The effects of father-absence on

Norwegian boys and girls. *Journal of Abnormal and Social Psychology,* 258-62.

McClelland, D. C. 1961. *The achieving society.* New Jersey: Van Nostrand.

McClelland, D. C., and Watt, N. F. 1968. Sex role alienation in schizophrenia. *Journal of Abnormal Psychology,* 73: 226-39.

McCord, J.; McCord, W.; and Thurber, E. Some effects of paternal absence on male children. *Journal of Abnormal and Social Psychology,* 1962, 64: 361-69.

McDermott, J. F. 1968. Parental divorce in early childhood. *American Journal of Psychiatry,* 124: 1424-32.

Madow, L., and Hardy, S. E. 1947. Incidence and analysis of the broken family in the background of neurosis. *American Journal of Orthopsychiatry,* 17: 521-28.

Maxwell, A. E. 1961. Discrepancies between the pattern of abilities for normal and neurotic children. *Journal of Mental Science,* 107: 300-307.

Meerloo, J. A. M. 1956. The father cuts the cord: The role of the father as initial transference figure. *American Journal of Psychotherapy,* 10: 471-80.

Miller, W. B. 1958. Lower-class culture as a generating milieu of gang delinquency. *Journal of Social Issues,* 14: 5-19.

Mischel, W. 1958. Preference for delayed reinforcement: An experimental study of cultural observation. *Journal of Abnormal and Social Psychology,* 56: 57-61.

Mischel, W. 1961. Father-absence and delay of gratification. *Journal of Abnormal and Social Psychology,* 62: 116-24.

Mishler, E. G., and Waxler, N. E. 1968. *Interaction in families.* New York: Wiley. 1968.

Mitchell, D., and Wilson, W. 1967. Relationship of father-absence to masculinity and popularity of delinquent boys. *Psychological Reports,* 20: 1173-74.

Monahan, T. P. 1957. Family status and the delinquent child. *Social Forces,* 35: 250-58.

Mussen, P. H., and Rutherford, E. 1963. Parent-child relationships and parental personality in relation to young children's sex-role preferences. *Child Development,* 34: 589-607.

Mussen, P. H.; Young, H. B.; Godding, R.; and Morante, L. 1963. The influence of father-son relationships on adolescent personality and attitudes. *Journal of Child Psychology and Psychiatry,* 4: 3-16.

Nakamura, C. V., and Rogers, M. M. 1969. Parents' expectations of autonomous behavior and children's autonomy. *Developmental Psychology,* 1: 613-17.

Nash, J. 1965. The father in contemporary culture and current psychological literature. *Child Development,* 36: 261-97.

Nelsen, E. A. and Maccoby, E. E. 1966. The relationship between social development and differential abilities on the scholastic aptitude test. *Merrill-Palmer Quarterly,* 12: 269-89.

Neubauer, P. B. 1960. The one-parent child and his Oedipal development. *Psychoanalytic Studies of the Child,* 15: 286-309.

Norton, A. 1952. Incidence of neurosis related to maternal age and birth order. *British Journal of Social Medicine,* 6: 253-58.

Oltman, J. E.; McGarry, J. J.; and Friedman, S. 1952. Parental deprivation and the 'broken home' in dementia praecox and other mental disorders. *American Journal of Psychiatry,* 108: 685-94.

Ostrovsky, E. S. 1959. *Father to the child: Case studies of the experiences of a male teacher.* New York: Putnam.

O'Connor, P. J. 1964. Aetiological factors in homosexuality as seen in R.A.F. psychiatric practice. *British Journal of Psychiatry,* 110: 381-91.

Parker, S., and Kleiner, R. J. 1966. Characteristics of Negro mothers in single-headed households. *Journal of Marriage and the Family,* 28: 507-513.

Pedersen, F. A. 1966. Relationships between father-absence and emotional disturbance in male military dependents. *Merrill-Palmer Quarterly,* 12: 321-31.

Pedersen, F. A., and Rabson, K. S. 1969. Father participation in infancy. *American Journal of Orthopsychiatry,* 39: 466-72.

Petersen, D. R.; Becker, W. C.; Hellmer, L. A.; and Shoemaker, D. J. 1959. Parental attitudes and child adjustment. *Child Development,* 30: 119-30.

Pettigrew, T. F. 1964. *A profile of the Negro American.* Princeton: Van Nostrand.

Pope, B. 1953. Socioeconomic contrasts in children's peer culture prestige values. *Genetic Psychology Monographs,* 48: 157-200.

Radin, N. 1972. Father-child interaction and the intellectual functioning of four-year-old boys. *Developmental Psychology,* in press.

Rebelsky, F., and Hanks, C. Fathers' verbal interactions with daughters in the first three months of life. *Child Development,* 1971, 42: 63-68.

Reuter, M., and Biller, H. B. 1972. Perceived paternal nurturance-availability and personality adjustment among college males. *Journal of Consulting and Clinical Psychology,* in press.

Risen, M. L. 1939. Relation of lack of one or both parents to school progress. *Elementary School Journal,* 39: 528-31.

Robey, A.; Rosenwald, R. J.; Snell, J. E.; and Lee, R. E. 1964. The runaway girl: A reaction to family stress. *American Journal of Orthopsychiatry,* 34: 762-67.

Rosen, B. C., and D'Andrade, R. 1959. The psychological origins of achievement motivation. *Sociometry,* 22: 185-218.

Rosenthal, M. S.; Ni, E.; Finkelstein, M.; and Berkwits, G. K. 1962. Father-child relationships and children's problems. *Archives of General Psychiatry,* 7: 360-73.

Rouman, J. 1956. School children's problems as related to parental factors. *Journal of Educational Research,* 50: 105-112.

Rowntree, G. 1955. Early childhood in broken families. *Population Studies,* 8: 247-53.

Rubenstein, B. O., and Levitt, M. 1957. Some observations regarding the role of fathers in child psychotherapy. *Bulletin of the Menninger Clinic,* 21: 16-27.

Russell, I. L. 1947. Behavior problems of children from broken and intact homes. *Journal of Educational Sociology,* 31: 124-29.

Santrock, J. W. 1970. Paternal absence, sex-typing, and identification. *Developmental Psychology,* 2: 264-72. (a)

Santrock, J. W. 1970. Influence of onset and type of parental absence on the first four Eriksonian developmental crises. *Developmental Psychology,* 3: 273-74. (b)

Schuham, A. I. 1970. Power relations in emotionally disturbed and normal family triads. *Journal of Abnormal Psychology,* 75: 30-37.

Schlesinger, B. 1966. The one-parent family: An overview. *Family Life Coordinator,* 15: 133-37.

Sears, P. S. 1951. Doll play aggression in normal young children: Influence of sex, age, sibling status, father's absence. *Psychological Monographs,* 65: No. 6.

Sears, P. S. 1953. Child-rearing factors related to playing of sex-typed roles. *American Psychologist,* 8: 431 (Abstract).

Sears, R. R.; Maccoby, E. E.; and Levin, H. 1957. *Patterns of child rearing.* Evanston, Illinois: Row, Peterson.

Sears, R. R.; Pintler, M. H.; and Sears, P. S. 1946. Effect of father-separation on pre-school children's doll-play aggression. *Child Development,* 17: 219-43.

Sears, R. R.; Rau, L.; and Alpert, R. 1965. *Identification and child rearing.* Stanford: Stanford University Press.

Seward, G. H. 1945. Cultural conflict and the feminine role: An experimental study. *Journal of Social Psychology,* 22: 177-94.

Siegman, A. W. 1966. Father-absence during childhood and antisocial behavior. *Journal of Abnormal Psychology,* 71: 71-74.

Sopchak, A. L. 1952. Parental 'identification' and tendency toward disorder as measured by the MMPI. *Journal of Abnormal and Social Psychology,* 47: 159-65.

Stanfield, R. E. 1966. The interaction of family variables and gang variables in the aetiology of delinquency. *Social Problems,* 13: 411-17.

Stendler, C. B. 1952. Critical periods in socialization and overdependency. *Child Development,* 23: 3-12.

Stendler, C. B. 1954. Possible causes of overdependency in young children. *Child Development,* 25: 125-46.

Stephens, W. N. 1962. *The Oedipus complex: Cross-cultural evidence.* Glencoe, Illinois: Free Press.

Stoller, R. J. 1968. *Sex and gender.* New York: Science House.

Stolz, L. M., et al. 1954. *Father relations of war born children.* Stanford: Stanford University Press.

Strodbeck, F. L. 1958. Family interaction, values and achievement. In *Talent and Society,* eds. D. C. McCelland et al., pp. 135-94. New York: Van Nostrard.

Suedfield, P. 1967. Paternal absence and overseas success of Peace Corps volunteers. *Journal of Consulting Psychology,* 31: 424-25.

Sutherland, H. E. G. 1930. The relationship between I.Q. and size of family in the case of fatherless children. *Journal of Genetic Psychology,* 38: 161-70.

Sutton-Smith, B.; Rosenberg, B. G.; and Landy, F. 1968. Father-absence effects in families of different sibling compositions. *Child Development,* 38: 1213-21.

Terman, L. M., and Oden, M. H. 1947. *The gifted child grows up.* Stanford: Stanford University Press.

Thrasher, F. M. 1927. *The gang.* Chicago: University of Chicago Press.

Tiller, P. O. 1958. Father-absence and personality development of children in sailor families. *Nordisk Psyckologi's Monograph Series,* 9: 1-48.

Toby, J. 1957. The differential impact of family disorganization. *American Sociological Review,* 22: 505-51.

Trenaman, J. 1952. *Out of step.* London: Methuen.

Troff, J.; Atkinson, J.; Feld, S.; and Gurin, G. 1960. The use of thematic apperception to assess motivation in a nationwide interview study. *Psychological Monographs,* 74: (Whole No. 499).

Wahl, C. W. 1954. Antecedent factors in family histories of 392 schizophrenics. *American Journal of Psychiatry,* 110: 668-76.

Wahl, C. W. 1956. Some antecedent factors in the family histories of 568 male schizophrenics of the U.S. Navy. *American Journal of Psychiatry,* 113: 201-210.

Warren, W., and Cameron, K. 1950. Reactive psychosis in adolescence. *Journal of Mental Science,* 96: 448-57.

West, D. J. 1959. Parental relationships in male homosexuality. *International Journal of Social Psychiatry,* 5: 85-97.

West, D. J. 1967. *Homosexuality.* Chicago: Aldine.

Wohlford, P.; Santrock, S. W.; Berger, S. E.; and Libernan, D. 1971. Older brothers' influence on sex-typed, aggressive, and dependent behaviors in father-absent children. *Developmental Psychology,* 4: 124-34.

Wylie, H. L., and Delgado, R. A. 1959. A pattern of mother-son relationship involving the absence of the father. *American Journal of Orthopsychiatry,* 29: 644-49.

Discussion

after papers by MICHAEL and BILLER

Prof. Fox: Are there any sex differences in the effects of paternal deprivation between boys and girls?

Prof. Biller: In general, there appear to be more effects on the male child than on the female child. We have some evidence which does indicate that the female is hampered by paternal deprivation and is positively influenced by very adequate fathering.

Prof. Fox: How is she affected?

Prof. Biller: For example, when taken together evidence from a number of studies suggests that high paternal expectations in the context of a warm father/daughter relationship are related to independence, initiative and creativity among females. (I did give a brief summary of findings relating to the father-daughter relationship in my paper but a much fuller description can be found in my book, *Father, Child and Sex Role*).

Dr. Kagan: Dr. Michael, I thought it rather surprising that the substances you extracted from the human vagina were attractive to the male monkey because cues to copulation are usually very species specific. Also out of curiosity I would like to ask you whether you find these same substances in what are generally regarded as erotic perfumes?

Dr. Michael: One would have thought that it was very important that if you have differing species that they should not have the same type of sex attractions. A point in this might be that the Anubis baboon is an East African animal and the Rhesus an Indian animal. Where the human fits in this I do not know. But the fact that there is cross species activity is an unusual situation in nature. As regards the substances, theoretically they should be active wherever you find them. As regards the human perfume industry, my colleagues tell me that all these substances have a negative effect on the human nose.

Dr. McKenna: You stated that normal animals housed in cages showed bisexual behaviour. Do you think it is valid to use the word normal in this context? Do you not think that bisexual behaviour may quite possibly be a result of the housing in cages? Lorenz for example writes that domestication with certain species increased the incidence of copulation and decreased the intensity of mother care behaviour.

Dr. Michael: Is a laboratory rat normal? Its species are bred in a laboratory, a laboratory rat is an animal preparation. Where do you find a normal human being when you are looking for your normal controls? This is the same problem. The point we are making is the behaviour distortion because of the conditions under which the observations are made.

Dr. McKenna: When you used the word normal it looks as if you are opposing this to abnormal. What I am suggesting is that when you cage the monkey you are changing the structure of the society in which the monkey is living, thereby changing his social patterns.

Dr. Michael: Certainly, this is perfectly true. The fact of the matter is that findings which were made in a laboratory have now been confirmed in field work when field workers knew what they wanted to look for.

Prof. Latane: I was very interested in the nice demonstration Dr. Michael gave of the effects of vagina-smears on sexual behaviour. I wonder if he could comment on the possibility that these effects could have been mediated by the behaviour of the females who smelling themselves 'all dressed up for the night' could have become more seductive.

Dr. Michael: You can check on this by blocking the sense of smell in the females and the effect is entirely on the male; the females in these experiments are extremely uninterested in matters sexual.

Dr. Daly: Dr. Biller, you touched on socio-cultural variables. I have just returned from America where I was acquainted with the American Negro and his similarity in many social and cultural aspects to the Irishman, particularly with regard to paternal relationships with children, and we have here the very frequent phenomenon of the absentee father. He may be working in England or in the local pub. The American Negro may be spending his time with another woman. Are there any cross cultural studies?

Prof. Biller: We have compared lower class white and negro boys, six year olds, and we found both father absence and socio-cultural effects. Negro father absent boys appeared to have the most insecurity in their sex role orientations: they seemed to be quite unsure of their masculinity although most had a knowledge of basic sex role norms and were generally masculine in their overt behaviour. A number of researchers have noted that the joint effects of paternal deprivation and the matrifocal family often are associated with psychological conflicts among lower class negroes.

Dr. Scott: I wanted to ask you a question about identification problems in the infant, when he has two objects with which he can identify, one the feeding object and the second the protection agency. When is the optimal point when the child moves from his feeding attachment?—complete identification with the mother figure; when then should the father take over in his protection area?—to my mind there should be a fairly statistically significant figure, to my mind twelve months.

Prof. Biller: This is a very provocative question and hopefully we
may be able to get some definitive answers. Many children do
form strong attachments to their fathers before they are a year
old, some at least as early as six to eight months of age. Our
observations suggest that an early attachment to the father as
well as the mother is conducive to the development of interpersonal skills. However, we need much more research regarding
father-infant interactions. Also, I doubt if there is any necessary
biological reason for the infant to have *an exclusive initial*
attachment to his mother.

Prof. Levine: One of the roles that fathers play as far as females
are concerned is presumably to establish gender roles. Now as
far as you see it, fathers have done this all wrong.

Prof. Biller: Many researchers have tended to oversimplify what
sex role development is; there are several components of sex
role, on the basis of our research it appears that the self concept
dimension is most critical; a person's positive acceptance of his
bodily and biological attributes seems particularly crucial. The
father can promote a positive feminine self concept in his
daughter without also expecting her to be passive, timid and
submissive. There is no fundamental incompatibility between a
woman having a strong pride in being a female and having the
ability to be assertive and independent as well as kind and
sensitive.

Dr. Michael: We found one site of production of these substances
but this does not preclude their being produced at other sites, by
the skin surface generally or other endocrine glands.

Prof. Lavelle: Dr. Michael you showed four patterns of sexual
activity in twelve pairs of monkeys. Have you tried the effect of
the sex phenomenon on the altering of that pattern in the
established pair? Take the ones that have the two peaks—the
ovulation and the premenstrual peaks—is the secretion of this
substance stronger at that time?

Dr. Michael: This is a difficult question to answer—I presented
this data in a terribly abbreviated form—first of all the mounting
cycle data that I showed on the slide was from the rhesus monkey
not from the baboon but can I come back to the baboon to
answer your question? If you take collections from the first
seven days of the cycle and the last seven days of the cycle and
compare with the seven days before the day of deflation of the

sexual skin, there is a very significantly higher production of these substances in the middle of the cycle in the baboon. The data from the rhesus monkey is much less clear cut.

Prof. Lavelle: Have you comparable pairs of baboons to what you have of rhesus showing different sex-activity patterns between pairs?

Dr. Michael: Yes, we have, but observed under different conditions. Some of our pairs of rhesus monkeys do not interact very well. There is a rather low level of activity throughout the cycle and if you get a series of male rhesus monkeys to rate a series of female rhesus monkeys, you can get a female that comes out very low on the popularity poll she is rather badly scored but you can convert her into a very popular female by some of the males but not all by using the application of these substances.

Prof. Lavelle: Can the proportion of these substances in the mix influence the acceptors and non-acceptors of the popularized females?

Dr. Michael: We do not know at the moment what is critical about the mix, we do not even know if there is one substance but we do know that though the substances are present in a large number of species the proportions of the mix are different in different species.

Dr. Cullen: I wanted to make one remark about the perfume business. I think humans have been empirically experimenting with this for a very long time. The vehicles carrying the more socially acceptable smells in perfumes are usually mammalian sex pheromones. I would like to come back to our dilemma in drawing up this programme. We had great difficulty in finding anybody working with animals who would say anything about fathers. I would like if we could this evening, to hear a little bit on the animal side about the father role. I know that Dr. Michael introduced the beginnings of the father relationship in the family group but we have tended to just talk about the mother.

Prof. Mitchell: I have films relevant to this. First of all adult male rhesus monkeys are capable of raising babies by themselves. They play much more frequently with their babies than do mother rhesus. They do not hold them as close to their ventral surface as do females. The male will punish more freely however. Separation of an infant from an adult male rhesus monkey, who is not supposed to be a very paternal beast, produces disturbance in the adult male, such as extreme self biting which is supposed to occur only in the social isolate adult male monkey.

Prof. Sackett: I have just got a report from a free environment situation where there are several natural groups of rhesus monkeys. A fully adult male monkey adopted a month old infant and has been 'mothering' it for almost one year. There is an extreme difference of philosophy between what Dr. Michael was talking about and what Prof. Biller was talking about. Somehow I get the feeling that I could not understand what was meant by father because I did not see it in any biological context or perspective. It seemed to me that 'the father' was simply a lable put on a second person in the family. Could not a female hold this role or could not a male serve equally well as a female in the role of 'mother'?

Prof. Biller: One of the reasons why fathers can have such a profound influence when they are actively involved with their children, is because they generally have some skills and abilities that mothers do not have. For example males in our society have more opportunities to learn assertive and independent behaviour, and they may be particularly good models for their children in this regard.

Dr. Michael: Professor Mitchell's remarks remind me that I would like to mention the studies of young Dean on Barbary apes. Here the infant is captured, almost abducted by what appears to be a sub-dominant male, and if this male can get his hands on the baby he does and he will tussle with the mother; the baby goes back to the mother for suckling and the infant is used by the sub-dominant male to get into relationship with the dominant male in the group. He uses the fact that he has got the baby and introduces the fact to the dominant male by giving the dominant male the baby.

Dr. Daly: Howell in Essex reported that the importance of father is that he is a multiple of mother. It is important to have two parents rather than one. This leads to an observation that I have encountered on at least two occasions in which mother has been deserted by father and has taken up a homosexual relationship and another woman has replaced father. Are there any studies that have been done on children raised in such a situation?

Prof. Biller: I do not know of any such studies, although I have heard of reports which suggest that such a parental situation is sometimes a factor in the development of severe sex role conflicts among children.

Prof. Fox: I would like to mention something about Canids; in this family (wolves, foxes, coyotes and jackals) fathers bring food to the cubs and mother and regurgitate it for them. There is an ecological factor working in relation to paternal behaviour; where food is abundant, the mother can forage for her own young and does not need the help of a mate. Where food is less abundant in other locales a more permanent pair bond is seen. Now in humans we do not have to forage for food anymore but we do have sex determined roles. So if a little boy does not have a father at home, his role and sex identification, his status and success orientation is going to be affected. Perhaps such sex-role stereotyping is a growth limiting cultural imposition upon children; are we not placing a distorted value upon mother and father roles now where roles and related acquired needs can set serious limitations to self-actualization?

Prof. Sackett: Would you find any deviations from normative variances of sex role behaviour and all the things that you were talking about if you had a group of individuals raised only by females or only by males? In other words, in a situation where every child had no experience with contrasts between behaviour of adult females and adult males.

Prof. Biller: The data we have for middle class families suggest that fathers are more concerned with sex roles than are mothers. Mothers differentiate their behaviour as a function of sex of child but the father appears to do this to a much greater degree and to be a more primary transmitter of sex typing when he is actively involved in the family.

Prof. Lifton: This is a question to Dr. Michael. Since there is so much confusion among human beings about the term that is called bisexuality and what you might call the enlarging of the possibilities of the male and female roles. Could you distinguish among such things as you presented: on the one hand the reversal of the positions in the sexual act, the mounting position, as opposed to concrete bisexuality, male monkeys seeking out other male monkeys, or females females, and then could you relate either or even just the mounting situation to the maleness in other more social ways such as protecting the female and the offspring and so on?

M

Dr. Michael: If you have a situation where you have a female-female pair which I can speak of with experience from the laboratory mounting of a female by another female, one female does all the active behaviour. If you introduce a male into the situation that pattern of behaviour disappears and she, the mounter, becomes the possessor, all things being equal, of the male.

Prof. Mitchell: Some of the work done at the University of Oregon at Portland by Alexander, has found that some of the most dominant males are also the most maternalistic in the sense that they will adopt infants, take care of infants and so on.

Prof. Lifton: In other words it may be that future research along these lines would give us better analogues in distinguishing between social possibilities and psychological possibilities which we are learning are much broader than we thought they were as designated culturally on the one hand and literal biological bisexuality which is something else again.

Prof. Levine: What evidence is there that the males are more stable than the females?

Prof. Biller: I did not intend to suggest that males were more stable but there are data which indicate that males in many situations are more likely to stand up for their rights, assert themselves and act independently.

Prof. Mitchell: We have compared adult male monkeys raising babies to adult females raising monkeys, in a separation situation where the parent has been with the infant for five to six months. When the male is separated from his little one, he is quite disturbed afterwards; this is a crisis situation. He pulls the barrier apart, trying to get back to the infant. Unfortunately, he also bites himself.

Prof. Biller: This certainly correlates with research on humans.

Prof. O'Doherty: There are so many different variables in all these things, I have to inject another one, but for your future research on paternal deprivations especially I think that we have been talking too much of the physical presence and physical absence of the father and I would like to see built into these studies the concept of the psychologically present father who is physically absent, the mother in other words keeping the father figure alive for the child and the psychologically absent father though physically present.

Madness — an ethological perspective

M. W. Fox,

Department of Psychology,

Washington University, St. Louis, Missouri

By definition, 'madness' refers to insanity, rashness, intense anger, rage, and in animals to any of several ailments marked by frenzied or irrational behaviour. The term mania was formerly used as a nonspecific term for any kind of 'madness'. It is currently used as a suffix with any number of Greek roots to indicate a morbid pre-occupation with some kind of idea or activity, and/or a compulsive need to behave in some deviant way (e.g., nymphomania, trichotillo-mania). Almost synonymous with 'madness' is the term insanity, being a label for a variety of emotional-behavioural disorders that do not accord with the cultural or species-norm. (The problem of defining the modal personality type is akin to deciding what range of actions is characteristic for a given species of animal in a given context.)

In addressing the problem of 'madness' or 'insanity' in animals, many factors must be considered; *species, context,* and also a variety of syndromes which are subsumed under the general title of 'madness'. In addition, *organic* causes must be differentially diagnosed from purely *psychogenic* or psychosomatic aetiologies. *Social* factors, either facilitating, inhibiting or modifying in some way the overt expression of disorder must be considered in both human and nonhuman species. Specific examples will be cited shortly. *Genetic* factors also play their part in determining response thresholds, emotionality and organization and sequencing of various action

179

patterns such as displacements, redirections and compromise movements in animals (see later); some of the latter action patterns are analogous to culturally modified displacements and self-directed actions or self adapters (Ekman and Friesen, 1968) in man. Such actions may serve to dearouse, to reduce the level of arousal, as well as having signal value as components of the 'body language' repertoire. *Early experience* during the sensitive or critical period of development may also have profound effects on emotionality and social and sexual preferences later in life.

With this brief sketch of some of the intervening variables which may be involved in the genesis of abnormal behaviour, it is obvious that a simple cause-effect relationship is an over-simplification and a rarity. The ethologist, like the psychoanalyst, is interested in the evolution, ontogeny and causality of behaviour, as well as in its 'fitness' or adaptiveness. Both fields take an aetiological approach to normal and abnormal behaviour respectively; the ethological method of observing, describing and later eliciting behaviours under certain contexts is very similar to the clinical method. This is in sharp contrast to the behaviourist's approach, where aetiology is rarely considered, lying far below the hierarchy of priority where behaviour modification via external reinforcement exemplifies the mechanistic posture of such a discipline. Although clinically often effective, behaviour therapy is a technique, not a science for it tells us little or nothing about the aetiology of normal or maladaptive behaviour.

AETIOLOGY AND SYMPTOMATOLOGY OF BEHAVIOUR DISORDERS IN ANIMALS AND MEN

In order to label a given behaviour or symptom-complex as abnormal or maladaptive, certain criteria should be considered. There should be no underlying organic cause (e.g., tumour or brain trauma).* The behaviour should be manifest at a high frequency under predictable circumstances, be persistent and consistent, and

---

*Although some toxic infections and metabolic disorders giving rise to 'madness' in animals should be considered, e.g.: rabies, 'dumb' and 'rage' forms; strychnine, DDT and organo-phosphorous poisons; 'ageine' bread bleach of the 1940s causing running fits in dogs; infectious encephalopathies, e.g., canine distemper; metabolic and nutritional disorders such as hypomagnaesmia ('staggers') and acetonemia (extreme nervousness) in cattle and copper deficiency (swayback) in sheep.

should be seen only in a minority of the population (or species). The behaviour is detrimental to the organism (maladaptive) in that it interferes with other maintenance behaviours or impairs the performance of some motivationally related and more appropriate (or adaptive) act. The behaviour may also be defined as abnormal if it is detrimental to the welfare of conspecifics or interferes with their maintenance activities (e.g., eating, sleeping, working, reproducing, etc.).

In addition, the behaviour in question may develop its own autonomy and stereotype (resembling normal 'rituals' in the ethological sense, see Morris, 1966). It may also undergo stimulus generalization or irradiation in that an increasing range of stimuli become effective releasers. There may be increasing impairment of function as the temporal duration of the behaviour increases and interferes with the organization and execution of other maintenance behaviours. 'Contamination' may spill over from one original motivational or situational context into others (e.g., social aggression to sexual aggression). All maintenance functions may be affected simultaneously as in the acute panic, hysteria, tonic immobility and anorexia nervosa often associated with separation-depression.

There are certain exceptional behaviour disorders which do not fit the above criteria, which are social-group phenomena. First are cases of *mass hysteria* (running fits) in groups of dogs and men (e.g., amok), stampedes in ungulates, mass panic reactions in domestic poultry. The possibility of a metacommunicative group 'mood', set, or predisposition acting in combination with social facilitation and allelomimesis (behavioural contagion) should be considered. Second are the effects of crowding stress. It may be better termed *interaction and proximity stress,* because at least wto factors are operating: *a)* there is a ghig frequency of reciprocal interruption of maintenance activities between conspecifics; *b)* the proxemic need for space is frustrated by constant invasion of personal and intimate distances by strangers, and there is no way to escape. Here, aggression may adaptively increase social distance and higher ranking individuals fare better. Another adaptation would be to completely filter out all exogenous stimuli (e.g., Calhoun's 'schizophrenic' ratts). Both forms of adaptation—hyperaggression and psychic withdrawal—are adaptive to the situation or context, but may be maladaptive to the individual and conspecifics. Clearly the situation or context must be rectified, but this is one of the last things that psychiatrists consider, although the analogies between rats and men under crowded living conditions are very real. The point is, *people behave like rats* (rather than rats behave like people) under certain circumstances; this is a relevant zoomorphism which in perspective is a reversal of the anthropocentric approach of attempting to find animal models that how how similar some species are to man.

When escape is possible out of the 'behavioural sink', the emigrating non-territory owning subordinates are metabolically wrecked. Lesions diagnostic of Selye's stress syndrome, coupled with changes in the CNS (brain colloids) and hypoglycemia may contribute to the disoriented, reckless behaviour of migrating lemmings. In a broader perspective this behaviour, although detrimental to the individual, is adaptive to the species, which may have regular four or seven year cyclic patterns of population explosions. Someone has to leave, otherwise the entire population would be eliminated by intraspecific fighting, famine, and disease. Crowding stress in a section of the population causes hyperactivity and the drive to emigrate, and this reaction may be 'programmed' in those species that have evolved this pattern of adaptive population regulation. Other species, such as deer, do not show this mass exodus madness under crowding stress, possibly because they have not yet adapted to crowding stress, this being a more recent experience attributable to man's mismanagement of wildlife ecosystems.

Trait and symptom disorders

Following is a tabulation of human traits or symptoms that are associated frequently with more generalized behaviour disturbances. References to comparable disorders in lower animals are cited in some instances.

Enuresis refers to urination at night during sleep, or during emotional excitement (fear). In the dog, this also occurs during submissive greeting.

Encopresis refers to defecation when the subject is emotionally excited (fear). This phenomenon is well recognized in lower animals.

Polyphagia may serve to diminish anxiety as a displacement (in the psychoanalytic sense, oral gratification) and has been reported in dogs (Brunner, 1968; Fox, 1968).

Polydipsia may serve similar functions as polyphagia and has been reported in dogs (Brunner, 1968).

Pica may have some underlying nutritional or metabolic disorder. It may include perversion of appetite as exemplified by coprophagy, autophagy, and aerophagy and has been reported in various animals (Brunner, 1968; Fox, 1968; Meyer-Holzapfel, 1968; Worden, 1968).

Catatonia refers to immobility, muscular rigidity, and occasional excitability, and has been described in lower animals (Chertok, 1968; Fox, 1968); it often follows some intense fear-evoking stimulus.

Flexibilitas cerea, a phenomenon in a schizophrenic whose arm or leg remains passively in the position in which it is placed, is observed only rarely in the dog.

Hyperesthesia refers to hypersensitivity to tactile stimuli; burning or tickling sensation (paresthesia) may be reported by the patient. These symptoms occur in neurologic disease and in psychoses in man. It is feasible that, in some animals, paresthesia may develop independent of parasitic, metabolic, nutritional, or other neurologic disturbance, and result in automutilation and autophagy (Meyer-Holzapfel, 1968). In the phobia known as 'touch shyness' in the dog, hyperesthesia may be the reason for the reaction; central neural filtering of afferent stimuli may be modified in states of vigilance or anxiety (Fox, 1968, 1971).

Hypoesthesia is essentially the reverse of hyperesthesia, namely, a decreased sensitivity to tactile and often painful stimuli, occurring in man in psychotic and hysteric reactions. In lower animals, hypoesthesia (determined by lack of pain withdrawal reflexes) occurs after induction of tonic immobility or catatonia (Chertok, 1968). Partial or complete tonic immobility, catatonia, or passivity occurs in extremely timid domesticated animals or in captured wild animals. Extreme fear seems to abolish or to interfere with normal pain withdrawal reflexes, but it is conceivable that the pain threshold is increased by intense arousal, resulting in true hypoesthesia. This arousal hypothesis (Fox, 1971c) is supported by the observed lack of withdrawal from nociceptive stimuli in animals that have been raised in isolation. (It has been noted that isolation-raised Scottish Terriers will repeatedly stick their noses into a candle flame) (Melzack and Scott, 1957). Some strains of laboratory Beagles, which are extremely timid but remain passive when placed on a table (and which occasionally have flexibilitas cerea), continue to remain passive and unflinching when blood is collected from the cephalic or jugular vein.

Hyperventilation may occur in man during acute attacks of

anxiety; it is also a normal autonomic reaction associated with rage and fear. A syndrome may develop when the individual hyperventilates to the point of alkalosis, at which time neurologic symptoms may develop. Hyperventilation (often coupled with hyperthermia, motor agitation, trembling, salivation, hypermotility with defection, urination, and pupillary dilation) is commonly encountered in fearful animals when restrained or during attacks of anxiety when they anticipate some particular traumatic stimulation (as in the conditioned emotional reaction). These autonomic and motor reactions are components of the 'fright, flight, or fight' reactions of emotionally disturbed animals, whether wild and non-socialized or socialized but anticipating psychologic or physical trauma.

Anorexia nervosa or refusal to eat food is often coupled with inability to retain food. It occurs commonly in late-adolescent human females, often as the sole symptom of a deep-seated sexual anxiety or conflict. In lower animals, this condition usually is associated with sudden environmental changes, such as captivity and isolation from peers, mate, or parent (Fox, 1968; Meyer-Holzapfel, 1968; Schmidt, 1968).

Behaviour disorders and specific syndromes

Anxiety is essentially the anticipation of dangers of unknown or imagined origins. This is distinct from fear, which is the emotional response to a consciously recognized external threat. Psychologic reactions include fear, depression, and apprehension. The psychologic changes described in persons subjected to voodooism are classic (Cannon, 1957), and in some ways are comparable to a phenomenon of sudden death in lower animals (Richter, 1957). A distinction has to be made between normal and pathologic 'anxiety'.

Many of the signs in dogs subjected to experimental neurosis suggest the combination of overt fear and anxiety in the form of conditioned emotional reactions (Broadhurst, 1961). As a sequence to sensitization to a particular noxious stimulus or situation, generalization (responsiveness to an increasing range of stimuli) may follow; the subject has a conditioned emotional reaction to an increasing range of stimuli which initially closely resemble the original disturbing stimulus or situation. Long after apparent recovery, when overt behaviour appears normal, autonomic reactions may persist. (Astrup, 1968; Gantt, 1962).

Conflict is essentially a struggle arising from the simultaneous operation of two opposing drives. In lower animals, simultaneous or successive combinations of behaviour indicating ambivalent motivation may develop, i.e., intentional and compromise movements (Marler and Hamilton, 1966). Frequently the behaviour of one opposing drive may be redirected to some substitute goal or object, or a motivationally and situationally unrelated act may appear as a displacement (Marler and Hamilton, 1966; Thorpe, 1964).

Aggression. The frustration-aggression hypothesis of Dollard and Miller holds that aggression is the consequence of frustration. Overt extrapunitive, self-directed, and redirected forms of aggression are well recognized in lower animals (Fox, 1968; Lorenz, 1966). Self-directed aggression may lead to auto-mutilation, which is not uncommon in zoo animals. It may also arise as a 'hypertrophy' of grooming and self-care (Meyer-Holzapfel, 1968).

Withdrawal may result from frustration; the patient may create protective fantasies, and in severe cases, even paranoid delusions and schizophrenic hallucinations may develop. Regression may occur, with the patient manifesting infantile, care-soliciting 'grooming ailments', or developing bulimia (excessive eating). Both types of behaviour have been described in lower animals (Brunner, 1968; Fox, 1968; Wickler, 1970). In some cases of frustration, apathy may ensue, with the patient giving up the urge to live (as also observed in lower animals) (Brion and Ey, 1965; Fox, 1968). In some instances, patients have developed frustration fixations comparable to cage-stereotypes in animals that are unable to escape. These are inflexible, obsessive, compulsive, and rigid stereotyped behaviours.

Sibling rivalry in man refers to the competition between siblings for parental love and attention, with underlying feelings of jealousy and frustration in one or more siblings. In pet dogs, sibling rivalry may take the form of extreme jealousy, aggression, and possessiveness of territory or favourite play objects when the owner acquires another pet or when the owner's affections are directed towards a visitor's child or pet. More extreme actions, including convulsions, anorexia nervosa, destruction of inanimate objects in the house, attacks on the owner (redirected aggression), hysteric bilateral posterior paraplegia, and compulsive eating have been reported in dogs whose owners have acquired another pet or their first offspring (Fox, 1965, 1968).

Stereotyped movements. In man, stereotyped movements such as rocking, pacing, arm waving, hand rubbing, flapping, clapping, waving the hands in front of the eyes, self-clutching, thumb-sucking, and head banging, or the adoption of bizarre statuesque postures (crucificial or Napoleonic) are seen in a variety of syndromes. These movements may develop in hospitalized (i.e. stimulus- and affection-deprived) children and provide a source of afferent stimulation to compensate for lack of varied input, or they may be comforting, rhythmic (perhaps parasympathetic arousing), and familiar activies that diminish anxiety. Autistic children may have bizarre motor stereotypes and occasionally vocal stereotypes. The sterotypes of the autistic may provide a repetitive proprioceptive feedback and motor output which is de-arousing or adaptive in diminishing chronic arousal of the reticular activating system, which has been proposed as a possible etiologic factor in this syndrome (Fox, 1968). Interestingly, if environmental complexity or social interaction is increased, the autistic child will increase its frequency of stereotype, although the movements per se may not increase in intensity (i.e., a typical intensity is maintained as a ritual). It has been logically

Fig. 1. Stereotyped swaying, a common cage-bar stereotype in the polar bear. (Arrows indicate direction of movement.)

Fig. 2A-C. Stereotyped sequence of 'rumination' in female siamarg. Food is regurgitated and reingested, as frequently as once every four to five minutes. (A) vomit posture; (B) vomitus is caught; (C) vomitus manipulated and ingested.

proposed, therefore (Fox, 1971c), that increasing the sensory input causes greater arousal which the autistic child attempts to reduce by increasing stereotypic movements. In some cases, such movements may be attention seeking, and if not reinforced may actually disappear, especially when alternative activities are substituted in the shaping of behaviour towards more adaptive and appropriate motor performance and attentiveness.

Epileptic children have been known to pass their extended fingers repeatedly before their eyes while looking towards the light; this produces repetitive visual flicker, and such 'neuronal masturbation' triggers a seizure. Similar hand waving has been observed in isolation-raised monkeys with corneal lesions (Berkson, 1968); such activity may result in varied stimulation which in some ways compensates for the animal's requirements for afferent input to the central nervous system. We may, therefore, propose that the stereotype of animals pacing in front of the cage bars (Fig. 1) may not only result from thwarted escape attempts (Meyer-Holzapfel, 1968) and from a need for motor output to diminish the activity drive, but may in some cases increase sensory stimulation by the visual flicker effect produced by walking past the cage bars.

Adult schizophrenics may derive some comfort (anxiety reduction) or pleasure from performing motor stereotypes or by adopting bizarre postures. In human psychiatry the term ritual is used to describe psychomotor activities that are sustained to relieve anxiety, as in certain obsessive compulsive neuroses (e.g., hand washing). Similarly, in confined animals, anxiety or frustration stemming from inadequate cover, inability to escape, or lack of varied stimulation to fulfil basic drives (notably hunting, prey catching and killing) may cause a variety of acquired, ritualized stereotypes to develop (Fox, 1968; Morris, 1966). These activities develop their own autonomy to the extent that the performance of the activity is rewarding in its own right; consummatory inhibition, or drive reduction appears to be weak, for many of these stereotypes are essentially consummatory. For example, a socially isolated siamang (Fig. 2) repeatedly vomited and ingested its food fifty-two times in two hours, while performing an almost unvarying sequence of movements.

Motor stereotypes not only have a highly predictable temporal sequencing of actions, but may also have great spatial consistency in that the actions are always executed at a particular place (Fig. 3). In a study of stereotypes in caged birds it was found that route tracing (locomotor stereotype) was associated with the physical restrictions imposed on movement by the cage, whereas spot picking (pecking at some particular place) resulted from some deficiency in laboratory conditions (Keiper, 1969). The latter was reduced when canaries had to work for food. There are several theories as to the cause of stereotypes (Keiper, 1969), which may be summarized variously as follows:

1. Displacement activities resulting from thwarted drives;

2. Mechanisms for modulating input from stressful stimuli;

3. Mechanisms for altering or controlling the general arousal level;

4. Remnants of escape movements;

5. Mechanisms for relieving boredom when opportunities for alternative activities are prevented;

6. Substitutes for normal behaviours which are denied by laboratory rearing conditions;

Fig. 3A-D. Stereotyped actions in Kodiac bear; the sequence begins with a bow (A), followed by two head and right forepaw swipes, the 1st (B) of greater amplitude than the 2nd (C). The same temporal sequence is again repeated (D) after the bear has circled the enclosure; note the similarity of spatial-postural relationships in A and D.

7. Substitutes for stimulation normally supplied to an infant by the mother; and

8. Activities resulting from movement restraint.

It has been shown in crab-eating macaques that as abnormal stereotyped behaviour developed, the different frequencies of various patterns were related to the age at which the infant was isolated from its mother (Berkson, 1968). Thus, younger subjects developed self-sucking, crouching, and self-grasping, whereas body rocking and repetitive locomotion began at a later age.

Neurosis in man refers to a less severe impairment of function in which maladaptive emotional reactions are the result of unresolved unconscious conflicts. The following types are amongst those recognized in man: anxiety neurosis, of which panic reactions and motor agitation are symptomatic, and depressive neurosis, a reactive type of depression due to an internal conflict or identifiable event such as the loss of a loved one. Both types have been described in lower animals (Fox, 1968).

Hysteric neuroses include: (a) conversion type, in which blindness, paresthesia, or paralysis of psychogenic origin may develop, and (b) obsessive compulsive type, in which there is intrusion of ideas, urges, or actions that the individual cannot inhibit—the latter ranging from simple movements (or tics) to complex rituals.

Phobia in man is defined as an obsessive, persistent, unrealistic and intense fear of an object or situation. In lower animals it may be extremely difficult to pinpoint what trigger from the perceptual environment releases such apparently irrational fear; it may be a particular odour or sound undetectable by the human sensory apparatus. In man, several specific fears are recognized, notably xenophobia (fear of strangers), claustrophobia (fear of confinement or restraint), agoraphobia (fear of open spaces), algophobia (fear of pain), and acrophobia (fear of heights). Generalization may occur and fear reactions develop when the subject is confronted with any novel stimulus or unfamiliar situation (panphobia). Similar phobias have been described in dogs subjected to experimental neurosis (Kurtsin, 1968), and also in pet dogs even after only one traumatic experience (e.g., fear of restraint, confinement, or of being touched or held) (Brunner, 1968). More severe autonomic and behavioural disturbances may follow some situational traumatic event; these disturbances in man are termed traumatic neuroses.

Character or personality disorders. In man, character or personality disorders are considered lifelong individual traits, comparable to individual character traits of lower animals, which may be species, breed, strain or sex related. Touch, sound, and sight shyness in dogs, for example, are character traits in that subjects are respectively fearful of being touched, of sudden or intense noises, or of suddenly moving or intense visual stimuli (Fox, 1965). These character or personality disorders appear to have a genetic basis, and a number of studies with dogs have shown how this genetic constitution may make the subject more susceptible to enviornmental disturbances, especially during development (Fuller, 1967).

Pavlov utilized classic conditioning to determine the nervous typology of dogs (sanguine, phlegmatic, inert, balanced, and others) (Fox, 1965; Kurtsin, 1968), and he showed that particular types were extremely prone to develop experimental neuroses, whereas others were more resistant (Astrup, 1968; Kurtsin, 1968). With this background, together with the theory that body constitution or somatotype is related to personality type in man (e.g., ectomorph or thin somatotype, mesomorph or average build, endomorph or fat type), studies have been made of several breeds of dogs and their hybrids (Stockard, 1941). These studies did not prove conclusively that somatotype and personality are directly correlated; however, there was some evidence that endocrine (especially thyroid gland) function has a genetic basis in the dog—there being breed differences in the histologic appearance of certain endocrine glands. Such a genetic basis may be correlated with body constitution (somatotype) and behaviour or personality.

Psychosis in man refers to a severe impairment of function, including delusions and hallucinations. In the category of psychoses, the major affective disorders (characterized by severe disturbance of mood ranging from depression to elation) include involutional melancholia, manic depression, or mania (or cyclic mania and depression). In lower animals, bizarre reactions suggestive of deranged perception, delusion, or hallucination are associated with toxic or organic psychoses. Psychotic-like reactions in the absence of any detectable toxic agent or neural lesion are relatively rare in lower animals; hysteric psychosis may be one example (Brunner, 1968; Fox, 1968).

Schizophrenia is the term given to an amalgam of severe behavioural disturbances in man. In lower animals, the existence of schizophrenia is questionable (Brion, 1965; Fox, 1968), although certain

N

signs do resemble schizophrenic-like reactions; lower animals raised in isolation do develop some signs that resemble those of infantile autism—impairment of social behaviour, affect, and development of stereotyped movements (Fox, 1968).

Anaclitic depression occurs when the symbiotic dependence of infant on mother is broken (Spitz, 1949). This has been studied extensively in nonhuman primates (Hinde, 1966; Kaufman and Rosenblum, 1967). In adult dogs, perpetual puppy syndrome occurs when the symbiotic relationship has been maintained by over-indulgent and permissive owners (child-substitute situation). Severe anaclitic depression may follow separation due to surgery, boarding or quarantine (Fox, 1968). Separation anxiety is most marked in the human infant between six and ten months of age, at which time fear and apprehension are marked when the infant is separated from its mother. This fear period is comparable to approximately seven to ten weeks of age in the dog. Crying, lethargy, and anorexia (to the point of marasmus) are symptomatic of this reversible transient situational disturbance. The correlation between acute illness and dependency behaviour in human infants has been stressed by child psychiatrists (Chess, 1969). After illness, the child attempts to maintain the interpersonal relationship that gave special attention during the illness. Similarly, some overindulged pets have been known to refuse to use one limb after surgery for congenital patellar luxation, because of the reinforcement of attention and petting by the owner when the animal was recovering postoperatively (Fox, 1965). In extreme cases, muscle atrophy develops; in other cases, surgical recovery is complete, but the subjects suddenly become lame and seek the attention of their owners when in some anxiety- or conflict-provoking situation.

It is clear from the aforementioned descriptions of neuroses and psychoses in man that a variety of maladaptive responses in lower animals fit within the category of neuroses. However, psychotic reactions and schizophrenia in lower animals are rarely recognized. This may be a phylogenetic limitation, i.e., psychoses and schizophrenic disorders may be encountered more frequently in more highly evolved species.

TOWARDS A COMPARATIVE PSYCHOPATHOLOGY

Since the excellent review of abnormal behaviour in animals and critique of Pavlovian terminology by Broadhurst (1961) and the edited collection of reviews by Zubin and Hunt (1967), Masserman (1968) and Fox (1968), there has been little attention focussed on comparative psychopathology. Psychiatrists are becoming increasingly aware of the limitations of studying the human species per se and can gain greater insights into the etiology of certain human disorders when the developmental and phylogenetic perspectives of comparative psychopathology are utilized. Scheflen (1965) for example has discussed quasi-courtship behaviour in psychotherapy, and Kaufman (1960) has shown the relevance of ethological studies to psychoanalytic theory; Wolpe (1967) examines the parallels between animal and human neuroses: Jones (1969) has reported an ethological type of study on motor behaviour in chronic schizophrenics and Pontinus (1967) has gone so far as to present a neuropsychiatric hypothesis about territorial behaviour. Ekman and Friesen (1968) have demonstrated the usefulness of studying non-verbal behaviour in psychotherapy. Among anthropologists, Callan (1970) and Tiger and Fox (1966) considered several areas where ethology is relevant to the study of social anthropology. Recently primates have been used as models for investigating the tiology of human developmental problems and Mitchell (1970) gives a detailed review of research on abnormal behaviour in non-human primates.

Ethology, psychoanalysis and man

One major area developed by ethologists is the comparative analysis of species-characteristic action patterns, the taxonomy of behaviour, and it is from such analysis that the genetics, phylogeny and ontogeny of behaviour can be followed. A number of psychoanalysts in the symposium ' Animal and Human ' edited by Masserman (1968) suggest that this approach of the ethologists may provide an invaluable contribution to the evaluation of their theoretical assumptions as to the origin and nature of inherited, unlearned responses of the human species. Marmor, in this symposium, states that ethological data could be used as a source of clues that can then be pursued in careful and objective observation and research with human beings. We may cite animal experiments on imprinting (Salzen, 1968), experimental neurosis (Astrup, 1968), maternal and peer deprivation (Bronfenbrenner, 1968), early handling stress (Ader and Plaut, 1968; Denenberg, 1964), effects of social stress and crowding studies (Calhoun, 1962, 1967; Ader and Friedman, 1965; Henry and Stephens, 1969) and genetics of abnormal behaviour (Peters, et al., 1967; Heston, 1970) as areas where useful clues may be found and applied to human development, psychoanalysis, psychodynamics, psychotherapy and psychosomatic disorders.

Beer (1968) discussed many limitations of applying ethology to psychoanalysis. For example, he showed the differences between ethological and psychoanalytic interpretations of displacement activity, but failed to emphasize the main point, that in animals, many displacements[1] are inherited (and species-characteristic) and may evolve through ritualization as important intraspecific communication signals (Marler and Hamilton, 1966). It is surprising that psychoanalysts have not picked up Thorpe's (1964) discussion of innate releasing mechanisms and fixed action patterns and his distinction between these and acquired releasing mechanisms and acquired action patterns.

The anthropocentric individual may claim that there is no point in studying comparative psychopathology, for man is too complex and is more a product of his environment or cultural milieu than a product of his genetically determined instincts. But it is only after a thorough comparative analysis of the biological foundations of psychopathology—from the functioning of the autonomic, endocrine and central nervous systems in different species under emotional stress, to the genetics, phylogeny and ontogeny of patterns of behaviour and of cummunication rituals—that we will be able to fully comprehend the influences of acculturation in man. The argument, therefore, that we need only study the influences of culture upon the development of man, because the biological contribution is insignificant, is as untenable as the time-worn argument of nature versus nurture. In animals, we study the influence of the environment upon development (i.e., genotype-environment interaction) in much the same way we should investigate the bio-cultural ontogeny of man.

This leads us to an important unit yof ethological and psychoanalytical theories relating to 'instinct' and the effects of experiences early in life on subsequent behaviour.

---

[1]See Delius (1967) for a valuable interpretation of displacement in animals as a de-arousal mechanism.

Chess (1969) in her introductory text to child psychiatry observes that '. . . our concepts of the forces operating in the child's development have been enlarged from many directions.' Freud called attention to the emotional and motivational factors involved in early parent-child relationships. The culturalists (such as Erikson and Fromm) emphasized the important influence of society at large. Pavlov demonstrated the conditioned reflex and its place in patterning behaviour. Watson and the later learning theorists explored the role that training and learning play in determining behaviour patterns. Gesell's work called attention to the schedule of neurologic and behavioural maturation, while Piaget showed that cognitive functions have their own sequential course of growth. Increasingly, serious workers in psychiatry and psychology have come to recognize that both normal development and disturbances in development, instead of being the products of any single factor, result from complex interactions between the child and his environment. The vital issue is not how heredity and environment are to be fractionated in the analysis of behaviour, but precisely how the two interrelate and simultaneously influence the development of the individual. The clinician cannot possibly diagnose and treat patients effectively in terms of the traditional 'nature versus nurture' concept. Constitutional determinants of behaviour are modified by the environment in which they operate, and in turn the environment does not have a uniform impact on genetically diverse individuals' (p. 17, 18).

It is of interest that there is a correlation between sociopathic personality and a child's early experiences of shifting environments, as from one foster home to another. It may be conceivable that such inadequate socialization where strong interpersonal bonds are not established (or are repeatedly broken) eventually leads to an asocial and in some cases an anti-social personality. These speculations also have relevance in some instances of social maladjustment in domesticated dogs (Brunner, 1968) in which a prior history of inadequate socialization may be correlated with poor trainability, timidity or aggression (fear-biting) with their owners.

The animal model may be useful for comparing with human disorders occurring at the pre-school level, when symptoms are expressed in overt behaviour and action. Chess states that 'Adult neurosis has its roots in the neurotic reactions of childhood and represents roganized reactions of anxiety or of defence against anxiety. Childhood neurosis is relatively rare, perhaps because of the immaturity of the child's personality, or, to put it another way, because the child is still in the process of maturation and his neurotic reactions have not yet had time to become organized. On the basis of this time-element concept, it is easy to see why the incidence of neurosis is greater in adolescence than in childhood' (p. 143).

We may add an evolutionary or phylogenetic concept, in that the frequency and range of neurotic reactions in animals is greater in more highly evolved social species, especially when adaptation to the environment (captivity, domestication) is impaired, or *contra naturam*. Wolpe (1967) in comparing animal and human neuroses points out that treatment is most effective when designed according to the laws of learning, for neurotic patterns appear to be acquired habits. This suggestion is supported by the high success rates of dynamically oriented psychotherapists employing techniques of systematic desensitization.

Deprivation effects

Studies in which dogs or monkeys were reared with restricted opportunity or with programmed opportunity to explore and man-ipulate novel objects have shown the importance of paced incre-ments of experience in determining or in 'setting' the qualitative and quantitative aspects of exploratory behaviour in later life. Thus well socialized dogs that have had no exposure to novel stimuli out-side of their home cage until twelve weeks of age are literally 'institutionalized' ('kennelosis syndrome'). They withdraw from and do not explore novel stimuli in an unfamiliar environment while littermates of the same age that have had a mere fifteen minutes prior experience with such objects in the same setting at five and eight weeks of age, are highly exploratory (Fox 1971c). Even slight increments of experience (perhaps during a critical period between five to eight weeks of age in the dog) have a profound effect on the subject's later exploratory behaviour and preference for environ-mental complexity. We may postulate an arousal-maintenance model of perceptual-motor homeostasis, where the optimal arousal or tolerance level is 'set' early in life as a result of the quality and quantity of early experiences. The level is set low in those animals having had little increments of experience. If the environment does not provide sufficient and varied stimulation the subject may compensate by creating its own varied input by elaborating stereotyped motor acts by directing specific activities towards inappropriate objects (e.g. copulating with its food bowl) (Morris, 1966). These stereotypes developed while in isolation may be performed when the subject is in a novel environment and may serve to reduce arousal or anxiety, as they are familiar activities and may be comforting, as for example thumb sucking, self-clutching and rocking in primates. (Berkson, et al., 1963; Berkson, 1967, 1968; Berkson and Mason, 1964). (This type of stereotype is to be distinguished from those locomotor cage-stereotypes described by Meyer-Holzapfel, 1968, which are derived from thwarted attempts to escape.) Mason (1965, 1967) has developed a comparable theory, in which he uses the term 'general motivational state' in reference to the influence of the degree of arousal on the organization of behaviour during different periods of development. Mirsky (1968) in discussing the psychoanalytic relevance of Mason's concept notes that 'His experiments on the systematic variations in the social behaviour of young chimpanzees as a function of the level of arousal revealed that the type of social interaction elicited on a particular occasion reflects the attempts of the animal to maintain optimal levels of behavioural arousal. In familiar situations the young chimpanzee seeks the more active and stimulating contact afforded by play, but, in new and unfamiliar situations, the animal prefers passive interactions such as clinging and other 'security-seeking' behaviours. These observations suggest that an estimate of the arousal properties of stimuli or situations may be obtained by quantifying the on-going social activities of the animal. Mason has proposed that the arousal level elicited by a stimulus is manifested by the young animal without specific differentiation, i.e., the particular stimulus characteristics, apart from their intrinsic novelty, do not alter the mode of the organism's response. It is the level of arousal per se which modulates the behaviour of the subject. This explanation of the changes in the character of the social response avoids the necessity of postulating specific drives which require fulfilment. In accord is the demonstration by Bridger (1962) that 'the major determinant for sucking by the human is the state of arousal in the behaviours of human infants is now a most important consideration among investigators of child development.' Impairment of arousal-regulating functions may contribute to a variety of disorders in both child and animal, including autism, hyperkinesis, hyperactivity, withdrawal (from excessive 'stimulus-overload'), hyperaggressiveness and motor stereotypy; some of these behaviours may be elaborated to effect de-arousal or serve some function as a perceptual filter preventing over-stimulation.

Socialization

If dogs are denied human contact until after twelve to four-teen weeks of age, they behave like wild animals towards human beings. Freeman et al. (1961) have shown that there is an optimal period of socialization in the dog, and it is common prac-tice to take pups at six weeks of age as pets. They develop strong attachments to man if acquired at this age. The later developing fear period may interfere with socialization if the pups are first acquired at eight or ten weeks, but in pups acquired at six weeks, the fear period may facilitate socialization: the pup will seek out its caretaker in order to reduce anxiety.

Although there is an optimal period for socializing pups, there is evidence that dogs may subsequently regress or become 'feral'. The social bond with man may be broken when well socialized pups are placed in kennels at three or four months of age; by six or eight months they are shy of strangers and often of their caretakers if they have not been handled much. In addition, they may be ex-tremely fearful when removed from their familiar quarters (i.e. institutionalization plus de-socialization). In wolves (personal obser-vation) and possibly in dogs, there appears to be a later fear period around five months of age, when the animal reacts violently to changes in its familiar environment, even though it is well socialized to people and is not unduly shy of strangers. This period may indicate that the animal has learned and become attached to its home range or territory (locality imprinting or primary localization). *A propos* of the phenomenon of desocialization, Woolpy and Ginsburg (1967) find that captive wild adult wolves can be social-ized after a period of six months of careful handling, and that when subsequently given less human contact, they do not regress or become desocialized. Wolf cubs, socialized early in life, will in con-trast (as in the dog) regress if subsequently given less human con-tact. These findings suggest therefore that although there is an optimal period later in life when socialization with man can be rapidly established, subsequent reinforcement is necessary because of some intrinsic instability of retention in young animals. Woolpy (1968) concludes that 'Apparently, an important aspect of socialization is learning to cope with a previously unfamiliar environmental situation in the presence of un-reduced subject fear.—We have interpreted the results of both the tranquillizer and the socialization experiments to indicate that the fear of the overt responses of fear appear very early in life, its subjective components continue to develop throughout at least the first year. Socialization must be conditioned in the presence of the fully developed subjective components of fear, and hence it cannot be permanently maintained in juveniles if they are left to develop fear responses subsequent to having become socialized in early life.'

We should also not forget the influence of gonadal activity which may increase intraspecific aggression and act as a dispersal mechanism in some species (Fox, 1968). This endocrine change, as seen in pet ocelots and raccoons who suddenly become aggressive occasionally and show extreme rage reactions (and even self-directed aggression) towards their handlers, is worthy of further investigation in relation to the proposed enduring nature of socialization and the interplay of ecologically adaptive dispersal mechanisms in various species.

The review of behaviour disorders under the general category of 'madness' in animals clearly demonstrates the validity of a comparative psychopathology. The present 'intrapsychic' processes conjectured in psychiatry could benefit from and be revitalized by a more descriptive phenomenological approach. This would not only facilitate animal-human comparisons, but would also enhance cross-cultural perspectives and values, is ethnocentric; in relation to com-cross-cultural dimension it is necessary to expand our horizons from a nearly exclusive interest in abnormality to a careful study of normal and even optimal personality functioning. There is also a need to return to a descriptive psychiatry in an era when etiology and treatment receive so much attention in psychiatry.' He notes that the present classification of psychiatric disorders, based on Western cultural perspectives and values is ethnocentric; in relation to comparative psychopathology, it is anthropocentric. Also the search for cultural universals in mental disorders is very similar to the search for inter-species similarities in behaviour disorders. Such research may lead to a better understanding of aetiology, symptomatology, prognosis and treatment.

CONCLUSIONS

In this overview of certain maladaptive behaviours in animals which might be labelled as examples of 'madness' or 'insanity', it is clear that such labels are both spurious and misleading. The behaviours are attempts to adapt to a particular situation or constellation of factors which are a cause of conflict, frustration or emotional disturbance. People do behave like animals in working around some situation or problem and in elaborating some psycho-motor response or behaviour complex to cope with a given problem. The range of responses and behaviour complexes or syndromes, both aetiologically and symtomatically, show certain consistencies between species (i.e., phylogenetically) as well as ontogenetically. Man and higher animals (carnivores and primates) possess complex brains and operate in complex socio-environmental milieus. The range of elaboration of possible disorders may be correlated with the degree of brain complexity and with the degree of socio-environmental complexity and interdependency. Recent work in trans-cultural psychiatry tends to support this latter correlation and also shows that although there may be pan-cultural disorders (as there are similar abnormal syndromes in various species) the culture may determine how a particular syndrome is expressed, accepted and treated. Research with animals does not seem to allow the researcher to enter the inner (intrapsychic) space of his subject while the analyst has access to his patient's past and present experiences via verbal communication. But the animal researcher is as much on the 'outside' as he wishes to be, and this is a function partly of his own self-esteem and lack of fear about losing prestige by being subjective (as distinct from biased objectivity which is either mechanistic or anthropocentric). The animal researcher has complete access to the animal's present via its non-verbal 'body language' and he may be able to fill in the information gap about past experiences by either programming the life history of the experimental animal or by questioning the owner or handler about the animal's prior experiences. This latter situation in small animal practice is analogous to child psychiatry, where the pet dog or cat has not only the neural or psychic apparatus to elaborate various behaviours similar to those observed in disturbed children, but is also exposed to a comparable interpersonal relationship; the similarities between the various relationships and family constellations that may develop between pet, owner and family and child, parents and other family members are very real. Similarly the syndromes which develop in some zoo species in isolation are often etiologically and symptomatically analogous to behaviour disorders reported in institutionalized and socially isolated, stimulus deprived mental patients and convicts.

As a dog, an ape and a man have ears and eyes and mouths which are structurally and fuctionally similar, so do they have similar brains, emotions and under similar stress can develop similar behaviour disorders. The inner world of a man may be phylogenetically a larger and more complex space, so that he may develop quantitatively and qualitatively a greater range of adaptive and maladaptive behaviours. In the Laingian sense, man may more easily get lost in this inner space (tied up in intrapsychic knots) but this may be counterbalanced by his neotenous or paedomorphic flexibility which greatly enhances his ability to elaborate new reactions, transcend or mature out of old beliefs and habits and to perceive or cognize and adapt to new sets of circumstances and opportunities (i.e., face up to 'future shock'). In the cybernetic sense, the human mind is more of an open system which is capable of continued accommodation and assimilation to form a new reintegrated persona structure of greater intrinsic complexity. The end point is a transcendental diffuse persona or for most of the species, a cultural-experiential fixation at one 'modal' point of personality development. As emphasized by Teilhard de Chardin, the evolutionary limits have already been set and actualized for non-human species, while the limits of human growth and potential have not yet been reached. These factors not only contribute to a greater range of behaviour disorders in man, but will also give rise to new disorders as culture and personality continue to evolve. With the exception of crowding stress, psychological castration and those arising from accidental loss of partner or parent, few behaviour disorders have been reported in wild animals in their natural habitats. Is this because the individual animal is in psychic as well as physiological equilibrium with its socio-environmental milieu? Is the high incidence of disorders in man not only attributable to his more complex and larger intrapsychic space, but to the historical disequilibrium between the individual and society? The range, severity and frequency of disorders may be less in those ancient, stable cultures (e.g., hunter-gatherers) where there is a greater degree of equilibrium or psychic harmony, while in those cultures experiencing rapid progress or acculturation, psychic stress is greater.

T. S. Szasz (1964) comments in his book *The Myth of Mental Illness* (Hoeber-Harper, New York) that the notion of a person 'having a mental illness' is scientifically crippling. 'It provides professional assent to a popular rationalization, namely, that problems in human living experienced and expressed in terms of bodily feelings or signs (or in terms of other "psychiatric symptoms") are significantly similar to *diseases of the body*. It also undermines the principal of personal responsibility, upon which a democratic political system is necessarily based, by assigning to an external source (i.e., the "illness") the blame for antisocial behaviour. We know that for the individual patient this attitude precludes an inquiring, psychoanalytic approach to problems which "symptoms" at once hide and express. Codifying every type of occurrence that takes place in a medical setting as, *ipso facto,* a medical problem makes about as much sense as suggesting that when physicists quarrel their argument constitutes a problem in physics.

Although powerful institutional pressures lend massive weight to the tradition of keeping psychiatric problems within the conceptual fold of medicine, the scientific challenge seems clear. The task is to redefine the problem of mental illness so that it may be encompassed under the general category of the science of man. Medicine itself contributes to this enterprise, as do numerous other disciplines. The psychiatric and psychoanalytic approaches to this task, however, must be defined more clearly. It is inevitable that these disciplines must stand or fall with whatever value their special methods possess. Since their methods pertain to the analysis of communications, and since their concepts involve those of psychosocial structure and sign-using behaviour, we should delay no longer in describing our work in terms appropriate to these methods and concepts. This, of course, would necessitate a thoroughgoing revision—and indeed, a scuttling—of many of our notions concerning both psychopathology and psychotherapy. The former should be conceived in terms of object relationships, sign-using, rule-following, social roles, and game-playing. As to psychotherapy, it should be systematized as a theory of human relationships, involving special social arrangements and fostering certain values and types of learning.'

Global acculturation-technoinvolution is now taking place, and certainly one of the most important fields for intensified research is in transcultural psychiatry, with sub-fields of social anthropology, human ethology, community psychology and guidance counselling. Animal models can take us only so far; many of the immediate social-psychiatric issues and more assuredly the problems of the future are uniquely human.

ACKNOWLEDGEMENTS

The preparation of this paper was supported in part by PHS Grant ES-00139 through the Center for the Biology of Natural Systems, Washington University. Segments of the review have been published earlier in the *J. Amer. Vet. Med. Assoc., 159*: 66-77, 1971 and *Z. fur Tierpsychol., 29*: 416-37, 1971.

References

Ader, R., and Plaut, S. M. 1968. Effects of prenatal maternal handling and differential housing on offspring emotionality, plasma cortisone levels and susceptibility to gastric erosions. *Psychosom. Med.,* 30: 277-86.

Ader, R., and Friedman, S. B. 1965. Social factors affecting emotionality and resistance to disease in animals. *Psychosom. Med.,* 27: 119-22.

Astrup, C. 1968. Pavlovian concepts of abnormal behavior in man and animal. In *Abnormal Behavior in Animals,* ed. M. W. Fox, pp. 117-28. Philadelphia: W. B. Saunders.

Beer, C. G. 1968. Ethology on the couch. In *Animal and Human,* ed. J. H. Masserman, pp. 198-213. New York: Grune & Stratton.

Berkson, G.; Mason, W. A.; and Saxon, S. V. 1963. Situation and stimulus effects on stereotyped behaviors of chimpanzees. *J. Comp. Physiol. Psychol.,* 56: 786-92.

Berkson, G. and Mason, W. A. 1964. Stereotyped behaviors of chimpanzees: relation to general arousal and alternative activities. *Percept. Motor Skills,* 19: 635-52.

Berkson, G. 1968. Development of abnormal stereotyped behaviors. *Dev. Psychobiol.,* 1: 118-32.

Berkson, G. 1967. Abnormal stereotyped motor acts. In *Comparative Psychopathology, Animal and Human,* eds. J. Zubin and H. F. Hunt, pp. 76-94. New York: Grune & Stratton.

Bridger, W. H. 1962. Ethological concepts and human development. In *Recent Advances in Biological Psychiatry,* vol. IV, pp. 95-107. New York: Plenum Press.

Brion, A., and Ey, H. 1965. Psychiatrie Animale. Paris: Desclée de Brouwer et Cie.

Broadhurst, P. L. 1961. Abnormal animal behaviour. In *Handbook of Abnormal Psychology,* ed. H. J. Eysenk. New York: Basic Books.

Bronfenbrenner, U. 1968. Early deprivation in mammals: A cross-species analysis. In *Early Experience and Behavior,* eds. C. Newton and S. Levine, pp. 627-764. Springfield, Ill.: C. C. Thomas.

Brunner, F. 1968. The application of behavior studies in small animal practice. In *Abnormal Behavior in Animals,* ed. M. W. Fox, 398-449. Philadelphia: W. B. Saunders.

Calhoun, J. B. 1962. A 'behavioral sink'. In *Roots of Behavior,* ed. E. L. Bliss, pp. 295-315. New York: Harper & Row.

Callan, H. 1970. *Ethology and Society.* Oxford Univ. Press, Oxford.

Cannon, W. B. 1957. 'Voodoo' death. *Psychosom. Med.,* 19: 182-90.

Chartok, L. 1968. Animal hypnosis. In *Abnormal Behavior in Animals,* ed. M. W. Fox, pp. 129-58. Philadelphia: W. B. Saunders.

Chess, S. 1969. *Introduction to Child Psychiatry.* New York: Grune & Stratton.

Delius, J. D. 1967. Displacement activities and arousal. *Nature,* 214: 1259-60.

Denenberg, V. H. 1964. Critical periods, stimulation input and emotional reactivity: A theory of infantile stimulation. *Psych. Rev.,* 71: 335-51.

Denenberg, V. H. 1968. A consideration of the usefulness of the critical period hypothesis as applied to the stimulation of rodents in infancy. In *Early Experience and Behaviour,* eds. G. Newton and S. Levine. Springfield, Ill.: C. C. Thomas.

Denenberg, V. H., and Rosenberg, K. M. 1967. Nongenetic transmission of information. *Nature,* 216: 549.

Ekman, P., and Friesen, W. V. 1968. Nonverbal behavior in psychotherapy research. *Res. in Psychotherapy,* 3: 179-216.

Fox, M. W. 1965. *Canine Behavior.* Springfield, Ill.: C. C. Thomas.

Fox, M. W. 1968. Ed., *Abnormal Behavior in Animals.* Philadelphia: W. B. Saunders.

Fox, M. W. 1971a. Towards a comparative psychopathology. *Z. fur Tierpsychol.,* 29: 216-437.

Fox, M. W. 1971b. Psychopathology in man and lower animals. *J. Amer. Vet. Med. Ass.,* 159: 66-77.

Fox, M. W. 1971c. *Integrative Development of Brain and Behavior in the Dog.* Chicago, Univ. Chicago Press.

Freedman, D. G.; King, J. A.; and Elliot, O. 1961. Critical period in the social development of dogs. *Science,* 133: 1016-17.

Fuller, J. L. 1967. Experiential deprivation and later behavior. *Science,* 158: 1645-52.

Gantt, W. H. 1962. Factors involved in the development of pathological behavior: schizokinesis and autokinesis. *Persp. Biol. & Med.,* 5: 473-82.

Henry, J. P., and Stephens, P. 1969. The use of psychosocial stimuli to induce renal and cardiovascular pathology in mice. *Psychosom. Med.,* 31: 454-55.

Heston, L. L. 1970. The genetics of schizophrenic and schizoid disease. *Sci.,* 167: 249-56.

Hinde, R. A.; Spencer-Booth, Y.; and Bruce, M. 1966. Effects of 6-day maternal deprivation on rhesus monkey infants. *Nature,* 210: 1021-23.

Jones, I. H. 1969. Motor behavior of chronic schizophrenics. *Brit. J. Psychiat.,* 115: No. 524.

Kaufman, I. C., and Rosenblum, L. A. 1967. Depression in infant monkeys separated from their mothers. *Science,* 155: 1030.

Keiper, R. R. 1969. Causal factors of stereotypes in caged birds. *Anim. Behav.,* 17: 114-19.

Kennedy, D. A. 1961. Key issues in the cross-cultural study of mental disorders. In *Studying Personality Cross-culturally,* ed. B. Kaplan, pp. 405-25. Evanston, Ill.: Row, Peterson & Co.

Kurtain, I. T. 1968. Pavlov's concept of experimental neurosis and abnormal behavior in animals, pp. 77-106. Physiological mechanisms of behavior disturbances and corticovisceral interrelations in animals. In *Abnormal Behavior in Animals,* ed. M. W. Fox, 107-66. Philadelphia: W. B. Saunders.

Lorenz, K. 1966. *On Aggression.* New York: Harcourt, Brace & World.

Marler, P. R., and Hamilton, W. J. III. 1966. *Mechanisms of Animal Behavior.* New York: Wiley & Sons.

Mason, W. A. 1967. Motivational aspects of social responsiveness in young chimpanzees. In *Early Behavior,* eds. H. W. Stevenson, E. H. Hess and H. L. Rheingold, Chapter V. New York: Wiley & Sons.

Mason, W. A. 1965. Determinants of social behavior in young chimpanzees. In *Behavior of Non-human Primates,* eds. A. M. Schier, H. F. Harlow and F. Stollnitz, vol. II: 335-64. New York: Academic Press.

Masserman, J. H. 1968. Ed. *Animal and Human.* New York: Grune & Stratton.

Melzack, R., and Scott, T. H. 1957. The effect of early experience on response to pain. *J. Comp. Physiol. Psychol.,* 50: 155-61.

Meyer-Holzapfel, M. 1968. Abnormal behavior in zoo animals. In *Abnormal Behavior in Animals,* ed. M. W. Fox, pp. 476-503. Philadelphia: W. B. Saunders.

Miller, N. E. 1969. Learning of visceral and glandular responses. *Science,* 163: 434-45.

Mirsky, A. 1968. In discussion in *Animal and Human,* ed. J. H. Masserman, pp. 112-18. New York: Grune & Stratton.

Morris, D. 1966. Abnormal rituals in stress situations. The rigidification of behavior. *Phil. Trans. Roy. Soc., B.* 251: 327-30.

Morris, D. 1964. The response of animals to a restricted environment. In The Biology of Survival, ed. O. G. Edholm. *Symp. Zool. Soc. Lond.,* No. 13, p. 99.

Peters, J. E.; Murphree, O. D.; and Dykman, R. A. 1967. Genetically-determined abnormal behavior in dogs: Some implications for psychiatry. *Conditional Reflex,* 2: 206-15.

Pontius, A. A. 1967. Neuro-psychiatric hypothesis about territorial behavior. *Percept. & Motor Skills,* 24: 1232-34.

Richter, C. P. 1967. Psychopathology of periodic behavior in man and animals. In *Comparative Psychopathology,* eds. J. Zubin and H. F. Hunt, 205-27. New York: Grune & Stratton.

Salzen, E. A. 1968. In discussion in *Animal and Human,* ed. J. H. Masserman, pp. 184-89. New York: Grune & Stratton.

Salzen, E. A. 1962. Imprinting and fear. *Symp. Zool. Soc. Lond.* 8 : 199-218.

Scheflen, A. E. 1965. Quasi-courtship behavior in psychotherapy, *Psychiatry,* 28 : 245-57.

Schmidt, J. P. 1968. Psychosomatics in veterinary medicine. In *Abnormal Behavior in Animals,* ed. M. W. Fox, pp. 365-97. Philadelphia : W. B. Saunders.

Spitz, R. A. 1949. The role of ecological factors in emotional development. *Child Develop.,* 20 : 145-55.

Stockard, C. R. 1941. *The Genetic and Endocrinic Basis for Differences in Form and Behavior.* Philadephia : Wistar Institute.

Thorpe, W. H. 1964. *Learning and Instinct in Animals.* London : Methuen & Co.

Tiger, L., and Fox, R. 1966. The zoological perspective in social science. *Man,* 1 : 75-81.

Wickler, W. 1970. Regressionen als normale elemente des Sazialverhaltens. *Praxis der Psychotherapie,* 15 : 150-51.

Wolpe, J. 1967. Parallels between animal and human neuroses. In *Comparative Psychopathology,* eds. J. Zubin and H. F. Hunt, pp. 305-13. New York: Grune & Stratton.

Woolpy, J. H. 1968. Socialization of wolves. In *Animal and Human,* ed. J. H. Masserman, pp. 82-94. New York: Grune & Stratton.

Woolpy, J. H., and Ginsburg, B. E. 1967. Wolf socialization : A study of temperament in a wild social species. *Amer. Zool.,* 7 : 357-74.

Worden, A. N. 1968. Nutritional factors and abnormal behavior in animals. In *Abnormal Behavior in Animals,* ed. M. W. Fox, pp. 238-60. Philadelphia : W. B. Saunders.

Zubin, J., and Hunt, H. F. 1967. *Comparative Psychopathology.* New York: Grune & Stratton.

Discussion

after paper

by Fox

Dr. Cullen : I would like to ask Professor Fox about some of these displacement activities in non-primates. You did mention that you had a difficulty in reproducing some of these behaviours at will say for demonstration or photographing procedures. The thought occurred to me that a long time ago, while working with Professor Russell Davis at Cambridge I managed to produce very rapidly a displacement activity in gold fish in an approach-avoidance situation. We very rapidly induced a feeding response to a light and later with an electric field across the large tank they displayed very quickly a displacement activity of chasing their own tails. As a demonstration it appeals very much to students because they can switch it on very rapidly and one can introduce it during a lecture.

Prof. Fox : Is that actually a displacement behaviour or is it a redirection or some kind of vacuum activity? Displacements are supposed to be something biologically irrelevant, while in a redirected behaviour, the behaviour spills over to another object, so that instead of attacking a partner an animal might attack itself or an inanimate object or a social inferior.

I should add that in the sexual behaviour in many species, aggressive males approaching the female show both sexual motivation and aggressive motivation. And what often switches him off in this double approach situation is frequently an infantile display or food-soliciting display by the female, which supposedly remotivates the male or cuts off the aggression.

Dr. Cullen : There was no evidence of aggression even when one or two other fish joined in and there was no self-directed aggression.

Prof. Brady : The kind of conflict we all like to have—We all have!

Prof. Lifton : I would like to raise a question about the consequent regression, because often I have felt that in clinical psychiatric work the term is used too promiscuously, because in its original evolution it has a psychopathological connotation with the moving back to earlier behaviour as an expression of some kind of breakdown of the individual. Professor Fox showed very clearly and importantly that what he called regression for the sake of bringing together the two fields was part of the useful life preserving repertory of behaviour and I wonder whether we do not need two terms for this rather diverse repertoire of behaviour, which includes say childlike elements in adult behaviour in the most desirable way and regression as breakdown in which the more advanced forms of function are not available? In this sense animal research would be useful for the clinician and in getting over some of his own conflicts in terminology.

Dr. Walsh : This concept has been approached by the author of a recent book—*Psychiatry in Medical Practice*. The author has described what he calls adaptive regression and maladaptive regression. A patient who on being admitted to hospital will not present a problem of psychological management if he regresses in

O

an adaptive fashion, but if he regresses in a maladaptive fashion he will become a management problem.

Prof. Lifton : Yes. In the way of maintaining the word regression, maybe adapted regression may in some way be a contradiction of terms. It is like the term 'regression in the service of the ego' which is a favourite psychoanalytical idea, but really what is meant is something of the early or profoundly unconscious elements of the imagination of the artist.

Syndromes resulting from social isolation—1

Lower animals

ROGER EWBANK,

Department of Animal Husbandry,
Faculty of Veterinary Science,
University of Liverpool

If one should attempt a definition of social isolation then, for the purposes of the present state of this meeting, one might suggest that it is the rearing of young animals after separation from their parent(s) and/or the maintenance of mature animals (sexually and/or socially) in isolation from other members of the same species. It should, perhaps, be remembered that many of the laboratory and domesticated animals are often removed from their parent(s) and/or weaned at an unnaturally early age, and so the apparent effect of social isolation at this time could be resulting from the interaction of several components. There is also the possibility that the isolated animal—and especially the young members of those species which have critical periods of socialization—may form unusually strong social bonds with their human attendants. These factors together with the variation in degree of isolation (e.g. sound and smell contact seems to have been possible in many of the social isolation experiments) make this whole subject complex and difficult to study.

I do not intend in this short paper to review either the extensive experimental work carried out on the effects of social isolation on laboratory rats and mice, laboratory reared chickens and laboratory maintained primates and dogs, nor the quite considerable volume of observational studies done on zoo animals kept under varying levels of isolation from other members of their own species. It is my aim, however, to try and indicate that in a rather special but common type of animal—the domesticated farm animal—we have a large population of creatures which are deliberately kept, as part of their management system, under varying degrees of social isolation and that this results, in some cases, in the development of abnormal behaviour patterns.

The tied-up dairy cow, the battery hen and even the fattening pigs are possible examples of social isolation. These and other forms can be classified, I think, into the following scheme.

Social isolation

(1) *near absolute form* e.g. the keeping of some bulls

(2) *partial form* a) no physical contact but smell, sight or sound communication, e.g. some calf rearing

b) restricted physical contact plus smell, sight or sound communication e.g. tied-up cow

c) full physical contact but limited to animals of same general status (monocaste society) e.g. pen of fattening pigs

Many of the abnormal behaviour patterns which possibly result from the social isolation have long been recognized by stockmen, agriculturalists and veterinarians, but they have not usually been scientifically investigated and are consequently often poorly documented. It is obvious that some of these resulting behaviours could be blamed at least partly upon 'boredom' (itself partly resulting from social isolation), sensory deprivation and/or movement restraint. I shall restrict myself now to considering briefly five of these abnormal behaviour patterns.

1. Temperament in the isolated bull

It has long been known that bulls kept tucked away in the darker and less frequented parts of the farmstead often suffer from a deterioration of temperament: they can become excessively aggressive towards both men and cattle. It is now generally recommended that housed bulls should be kept near the busiest part of the farm. And certainly bulls mixing outside with other cattle are usually quieter than confined ones.

2. Breeding difficulties in calves reared in isolation

The U.K. Code of Recommendations for the Welfare of Livestock (No. 1 Cattle) suggests that calves should be reared in view of each other. As far as I know there is no scientific evidence to back this recommendation. Professional cattle breeders, however, believe that sometimes isolated calves are difficult to breed; they don't seem to behave normally towards other cattle.

3. Bar-gnawing shown by stall confined sows

In this system of husbandry the pregnant sows may be isolated in the 6′ long and 2′ wide stalls for some sixty to seventy days. Quite a number of the animals show, on arousal, excessive bar-gnawing activity (Fig. 1).

4. Head-shaking in battery cage confined poultry

Laying birds isolated in battery cages often show excessive head-shaking movements which disappear when they are placed with others in floor pens. It has also been suggested that when first put together the post-battery birds show a type of ' social-lethargy'.

5. Excessive aggression in the monocaste pig group

The fattening pig group is set up by putting together animals of the same breed, weight and sexual status (castrate males, immature females). There is some suggestion that these groups of very similar individuals may have difficulty in recognizing and remembering each other and consequently cannot easily form a stable dominance hierarchy (Meese and Ewbank, 1972). This seems to result sometimes in excessive amounts of aggression within the group.

Fig. 1.

It may strike you that these clinical examples are neither clear cut nor possibly even truly resulting from social isolation. But I believe that the domesticated farm animal and especially the domesticated pig do show signs of abnormal behaviour when they are isolated, and that further investigation of the effects of these non-experimental forms of social isolation is surely needed. It could produce results of value both to the welfare of farm animals and to the understanding of the biological/ethological process involved.

Reference

Meese, G. B., and Ewbank, R. *Anim. Prod.* 14, 359 (1972).

Syndromes resulting from social isolation—2

Primates

G. MITCHELL,

Department of Psychology,
University of California, Davis

I will summarize several different projects which have been completed in my laboratory and relate these findings to those published by others including Drs. Harlow and Sackett who have already addressed this conference. The projects I will discuss deal with the development of disorganization in the behaviour of the rhesus monkey. This disorganization in behaviour is produced by rearing the monkeys in social isolation from birth to six months or more. I think that you will all agree that isolation rearing of rhesus monkeys provides a good model for mental illness in man. The monkeys referred to in the comments which follow will range from a few days to twelve to fourteen years of age and the methods employed will vary with each particular study. Most of the research discussed herein that originated in my laboratory is still being carried out in collaboration with Brandt, Copp, Erwin, Gomber and Redican.

1. Postural communication and bodily movement

a. *Mode of movement.* Isolate-reared rhesus differ from socially-reared monkeys with regard to bodily posture and movement. In the first month of rearing, socially reared monkeys do more climbing and jumping than do isolates, whereas isolates are more inclined to walk. In addition, the movements of isolates are slow, awkward, and rigid. These differences are maintained throughout life but diminish as the animals pass puberty. Isolates, however, remain awkward in their movements up to twelve or thirteen years of age.[1][2] These differences in movement and posture convey information to human observers concerning the monkey's confidence and/or degree of relaxation. They probably also convey similar information to conspecifics.

b. *Submissive and dominance-related postures.* Early in life (the first two years), isolates display more crouching and cowering than do socially reared animals. As the isolates near puberty, this crouching and cowering spontaneously decreases. By the time the monkeys are adults, there are no longer significant differences in these behaviours. Because of these changes in posture, young isolates are usually subdominant when compared to socially reared monkeys whereas isolates past puberty are less different from controls in dominance.[3][4]

c. *Sexual posturing.* Isolate-reared rhesus at all ages show both qualitative and quantitative abnormalities in sexual posturing. This is particularly true of males but also true of females.[5]

d. *Stereotyped movements.* Isolate-reared monkeys display more frequent deprivation stereotypes and more frequent cage stereotypes than do socially-reared monkeys.[6][7] The deprivation stereotypes, such as rocking, wane with age so that by the time the isolate is two or three years of age he usually no longer rocks. The rocking is replaced by cage stereotyped movements such as repeated jumping, pacing or somersaulting.[8][4]

e. *Bizarre postures and movements.* A wide assortment of bizarre postures and movements appear in isolates within the first month of life[1] and some of these remain throughout life. The number of bizarre postures and movements displayed by an individual decreases as the animal matures. When the isolate-reared rhesus monkey is a fully mature adult he usually displays only two or three idiosyncratic bizarre movements.[2]

All of the abnormalities in postures and movements discussed above interfere with effective social communication.

2. Vocalizations

a. *Coo.* The coo vocalization is a clear call which generally occurs in the rhesus monkey when there is a stimulus change. Separation of an infant from its mother or from a familiar environment produces increases in the frequency, intensity and quality of these calls.[9] These calls occur less frequently in adults than in infants. Facial expressions to some extent replace vocalizations of this sort as the monkey matures.[10] Both infant and adult isolate-reared monkeys emit the coo less frequently than do socially-reared monkeys of similar age and, in addition, the coo is not used in the appropriate context by isolates.[7 4 10]

b. *Screech.* The screech is associated with withdrawal or fear. It occurs more frequently in infant isolates than in infant controls, but the difference disappears as the animals mature.[7 4 2]

3. *Facial expressions*

a. *Lipsmacking.* Little is known concerning development of lipsmacking in isolate-reared animals. Since this expression is related to affection, pacification, affiliation or appeasement,[11 12] its value in promoting peaceful interaction between animals is substantial. Since it is also the *first* facial expression to develop ontogenetically,[13] its importance may be still greater.

b. *Fear grimacing.* The fear grin occurs more frequently in young isolates than in young controls (under two years) but the difference decreases markedly at or near puberty.[7 4]

c. *Threats.* The stare threat and open mouth threat, often accompanied by furrowed brows and head bobbing, occur less frequently in young isolates than in young controls but the difference disappears at or before puberty and *reverses* following puberty.[4]

d. *Looking.* The most frequently used mode of communication among rhesus monkeys, and perhaps among all terrestrial non-human primates, is looking. Rhesus monkeys do more looking than they do anything else.[14] The duration of each look appears to be related to three basic emotional states. Wide-eyed, expressionless looks of longest duration are associated with affection, interest or curiosity. They are most evident in neonates and seem to be related to the lipsmack facial expression. Short, quick glances appear later in the first year and seem to be related to the fear primace. Looks of intermediate duration are most often stares. The areas around the eyes look tense and a minimum amount of eye movement is displayed. These looks are related to threats and generally develop after looks of affection and looks of fear.[13 14] Infant monkeys display few facial expressions but their looking behaviour is extremely im-

Fig. 1. A rhesus infant reared in social isolation exhibiting autoerotic activity. The infant is manipulating the anogenital region.

Fig. 2. Self-threatening behaviour in an adult male isolate-reared rhesus monkey.

Fig. 3. The same male clasping and biting himself.

portant. Isolate infants display greater frequencies of quick glances
than do controls. Adult isolates display a greater average duration
per look than do control adults. These looks are apparently interpreted as stare threats by normal adults but they may be infantile
wide-eyed looks.[14]

4. Object of the display

Isolate infants and adults direct significantly more behaviour of
all kinds toward themselves than do socially-reared monkeys. These
self-directed behaviours develop through the following sequence:
affection related, fear related, aggression related.[7] This sequence is
the same as for normal animals[13] but the direction in which the
behaviours are displayed differs. The isolates apparently do not
develop a clear idea of self versus not self and as they reach adulthood they direct more and more hostility toward the self. Gallup[15]
has shown that isolate-reared chimpanzees do not recognize themselves in mirrors as do socially-reared chimpanzees. Perhaps the
precursors of self-recognition are present in normal rhesus monkeys
but are lacking in isolates. Since the isolates are also hostile toward

themselves, it may be that the distinction between self-recognition and self-love is as difficult to make in monkeys as in man. The failure to know the self certainly interferes with peaceful social communication.

5. Therapy for adult male isolate-reared rhesus

Most studies of early social isolation in non-human primates have focused on the production of psychopathology.[16][17] Recently, however, some of the research attention in this area has shifted toward psychotherapy on isolation-induced behavioural abnormalities. The success of Harlow and Suomi[18] in producing complete social recovery in six-month-old isolate monkeys via social exposure with three-month-old normal 'therapists' suggests that primates can be used in testing psychotherapeutic models for human clinical disorders.

In our laboratory Jody Gomber and I have three fully mature male isolate rhesus monkeys who have exhibited severe behavioural pathology throughout most, if not all, of their lives. We are attempting rehabilitation of these males by pairing them with infants or young juveniles who have had either normal or restricted social experience. The procedure for pairing has been established as successful with fully mature normally-reared males in our laboratory by Redican. We have reasonable cause to believe that this pairing procedure can be employed with the adult isolates and that a therapeutic effect is feasible. Mitchell,[19][20] pairing three-and-a-half and four-and-a-half-year-old isolates with adults, age mates and infants, found that although the isolates exhibited increasing hostility toward age mates, their infant-directed hostility declined with age, and that they interacted positively most frequently with the infants. Eight-year-old female isolates exhibited lower levels of hostility toward infants than did four-and-half-year-old isolates, indicating a probable continuation of decreased infant-directed aggression with age.[21]

An effective social rehabilitating agent, according to Harlow,[22] must provide contact acceptability without a threat of aggression, as well as a learning opportunity for the development of more sophisticated social skills. Since young monkeys, which are gradually expanding their own social repertoires, exhibit very little threat or aggression when paired with isolates,[19] and since adult isolates are less hostile toward and positively interact more with juveniles and infants, our expectations of producing significant social recovery in the adult male isolates are high. Differences between attachment for infants by control males and attachment for infants by isolate-reared males are being assessed utilizing a separation paradigm.

Besides producing data on the therapy of adult isolate animals, this study has provided valuable comparisons with other work in our laboratory. Differences between normal and isolate males in their initial reaction to the infants have added to our comprehension of the isolation syndrome. In terms of the young animals (or 'therapists') themselves, comparisons between their social development and that of infants reared by control male monkeys and infants reared by mother monkeys have been of some importance in the investigation of the role of learning in the development of sophisticated social capabilities. Finally, the study has contributed to our increasing understanding of paternalistic behaviour in primates and of the nature of attachment and separation in primates.

Therapy for isolate-reared infants. Edna Brandt and I[23] have used older therapists as well as infant therapists. Each of eight male or female isolate or control infants was paired for three weeks with either a male or a female preadolescent. The male preadolescents were more aggressive toward the infants than were the females who were at times very gentle. The males did show some affection for the infants, especially female infants, but it was awkward and often rough. The male infants both elicited and emitted more aggressive behaviour in their pairings with preadolescents than did the female infants. However, they also elicited and emitted play. There was more social behaviour directed toward control infants than toward isolate-reared infants, but social interaction between preadolescents, particularly females, and the isolate infants increased significantly over time. Thus, normally socialized female preadolescents may provide good social therapy for isolate-reared infant rhesus monkeys.

References

1. Baysinger, C.; Brandt, E. M.; and Mitchell, G. *Primates,* in press.
2. Fittinghoff, N.; Lindburg, D. G.; and Mitchell, G. *Primates,* submitted.
3. Rowland, G. 1964. Doctoral dissertation. Madison: University of Wisconsin.
4. Mitchell, G. 1968. *Folia primat.,* 8: 132-47.
5. Mason, W. A. 1960. *J. comp. physiol. Psych.,* 53: 582-89.

6. Berkson, G. 1967. *Comparative psychopathology,* eds. J. Zubin and H. F. Hunt. pp. 76-94. New York: Grune and Stratton.
7. Mitchell, G.; Raymond, E. J.; Ruppenthal, G. C.; and Harlow, H. F. 1966. *Psychol. Rep.,* 18: 567-80.
8. Cross, H. A., and Harlow, H. F. 1965. *J. Exp. Res. Pers.,* 1: 39-49.
9. Seay, B. M.; Hansen, E. W.; and Harlow, H. F. 1962. *J. Child Psychol. Psychiat.,* 3: 123-32.
10. Brandt, E. M.; Baysinger, C.; and Mitchell, G. *Int. J. Psychobiol.,* in press.
11. Hinde, R. A., and Rowell, T. E. 1962. *Proc. Zool. Soc. Lond.,* 138: 1-21.
12. Redican, W. K.; Kellicutt, M. H.; and Mitchell, G. 1971. *Develop. Psych.,* 5(3).
13. Rowell, T. E. 1963. *Determinants of infant behavior,* ed. B. M. Foss, vol. II. pp. 35-49. London: Methuen.
14. Mitchell, G. *J. Phenom. Psych.,* submitted.
15. Gallup, G., and McClure, M. K. 1971. *Psych. Rec.,* 21: 69-74.
16. Mitchell, G. 1965. 'Long-term effects of total social isolation upon the behaviour of rhesus monkeys.' Unpublished master's thesis, University of Wisconsin.
17. Mason, W. A., and Sponholz, R. R. 1963. Behavior of rhesus monkeys raised in isolation. *Psychiat. Res.,* 1: 1.
18. Harlow, H. F., and Suomi, S. J. 1971. Social recovery by isolation-reared monkeys. *Proc. Nat. Acad. Sci. U.S.A.,* 68.
19. Mitchell, G. 1966. 'Deferred effects of total social isolation in the rhesus monkey.' Unpublished doctoral dissertation, University of Wisconsin.
20. Mitchell, G. 1968. Persistent behavior pathology in rhesus monkeys following early social isolation. *Folia Primat.,* 8: 132.
21. Arling, G. L.; Ruppenthal, G. C.; and Mitchell, G. 1969. Aggressive behavior of the eight-year-old nulliparous isolate female monkey. *Animal Behavior,* 17: 109.
22. Harlow, J. F.; Harlow, M. K.; and Suomi, S. J. 1971. From thought to therapy; lessons from a primate laboratory. *Amer. Sci.,* 59: 538.
23. Brandt, E. M., and Mitchell, G. Pairing preadolescents with infants (*Macaca mulatta*): Therapy for isolate-reared infants? *Develop. Psych.,* in press.

Syndromes resulting from social isolation—3

Abnormalities of personal space in violent prisoners

AUGUSTUS F. KINZEL

NEW YORK STATE PSYCHIATRIC INSTITUTE

Man's capacity to form social bonds probably depends largely on the degree to which he feels comfortable with emotional and physical closeness to others and the degree to which he has drive autonomous interest available for other individuals and groups. If there is impairment in closeness tolerance or in the normal resolution of narcissistic interest in his personality development, he suffers the consequences of asocialization, namely, the imposition cf restraints by society.

There is probably no group naturally occurring in our society today less social and more oppressed than violent criminals. These men are conspicuously socially deficient. Their mental lives are dominated by the constant fear of violent assault from others, and yet they are convinced that violent assault is the only effective way to solve problems. In fact, until recently, these men were labelled incurable asocial, and were isolated in single prison cells where life was barely sustained. What accounts for the severe degree of social deficit in these men which prompts such an isolating response from society?

As staff psychiatrist at the U.S. Medical Center for Federal Prisoners assigned to the maximum security unit, the author noted that simple physical closeness of one inmate to another was at least as powerful a trigger of violence as were threats, thefts, or other provocations. When individually interviewed at the doorway of their cells, they tended to keep a considerable distance from the interviewer, especially when troubled. A softly misthrown basketball, or a comment such as, 'You've got dandruff', was sufficient to provoke violence. One victim was seen as 'coming up in my face', when in fact he was not. What was this extraordinary sensitivity that seemed to trigger so much violence?

Ethologists have long known that many species keep invariable inter-individual distances. The even spacing of sparrows on a telephone wire suggests some innate sense of constant space around the body, which they will try to maintain by moving away when crowded. Moreover, some species when approached within their reaction distance do not retreat to maintain the space but begin to attack directly and reflexly toward the approacher. The circus trainer knows that the lion must move directly onto a platform in front of him when crowded. Sommer has described how people space themselves in different social settings. Hall has described the cultural variations in interpersonal distancing. Some attempts have been made to correlate interpersonal distancing with personality types, but it was principally Horowitz who actually measured a zone of intolerance to physical closeness to others, and discovered abnormal personal space enlargement in schizophrenic patients. This was the first suggestion that an abnormality in personal space might indeed be one sign of a clinical syndrome. He defined the 'Body-Buffer Zone' as the area around a person within which anxiety is aroused when another enters. This concept showed promise in elucidating what appeared to be an even greater hypersensitivity in violent prisoners.

A procedure was devised to measure the body-buffer zones of most violent and least violent prisoner groups. The violent group was repeatedly violent with little provocation, frequently needed forcible restraint, often carried weapons 'for protection', was more aggressive than sensual in their sexuality and gave histories of frequent violence between parents. All reported episodes of cruelty toward domestic animals. The non-violent group showed none of these characteristics. Each prisoner was asked to stand in the centre of a bare 20' x 20' room, and to say 'stop' when he felt the experimenter had approached too close. Starting eight feet in front of the prisoner, the experimenter inquired, 'Here?', waited two to three seconds for a response, took a step toward the prisoner, repeated the inquiry, and proceeded in like fashion until the prisoner indicated

P

he should stop. At this point the distance between his toes and the centre of the room over which the prisoner was standing was recorded. The experimenter then made similar approaches from seven more directions around the prisoner. The area within the eight closest distances tolerated was taken as the prisoner's body-buffer zone. The procedure was repeated on each individual at approximately weekly intervals for twelve weeks.

The results were quite striking. The violent group zones were, on the average, four times larger than the non-violent group zones. The zones of both groups diminished 50% in twelve weeks, but the zones of the violent group remained significantly larger. In a later independent study done by Hildreth, these findings were confirmed on much larger samples with a more rigorous blind technique.

As the prisoners told of 'rushing in' and 'looming' sensations when the experimenters slowly approached their zone threshold, the similarity of their anxiety to stranger anxiety in children became apparent. Unfortunately it was not possible to get histories of childhood development in these men. It is known from other research, however, that, when infants develop stranger anxiety (which happens by no means universally), one can repeatedly get the same alarmed response including clutching the mother or burying the head in the mother's flesh by having a stranger approach exactly the same distance. Further support for a correlation came from the psychoanalytic psychotherapy of two of the most dangerous and alienated prisoners. One insisted he felt like a mountain lion, and wished to live like one, alone, and on the prey, until, following a simple Christmas Card from the mother, he made a desperate escape attempt, with overtones of reunion with the mother. The other insisted he was a homosexual and hated all parental figures, only to reveal in repeated dreams images of feminine sweaters, which we were able to trace back to the mother, at least in ownership. In addition, Benjamin states, 'We have also speculated on the basis of suggestive but inadequate data that the child with extremely high infantile stranger anxiety will tend later more toward the development of the castration-mutilation anxiety series than will the child who shows more infantile separation anxiety.'

An interesting additional finding of the research was that the violent group showed disproportionately larger rear zones. With better sampling techniques, Hildreth noted that both the most and the least aggressive prisoners had larger rear zones. Both of our

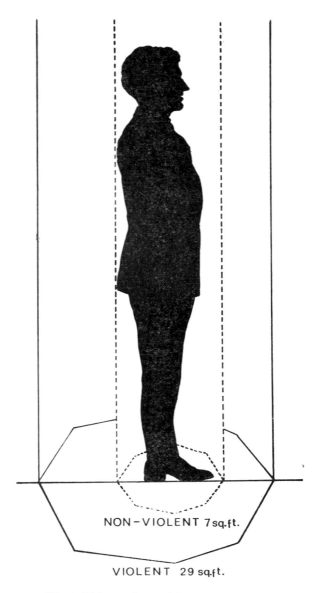

Fig. 1. Violent and non-violent group zones.

Fig. 2. Weekly violent and non-violent zones.

corollary clinical data suggest that the hypersensitivity in these men to approach from the rear represents homosexual anxiety. If so, the body-buffer zone may be the first actual measurement of this specific form of anxiety. It does not, however, appear to be primary as an accompaniment of violent potential.

It is important to distinguish the psychopathology described in the prisoners from the more common paranoid psychopathology. In the latter, the infantile mother image is suspect and devouring, whereas in the prisoners I have described she is seen as a haven of safety.

Thus, we appear to be dealing with a syndrome characterized by repeated violent behaviour with little provocation, extreme hypersensitivity to physical closeness to others, manifested by abnormally large and abnormally shaped body-buffer zones, with resultant major defects in socialization. We hypothesize that this syndrome is based on a failure in modulation of extreme stranger anxiety during development, and look forward to data that would refute or support this formulation.

What can we do to alter this rather specific and grossly deviant pathology? It is possible that the large body-buffer zones could be decreased by the desensitization of repeated approaching by a neutral figure. Taking Harlow's lead that peer relationships might go a long way toward diminishing aggressivity, we would certatinly want to encourage peer interaction. The isolation cells must go. These individuals deserve specialized treatment facilities that will meet their particular needs, and will counteract, not reinforce, their pathology. If our formulation is accurate, treatment actually involving the mothers might be necessary to begin to break down the monistic delusion that she offers omnipotent security. Above all, these men need for identification figures individuals for whom violence is an unacceptable mode of adaptation.

The author wishes to acknowledge his gratitude to those whose attention to animal behaviour has contributed so much new stimulation to our understanding of human behaviour, and who provided the models for the conceptual basis of this research.

References

Ardrey, R. 1966. The Territorial Imperative. New York: Dell Publishing Co.

Benjamin, J. D. 1963. Further Comments On Some Developmental Aspects of Anxiety. Counterpoint, ed. H. S. Gaskill. New York: Int. Univ. Press.

Bowlby, J. 1969. Attachment and Loss, vol. 1. New York: Basic Books.

Hall, E. T. 1966. The Hidden Dimension. New York: Doubleday and Co.

Harlow, H. Abnormal Social Behavior in Young Monkeys. Exceptional Infant, vol. 2, J. Hellmuth, Seattle, Wash.

Hediger, H. Studies of Psychology and Behavior of Captive Animals in Zoos and Circuses. New York: Criterion Books, 1955.

Hildreth, A. M., et al. June 1971. Body Buffer Zone and Violence: A Reassessment and Confirmation. Amer. J. Psychiat. 127:12.

Horowitz, M. J., et al. 1964. The Body Buffer Zone: An Exploration of Personal Space. Arch. Gen. Psychiat. 11:651-56.

Kinzel, A. F. July 1970. Body-buffer Zone in Violent Prisoners. Amer. J. Psychiat. 127:1.

Kinzel, A. F. 1971. 'Violent Behavior in Prisons', in Dynamics of Violence, ed. Jan Fawcett, M.D. Chicago: American Medical Association.

Lorenz, K. 1963. On Aggression. New York: Harcourt, Brace & World, Inc.

Sommer, R. 1969. Personal Space. Englewood Cliffs, N.J.: Prentice-Hall, Inc.

Syndromes resulting from social isolation—4

Need for experimental evaluation of the role of psychosocial stimuli in disease as a guide to rational health action

AUBREY KAGAN,
Unit of Research in Epidemiology,
Division of Research in Epidemiology and Communications
Science

1. The supposition

The organizers' description of this section implies that lack of stimuli, when accompanied by a low or flat emotional response, results in mental illness. I will attempt, briefly, to support and then contest this notion, refer to a unifying hypothesis, show the importance of knowing whether it is true, and suggest how one might find out.

2. Support

There is a good deal of evidence to support the notion that the social outcast, whether red grouse, rat, or man, is at high risk to disease. To focus on the possible relevance in man, I have chosen more specific situations, e.g. there are innumerable papers that show that, compared with 'controls', a high proportion of children with behaviour disorders are deprived of normal parental care—such as unmarried mother, father died when they were young, child was admitted to a foster home. We are tempted to say that the behaviour disorder is due to deprivation of parental care, i.e. a form of social isolation.

Similarly, we associate:

— suicide and attempted suicide in adolescents and young adults with early loss of a parent;
— schizophrenia with lack of mothering;
— suicide in young adults with the loss of a spouse;
— 'long range penetration strain', apathy and abnormal behaviour, in Chindits, Artic explorers, Eskimos, or 'special prisoners', with general sensory deprivation.

3. Contestation

Although, at a first glance, this supports the idea that social isolation, accompanied by low, emotional response, results in mental illness, it does not stand up to closer scrutiny.

First, there is no proof that the social situation is the cause of disease.

Secondly, the associative evidence is usually not well based: there are to many confusing variables. Biller's paper on paternal roles brought this out yesterday.

Thirdly, we think of the social situation as isolation, i.e. a deficit. May it not be the reverse, i.e. an excess of stimuli, for example, the child of an unmarried mother may not have a father, but a series of 'uncles'; or when there is a lack of parental care, the child may be exposed to more situations that he has to deal with himself. Similarly, adults, when suddenly deprived of a spouse, may be exposed to more psychosocial stimuli, rather than less.

Fourthly, the emotional response may not be deficient; it may be elevated. I don't know of data that indicate whether children with behaviour disorders, adolescents' suicide, suicide in young widowers or widows, respond initially or eventually with little or much emotion. It seems quite likely that the flat, emotional response, characteristic of the majority of chronic schizophrenics, is not at all characteristic of acute schizophrenia, and emotional deficit may be secondary. It is possible, for example, in the case of 'long range penetration strain', that the first reaction is an over-response to over-

Fig. 1

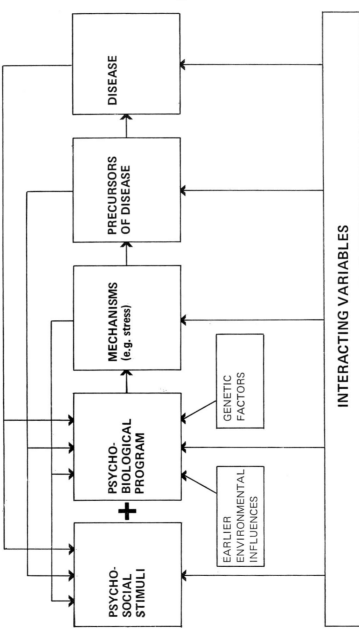

Fig. 2

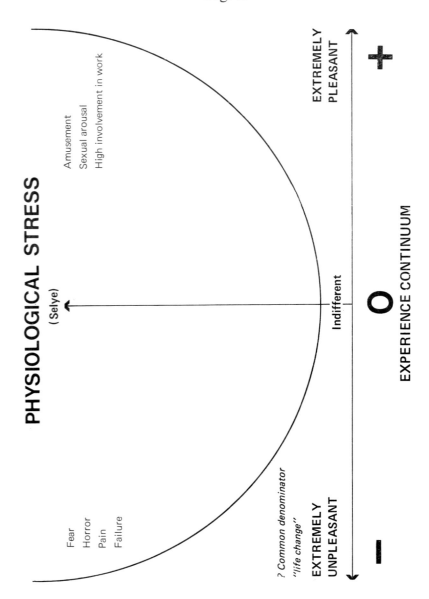

Fig. 2: Hypothesis regarding the relation between physiological stress as defined by Selye and pleasant, indifferent, and unpleasant experiences of various environmental stimuli, e.g., 'life change'. Note that the physiological stress level is lowest during indifference but never goes down to zero. Pleasant as well as unpleasant emotional arousal is accompanied by an increase in physiological (but not necessarily in psychological) stress.

Fröberg, Karlsson, Levi, and Lidberg 1971.

whelming external stimuli, and that subsequent flat response is a protective device that overdoes things and fails in its purpose.

4. A unifying concept

Fig. 1 shows in diagrammatic form a concept of the relationship between psychosocial stimuli to disease that Dr. Levi and I[1] have found useful.

The notion is that stimuli arise from a social situation (Box 1) which, according to the present state of the organism (Box 2), may or may not produce an emotional or other physiological response (Box 3). Under certain circumstances this prevents or gives rise to precursors of disease or disease (Box 5). This process can be promoted or prevented by interacting variables (Box 6).

Social situations may be pleasant or unpleasant (e.g. electric shocks, handling by the keeper or by the mother as in Levine and Denenberg's rats and mice).

A physiological response that frequently occurs is the increased excretion (and presumably secretion) of catecholamines and 17 OH Keto Steroids—Fig. 2 from Fröberg, Karlsson, Levi and Lidberg (1971).[2]

The work of Levi and Frankenhauser, and others, indicates, as many would expect, a great variation between individuals in physiological response of the Selye type, and that the physiological response is highly co-related with the degree of emotion perceived.

This response is associated with a large number of physiological changes that resemble precursors of disease (e.g. raised blood pressure, serum cholesterol, protein bound iodine, etc.)[3] It may be a mechanism by which disease is caused either if it is frequent, intense or prolonged, or if it is not followed by the proper activity—flight or fight. It may be only an index of neuroendocrine activity resulting from environmental change.

Rahe[4] and his colleagues have defined a list of forty-two 'life events', pleasant and unpleasant, that people think affect them (Fig. 3). Examples are: death of a spouse, marriage, change in responsibilities at work, change in residence, change in eating habits, vacation, minor violations of the law.

They have shown that these life change events:

(a)—can be ranked in order of importance (as shown in the figure);
(b)—a relative weight can be given to each event;

Fig. 3

Results of Social Readjustment Rating Questionnaire

Life Event	Mean Value
Death of spouse	100
Divorce	73
Marital separation	65
Jail term	63
Death of close family member	63
Personal injury or illness	53
Marriage	50
Fired at work	47
Marital reconciliation	45
Retirement	45
Change in health of family member	44
Pregnancy	40
Sexual difficulties	39
Gain of new family member	39
Business readjustment	39
Change in financial state	38
Death of close friend	37
Change to different line of work	36
Change in number of arguments with spouse	35
Mortgage over $10,000	31
Foreclosure of mortgage or loan	30
Change in responsibilities at work	29
Son or daughter leaving home	29
Trouble with in-laws	29
Outstanding personal achievement	28
Wife begins or stops work	26
Begin or end school	26
Change in living conditions	25
Revision of personal habits	24
Trouble with boss	23
Change in work hours or conditions	20
Change in residence	20
Change in schools	20
Change in recreation	19
Change in church activities	19
Change in social activities	18
Mortgage or loan less than $10,000	17
Change in sleeping habits	16
Change in number of family get-togethers	15
Change in eating habits	13
Vacation	13
Minor violations of the law	11

(Taken from 'Psychotropic drug response. Advances in prediction', Rahe, R. Illinois, C. C. Thomas, 1969, page 97.)

(c)—the ranking and weight are similar for people cf different
    social class and ethnic group.

Further, they have shown that when subjects are characterized for
life change event scores by summating the number of times each
event occurs in a particular interval of time, multiplied by the
'weight' appropriate to the event:

(a)   that the score is co-related positively with a subsequent illness;
(b)   that in a particular group of subjects it was co-related positively
       with catecholamine excretion.

We now have a general concept that exposure to psychosocial
stimuli in sum, whether pleasant or unpleasant, may prevent, predispose to, or cause disease. Stimuli arising from social incongruity,
parental deprivation, loss of a spouse, etc. could be special cases of
the general concept. Man being a biological phenomenon, it is
certain that there is an optimum level of stimulation, and so we
would expect too few stimuli to be dangerous as well.

5. The importance of evaluating the role of psychosocial stimuli in the causation or prevention of disease

To be even more general, we can summarize current and well
supported speculation by the concept that 'stimuli arising from
psychosocial situations can promote health or cause disease'. If such
situations are adapted to the organism's needs or the organism can
adapt to the situation, health ensues. If not, disease results.

To see this notion in its present-day importance, it is necessary to
take a broad view.

When changes are frequent and extensive, the chances of failure
of adaptation increase.

When changes are slow—over periods of 10,000 years or so—
natural selection and survival of the fittest is nature's method of
adaptation.

Our innate characteristics must still carry the lessons of our
formative aeons up to a few thousand years ago.

When changes are faster, but still over periods of two or three
generations, the process of adaptation depends much more on man-
made efforts. The time-honoured method is to see trouble coming,
or, more usually, after it has come, and to make environmental
corrections. This has sometimes been described as planning from
crisis to crisis.

The fear today is that changes are so fast and so extensive, that ill effects might occur on too large a scale, with too little warning to be able to make a rational correction.

This is the prospect of people in developed and developing countries today. Environmental change, physical or psychical, is frequent, extensive, often unplanned, and, when planned, its significance is, at best, only partly known. The rate of change is probably still increasing.

Since these changes are man-made, we can, in theory, reduce risk by trying to slow the tempo, obtaining a better understanding of the events and introducing rational control—of environmental change.

We are unlikely to be effective in stemming the rate of social change in the next twenty years, but we might be very effective in understanding its effect and I think it to our advantage if we were to test some of the present hypotheses and evaluate health actions based on them, e.g. instead of continuing to look for supporting evidence of ideas put forward by Spitz and Bowlby of twenty-odd years ago.

6. An approach to hypotheses testing and health action evaluation

Remaining for one more moment at the general level, Lambo, Levi and I have proposed that four general types of hypotheses are ripe for testing:

(a)   modification of psychosocial environment (Box 1, Fig. 1) reduces disease and promotes health;

(b)   modification of psychological reactions or physiological response by social, psychological or pharmacological means (Box 3, Fig. 1) reduces disease and promotes health;

(c)   effects of psychosocial environment and psychological or physiological response are inter-related through neuro-endocrine mechanisms as a final common pathway;

(d)   minimizing 'pre-disposing' factors or promoting 'protecting' factors prevents disease and promotes health (Box 6, Fig. 1).

Let us consider now how several specific hypotheses of the general type mentioned above could be tested in relation to a specific problem. We will take the handling of premature babies, because much thought and some activity have been given to this problem already and it illustrates the principles that could be applied under suitable circumstances to other conditions.

A practical problem is to know what degree of stimulation is beneficial to premature babies, what type of stimulation and under what conditions.

For this purpose, we can assign them at random to three types of treatment:

T.1—is the ordinary incubator treatment, in which the baby is, to a large degree, isolated from stimulation (rather like Sackett's isolated infant monkeys).

T.2—is incubator treatment, with extra stimulation, e.g. by rocking the cot gently for six hours out of twenty-four, in two batches of three hours.

T.3—is incubator treatment with extra stimulation, e.g. by rocking the cot every alternate hour.

The daily catecholamine excretion in each case would be measured and assigned to one of three groups: low (M.1); medium (M.2); and high (M.3).

Another observer, who has no knowledge of the treatment group to which the baby is assigned, assesses the outcome in terms of gain in weight, physical activity, co-ordination, mental alertness, reaction time, date at which 'mile stones' are reached, illness—at three months, six months, one year, five years (and perhaps ten years).

This type of design of study, in which Boxes 1, 3 and 5 (Fig. 1) are assessed—Box 6 is kept constant and 2 is equal for the three groups—enables us to test several hypotheses.

For example, if the outcome for T.2 is better than T.1, which is equal to T.3, we know that moderate stimulation is a good thing in general.

But, some in T.1, T.2 and T.3 will have done well, and some badly:

— if T.1 with M.2 are better than T.1 with M.1 and M.3;
— T.2 with M.2 are better than T.2 with M.1 or M.3;
— T.3 with M.2 are better than T.3 with M.1 or M.3.

we will have demonstrated that the important thing is to maintain a moderate degree of physiological response.

Many other hypotheses can be explored in this type of study design and many other conditions can be considered when this type of controlled intervention can be carried out. For example, in some communities, it may be possible to study:

— the effect of different types of day care on the development, health and behaviour of children or health of families;
— the effect of crisis counselling on prevention of suicide;
— the effect of parental care on behaviour disorder;
— the effect of high rise dwellings on people who live in them.

The important thing is that this approach increases our knowledge, and enables us to propose health action with the maximum good and the minimum harm.

There are a number of problems of ethics, numbers and other details I have glossed over, but time dictates that this must be left for discussion, or another occasion.[5][6][7]

References

1. Kagan, A. R., Levi, L. 1972. 'Health and Environment—Psychosocial Stimuli: A Review', in press.
2. Fröberg, Karlsson, Levi, and Lidberg. 1971.
3. Levi, L., 1966. 'Physical and mental stress reactions during experimental conditions simulating combat' (Försvarsmedicin 2, 3).
4. Rahe, R.; Gunderson, E. K.; and Arthur, R. J. 1970. 'Demographic and Psychosocial Factors in Acute Illness Reporting.' Journal of Chronic Diseases, 23: 245-55.
5. Kagan, A. R. 1972. 'Evaluation of Mass Screening for Health: Needs, Difficulties and Possibilities.' Public Health, 86: 3.
6. Kagan, A. R. 1971. 'Epidemiology and Society, Stress and Disease'. In 'Society, Stress and Disease: The Psychosocial Environment and Psychosomatic Disease', ed. L. Levi, pp. 36-48. London/New York/Torono: Oxford University Press, 1971.
7. Kagan, A. R. 1972. Society, Stress and Disease: Psychosocial Disease in Childhood and Adolescence. Prevention and Research'. In 'Society, Stress and Disease: Childhood and adolescence,' ed. L. Levi, —— London/New York/Toronto: Oxford University Press.

Discussion

after papers

by EWBANK, MITCHELL, KINZEL AND KAGAN

Prof. Biller : I wanted to ask Professor Mitchell if there is any evidence of deterioration in rhesus monkeys in terms of central nervous system function?

Prof. Mitchell : Data are scarce here.

Prof. Biller : I was wondering if some of these stereotypic behaviours in the older animals could have some association with cerebral dysfunctioning?

Prof. Mitchell : There is some work going on. I think that Professor Fox perhaps might be able to answer that better, as he has done some with EEG in isolate reared dogs.

Prof. Fox : EEG and evoked potential studies have been conducted on isolation raised dogs but I know of no work on primates.

Dr. Carino : I have two questions for Dr. Kagan: 1) You spoke about the precursors to disease—can you define what you meant by disease? 2) You call for the introduction of a rational control. I would like to know how you identify a norm or who would define this norm and who would carry out the control?

Dr. Kagan : A general definition of disease that I find useful is 'Disability due to mental or physical dysfunction'. Disability is inability to perform and may be considered in various degrees at different levels of hierarchy, e.g. individual, family or community. A fairly clear cut definition at individual level would be inability to perform tasks considered essential in that community—e.g. to earn a living, to look after oneself in our culture. Sleeping sickness epidemic, in a community at subsistence level, that prevents timely crop sowing could wipe the community out by the following winter. There are other degrees of disability that could be considered but I would like to have a go at your second question now. Would you please repeat it?

Dr. Carino : Who would define your norms and what method of control would you use?

Dr. Kagan : I wonder if you would put this in a more specific way as I do not think that I can answer it in a general way.

Dr. Carino : I have a different concept of 'disease' from the one that you define. This same question was asked of Dr. Skinner, but he could not answer who would describe or put together the kind of uniform society he idealised and he sort of left the obligation to control to the individual societies.

Dr. Kagan : I think that is it best to give an example. Suppose the hypothesis to be tested is that admission of a sick child to hospital with its mother is better for the health of the child than admission without its mother. The cases would be children admitted with mothers, the controls would be admission of similar children with similar diseases without their mothers. Assignment to case and control would be random. The criteria could be speed with which the child is restored to health, drugs in hospital, freedom from secondary effects or relapse, etc. The norm here is return to freedom from the disease (and its complications) for which the child was admitted. This study could only be carried out if the subjects (or their parents in this case) thought that it was reasonable and desirable.

Syndromes resulting from over-rigid control—1

Psychophysiological syndromes resulting from overly-rigid environmental control: concurrent and contingent animal models*

JOSEPH V. BRADY,
The Johns Hopkins University School of Medicine

Animal laboratory studies over the past several decades have provided an important point of departure for the psychcphysiological analysis of emotional interactions in general, and for investigating the role of environmental influences in the development and maintenance of psychopathological disorders, in particular. Experimental attention has, for the most part, focused upon endocrine and autonomic functions under conditions of behavioural stress, and numerous investigators following the pioneering research of Pavlov[1] and Cannon[2] have called attention to the psychophysiological consequences of overly-rigid enviornmental control.[3-25]

The current status of such animal laboratory approaches appears to reflect the emergence of two general models for the analysis of overly-rigid environmental influences upon psychophysiological interactions. The first and more traditional *concurrent model* empha-

*This work supported in part by Grant HE–06945 from the National Heart and Lung Institute.

sizes the effects of *antecedent* (but contiguous and correlated) environmental events upon the elicitation of physiological responses. Environmentally-induced 'fear', 'anger', and 'rage' responses have been convincingly demonstrated to elicit a wide range of visceral and autonomic changes in laboratory animal studies within the framework of this concurrent psychophysiological model.[3-25] The second and more contemporary *contingent model,* in contrast, focuses upon the controlling *consequences* which *follow* physiological responses and bear a close temporal relationship to their occurrence. Recent studies of instrumental or operant visceral and autonomic conditioning provide dramatic examples of the extensive environmental influences available for experimental analysis within the framework of this *contingent* psychophysiological model.[26-43]

Significantly, laboratory animal studies within the framework of both concurrent and contingent models continue to provide a vigorous and productive research base for the experimental analysis of emotional interactions and the psychopathological effects of overly-rigid environmental control. In the present report, some current

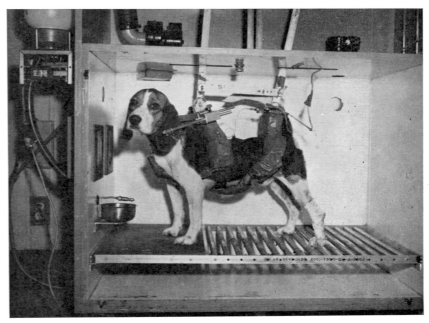

Fig. 1. Restraint harness and experimental chamber for the laboratory dog.

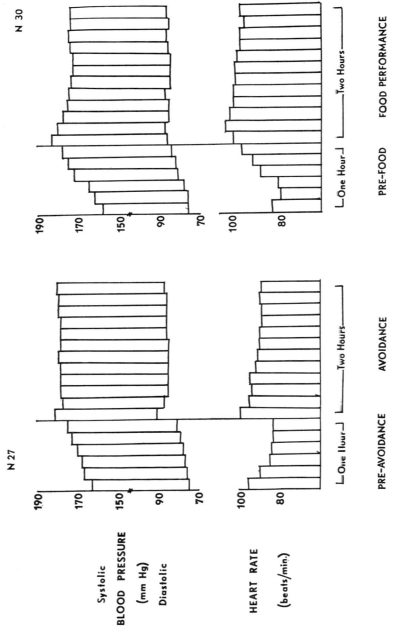

Fig. 2. Average blood pressure and heart rate values during consecutive ten-minute pre-performance and performance intervals for twenty-seven 'avoidance' sessions (left panel) compared with thirty 'food' sessions (right panel).

research at The Johns Hopkins University School of Medicine will be briefly reviewed within the context of such approaches to the experimental basis of psychophysiological disorders. Specifically, the effects of controlled environmental influences upon behavioural-cardiovascular interactions will provide the focus for this presentation.

The subjects in these studies are dogs and baboons restrained in specially-designed experimental chambers, as illustrated for the dog[44] in Fig. 1. Typically, these experiments have been directed toward an analysis of changes in heart rate and blood pressure (measured concurrently and continuously by means of permanently implanted arterial catheters) related to behavioural conditioning involving both concurrent and contingent procedures. Fig. 2, for example, compares the preparatory cardiovascular responses to aversive and appetitive conditioning situations with laboratory dogs.[45] The animals were required to press a response panel either to avoid shock or obtain food during a two-hour experimental session *preceded* by a one-hour interval during which no environmental consequences were programmed for panel pressing. Fig. 2 compares the concurrent changes in blood pressure and heart rate during the pre-avoidance and avoidance performance (left panel) with the concurrent changes in blood pressure and heart rate during the pre-food and food performance periods (right panel). Fig. 2 shows consecutive ten-minute interval averages and summarizes the stable response pattern which characterized the twenty-seven avoidance sessions on the one hand, and the thirty food sessions on the other. Progressive elevations in both systolic and diastolic blood pressure accompanied by progressive *deceleration* in heart rate were consistently observed during the pre-avoidance hour, while progressive increases in both heart rate and blood pressure characteristically occurred during the pre-food hour.

That these pre-performance group differences were in fact representative of the observed individual animal effects of these procedures is illustrated in Fig. 3 which shows the changes in blood pressure and heart rate during successive exposures to both aversive and appetitive conditioning with the same dog. The left panel shows the ten-minute interval averages for blood pressure, heart rate, and panel pressing responses associated with ten initial avoidance sessions. The middle panel shows the changes observed during ten food sessions following the avoidance series, and finally, the right panel

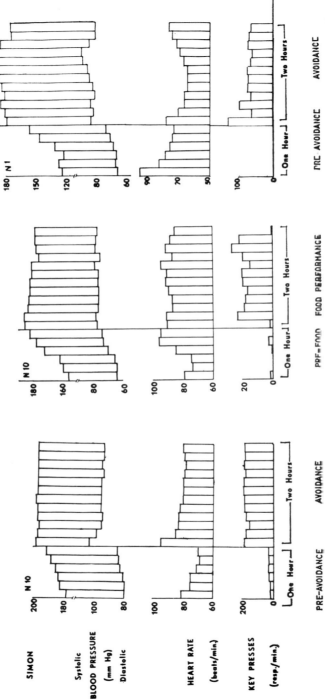

Fig. 3. Average blood pressure, heart rate, and panel response rate during consecutive ten-minute pre-performance and performance intervals for ten 'avoidance' sessions (left panel), ten 'food' sessions (middle panel), and one additional 'avoidance' session (right panel) following exposure to the ten 'food' sessions (middle panel) with the same dog ('Simon').

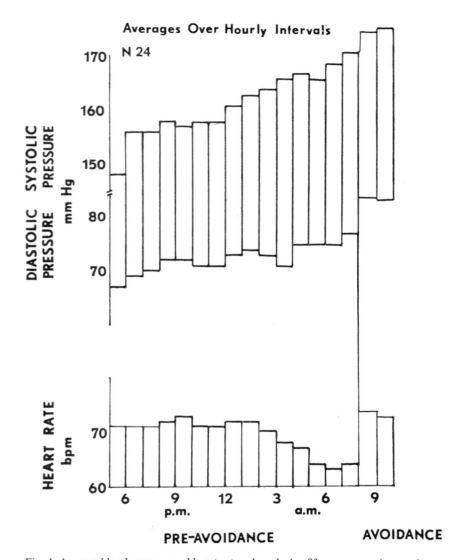

Fig. 4. Average blood pressure and heart rate values during fifteen consecutive one-hour pre-avoidance intervals followed by two consecutive one-hour avoidance intervals for twenty-four terminal sessions.

shows the reversal in the cardiovascular response pattern which accompanied a single avoidance session following the food series.

Of particular interest, of course, is the divergent and sustained change in blood pressure and heart rate consistently observed during the pre-avoidance interval.[46] Previous reports of similar experimentally-induced divergencies have, for the most part, described such changes as being limited to brief periods of only seconds, and have suggested the participation of homeostatic autonomic reflex mechanisms.[23][47] Recently, however, we have observed that this divergent pattern can be sustained for at least fifteen hours under conditions which generate extended delays during the pre-avoidance interval before onset of the required shock-avoidance performance.[48] Fig. 4, for example, illustrates these progressive changes in blood pressure and heart rate in the form of consecutive one-hour interval averages for twenty-four sessions taken from the experimental records of three dogs during a fifteen-hour pre-performance interval followed by the required two-hour shock-avoidance performance.

Similar divergent changes in blood pressure and heart rate have been observed on a somewhat more acute basis in a series of three baboons studied over extended periods during prolonged exposure to concurrent behavioural performance requirements.[25] The animals were restrained in a specially designed chair, as illustrated in Fig. 5, and positioned in a sound-attenuated experimental chamber facing a work panel with accessible stimulus lights, push button switches, a lever manipulandum, and a food-pellet tray, as illustrated in Fig. 6. The baboons were monitored for over a year in an experiment involving continuous recording of heart rate and both systolic and diastolic blood pressure through indwelling femoral artery catheters during shock-avoidance and food-reinforced performances within the context of a twenty-four-hour (per day), behaviour control programme represented diagramatically in Fig. 7, which provided scheduled rest and sleep periods. Comparisons of the acute cardiovascular changes occurring during the rigidly controlled escape-avoidance activity with those recorded during food and sleep activities revealed dramatic differences. Figs. 8 and 9 show typical polygraph recordings of blood pressure and heart rate during intervals of escape-avoidance, food-maintained responding, and sleep. Fig. 8, for example, compares the acute changes in blood pressure and heart rate observed during an escape-avoidance performance (top panel) for one of the baboons (Sport) with those recorded during

Fig. 5. Baboon confined to restraint cart by arm cuffs and waist plate. The arm cuffs may be moved forward and backward on a track and allow considerable freedom in movement of the upper body.

Fig. 6. Experimental chamber with animal and cart placed inside facing intelligence panel. Blood pressure transducer, calibration equipment and infusion pump are shown on top of chamber.

a topographically similar food-maintained performance (bottom panel) for the same animal. Though identical performance requirements (FR 150) were programmed (top pen, each panel), the elevations in blood pressure during escape-avoidance (approximately

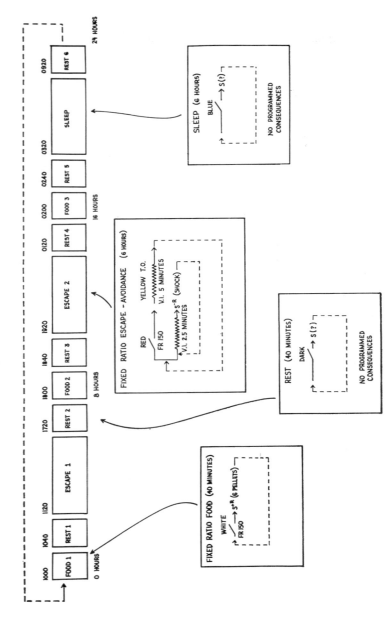

Fig. 7. Sequence of activities comprising the twenty-four-hour behaviour programme.

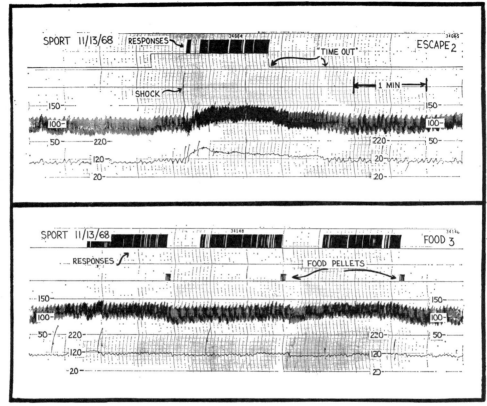

Fig. 8. Sample polygraph recording for baboon 'Sport' comparing typical blood pressure and heart rate changes during escape activity (top panel) with typical changes during food activity (bottom panel).

40mm Hg for both systolic and diastolic, as shown on the middle pen, top panel) contrasted sharply with the more modest increases recorded during the food performance (approximately 10-20mm Hg, as shown on the middle pen, bottom panel). Similarly, acute elevations in heart rate approximating 40 beats/min. or more accompanied onset of escape-avoidance responding (bottom pen, top panel) while virtually no heart rate change can be observed during food activity (bottom pen, bottom panel). Over the extended course of the experiment, virtually thousands of such comparisons confirm the differential cardiovascular effects of the aversively and appetitively maintained components of the programme.

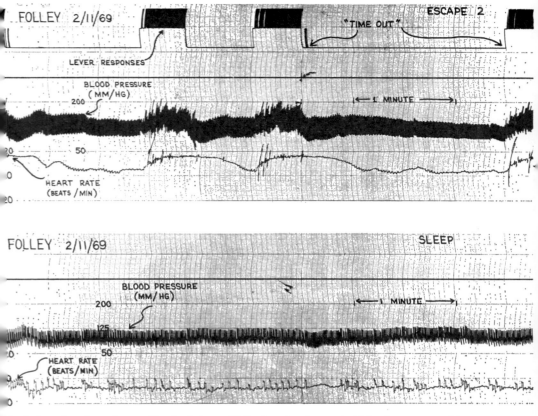

Fig. 9. Sample polygraph recording for baboon 'Folley' contrasting typical blood pressure and heart rate changes during escape activity (top panel) with typical levels during sleep (bottom panel).

Fig. 9 compares the acute elevations in blood pressure and heart rate during an escape-avoidance performance (top panel) for the second baboon (Folley) with the cardiovascular levels observed for the same animal during sleep (bottom panel). Again, elevations in blood pressure of the order of 40-50mm Hg (middle pen, top panel) and increases in heart rate of approximately 50-60 beats/min. (bottom pen, top panel) during the escape-avoidance performance even in the absence of shock contrast sharply with the stable lower blood pressure (middle pen, bottom panel) and heart rate (bottom pen, bottom panel) maintained throughout sleep.

Acute changes in blood pressure and heart rate of considerable interest have also been consistently observed *within* the escape-avoidance activity and in comparison with other activities. Specifically, with the onset of the red light, and as the animal began responding on the fixed ratio requirement, blood pressure typically rose at least 30-40mm Hg and heart rate rose on the order of 60-80 beats/min. These acute elevations in pressure and heart rate were both reliable and clearly not directly dependent upon the delivery of the electric shocks. Following completion of a typical escape from the red light, the pressure declined abruptly, predominantly showing a greater decline in diastolic, and hence an increased pulse pressure. Systolic pressure, after this initial drop, generally remained stable, while diastolic gradually increased on the order of 15-20mm Hg as the heart rate continued to decline to the minimum resting level found during the 'safe' period. This divergence from the more usually observed positively correlated changes in blood pressure and heart rate was consistently found in both animals, and has been tentatively interpreted as reflecting peripheral changes in the cardiovascular system mediated by the central nervous system. Both the avoidance experiments with dogs and these observations with baboons, indicate clearly that the divergent changes in blood pressure and heart rate are related directly to the programmed behaviour-environment interaction contingencies, and suggest that the prospects for developing useful animal experimental models for at least the laboratory condition of overly-rigid control which produces more chronic psychophysiological disorders may not be unduly remote.

The results of these studies clearly demonstrate the adequacy of the subject restraint, cardiovascular monitoring, and behavioural programming systems for continuous long-term psychophysiological observation and experiment with laboratory animals. In addition, the results reliably demonstrate that substantial elevations in both blood pressure and heart rate can be selectively and differentially related to behavioural performance requirements involving aversive contingencies. These acute elevations in blood pressure and heart rate during escape-avoidance were consistently observed even in the absence of shock. This fact, plus the failure of topographically similar food-maintained performance to produce comparable elevations, confirms the importance of the contingency relations between environmental events, rather than work requirements or the occurrence of stimuli and responses *per se*, as critical determinants of psychophysiological changes.

One important feature of these studies within the framework of a concurrent spychophysiological model, however, is the lack of any explicit contingency relationship between the psychophysiological response levels and the occurrence of either escape-avoidance responses or shocks. With the baboons in the present experiment for example, escape from the aversive condition, which can be assumed to be positively reinforcing, occurred equally as often following either rising or falling blood pressure changes. Although the predominance of these reinforcing events might be assumed to favour reinforcement of elevated pressure, the actual relationships provided were noncontingent, and chance reinforcement of lowering blood pressure could have occurred on numerous occasions.

In fact, several recent experimental reports have provided convincing evidence that the arrangement of explicit contingent relationships between selected autonomic responses (e.g., heart rate, blood pressure) on the one hand, and the occurrence of specific reinforcing environmental consequences, on the other, can produce significant modifications in such physiological functions.[26-43] While it is not surprising that cardiovascular functions have provided an important focus for such instrumental visceral learning studies with both animals and humans, the reported changes have, for the most part, been limited in both magnitude and duration. In addition, numerous theoretical and methodological questions have been raised concerning the role of 'voluntary mediators' (e.g., respiratory or skeletal responses) in the development and maintenance of such operant autonomic conditioning effects.[30]

Significantly, however, some more recent animal experimental studies within the framework of such contingent psychophysiological models of behavioural-cardiovascular inter-relationships have attempted to extend the limits of available instrumental cardiovascular conditioning procedures with particular reference to the control of blood pressure. In our laboratories, for example, the effects of controlled environmental consequences contingent upon changes in diastolic blood pressure are being studied with chair-restrained baboons in relationship to effects upon both heart rate and blood pressure.[41-43] Animals, surgically prepared with indwelling femoral artery catheters, are initially trained, using an operant 'shaping' procedure, to raise and maintain diastolic pressure levels.

This involves the programming of continuous twelve-hour 'work' periods alternate with a twelve-hour 'rest' interval each twenty-four hours, and two feedback light signals to the babocns when the diastolic blood pressure is either above or below the prescribed criterion. Beginning with very modest increase requirements, both animals have been gradually 'shaped' over several months on the programme to produce elevations in diastolic pressures approximately 30-40mm Hg above pre-experimental resting baseline levels and to maintain such increases continuously throughout virtually the entire twelve-hour recurrent 'work' periods. Characteristically, blood pressure levels during the alternating twelve-hour 'rest' intervals were initially observed to return to basal levels shortly after termination of the programmed 'work' period. After several months on the programme however, blood pressure levels during the 'rest' periods have gradually increased over the pre-experimental baseline, and both animals currently maintain diastolic levels during the twelve-hour 'rest' intervals which are 15-20mm Hg above such pre-experimental basal values. Significantly, heart rate changes developing during latter phases of the experiment appear to be following a course which in inversely related to the blood pressure response. Although substantial elevations in heart rate have continued to accompany the blood pressure changes during the twelve-hour 'work' periods, heart rate levels have appeared to decline somewhat during later monthly intervals despite progressive elevations in blood pressure. Significantly, similar divergencies in heart rate and blood pressure changes have been observed during the twelve-hour 'rest' periods over the extended course of this experiment.

Fig. 10, for example, compares the concurrent changes in blood pressure and heart rate during the twelve-hour 'work' periods with the changes in blood pressure and heart rate during the twelve-hour 'rest' periods for one of the experimental animals over the first seven months of this study. Fig. 10 shows conservative monthly averages for heart rate and both systolic and diastolic blood pressure during exposure to the alternating twelve-hour 'work-rest' programme and includes pre-experimental basal values for both heart rate and blood pressure. Characteristically, progressive elevations in both systolic and diastolic blood pressure can be seen to have developed in response to the experimental requirements during the twelve-hour 'work' periods. Heart rate, on the other hand, while substantially elevated over basal values during these twelve-hour 'work' periods,

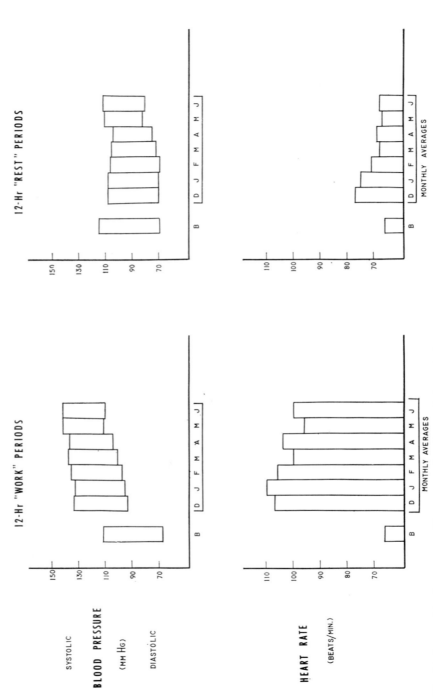

Fig. 10. Average blood pressure and heart rate values for one baboon during consecutive monthly intervals for the twelve-hour 'work' periods (left panel) compared with the twelve-hour 'rest' periods (right panel).

appears to decline over the course of the same observation interval. Similarly, divergent changes in blood pressure and heart rate can be seen to characterize the cardiovascular response pattern developing during the twelve-hour 'rest' periods. Blood pressure levels, initially approximating baseline values over the first few months of the experiment, have shown modest but progressive elevations during the latter months of this study. In contrast, initially elevated heart rate levels during the twelve-hour 'rest' periods appear to have declined progressively to approximately basal values over this same interval.

The relationship between these varied physiological-behavioural interaction patterns in experimental animals on the one hand, and similar functional changes characteristic of psychosomatic disorders in humans on the other, is, of course, far from clear. The temporal course and complex inter-relationships characterizing the blood pressure and heart rate changes observed in response to these chronic laboratory behavioural stress situations, however, are not inconsistent at least, with clinical accounts of the dynamic physiological interactions observed to occur in essential hypertension. Under any circumstances, animal studies within the framework of the laboratory psychophysiological models reviewed in this report would seem to provide a systematic experimental basis for identifying and defining the role of overly-rigid environmental control in the development and maintenance of a broad range of psychopathological disorders.

References

1. Pavlov, I. P. 1879. Uber die normalen Blutdruk-schwankugen bien hunde. *Arch. Gesamte Physiol.* 20: 215.
2. Cannon, W. B. 1915. *Bodily changes in pain, hunger, fear, and rage.* New York: Appleton.
3. Gantt, W. H., and Hoffman, W. C. 1940. Conditioned cardio-respiratory changes accompanying conditioned food reflexes. *Am. J. Physiol.* 129: 360-61.
4. Gantt, W. H. 1942. Cardiac conditioned reflexes to painful stimuli. *Fed. Proc.* 1.1.
5. Mahl, G. F. 1949. Effect of chronic fear on gastric secretion of HCL in dogs. *Psychosom. Med.* 11: 30.
6. Dykman, R. A., and Gantt, W. H. 1951. A comparative study of cardiac conditioned responses and motor conditioned responses in controlled 'stress' situations. *Amer. Psychol.* 6: 263.

7. Mahl, G. F. 1952. Relationship between acute and chronic fear and the gastric acidity and blood sugar levels in macaca mulatta monkeys. *Psychosom. Med.* 14: 182-210.
8. Sawrey, W. L.; Conger, J. J.; and Turrell, E. S. 1956. An experimental investigation of the role of psychological factors in the production of gastric ulcers in rats. *J. Comp. Physiol. Psychol.* 49: 457-61.
9. Dykman, R. A., and Gantt, W. H. 1956. Relation of experimental tachycardia to amplitude of motor activity and intensity of the motivating stimulus. *Amer. J. Psychol.* 185: 495-98.
10. Fronkova, K.; Ehrlich, W.; and Slegr, L. 1957. Die Kreislaufanderung bein Hunde wahrend des bedingten Nahrungsgeflexes und seiner Hemmung. *Pflug. Arch.* 263: 704.
11. Brady, J. V.; Porter, R.; Conrad, D.; and Mason, J. 1958. Avoidance behavior and the development of gastroduodenal ulcers. *J. exp. Anal. Behav.* 1: 69-72.
12. Dykman, R. A., and Gantt, W. H. 1960. Experimental psychogenic hypertension: blood pressure changes conditioned to painful stimuli (Schizokinesis). *Bull. Johns Hopkins Hosp.* 107: 72-89.
13. Black, A. H. 1959. Heart rate changes during avoidance learning in dogs. *Canad. J. Psychol.* 13: 229-42.
14. Gantt, W. H. 1960. Cardiovascular component of the conditioned reflex to pain, food, and other stimuli. *Physiol. Rev.* 40: 266-91.
15. Stebbins, W. C., and Smith, O. A. 1964. Cardiovascular concomitants of the conditioned emotional response in the monkey. *Science,* 144: 881-83.
16. Brady, J. V. 1965. Sxperimental studies of psychophysiological responses to stressful situations. *Symposium on Medical Aspects of Stress in the Military Climate,* Walter Reed Army Institute of Research, Washington D.C. Government Printing Office, page 271.
17. Mason, J. W.; Brady, J. V.; and Tolson, W. W. 1966. Behavioral adaptations and endocrine activity. *Proceedings of the Association for Research in Neurons and Mental Diseases,* ed. R. Levine. Vol. 43. Baltimore, Md.: Williams and Wilkins Co.
18. Brady, J. V. 1966. Operant methodology and the production of altered physiological states. *Operant Behavior: Areas of Research and Application,* ed. W. Honig. New York: Appleton-Century-Crofts.
19. DeToledo, L., and Black, A. H. 1966. Heart rate: changes during conditioned suppression in rats. *Science,* 152: 1404-06.
20. Brady, J. V. 1967. Emotion and the sensitivity of the psychoendocrine systems. In *Neurophysiology and Emotion,* ed. D. Glass, p. 70. New York: The Rockefeller Univ. Press.
21. Brady, J. V.; Kelly, D.; and Plumlee, L. 1969. Autonomic and behavioral responses of the rhesus monkey to emotional conditioning. *Ann. N.Y. Acad. Sci.* 159: 959-75.
22. Forsyth, R. P. 1969. Blood pressure responses to long term avoidance schedules in the restrained rhesus monkey. *Psychosom. Med.* 31: 300-309.
23. Katcher, A. H.; Solomon, R. L.; Turner, L. H.; LaLordo, V.; Over-

meier, J. B.; and Rescorla, R. 1969. Heart rate and blood pressure responses to signaled and unsignaled shocks: effects of cardia sympathectomy. *J. Comp. Physiol. Psychol.* 68: 163-74.

24. Herd, J. A.; Morse, W. H.; Kelleher, R. T.; and Jones, L. G. 1969. Arterial hypertension in the squirrel monkey during behavioral experiments. *Am. J. Physiol.* 217: 24-29.

25. Findley, J. D.; Brady, J. V.; Robinson, W. W.; and Gilliam, W. J. 1971. Continuous cardiovascular monitoring in the baboon during long term behavioral performances. *Commun. Behav. Biol.* 6: 49-58.

26. Engel, B. T., and Hansen, S. P. 1966. Operant conditioning of heart rate slowing. *Psychophysiol.* 3: 176-87.

27. Engel, B. T.; and Chism, R. A. 1967. Effects of increase and decrease in breathing rate on heart rate and finger pulse volume. *Psychophysiol.* 4: 83-89.

28. Engel, B. T. and Chism, R. A. 1967. Operant conditioning of heart rate speeding. *Psychophysiol.* 3: 418-26.

29. Miller, N. E., and DiCara, L. 1967. Instrumental learning of heart rate changes in curarized rats; shaping and specificity to a discriminative stimulus. *J. Comp. Physiol. Psychol.* 63: 12-19.

30. Katkin, E. S., and Murray, E. N. 1968. Instrumental conditioning of autonomically mediated behavior: theoretical and methodological issues. *Psychol. Bull.* 70: 52-68.

31. Plumlee, L. A. 1969. Operant conditioning of increases in blood pressure. *Psychophysiol.* 6: 283-90.

32. Miller, N. E. 1969. Learning of visceral and glandular responses. *Science,* 163: 434-48.

33. Engel, B. T., and Melmon, K. L. 1968. Operant conditioning of heart rate in patients with cardiac arrhythmias. *Cond. Reflex,* 3: 130.

34. DiCara, L. V., and Miller, N. E. 1968. Instrumental learning of systolic blood pressure responses in curarized rats: disassociation of cardiac and vascular changes. *Psychosom. Med.* 5: 489-94.

35. Benson, H.; Herd, J. A.; Morse, W. H.; and Kelleher, R. T. 1969. Behavioral inductions of arterial hypertension and its reversal. *Amer. J. Physiol.* 217: 30-34.

36. Shapiro, D.; Tursky, B.; and Schwartz, G. E. 1970. Differentiation of heart rate and systolic blood pressure in man by operant conditioning. *Psychosom. Med.* 32: 417-23.

37. Miller, N. E.; DiCara, L.; Solomon, H.; Weiss, J. M.; and Dworkin, B. 1970. Learned modification of autonomic functions: a review and some new data. *Cir. Res. 26, Suppl:* 3-11.

38. DiCara, L. 1970. Learning in the autonomic nervous system. *Sci. Amer.* 222: 30-39.

39. Schwartz, G. E. 1972. Voluntary control of human cardiovascular integration and differentiation through feedback and reward. *Science,* 175: 90-93.

40. Weiss, T., and Engel, B. T. 1971. Operant conditioning of heart rate in patients with premature ventricular contractions. *Psychosom. Med.* 33: 301-321.

41. Brady, J. V.; Findley, J. D.; and Harris, A. H. 1971. Experimental psychopathology and the psychophysiology of emotion. In *Experimental Psychopathology,* ed. D. Kimmel. New York: Academic Press.

42. Harris, A. H.; Findley, J. D.; and Brady, J. V. 1971. Instrumental conditioning of blood pressure elevations in the baboon. *Cond. Reflex,* 6.4: 215-26.

43. Brady, J. V.; Anderson, D. E.; and Harris, A. H. 1971. Behavior and the cardiovascular system in experimental animals. In *Proceedings of the International Symposium on Neural and Psychological Mechanisms in Cardiovascular Disease,* ed. A. Zanchetti. Milan: Publisher Il Ponte (in press).

44. Anderson, D. E.; Daley, L. A.; Findley, J. D.; and Brady, J. V. 1970. A restraint system for the psychophysiological study of dogs. *Behav. Res. Instr. & Meth.* 2: 191-94.

45. Anderson, D. E., and Brady, J. V. 1972. Differential preparatory cardiovascular responses to aversive and appetitive behavioral conditioning. *Cond. Reflex,* 7.2: 82-96.

46. Anderson, D. E., and Brady, J. V. 1971. Pre-avoidance blood pressure elevations accompanied by heart rate decreases in the dog. *Science,* 172: 595-97.

47. Yehle, A.; Dauth, G.; and Schneiderman, N. 1967. Correlates of heart rate on classical conditioning in curarized rabbits. *J. Comp. Physiol. Psychol.* 64: 99-104.

48. Anderson, D. E., and Brady, J. V. 1972. Prolonged preavoidance upon blood pressure and heart rate in the dog. *Psychosom. Med.* (in press).

Syndromes resulting from over-rigid control—2

Man—Family

DEREK RUSSELL DAVIS,

Department of Mental Health, University of Bristol.

A parent has expectations of his child and becomes upset when he is disappointed. About a parent it may be asked: what expectations does he, or she, have in particular respects? In what degree have the expectations been determined through interaction with the child, in what degree through experience in other relationships? How has he behaved when he has been disappointed?

'Battering' Parents

Consider some of the descriptions given of battering parents (e.g. Helfer and Kempe, 1968). Deprived themselves of parental care and affection, these parents have often been depressed and have looked in their relationships with their children for satisfactions the children have not given them. Parents whose memories of their own childhoods are painful tend to expect their children to be affectionate and good. Disappointment revives painful feelings. Unrealistic expectations then reflect needs not met in other relationships. Usually the parents lack support from kin and neighbours and are relatively isolated socially. They become desperate and then violent when their children cry and do not respond to comforting. An example of the odd expectations of battering parents is Mrs. S. who was angry at her five-month-old son's soiling which she thought quite abnormal.

Misunderstandings by Parents

A battering parent who feels rejected by his baby is not alone in reading much more into an infant's behaviour than is warranted. An unhappily married mother, for instance, thinks that the cries of her new-born son reflect his father's temper. A nurse feels insulted by the penile erection of a thousand-gram 'prem' infant when he is roughly handled.

Dwarfs

A mother's expectations affect the establishment of food habits— especially in the middle of the first year at about the time of weaning. This is the age (between five and nine months) at which two-fifths of the dwarfs without physical abnormalities studied by us in Bristol (Apley *et al.*, 1971; Davis, 1971) had shown slowing in growth. When a child goes over at this age to a mixed diet, the mother tends to adhere to a system based on her understanding of his dietary needs. The dietary habits of some of the families of dwarfs are strange. The evening meal of one family—the father a university lecturer, the mother a school-teacher—consisted of white bread covered with chocolate spread liberally sprinkled with sugar. As a general rule, however, the diets of dwarfs are relatively better off for protein than for calories.

Some mothers allow the child a free choice of food, as in a 'cafeteria' system. He then shows a much greater variability in choice and amount than any that the more rigid 'table d'hote' system allows. Dwarfs have developed highly restrictive food habits, with fussiness and fads, which have given them a calorie intake falling far short of their needs (Table 1). Bobby, eleven-and-a-half-years old, and well below the third percentile in height, eats about 850 calories a day—40% of his needs on the usual standards. Of the 850 calories, 600 come from four packets of potato crisps. His twin sister is just above the sixtieth percentile.

Disorders of food habits like these have been attributed to 'maternal deprivation' (e.g., Patton *et al.*, 1963; Togut *et al.*, 1969). In some cases the under-eating has been part of a reaction to separation from the mothering person, perhaps the maternal grandmother. In other cases it has been part of a negativistic reaction to over-rigid control by the mother. Evidence in support of this last

TABLE 1

Calories and Proteins in the Diet

Percentage of standards for children of like—

	N	Calories		Proteins	
		age	size	age	size
dwarfs	36	57·2	63·4	78·8	88·0
controls	23	93·6		104·6	

view is that on average one third to one half of the calories in the diet of the dwarfs in our series was derived from food eaten outside meal-times—typically potato crisps, sweets and Lucozade.

I am interested not so much in physical as mental stunting, but physical stunting provides a paradigm in that the child's behaviour serves to restrict his experience severely, his responses are stereotyped.

Other syndromes

Many other habits developed during childhood may become disordered as a result of over-rigid discipline by the parents, e.g., bowel habits, when the disorder may be soiling, or speech stammering.

About a child it may be asked: In what degree, and in what ways has his behaviour been modified by his parents' expectations of him?

High verbal ability

The pattern of intellectual development during childhood depends, it has been shown (e.g., Kent and Davis, 1957), upon the parents' expectations. About a third of the mothers in a sample of 118 eight-year-old school children were classified as 'demanding' because they set high standards for their children and were ambitious for them in their school work. These parents expected their children to conform to a model of what they should be and were intolerant of any departure from it. This model was imposed by the parents with little regard to the child's wishes or real needs.

Compared with the children with 'normal' mothers, those with demanding mothers tended to score highly on tests of verbal ability (Table 2). Scores on tests of 'performance' did not differ between the two groups. Nine of the twelve children in the sample with I.Qs. over 140 had mothers who had been classified as demanding.

TABLE 2

Maternal Discipline and Test Scores (IQs)

		Normal Group n=41	Demanding Group n=38	P for difference
Verbal test	mean	109·9	124·2	<0·01
	s.d.	14·8	23·0	
Performance test ..	mean	110·4	113·4	—
	s.d.	11·0	12·3	
Reading age	mean	8·4	9·1	—
	s.d.	1·75	2·1	

(Kent and Davis, 1957.)

The children with demanding mothers tended to be tense, restless, ill-at-ease and unduly anxious to succeed, and to go to pieces in the face of failure. They tended to learn facts rather than principles. Their knowledge tended to be narrow and specialized, and they were relatively poor in applying it in novel situations.

The children with the demanding mothers were as a group doing relatively well in their school work, although not invariably so. Progress in school work depends upon the expectations of teachers as well as parents, as numerous investigators have now shown.

Not all the children of demanding parents do well academically. Some break down into psychiatric illness. This is more likely to happen when the child has been stimulated excessively, and rewarded infrequently. Also, demanding disciplines were found in a sample of children appearing in Court. About one quarter of the parents in this sample were classified as 'demanding', nearly one half as 'unconcerned'. The offending children of demanding parents were more likely to show 'psychotic' than 'psychopathic' features.

Over-anxious mothers

Some of the mothers interviewed in the same investigation were classified as 'over-anxious'. Like the demanding mothers, they too were ambitious for their children, but the models they held out for them were inconsistent and shifting, although they might be emphatic. They were ceaselessly anxious lest the children should fall short in some way. They were sometimes intolerant when they did do so, sometimes indulgent. They sapped the children's confidence, and tended to restrict the children's activities outside the home for fear of what might happen to them. The children tended to score relatively poorly on 'performance' tests (Table 3), and to show a con-

TABLE 3

Maternal Discipline and Test Scores (IQs)

		Normal Group n=41	Over-anxious Group n=30	P for difference
Verbal test	mean	109·9	107·3	—
	s.d.	14·8	15·2	
Performance test	mean	110·4	100·7	<0·01
	s.d.	11·0	12·7	
Reading age	mean	8·4	8·0	—
	s.d.	1·75	2·0	

tinual need for attention, praise and reassurance from the tester. They lacked spontaneity and initiative. When separated by the tester from their mothers, they tended to become highly anxious, with disorganization of their behaviour both within and outside the test situation.

[*Robert*. The tester did not succeed in separating Robert, aged eight-and-a-half, from his mother, or she from him. Despite a reading age a year in advance of his chronological age, he was subsequently transferred to a special school. On his first morning there, he suffered —'out of the blue'—his first grand-mal attack. A few months later, put down by the school bus at an unfamiliar spot, he ran heedlessly across the road and was killed in a collision with a car.]

Emancipation

Although the control of the demanding discipline is the more rigid, the shifting and inconsistent character of the over-anxious discipline makes its control more difficult to escape. This is of importance to the teenager while emancipating himself from the influence of his parents and establishing his independence and social and sexual identity. Emancipation is more difficult when models have been shifting and inconsistent, and confidence has been sapped. The young person tends then to be tied into an unhappy home situation. Outside it he is incompetent.

Rules if they are inflexible can be broken. The teenager can rebel against rigid rules, and can establish his independence if he has acquired the intellectual and other skills which enable him to cope on his own.

The processes of emancipation can be shown to have gone awry in patients suffering from schizophrenic types of illness. In such cases the patient has remained tied into a close, exclusive relationship with an over-anxious mother (or father) who has over-protected him and discouraged him from developing independent interests. She has thus handicapped him in developing autonomy and identity, and has 'engulfed' him, as Laing (1960) has put it. 'Mystified' or caught up in a 'double bind', he cannot define and therefore cannot break away from parental controls.

Failure in emancipation during adolescence or earlier cannot be understood without reference to the needs and expectations of the parents, which are incorporated into the family's rules for the young person. Laing's (1971) nine-year-old patient, David Clark, is expected by his mother to play the parts once played by her father, whose name he has been given. The family's rules for David, formulated partly by Mrs. Clark's mother, are intended to stop the bad behaviour, as perceived, of Mrs. Clark's father from coming out in David. To David the rules are incomprehensible and unrealistic and inescapable.

References

Apley, J.; Davies, J.; Davis, D. R.; and Silk, B. 1971. Non-physical causes of dwarfism, *Proc. roy. Soc. Med.* 64: 135-38.

Davis, D. R. 1971. Physical and mental stunting, *Proc. Internat. Congress Pediat.* 111: 181-86.

Helfer, R. E.; and Kempe, C. H., eds. 1968. *The Battered Child,* London: Chicago University Press.

Kent, N., and Davis, D. R. 1957. Discipline in the home and intellectual development, *Brit. J. med. Psychol.* 30: 27-33.

Laing, R. A. 1960. *The Divided Self,* Harmondsworth: Penguin.

Laing, R. A. 1971. *The Politics of the Family,* London: Tavistock.

Patton, R. G., and Gardner, L. I. 1963. *Growth Failure and Maternal Deprivation,* Springfield, Ill.: C. C. Thomas.

Togut, M. R.; Allen, J. E.; and Lelchuck, L. 1969. A psychological exploration of the non-organic failure to thrive syndrome, *Develop. Med. Child Neurol.* 11: 601-607.

Syndromes resulting from over-rigid control—3

Man — Society

EILEEN KANE

UNIVERSITY OF PITTSBURGH

The selection of titles and demarcation of foci in a multi-disciplinary symposium often presents the individual speaker with a frame of reference or a division of the field of inquiry which conflicts, or even more perturbingly, vaguely mis-articulates with the conventions observed in his own academic domain. Few of my fellow anthropologists, for example, would choose to organize their research and material in such a way that the title 'Syndromes Resulting from Over-Rigid Control' would be appropriate. Fortunately, this experience, which at first reaction strikes one as academic miscegenation, has two happy consequences: it reminds us, first, of a fact which we are in danger of forgetting: that human experience is not artificially subdivided into the academi-centric categories which the various disciplines have assigned themselves; and secondly, it forces a reexamination of the conventions and perspectives of one's own particular discipline.

Taking 'Syndromes Arising from Over-Rigid Control' as the universe of inquiry, the most profitable research areas would appear to be

a) animal, particularly primate, response to control, where a wide range of experimental situations can be established using the living species most closely related to modern man;

b) fortuitously-occurring pathological situations in human populations, such as those which occur as a result of natural disaster, war, imprisonment, injury, etc.; and limited experimental situations, restricted by the ethical considerations associated with research upon humans;

c) cross-cultural research, which provides information on the range of human responses to the current universe of cultural and biological controls which mankind, in a diversity of approaches to human organization, imposes in various societies.

The extent of this repertoire provides us with an insight into the absolute range of biological and cultural control which the species currently imposes and within which it functions; the variety within this repertoire enables us to analyse responses to variations in form of control.

The limitations of each area of inquiry make a combined approach necessary: primate research, for example, can provide assistance in determining what is biologically universal in man's behavioural responses; cross-cultural research helps to determine what are culturally universal in man's behavioural responses and what aspects of behaviour are locally specific to particular societies. It is essential, in cross-cultural research, to realize that currently-existing societies do not necessarily exhaust all possible varieties of form of control; it is equally essential to bear in mind that by extrapolating from primate behaviour implications for human behaviour we may be confused by attempts to relate possible biologically universal-hominoid responses to certain of our own locally-specific cultural responses. We must bear in mind, of course, that within absolute parameters of human tolerance response to 'control' is culturally-associated, as is definition of what constitutes 'control'. The term 'over-rigid', however, connotes a normative aspect which many anthropologists, steeped in a theoretical tradition of cultural relativity, would reject. Over-rigidity resulting in pathological syndromes would have to be restricted to a minority of a population if the culture is to survive; or, if one can accept the conclusion of some authors that widespread pathological characteristics exist in certain populations, such as the Alorese, the Marquesans and the Trukese, one must examine evidence such as Kardiner's for the Alorese, which attributes survival to geographical isolation and lack of enemy challenge. One legitimate approach, however, which does not violate the concept of cultural relativity, is the use of the 'emic' (borrowed from the linguistic term 'phonemic') perspective. In this perspective, cultural behaviour is viewed from the inside view or the actors' view: 'the units of conceptualization in anthropological theories should be "discovered" by analysing the cognitive processes of the people studied, rather than "imposed" from cross-cultural (hence ethnocentric) classifications of behavior.' (Pelto, 1970: 68). The theoretical counterpart of this is the 'etic' (from 'phonetic') approach, in which the researcher analyses cultural traits and patterns on a cross-cultural comparative basis, to determine differences and similarities.

Most of the more recent explorations in the field of culture and personality fall into the second category; most relevant for the approach taken in this conference are the studies undertaken by Whiting and others using a cross-cultural statistical approach; however, the majority of these have been reviewed extensively by Barry (1969: 155-79) in an article which classifies studies of cross-cultural evidence on determinants of mental illness in terms of four major conflicts: trust and fear of other people; love versus hatred; independence versus dependence; and expression versus control of bodily functions, following Freud's and Erikson's theories of personality development.

Most readers will be familiar with the difficulties associated with using cross-cultural approach: the problem of ensuring the comparison of like phenomena; the differing quality and lack of standardization in the ethnographic accounts used; the distortion associated with the process of converting material from ethnographic accounts into quantitative categories; the fact that the original research usually had foci not entirely conducive to the purpose which the cross-cultural researcher is now putting it; lack of complete independence between the societies, as well as between the variables studied; the inability, because of the use of human populations, to manipulate complexly-interrelated variables, and the problem of ensuring independence of variables. Cross-cultural tests, ratings and scalings form a considerable literature in itself. Some of these obstacles have been overcome in more recent studies by standardizing field work and focus (Six Cultures, Whiting, 1963, Mothers of Six Cultures, Minturn and Lambert, 1964). The problem of possible interrelatedness has been dealt with through the use of techniques such as multi-variate analysis and factor analysis.

Although some of the problems associated with cross-cultural studies will never be entirely obviated, future studies will undoubtedly avoid the major difficulties which have characterized the earlier research.

INDUCED CULTURE CHANGE

I stated initially that the normative aspect of determining 'over-rigidity' and the fact that form, in most instances, and response to control are culturally-associated and present theoretical difficulties for many anthropologists. However, among the areas of inquiry in which form of control is determined by forces external to culture, are situations in which non-local cultural patterns and elements are introduced through induced culture change. Culture-change is a continuously-occurring process although its rate differs from one society to another. A culture which did not change would ultimately disappear. An analysis of the pathological consequences of culture change as a phenomenon, therefore, would have a utility similarity to that of analyzing the pathological consequences of growing up, or of having sunrises; the alternatives make an imputation of pathology inappropriate.

However, some forms of culture change have a higher potential for introduction of non-adaptive elements, with consequent pathological effects. Among these forms are those which can, for the sake of convenience, be seen as occurring mainly in response to internal factors, and those which occur mainly in response to external factors. Kroeber has categorized the former into changes associated with the subsistence-economic technological level such as the Neolithic Revolution and the Industrial Revolution; the 'biological play impulse' of cultural expression, such as fashion changes or changes arising from affective factors such as boredom, fatigue, etc.; and growth changes leading to new idea systems and social reconstructions. Changes from outside may arise from process of diffusion, bringing new culture traits; the spread of larger patterns or complexes, and finally, the changes arising from contacts of whole cultures, i.e., acculturation. It is in the latter category of external change that the potential for disruptive change is greatest. Much diffusive change is due to erratic, uncontrolled happenstance in which there is no deliberation on the part of the giver or receiver; however, in the last generation, with the increasing awareness of the 'underdeveloped nation' and the Third World, Western industrialized nations have regularly initiated and implemented deliberate programmes of induced culture change for less technologically-developed countries.

Social scientists involved in induced change have been able to isolate, on an *ad hoc* basis, some of the psychological factors involved in resistance to innovation (Foster, 1962; Arensberg and Niehoff, 1971) and have predicted methods for implementing change upon a rough understanding of the psychological implications and consequences of change. A considerable body of literature exists on the consequences of cultural disorganization arising from externally-induced change or change in response to catastrophe; and Anthony Wallace has incorporated into his process structure of stages of revitalization movements, two intermediate stages which reflect, respectively, individual stress resulting from cultural disequilibrium, and institutionalized deviance in the form of alcoholism, and crime. Wallace cites the 'quasi-pathological' response of the Seneca to sociocultural disorganization: drunkenness, fear of sorcery and the disruptive increase of factionalism (Wallace, 1961). More specifically, Hallowell, through the use of Rorschach tests, found that the personality structure of the acculturated Ojibwa with deprivations and cultural restrictions, was a quasi-pathological form of the relatively unacculturated personality of the Lake Winnipeg Ojibwa (Hallowell, 1967: 462). In such situations, 'over-rigid control' can be viewed as felt lack of choice on the part of the individual, with little perceived opportunity for meeting the new situation in a way which would be considered adequate by the individual.

a. Consequences of induced economic change

Certain characteristics of social organization associated with various forms of pre-industrial economy are known, as are the essential characteristics of and pre-requisites of the industrial process and industrialization. It is possible, therefore, in situations of rapid technological change in underdeveloped countries, for example, to isolate the cultural areas in which conflict is likely to occur, and in which the individual may encounter lack of reinforcement of previously learned patterns of behaviour, expectations which cannot easily be met from the cultural repertoire of patterns which he has mastered as part of the socialization process, and significantly altered sources for maintenance of security, reduction of anxiety and formulation of a coherent world-view.

Industrial nations have involved themselves in attempts to ameliorate the political, economic and social consequences of under-development through economic and technological assistance. In some instances, this has resulted in directed programmes of change; in others, it has simply involved a dissemination of information on the desirability of modern western technological processes, prompting, in some instances, an initiative for change from within the culture. Often, changes occurring in these circumstances have unexpected and unforeseen non-adaptive consequences. Frequently, practices which could be introduced with minimal consequences for the culture, for particular institutions, and for the individual, if stripped to bare essentials, are introduced instead with all of their original cultural accretions : health programmes which incorporate foods aesthetically or religiously repugnant to the recipients; factory schedules which conflict unnecessarily with the agricultural cycle of the part time farmer-factory worker; personnel management schemes which are based upon American conceptions of the nature of the relationship between manager and worker or between men generally; or educational programmes which use competitive exercises in a society which may abhor aggressive distinctiveness. The general mental health implications of technological change in such circumstances have been outlined by, among others, Mead (1961), although there is little actual research which focuses specifically upon this aspect of change. Generally, however, we know that institutional crescivity generally decreases with change from pre-industrial to industrial economy. The kin-based unit loses some of its multi-purposiveness; its function as a productive unit disappears as individuals leave the family-based subsistence economy for the wage-labour force. In this new situation, the individual may extra-unit, and expect, as is frequently seen in the western rural Irish community, that the factory, for example, will be bound by the social conventions which characterized his relationship to the agricultural subsistence production unit: e.g., that it will be sufficiently flexible to incorporate him when his work is not required elsewhere, and to release him when other obligations or opportunities exist; that as a member of a social unit (here, the community) he should have preference above non-parish residents in employment, regardless of his technological skills, just as he had preference previously as a family member, in relation to family farm employment. Certain social functions once fulfilled by the kin-based unit, such as care of the elderly, occupational training, and social control are now performed by special-purpose institutions.

Other functions once assumed by the family are assumed, nearly by default in some instances, by other institutions: prevention of divorce, for example, becomes less a kin-unit function as marriage no longer functions as a necessary alliance between two kin groups, and becomes, instead, the concern of the church, or in some instances, the state, which frequently can bring little more than negative sanctions to bear. The corporation as a non-social entity develops.

Culture change is a process, and industrialization may be viewed as a process in itself. However, we can isolate more specific processes for potential conflict in induced technological change. The content of the socialization process, for example, changes, but more pertinent to the point, attitudes inculcated in the socialization process may become, in the course of rapid change, less relevant or irrelevant to successful adult functioning; and adults may no longer have the requisite knowledge and experience to pass on relevant attitudes and skills to youth. Attitudes heavily reinforced in childhood may assume a negative value in rapid change.

We also know that the characteristics of roles and role-associated behaviour may be altered; former economically-related patterns of behaviour for youth, women, household heads, community leaders and the elderly may be inappropriate in the new situation, in which the young may require extended schooling and lose their economic contributory role to the family; women who formerly participated in family agricultural work may find their contributions now limited to domestic services, while the household head becomes the sole cash contributor as he enters a wage labour force; the entrepreneurial behaviour of the broker may become more strategic to the community than the traditional role-associated behaviour of occupants of former high-status positions such as the religious leader or the teacher; and the elderly may find that they are no longer considered to be experienced respositories of useful traditions and values.

Finally, we know that differing conceptions of what constitutes work, unfamiliarity with the market system and the integration of

production processes, and difficulty of reconciling the factory conception of division of labour with traditional patterns of community
co-operation are major problems of adaptation of attitudes to
factory work on the part of a traditional subsistence economy.

b. Induced economic change in rural Ireland

My own research, although not specifically focussed upon psychopathological consequences of change, was undertaken to provide an
analysis of the social and cultural factors affecting the development
of government-subsidized industrialization and the effects of the
industrial process in nine rural Irish-speaking (Gaeltacht) communities in western Ireland, whose populations ranged in size from 200
to 1,000. Included in the study were surveys of twelve government-
subsidized or semi-state associated factories, with a total work force
of 1,750 full and part-time employees. The results of this five year
research programme are reported in considerable detail elsewhere
(Kane, 1971); however, one aspect of the problem, which must of
necessity be radically condensed here, usefully illustrates the consequences of an over-rigid application of industrial practices which,
because of their historical development in Britain and the United
States, had cultural accretions which were inimical to the successful
introduction of basic manufacturing enterprises in rural Irish
communities.

In the past decade, culturally-oriented nationalism has assumed
a new and increasingly greater importance in the formulation of
national economic, political and social policy in Europe. This is
particularly true of Ireland; what is now a minority language is the
first official language, by Constitutional article, of the State; and
government policy promotes its use as a general medium of communication. A concomitant of this policy is government acceptance
of the responsibility for encouraging the development of economic
viability in the rapidly depopulating Gaelic-speaking areas of
western Ireland which are thought, through their maintenance of an
unbroken tradition of Gaelic as the vernacular, to represent the
'national identity' in its purest context. To this end, the Third
Programme for Economic and Social Expansion has fostered a programme of light industry, additional agricultural subsidization,
facility development for tourism, and other special aid programmes
to farmers and manufacturers in Gaelic-speaking communities.

For a complex of reasons, some of which are not traditionally the concern of the anthropologist, the introduction of factories into Gaeltacht communities did not significantly affect the Gaeltacht resident's decision to remain or emigrate, nor did it have a significant effect on his family economy or that of the community generally. Factory programmes were frequently judged to be irrelevant to the community and were met with apathy, misunderstanding, erratic productivity, high labour turnover and in some instances, active hostility. Among the factors which help to account for this negative response are the following:

i. Structural rigidity: the attempt to replace the Gaeltacht worker's agricultural subsistence base through the introduction of factories, or to involve him in a binary agriculture-factory economy was predicated on the assumption that the Gaeltacht worker is a farmer. In fact, however, the Gaeltacht worker's economy is based upon an intensive complex of cash, produce and service sources, using the farm mainly as a living unit and only incidentally as an extensive agricultural productive unit. His complex may contain, in addition to agriculture, income from seasonal tourism, government, social assistance and emigrants' remittances from children, knitting for a commercial agent, keeping poultry, tending a kitchen garden, cutting turf for family fuel, operating a small shop or pub, participating in seasonal migration to Britain, working in a local hotel seasonally, working for the county council part-time, and driving a hackney car, among other activities. This integration of cash and productive sources allows for considerable flexibility in adjustment to changes in the biological life cycle of the family, to market trends, and to natural disasters. It provides community services in the absence of enough cash and demand to attract a commercial interest. The integration is feasible only as long as cash in some form, very often in the form of government social assistance, enters into its composition. Why isn't the Gaeltacht worker replacing this precarious balance with cash-paid factory work in the local community? First, full-time factory work (part-time factory work for adult males is limited) destroys the balance of the complex; the worker is being asked to risk a flexible set of cash, income and produce sources for a single cash income source. Moreover, full-time employment would prohibit self-provision of necessary services such as turf-cutting, which cannot be hired, and which, if they could be, would elevate the hirer to an undesirable social status which would leave him open to payment for all services now performed as a matter of course, or on the basis of personal exchange.

Although the introduction of industry as a solution to the problems of underdevelopment is common, a more flexible approach, given the structure of the Gaeltacht worker's economy, would be the substitution on a cash basis of schemes based upon the original economic structure, i.e., a complex of integrated sources. Through government grants for horticultural schemes, tourism, etc., the Gaeltacht worker can gradually replace, on a cash basis, his former system without sacrificing its essential element: security. Moreover, as items are re-created on a cash basis, balance is no longer an integral feature; since all yield cash, economically feasible items can be substituted for one another, and ultimately, the surrender of some to take up factory work does not necessarily involve the collapse of the whole as it did in the precarious balance of the old system. Nor would it be impossible to return to the cash-based complex, if factory work failed, since the sources, or similar ones, which are entirely independent of one another, could be re-established.

ii. A second, socio-demographic factor hinders the successful establishment of industry in the Gaeltacht community. Since only six per cent of the farmers in Gaeltacht counties are under thirty-five years of age, the potential factory force is to be found among the underemployed, the unemployed, the current school population and returned emigrants. As discussed elsewhere, only the first category is relevant. The unemployed is an amorphous category which includes any person under the age of seventy who is without work, the voluntary idle, and adult sons of retired farmers who have not officially surrendered their farms. In the third category, my own research indicates that Gaeltacht vocational school students rank factory work either low or last in any list of ranked occupations, and no student surveyed listed any type of factory work in questions concerning either aspirations or actual future expectations. In the fourth category, to date, few attempts to attract returned migrants have been successful, and no industrial plan could plan a programme, at present, predicated upon the attraction of returned emigrants. The underemployed category includes, in addition to 'male relatives assisting,' whose numbers appear to be declining to the point of statistical insignificance, many of the Gaeltacht residents described above, who base their incomes on a complex of sources, and who may therefore be underemployed but restricted in their ability to assume factory work.

This simple example of a structurally inappropriate application of the 'industrial solution' to a rural subsistence community does not, of course, entirely account for the 'farmer's' rejection of industry or for the rural factory worker's difficulty in adapting to the factory. In addition to this lack of correlation of basic facets of the industrial process with existing patterns of community life and with traditional economic orientation other factors, such as the over-rigid application of unnecessary cultural accretions, are pertinent.

i. Characteristics of the organizational structure of the industrial enterprise conflicted with the cultural patterns of community organizations: hierarchical differentiation of occupations, for example, prevented some workers in communities with little social and economic differentiation from seeking promotion above peers. Interaction with managerial staff was stilted, since few middle-level statuses existed in the pre-industrial community.

ii. The agents of induced change were themselves the victims of over-rigid introduction of change; non-local managerial staff, for example, had to re-adapt their concepts of management practice, of worker-personnel relations, and of effective incentive schemes; they also had to adapt to different sub-cultural premises and patterns of behaviour on the part of the community. Those who could not make these adjustments exhibited a variety of behaviours and attitudes: some doubted the sincerity of the Gaeltacht workers; others doubted the feasibility of the entire industrialization programme, concluding that the rural worker and community were not capable of adjusting to factory work, or that the Irish language was an inappropriate medium for modern industrial society (this in spite of the fact that most managers were committed urban Irish speakers); and finally, some doubted the validity of their managerial training or were forced to question their own personal ability to function in the situation.

iii. The rural factory worker had to change or integrate past work patterns and experiences with those required by the new situations; motor patterns, economic attitudes and social relations between himself, managerial staff and fellow workers also required change.

iv. In the community, the educational process and the content of the process had increasingly less relevance for the inculcation of skills and attitudes necessary to the changed technological base with its concomitant social and cultural changes; traditional aspirations were no longer met; or, conversely, new aspirations were inculcated which could not be met, due to lack of sufficient employment opportunities on appropriate levels. Within the community, groups necessary to the integration of the community into the national commercial network, such as development groups, were recruiting members on inappropriate bases, such as on factional or social status basis, rather than on skill or technical suitability.

CONCLUSION

It is obvious from the above that the concept of 'control' is a complex one which cannot be restricted to its physical form or to strictures which would engender psychopathological responses in purely Western, non-acculturative situations. The absolute physical parameters of control must be determined through primate and other animal research, and through studies of human disaster. Cross-cultural research is relevant here in presenting the current range of levels of control. Response to non-physical forms of control can also be profitably pursued on a cross-cultural basis, as well as within our own society. It is essential, however, that specific research be undertaken on psychopathological responses to emically-defined forms of control: one of the most obvious areas for such investigation lies in the realm of induced culture change or acculturation, which, by its very nature, can be defined as over-rigid applications of the patterns of one culture to another.

References

Arensberg, C. M., and Niehoff A. H. 1971. Introducing Social Change: a Manual for Community Development, 2nd ed. Chicago: Publisher (?).

Barry, H. III. 1969. Cultural Variations in the Development of Mental Illness, in Plog, Stanley G. and Robert B. Edgerton, Changing Perspectives in Mental Illness, 155-79. New York.

Foster, G. M. 1962. Traditional Cultures and the Impact of Technological Change. New York.

Hallowell, I. 1967. Culture and Experience. New York.

Kane, Eileen. The Development of the Industrial Process in the Gaeltacht, a volume of extracts prepared for Comhairle na Gaeilge from a study commissioned by Gaeltarra Eireann. Unpublished (forthcoming).

Mead, Margaret. 1961. Cultural Patterns and Technical Change. New York.
Minturn, L., and Lambert, W. W. 1964. Mothers of Six Cultures. New York.
Pelto, Pertti. 1970. Anthropological Research: The Structure of Inquiry. New York.
Wallace, A. F. 1961. Culture and Personality. Philadelphia.
Whiting, M. B. ed. 1963. Six Cultures: Studies of Child Rearing. New York.

Discussion

after papers by BRADY, RUSSELL DAVIS and KANE

Prof. Russell Davis: A comment on Dr. Kane's paper. Kwashiorkor is of interest. The illness commonly starts when the child is transferred from the mother to the maternal grandmother. It does appear to be the break of the bond with the natural mother which is of crucial importance.

Prof. Lifton: I have two questions—one for Professor Russell Davis and one for Dr. Kane. I wonder whether in your impressions of the parents in the most extreme treatment of children—say the battering parents—how much could one sense that they must feel profoundly threatened, even something in their very lives symbolically threatened, by the growth and autonomy of those children— is that in keeping with your observations and what is the nature of that threat to the parents that makes them lash out violently.

Prof. Russell Davis: They have an entirely fantasy infant to look after who is expected to do certain kinds of things but does not. The reality of the infant is something which is quite different. He is beginning to be autonomous. It is at this point that the anger begins to mount.

Prof. Lifton: The remark I had for Dr. Kane is that I was fascinated by one of the last points you made, when you were cut off by time, about the new problem of the way which a very rapid cultural change and the various programmes for innovation in which the rigidity of the innovating programme becomes a kind of superimposed rigidity. I think that you are making a distinction between a kind of cultural natural rigidity which can be managed because it is of the culture, it is called rigidity from the outside but it works within the culture and an imposed rigidity from the outside which is felt to be a foreign body—can you give an example of that?

Dr. Kane: The introduction of factories, e.g. the Western European concept of factory with all the cultural factors attached to the industrial process which arose in British and American society which have been transferred in this country to the West of Ireland, to Irish speaking areas in the Gaeltacht, agriculture schemes which have completely different conceptions of what constitutes what is suitable to male and female, or whether there would be co-operation between working partners, these kinds of things. I have seen no studies of the mental strain induced in the workers because they simply for the most part pack up and leave but I have certainly seen it in the case of the managers. They are trained in Irish Management Institute techniques, personnel management techniques, these sort of things, they are brought in from Dublin, go into the factory, expect that these kind of procedures are going to work, they do not, and there was one instance even of suicide arising out of this.

Dr. McKenna: One of the remarks that Professor Russell Davis made about a clinical case—'he *had* to be transferred to a special school'—suggested that there was an inevitability about this procedure as if it were preordained that special schools were for certain people. This highlights one of the areas where there is a great dearth of research, that is in the administration of programmes. We have clinical research directed to persons, we have disability research directed to diseases but we have very little administrative research directed towards the delivery of mental health services to the consumers. One of the things that we are missing at this Conference is a consideration of the delivery of mental health services. Mr. Ewbank pointed out in his paper this morning the way that we create huge litters or monocaste societies of pigs and affect their subsequent health. In much the same way, some special residential schools create somewhat similar societies. In some orphanages we have children housed in dormitories all of the same age group, without any reference to the natural family pattern of stagger of ages. Again we accept the separation of children's hospital and adult hospitals without reference to what the effects of this particular type of delivery of these health services to the consumer may be.

Prof. Russell Davis: I would like to comment on that—my phrase was euphemistic—I was the wicked man responsible for transferring Robert to a special school because I thought it was going to be good for him. The separation from his mother in the ordinary school meant that he was nearly paralysed throughout the whole day—I thought he could be managed better in the special school. As it turned out things went worse. We are still stuck with the Victorian idea of education. You take the child out of the family because it is good for the child to get him out of the family. You put him into a school. You do not bring the parents into it and so you make sure that the separation actually takes place. This is particularly important I think as a factor in the development of special schools and adds very considerably to the management problems of children as vulnerable as Robert.

Dr. Lewis: On the question of battered babies, Professor Russell Davis's view may be quite correct but at the same time there is possibly a simple explanation as well. Babies naturally cry; babies cry in the middle of the night and therefore they wake their parents up. Both parents inevitably become partially sleep deprived. One of the effects of sleep deprivation is increasing irritability and increasing inability to cope with frustration. If they have in their personality a low tolerance of frustration and inability to cope this additional sleep-deprivation induced decrease in tolerance threshold may well give rise to the aggressive outburst.

Dr. Murray: I am afraid that the concept of the battered baby limited the picture that was introduced at first. Initially there was a failure to recognize that there was a wide spectrum starting with the crying baby who is battered going on to the child who sustains burns at the peak age of two to four years. There is now good evidence to suggest that some of these may be battered baby equivalents resulting from unconscious neglect which is a manifestation of rejection. This rejection may present later in different ways—one mother I have in therapy—she rejects her eight year old daughter and inflicts physical punishment on her, said 'I became very disturbed when she sat down yesterday in front of her nine year old brother and opened her legs wide'. This was competitive anxiety and is a further extension of the spectrum. I wonder whether Professor Russell Davis's stunted children were stunted for physical or emotional reasons or both?

Prof. Russell Davis: There are two questions here about battered babies. In the shortness of my delivery I did not make clear that the parents described are common in type, but not perhaps universal. Since we have been collecting systematic data on their expectations about infants' behaviour, it turns out that the tendencies are more general than we had supposed. In our studies of physically stunted children we have been separating out those children who are normal in every other respect except their height and weight, which is below the third percentile.

Dr. Scott: I am addressing this to Dr. Kane as she can take an objective attitude towards the male society. Males live in a very controlled rigid society and with the changing labour practices which you noted in your last remark, man has more 'free time'. In this free time it appears that man perhaps is regressing if I can use the word, going back primitively to types of activity which will fit this time so we have in our activity programmes for leisure time all the primitive acts, namely food/sea searching, namely the fisherman, we have food/land searching, namely the hunter, we have the gardener with his roses, namely the farmer, we have the fire watcher, we have got the modern male, he can get these primitive elements and put them into his leisure activity and we know what the monkeys do in their leisure activities, but the question I raise is how in this free time that is available to man, is it going to be available to the cultured woman in our society what she is going to do with her primitive activities as we take the hunter, the fisherman, the farmer, in the male frame of references?

Dr. Kane: The first thing she does is take up anthropology. I think that someone else will have to comment on primitive drives; I would have to take exception to the classification of these economic activities as primitive.

Prof. Latane: I would take exception to the idea that modern man has more 'free time' than primitive man. My understanding of most of the sociological, economic and anthropological evidence is that primitive man and man in the underdeveloped countries suffers more from the fact that he has nothing to do all day, than from an excess of demands on his time. Modern affluent urban man is rather more harried than leisured.

Dr. Crawley: I was wondering about the question of measurement in terms of personality and culture. It seems to me that there must be a great difficulty in attempting to assess personality by methods which are surely culturally biased, in a transcultural way. How can this difficulty be overcome?

Dr. Kane: I think that the first thing that will have to be done is a recognition on the part of people devising psychological tests that this is a problem. Secondly, I think that a complete understanding of the cultures concerned have to be taken into account before the devising of any test. If you give a test in a society where competitiveness is completely proscribed, you are not going to have people trying to achieve success in the test. Secondly, in a society where co-operation is involved we find, especially in the case of the Australian aborigines, that they tried to make the tester an honorary member of the tribe and tried to get him to help on the test. So you are going to get a reaction to the test situation for a start. Certainly the use of tests has been very difficult in many societies.

Syndromes resulting from over-lax control—1

Causes and consequences of social contact in lower animals

BIBB LATANÉ,
Ohio State University

As an experimental social psychologist who only in the last few years has started to do intensive research with animals, I am honoured and pleased to be invited to this conference, and especially to be asked to speak on the behaviour of animals. I must say that my delight was somewhat tempered when I read the title originally proposed for my talk—'Syndromes resulting from over-lax social control in lower animals.' I am afraid that I do not understand what social control in lower animals involves, and as a result am even less clear as to just what the absence of it might entail.

Therefore, I would like to shift ground somewhat to talk about a different and, I think, more basic topic, namely, the causes and consequences of social contact in animals. What are the forces that bring animals together in pairs and groups? What motivates individuals to come together in herds, flocks and swarms? What motivates us to come together in rooms like this? Equally important, what are the consequences of this behaviour? The answers to these questions will require a great deal of research, and they are likely to be complicated. They are also likely to differ from one species to another. For example, consider the laboratory rat.

Professor Harlow has discarded his early dualistic conception of animate matter as consisting of rats and man in favour of another dualistic conception involving man and monkey. I would like to

286

propose a tripartite division including the best features of each of these formulations: a tripartite division into monkey, man and rat (not necessarily in that order). I hope to convince you tonight that there is value in studying the social behaviour of the albino laboratory rat. Rats, as I will try to show you, are quite gregarious animals, very attractive and attracted to each other, if not to monkeys and men. Their lives in this respect, however, are not nearly so complicated as ours and they provide, I think, a useful case study.

Albino rats when given the opportunity are extremely sociable. A good way to demonstrate this is to take a pair of same sex albino rats, place them in a large featureless circular open field, say four feet in diameter, and allow them freely to run around with no restraint, so that they can do whatever they want. If you were to do this, you would notice that rats will spend a lot of time exploring their environment—sniffing the walls, running around, rearing up and trying to look over the wall, and perhaps poking their noses out into the centre of the field. You would also notice, however, that rats spend a good deal of time, and an increasing amount of time, in social contact—interacting with each other, chasing each other about, climbing over and under each other, nosing each other, rubbing against each other. In fact, if you were to keep a stop watch on them, as my students and I have now done over 15,000 times in a great variety of experiments, you would probably find that they would spend somewhere in the vicinity of 40-70% of their time in direct physical contact.

Rats spend a lot of time in contact and this contact in no way compares with the amount of time that rats might spend touching non-social objects. The most seductive of the many kinds of non-social objects we have studied, an opaque tunnel, has elicited only 30% time in contact, and most non-social objects elicit well under 10%.[7 9 11 15] So we have almost a gulf between the amount of time that rats will engage in social contact, as oppose to contact with any of a variety of other kinds of objects.

I would like to summarize this evening a great deal of research very briefly and to help me I have prepared a list of ten characteristics of social behaviour in rats. Let's see how far down this list we can get.

1. Physical
2. Friendly

3. Asexual
4. Indiscriminate
5. Species-specific
6. Not based on early learning
7. Not based on static stimulus qualities
8. Interactive
9. Regulated
10. Fear-reducing

I should start off by saying that social behaviour in rats is very *physical*. If rats are not in direct physical contact, they seem to show virtually no interest in each other. If you prevent direct physical contact by interposing a screen or some other barrier between rats, you will find that they show very little attraction to each other.[4 18] I suppose this should not surprise us too much because rats have rather imperfect distance receptors and no means of communicating symbolically across space. Rats do not show, at least in this kind of situation, any sign of individual distance preference greater than zero. Physical contact is the important thing.

The contact that rats engage in is predominantly *friendly* and playful, rather than aggressive or hostile. Rarely do you see behaviour that can be coded as aggressive and we have seen virtually no instances of direct fighting between rats in a pair. I suspect this has to do with the fact that the laboratory rat, like man, is a domesticated animal and has undergone many generations of selection pressure against fighting each other or biting experimenters.

The kind of behaviour I am describing seems to be *asexual,* at least in the sense that sex is not its primary motivation. Unlike Professor Fox's impression of primates, rats do not seem to be motivated in their social behaviour by underlying sexual drives. Rats are no more sociable in cross-sex pairings than they are in same-sex pairings, and manipulations that strongly affect their sexual behaviour, such as giving females hormone injections, giving males experience to make them more sophisticated copulators, or satiating them through unlimited access to receptive partners, have no effect on social attraction.[16] I don't think that we can call the kind of behaviour I am talking about sexual or sexually motivated.

I should mention briefly that rats are rather *indiscriminate* in their social life. They don't prefer their cagemates over strangers, and they don't seem to develop individual friendships or preferences for one rat over another.[12] Other rats of the same general age and sex seem pretty much interchangeable.

However, social attraction in rats is *species-specific*. As I said before, if you put rats together in an open field they will spend 40-70% time in contact. If you put a pair of gerbils in the same kind of field, you will find that they spend 25-30% time in contact, but if you were to put a rat and a gerbil in a field together you would find a substantial decrease in attraction, down to a range of 10-15% time in contact.[17] Rats prefer rats over gerbils and gerbils prefer gerbils to rats.

Now, what causes this high level of attraction—what is it about a rat that makes it so attractive to other rats?—what makes rats so interested in spending so much time with each other? You are familiar with a number of explanations, explanations which use concepts like 'imprinting', 'social learning', or 'innate releasing mechanisms'. These explanations do seem to work for some species. Rats, however, do not always follow laws laid down for insects, fish, or precocial birds. I would like briefly to describe an experiment that makes such explanations unlikely for rats.

This experiment was designed to determine whether social attraction in rats depends on the quality of their *early contact*, on the fact that rats are raised by rats and with rats. The ideal experiment to determine this would be a maternal deprivation experiment, in which rats are raised without ever seeing another rat. Professor Levine described procedures he and Evelyn Thoman have developed to raise rats without exposure to their mother. This is a laborious and difficult, but very valuable, technique. We have taken another tack. Instead of raising rats with no mothers, we have raised them with altered mothers, mothers that have been changed so as to differ in appearance and stimulus qualities as much as possible from other rats.

We have taken expectant mothers and removed their hair by shaving them and using repeated applications of a commercial depilatory, which, by the way, is remarkably effective on rats. We fed these mothers on a garlic-infused diet which, I am told by metabolic experts, markedly changes their body odours. We clipped their whiskers and, in general, did as many different things as possible to alter their appearance, feel, and smell. For the sake of preventing possible injury, we did leave intact the hair on the mothers' heads and around their genitals. Despite their rather bizarre appearance

T

(they looked like nothing so much as miniature albino lionesses) the mothers on the whole behaved quite like normal mothers. Rats were raised either with normal or altered mothers, and either in litters with sibs, or as only children.

If social learning in rats depends on early contact with rats, raising a rat with an altered mother, or without exposure to litter mates should interfere with the development of social attraction. It turns out that these variations do not decrease the degree of attraction that rats show to other rats, either normal or altered, either at weaning or later after a period of individual housing.[11] It seems unlikely that imprinting or early social learning is crucial to the development of social behaviour in rats.

Similar evidence shows that the *static stimulus qualities* associated with a rat, its ratty appearance, feel, or smell, seem to have little importance in leading to social attraction.[9] It seems unlikely that innate releasing mechanisms are very important to social behaviour in rats.

What does seem to be important is the fact that rats are optimally and appropriately responsive to each other: they are able to *interact* (as distinguished from being able merely to act on or be acted upon).[8] If you create a surrogate rat, something that bears no superficial resemblance to another rat, but does have the capacity to interact, for example, a responsive human hand, you will find that it can, when maximally effective, be as seductive as another rat.[19] I think interaction is a necessary concept, not only to describe the social behaviour of rats, but also to understand the motives underlying it. Interaction, I think, is the basic source of social attraction in rats, and in this respect I think they are similar to man.

At the beginning I promised to talk about the consequences as well as the causes of social contact. I will have time to mention only two: its effect on further social contact, and its effect on emotional arousal or fear.

Social contact in rats is *regulated*. By this I mean only that social isolation, whether short-term or prolonged, has profound effects on the social behaviour of rats, but in the direction of making them more, not less, sociable.[1 5 10 11 14 18] A rat housed alone, in isolation, for periods as long as fifteen months or well over 90% of their lives, shows not a severe social deficit but rather an increase in social motivation, an increased desire to interact with other rats. It appears that social learning in rats is accomplished quickly and that social isolation primarily affects social motivation, for these effects are quickly reversible. The present degree of social isolation is more important than past amounts of social contact in determining sociability.

Finally, let me mention that social contact seems to have strong effects on *fear*-like behaviours. Some time ago, I left an imagined pair of rats running around in an open field, spending a great deal of time with each other. If you were to compare the behaviour of these animals, tested in pairs, with that of other rats exposed to the same situation alone you would probably notice two things:

First, you would notice that animals tested alone are much less active than animals tested in pairs, spending much less time running around the open field and up to twice as much time immobile. Single animals exposed to an unfamiliar test situation are much more likely to freeze than animals exposed to the same situation in pairs.

Second, although you might not notice it during the test, when you went to clean up the field afterward, you might be surprised to find more fecal boluses in the field to which only one rat had been exposed than in the field which contained two rats. Animals tested individually often defecate over twice as much as animals tested in pairs. Thus, it appears that the presence of another animal markedly reduces two different manifestations of fear in rodents— namely immobility or freezing, and defecation.[4][6][11][15]

From this evidence, one might think that the reason why rats like each other may be because they do reduce fear for each other. This, I hasten to add, is probably not very tenable. Experiments varying potential sources of fear show either no effects or contradictory effects. Although autonomic arousal, which should magnify fear, does lead to increased gregariousness,[3] unfamiliarity with the enviornment, which also increases fear, leads to decreased attraction.[2][14] Likewise, application of stresses, such as shock or threat of shock, decreases attraction.[6] And correlational techniques, across different strains of rats or across different individuals within a strain, show no consistent relationship between the level of expressed fear and level of attraction.

A final bit of evidence, however, does support the possibility that fear motivates affiliation in rats. Alcohol, which seems to reduce fear, at the same time makes rats less sociable.[1] In this respect, unlike many of the others I have dealt with so far, rats differ from humans. Humans tend to become more sociable and gregarious under the influence of alcohol. This is probably because humans lose some of their inhibitions about engaging in social contact. Rats on the other hand, seem to have few such inhibitions. Perhaps this is why it is remarkably hard to convince a rat to take a drink.

I hope I have been able to convince you tonight that men and rats do have something to learn from each other. Thank you.

References

1. Cappell, H., and Latané, B. 1969. Effects of alcohol and caffeine on the social and emotional behavior of the rat. *Quarterly Journal of Studies on Alcohol,* 30: 345-57.
2. Eckman, Judith; Meltzer, J.; and Latané, B. 1969. Gregariousness in rats as a function of familiarity of environment. *Journal of Personality and Social Psychology,* 11: 107-114.
3. Joy, Virginia, and Latané, B. 1971. Autonomic arousal and affiliation in rats. *Psychonomic Science,* 25: 299-300.
4. Latané, B. 1969. Gregariousness and fear in laboratory rats. *Journal of Experimental Social Psychology,* 5: 61-69.
5. Latané, B.; Cappell, H.; and Joy, Virginia. 1970. Social deprivation, housing density and gregariousness in rats. *Journal of Comparative and Physiological Psychology,* 70: 221-27.
6. Latané, B.; Friedman, Lucy; and Thomas, J. 1972. Affiliation in rats under stress. *Psychonomic Science,* 27: 39-40.
7. Latané, B. and Glass, D. C. 1968. Social and nonsocial attraction in rats. *Journal of Personality and Social Psychology,* 9: 142-46.
8. Latané, B., and Hothersall, D. Social attraction in animals. In *New Horizons in Psychology II,* ed. P. C. Dodwell. Penguine Books, in press.
9. Latané, B.; Joy, Virginia; Meltzer, J.; Lubell, B.; and Cappell, H. 1972. Stimulus determinants of social attraction in rats. *Journal of Comparative and Physiological Psychology,* 79: 13-21.
10. Latané, B.; Nesbitt, P.; Eckman, Judith and Rodin, Judith. Long- and short-term social deprivation and sociability in rats. *Journal of Comparative and Physiological Psychology,* in press.
11. Latané, B.; Poor, D.; and Sloan, L. 1972. Familiarity and attraction to social and nonsocial objects by rats. *Psychonomic Science,* 26: 171-72.
12. Latané, B.; Schneider, Emily; Waring, P.; and Zweigenhaft, R. 1971. The specificity of social attraction in rats. *Psychonomic Science,* 23: 28-29.
13. Latané, B.; Sloan, L.; and Walton, D. Effects of early contact with normal or altered rats on later social behavior. In preparation.
14. Latané, B., and Walton, D. 1972. Effects of social deprivation and familiarity with the environment on social attraction in rats. *Psychonomic Science,* 27: 9-11.

15. Latané, B., and Werner, Carol. 1971. Social and nonsocial sources of attraction in rats. *Psychonomic Science,* 24: 147-48.
16. Sloan, L., and Latané, B. 1971. Sex and social attraction in rats. St. Louis: Psychonomic Society.
17. Walton, D. and Latané, B. 1971. Effects of prior contact on cross- and within-species attraction in rats. Washington: American Psychological Association.
18. Walton, D. and Latané, B. 1972. Effects of social deprivation and familiarity with the environment on social attraction in rats. *Psychonomic Science,* 26: 4-6.
19. Werner, Carol, and Latané, B. 1970. Rats are attracted to the human hand. San Antonio: Psychonomic Society.

Syndromes resulting from over-lax control—2

Man—Family

JULES H. MASSERMAN,
President, International Association of Social Psychiatry

Professor Fox, colleagues and fellow captives, I presume Dr. Cullen intended it as a compliment when he presumed that I could summarize some thirty years of research in half that number minutes so I shall have to talk in headlines which are notoriously misleading. Permit me then to do what I can about co-relating animal research, my own and others with human experience because after all I am a card carrying analyst and I am most interested in the human aspects of it. May I indeed presume to give you certain inferences from both sets of experience, in the laboratory and in the office, which I have with some risk called bio-dynamic principles.

The first of these is that all organisms, four-footed, two-footed and I mean not only kangaroos, do act in response to physiological needs so that any organism will escape from cold, from confinement, will try to satisfy a thirst or sex. As a psychoanalyst I must admit that sex is not the only motivation.

Second, all organisms are born differently, with different capacities and have different experiences, and therefore see the world differently, each as an individual, with some ipsistic views. This brings into sharp focus what we mean by an interview clinically, an exchange of views of the universe. In order to understand any person we are communicating with we have to see how he sees it, not just as we think he ought to see it.

294

The third principle is that as we go up the evolutionary scale and I do not place man at the top of it at all, each organism develops a certain versatility, a behaviour. Sometimes it gets quite confusing for us, it is most disconcerting because we have so many choices that it is really difficult.

Then the fourth is whenever the environment seems to present problems, we have the capacity of an individual organism to cope. I shall try to confine that not only to our organism but to lower organisms than man, then it develops various behaviour patterns that to the observer were aberrant. We can label them all sorts of things in our peculiar psychiatric jargon. I shall have no time to demonstrate any of these premises, in fact they cannot be demonstrated, just might be illustrated. You can take a cat or a dog or a monkey or a rat and get it cold, confine it, get it hungry or thirsty and it will adopt various modes of behaviour, to relieve it of this physiologic stress. I have never seen a Pavlovian reflex, like an American who is for Vietnam, I hope never to see one. The responses are always contingent on the environment and there are many factors that have to be analysed, it is a gestalt response.

The second and third principles about versatility and about different views of the environment can be illustrated in various ways because they also take up social interaction. Let me give you just two instances which might illustrate the altruism, co-operation and so on among animals under laboratory conditions. Suppose you take a monkey in a divided cage with a transparent barrier and the monkey cannot get through if it sees a sign. We taught the monkey to read German. It pulls a chain and gets its food. If at the same time through the transparent barrier it sees another monkey getting an electric shock, it may refrain from pulling the chain. Like all humans it does not refrain from it very long but it does for a considerable significant period. And so we have what you could call co-altruism. One can also demonstrate that it does not depend on dominance, on sex, on comparative ages. It does depend on the previous acquaintance of the animals and their friendly relationships. You can get co-operation, even among cats, of all individualistic creatures. Suppose you have again a divided cage with a transparent barrier, and you have taught a cat to push switch, in response to a signal, go around the barrier and get the food on the next side. If you put two cats similarly trained in the same cage, one cat pushes the switch, the other one gets the food. This is a problem of course—you work, you do not eat, you hang around the trough, you do eat. They may co-operate for a little while, push a switch, eat, the one who just ate comes back and pushes the switch for its partner. That lasts about as long among cats as it does among humans—a very short time. The result is that one animal will sit by the switch which is no longer effective as a food getting device, the other will sit by the trough, because that is where it has learned to eat and have a sit-down strike. They are looking at each other. This is no biologic solution, and one animal learns, like most of us do learn, that if you work very hard, push the switch eight, ten times and get eight or ten pellets, the parasite will get about six of them, you can get around in time to get the last two. Then you have a stable social system, again as in humans. I thought that that was the end of the experiment but cats are always smarter. Some of them learn that if they pick up the switch and push it into a corner so that the electro connection always works, the automatic feeder will continue to work and nobody else has to work. And so you have this versatile adaptation among various animals.

The fourth principle I have had to revise, like most of the others, continuously. I started out in the good old analytic doctrine that neurosis comes from conflict, the Oedipus Complex. You want something very badly that you should not want and you are afraid of terrible consequences if you try to get it. And so at first we set up this business of pushing a switch, going over to feed and getting an air blast. Or in the case of a monkey, if you want a symbolic deterrent—a little toy green snake comes out at the monkey at the moment of feeding. You can call it a phallic symbol: explain that to the monkey if you like. But what happens is a terrific dilemma is set up. If you work for food and you go over and get it, there is this threat of destruction which seems to be innate in some monkeys, they can be raised in a laboratory and there is still the fear of anything sinuous which looks like a snake. You can raise them in such a way that they are not, but that is another story. Well there you have every evidence for what in humans we will call anxiety, physiologic and bio-medic. You have stereo-typed behaviour, you have, of course, inhibition not only about feeding in a cage, but anywhere else, or anything that looks like food that is in a cage. You have depressive reactions. I do wish I could show you films about this, it is awfully difficult to just state it. You have psychosomatic disturbances of severe degree. Then you have hallucinations and delusions.

Now how do you know when a monkey cannot tell you? Well how does a human tell you? By his behaviour. You have a monkey go to the food box and pick out a pellet of food and chew it and eat it. There is no food there at all. If you put real food there he will go through the glass wall of the cage. He is now living in an imaginary world. Well I am not merely interested either in inducing neurosis in cats or monkeys or humans. I am much more interested in what you do about it. Let me then point out the sort of techniques that do have human parallels, that work in a laboratory. And again I can only speak in headlines, again misleading and inadequate.

First technique is to satisfy basic needs, one of the physiologic needs. The monkey is hungry, feed it. For the time being, until it gets hungry again the dilemma is temporarily solved, just the same as we have to abolish poverty and so on in people we call neurotic in case they are hungry, starved or confined in ghettos.

Second technique is to force a solution. This is sort of drastic. The behaviour therapists do this. You push the cat or the monkey closer and closer to the food box, arousing great inhibitions, attempts to escape, but there is no escape possible. Hunger mounts —the food is very attractive, you can break through an inhibition and start feeding, almost compulsively and then the next time you do not need so much pressure.

A third technique is, just permit the monkey, once it has learnt control of the way to get food, it had learnt to push a switch and so on, to tentatively work out its own problems. It will regard the switch and sort of look at it and touch it and after a while press it and get the signal and run away, and then press it again and then get the signal and look at the food box, gradually work through a previously conflictful situation by its own techniques that it had previously acquired in its own education, as most of us do without benefit of the clergy or psychiatry.

Fourth technique is what we call group therapy. Take a neurotic cat crouching in the corner, cataleptic and so on, and put it in with normal cats that are feeding in response to this signal, it eats more readily than it would have done by itself even if you had given it the technique for resolving its situation. It will follow the crowd back to the food box and re-explore it just the same as we send the problem child to a good school, a good school meaning where the kids do what we want our child to do, and it learns that there are far better rewards for behaving in ways that are not regressive.

Fifth technique, if none of these others works, is what may be called individual psychotherapy, which simply means having some other organism than the neurotic one, the regressed evasive one trusts, and there can be any surrogate organism that it trusts. Gradually pet it, lead it, bit by bit, feed it by hand over to the food box, sound the signals at the proper time so that they are not aversive. This process of reorientation, reguidance we humans do verbally mostly, although not necessarily. We can do it in a school yard, in a classroom. We are able to do it by occupational therapy and so on. Gradually, you have the neurotic organism face, re-explore and re-master a situation which previously had been traumatic.

That leaves out what some of us psychiatrists keep doing, that is using drugs, doing various operations, electric shock and so on. We tried these in the laboratory too. What most of the drugs do and especially alcohol, is disorganize complex behaviour. Just as you know, you think you drive well, you think you drive even better if you take a few drinks, but everybody who drives with you knows you drive a lot less well when your judgement is impaired. It is simply that a very complex behaviour is disorganized. Now neurotic behaviour is a highly complex compendium of responses and if you feed a neurotic cat—not so much as a monkey, they do not take it that way—alcohol, it disorganizes some of the phobias, the aversions, the regressions and so on. It begins feeding, in sort of a drunken fashion, but it is feeding again. The trouble is it learns the effects of alcohol. I wish I could show a film in which these neurotic cats, once they have experienced the effects of alcohol, start becoming alcoholic cats. If you give them a choice of a mug full of milk and an Alexander Cocktail which is milk with ten per cent alcohol, they will go straight for the cocktail and drink it. Until you clear the neurosis by other means, in which case the alcohol consumption goes down just the same as is clinically true. Electric shock, and various brain operations work the same way by disorganizing the capacity of the central nervous system to process highly complex behaviour which is what we call neurotic or psychotic, but these leave permanent effects in the animals, whereas alcohol not so much, other drugs not so much either. And they leave permanent effects in humans too. Well what then shall we add with regard to human behaviour? Again permit me to talk in unconscionable brevity. We have to consider what I would call the ultimate UR adaptations of humans. Humans have three primary motivations.

First to preserve their physical well-being and longevity in skills; we all need these.

Second to assure our social securities, and here I can just gently touch on what I was supposed to talk about—family relationships. They start with the family relationships, and go on to the tribe, the clan, the nation and eventually human brotherhood.

Third, humans need, what dogs also have by the way, a faith in some sort of superior being that seems to order their environment. So we have our philosophies, our theologies, our religions too. If any of these are transgressed we lose our faith in our own health. If we lose our faith in our social belongingness, and lose our faith in our philosophies or our theologies we are terribly distressed. Then all psychotherapy, which is a bastard word, really consists, if it is going to be effective at all, in restoring physical well being, in restoring social hegemony, social relationships, through the medium of the therapist, who is for the time being a surrogate friend, trying to restore a philosophy in which we can attain serenity. If any method of psychotherapy does that it is successful, if it does not it is not.

Syndromes resulting from over-lax control—3

Man—Society

R. CARINO,*
State University of New York

The type of control I have chosen to talk about today is self-control. In this paper I will try to show that the more irresponsible an individual is made to appear, the more responsible the state becomes for controlling him. Once a person is relieved of the obligation of responsibility for his actions, his personal freedom becomes a threat to the preservation of social order. Society and its leaders then demand external enforcement to protect the individual from harming himself and others. This power and authority to control is delegated to the state as a necessity to the creation of irresponsibility. Lawmakers, physicians, and social reformers all take part in the administration of this concept and have disguised the stigma and discrimination of incompetence with benevolent concern. The syndrome resulting from this creation of personal irresponsibility is society's misguided attempt to dehumanize humans 'for the sake of humanity'.

At a time when peace and love are considered basic to the solution of life's problems, it has seemed humanitarian to look upon society's deviants as bereft of reason, and incapable of restraining themselves from acts which are offensive or injurious to their

*Nominated by D. T. Szasz. We are grateful to Dr. Carino for his participation at short notice.

fellow man. The term used to describe such people is 'mentally ill' —the so-called 'sick' people who cause discord in an otherwise harmonious symphony of community life. If the madman is a sick man who lacks reason and self-control, then the only morally proper reaction is to control him for his own welfare, the welfare of others, and that of the community.

Although, to this day, no suitable definition of 'mental illness' has ever been made, nevertheless, it continues to be the label which justifies the denial of human rights. Sick, incompetent, irresponsible, unable to know his own needs, the psychiatric patient is forced to submit to being controlled—that is the logic of involuntary psychiatric intervention. But the label is a mistake, problems in living are not diseases, and the logic is weak. The madman is not a sick man; he may be troubled, stupid, criminal, or psychotic, but he is not diseased. Controlling him is not a cure—it is coercion. The denial of human rights in order to treat, seems sometimes logical—but it is always unjust.

The striking thing about freedom is that the world appears threatened by it. Free choice has dropped in rank from a cherished virtue to a decision capable of error and therefore is seen as too dangerous to allow. Psychiatry is being called upon to stamp out autonomy and build a uniform society greater than that manufactured by the gods. From this behaviouristic point of view, what the world needs now is genetic manipulation and chemical control of emotion so that in time, only physical and mental masterpieces will be delivered from artificial wombs. Genocide for the sake of love. Dehumanization for the sake of humanity.

Obviously, something went wrong somewhere. The sciences which claim to aid humanity could not have been fooled unless the disguise was clever and altruistic.

When the psychiatrist came upon the scene of public life he was confronted with the massive power of common law—the body of general rules and principles that must be applied impartially in all cases. Two major characteristics inherent in the psychology of this relationship between psychiatry and the law can be discerned. The first is the fact that the psychiatrist is a citizen who, like the law giver or law officer, is concerned with the proper protection of his community, biased by its traditions, and subject to its failings, prejudices and more positive trends. The second characteristic is that, inspired and armed with new knowledge, he is a humanitarian reformer frequently thrown into the inevitable conflict with the old traditions of the law.

As a citizen he seeks protection by the law—as a humanitarian he seeks the abolition of certain laws and legal procedures as useless, injurious and offensive to psychiatric theory and to the ultimate good of man and society.

Never clearly differentiating for himself the situations in which he was a servant of the law and those in which he challenged its validity, the psychiatrist only gradually developed his attitude through his own experience and education. The criterion of his scientific evolution can be found only in the psychiatrist's attitude toward mental conflict and the degree to which he is guided by the therapeutic intent.

At that point in history when the psychiatrist called for commitment and the courts called for imprisonment, psychiatry and the law faced its fatal battle—how to treat the human sufferer with respect for his human rights. Could the madman be handled without forcing him to leave his madness? Could he be made better without denying his freedom? Could incarceration be justified?

On the battlefield, psychiatry and the law decided upon a series of adjustments of their various differences and developed an agreement as to the importance of stressing that madness is a disease. Thus the notion that the insane defendant is a sick man, irresponsible for his behaviour, who should not be punished with justice but rather incarcerated with love.

Psychiatry and the law then ceased to consider what an individual deserves and considered only what would cure him. As a result he was tacitly removed from the sphere of justice altogether and instead of a person, a subject of rights, we now had a mere object, a patient, a case. The demand for cure then became more important than the demand for justice and it was considered morally correct to deny individuals their human rights in order to treat them.

In the battle neither law nor psychiatry was victorious; rather, both were defeated, with error and stupidity conquering by default. For mental illness is indeed a myth, 'a metaphor which we have come to mistake for a fact. We call people physically ill when their body-functioning violates certain anatomical and physiological norms' (Szasz, 1963). There is no illness when personal conduct violates certain ethical, political and social norms.

The idea of mental conflict as illness has corrupted both law and psychiatry. Together they have decided to consider problems in living as medical maladies. Together they have removed self-control as a personal necessity and replaced it with necessary mental institutions and their contraptions. Together they have failed to recognize that justice is a form of love, and have agreed to treat man as something less than human—as an incomplete being that requires programming and control. As a result, laws are more unjust and psychiatry more inhuman; human rights fall second to the greater good of humanity; incarceration is the loving, helping hand to the threatened community; and we are left with the control of some for the sake of all.

With a misguided attitude toward mental conflict, therapeutic intent has become the poison camouflaged by the sweetness of the wine.

In 1970 the United States Department of Health, Education and Welfare advised its nation: 'What can the average citizen do about mental illness? The most important thing to do is realize that mental illness is an illness and that the mentally ill are people who are troubled and need help. The mentally ill may say and do things that seem inappropriate or unusual or even shocking, but they say and do things because they are sick.' What kind of denigration is this? Is a woman saddened by the fact that she can't have children, mentally ill? Is an individual who uses drugs to cope with or rebel against an intolerable family situation, mentally ill? Is a cigarette smoker who is not only a danger to himself but also to others, mentally ill? Is an old man who wants to die because he has been rejected by his selfish children, mentally ill? Is a man who claims to be the Son of God and allows Himself to be crucified, mentally ill? Is a state that forces people to submit to electrical stimulation, chemical restraint, neurosurgery and calls it therapeutic, mentally ill? Is a country that justifies its murders by calling it war, mentally ill? Is this the inappropriate, unusual and shocking behaviour that is labelled 'sick'? When did morality, ethics, and politics become medical phenomena? Why are human tragedies treated as medical problems?

Like so many times in the past, a transient sense of value has caused some people to suffer and endure unnecessary and illogical punishment. Christians have been crucified, lepers exiled, blacks enslaved, heretics murdered, witches burnt, Jews gassed, homosexuals humiliated, women oppressed. The reasons for these tragic

examples of human error seemed morally justified at the time; today
they draw outrage from the general public. Involuntary psychiatric
intervention seems morally justifiable to many; to some it is out-
rageous. Mental patients across the United States are beginning to
organize and demand the decency and respect accorded to other
human beings—and rightly so. It is amazing that in this day, the
people most concerned with maintaining the humanness of our race
are those that have been so unjustly abused by it. Perhaps one can
realize what freedom of choice and personal responsibility mean
only when these human virtues have been lost. These stigmatized
people who have *lived* beyond freedom and dignity are warning
us to stop and take notice of the direction in which we are heading
—but few will listen. Instead the public ear is turned towards the
state—like the National Institute of Mental Health which claims
that the mentally ill say and do inappropriate, unusual and shocking
things because they are sick. Once again the masses may be march-
ing in the wrong direction under the leadership of prominent, powerful and ignorant men.

Kenneth B. Clark, President of the American Psychological
Association, recently stated: 'It is now possible—indeed, imperative
—to reduce human anxieties, tensions, hostilities, violence, cruelty,
and the destructive power irrationalities of man which are the basis
of wars. It is an awesome fact that a few men in the leadership
positions in the industrialized nations of the world now have the
power to determine among themselves the survival or extinction of
human civilization. There is no way of predicting the personal and
emotional stability of these leaders with the life-and-death power
over mankind. . . . The masses of human beings are now required to
live and continue to work on faith, hope, denial and the acceptance
of the chances that their powerful leaders will have the strength to
use their power wisely and morally. Given these contemporary facts,
it would seem logical that a requirement imposed upon all power-
controlling leaders and those who aspire to such leadership would
be that they accept and use the earliest perfected form of psycho-
technological, biochemical intervention which would assume their
positive use of power and reduce or block the possibility of their
using power destructively.'

No longer is it enough to fear the insane; we must now also fear
the same. Eminent leaders must be chemically protected from
human error. Not only must we prevent the assassination of a head

of state, we must prevent our assassination by a head of state. Obviously this isn't enough because it still leaves the rest of us open to the error flowing from freedom of choice. B. F. Skinner claims we must all be protected from one another. No longer demanding justice, the world is satisfied only with success. Total control for the sake of preservation. Dehumanization for the sake of humanity.

Dr. Thomas Szasz ends his book *Law, Liberty and Psychiatry* this way. 'Many modern psychotherapists have adopted as their credo, Socrates' declaration that the unexamined life is not worth living. But for modern man this is not enough. We should pledge ourselves to the proposition that the irresponsible life is not worth living either.'

References

1. Szasz, T. S. 1961. The Myth of Mental Illness: Foundations of a theory of personal conduct. New York: Hoeber-Harper.
2. Szasz, T. S. 1963. Law, Liberty, and Psychiatry: An inquiry into the social uses of mental health practices. New York: The Macmillan Company.
3. Szasz, T. S. 1970. Ideology and Insanity: Essays on the psychiatric dehumanization of man. New York: Anchor.
4. Szasz, T. S. 1970. The Manufacture of Madness: A comparative study of the inquisition and the mental health movement. New York: Harper & Row.
5. Zilboorg, G., and Henry, G. 1941. A History of Medical Psychology. New York: Norton.

Discussion

after papers

by LATANÉ, MASSERMAN AND CARINO

Prof. Lavelle: What is the evidence that the rats do not recognize other rats as individuals?

Prof. Latané: Over a series of days some rats have been paired with the same partners, while others have been paired with different partners each day. The first condition thus would allow the development of specific 'friendships', the second, of course, would not. There is no difference in the amount of contact between these two conditions.

Rats housed in pairs were tested with either their cage mate

U

or with a pair-housed animal from a different cage. Again, there is no difference in their degree of attraction.

Rats are as much attracted to a strange rat as to a familiar rat. Although it may be possible to train rats to show individual recognition, their attraction to other rats appears to be general.

Prof. Russell Davis: How does the cat given a greater degree of control over the experimental situation work through to his own kind of solution? Has he to be taught the technique of control before he is made neurotic or does he find the solution after he becomes neurotic?

Dr. Masserman: The cat has to be taught ahead of time the technique which it can later use to re-explore and master its dilemma. In the Air Force if a good pilot crash lands, he is immediately made fly again to reassert his previous mastery.

Dr. Scott: Running throughout the conference there is a very enigmatic problem that I have been trying to understand. We think in my prison language of the captive and captor, what about the 'captive experimenter' and his 'captive'—have you any observations about their pathological interdependency? What happens to the experimenter in relation to his animals, in other words his reversed conditioning or reactions in terms of personality?

Dr. Masserman: Some years ago, I had a Korean laboratory assistant. Koreans raise dogs without devotion and kill and eat them any time and my assistant could never cure a neurotic animal. They would sense immediately that here was a person who did not really care about them.

Prof. Fox: A number of people during the discussion are stereotyping certain individuals from their experience of one or a few members of some racial group and this is to be avoided.

Prof. Lavelle: Has the case been tested in which three animals were put into a situation where one was required to help another in distress. Does the 'apathetic bystander' have a biological basis in other animals?

Dr. Masserman: If a dominant animal becomes particularly traumatical, two or three of its subordinates may gang in an alliance and put him in his place.

Prof. Latané: There have been a number of experiments in which rats and other animals appear to perform or learn responses which in some way 'help' other animals. These behaviours can often be explained in terms of more self-centred motivations. I have done one direct experiment on 'bystander intervention' in rats by putting pairs of free-roving rats in a field, establishing a base line of social contact, and then attaching a large alligator clip to the tail of one of the rats. This, of course, causes it considerable distress. For the first few minutes after application of the alligator clip we saw no change in approach behaviour whatsoever. However, this was followed by gradually increasing avoidance. The 'victims' tended to attack anyone who approached them. I suspect that this operates among people also—those in distress sometimes are likely to resent or repel help.

Prof. Fox: Pheromones are produced in the urine when rats are psychologically or physically traumatized, while other species vocalize and may display fear; this could certainly stop a partner from performing for a while. I am therefore disputing many experimental situations that claim to demonstrate 'altruism' when simply the traumatized animal's behaviour 'cuts-off' the ongoing operant behaviour of its so-called altruistic partner.

Prof. Lifton: I would like to respond to Dr. Carino. I do not think that his very impassioned statement about very important matters should be ignored. I agree with two major themes of his paper that the so-called normal people in our society are more likely to do us in than the abnormal ones—certainly, my own studies regarding Vietnam and Hiroshima bear this out. The second point I would like to agree with is that the whole relationship of psychiatry and the law has gotten mired down. The point I would like to raise and ask him to comment more about is the whole issue of responsibility, whether there are situations where he would feel that the State or certain groups in the State should take responsibility towards each citizen having minimal income, minimal living conditions and related to that the fact that so called normal people are more dangerous to us than so called abnormal people. It does not necessarily mean that people we label as schizophrenic would be able to fend for themselves without various kinds of assistance and indeed at times unable to assume certain kinds of responsibilities that it would be much better for all if they could assume.

Dr. Masserman: Does Dr. Carino hold that man has a regard as to what this does to others? And what does he really mean by mental disease? There are a great many people who try suicide at times. If they are rescued by a psychiatrist or by a society, 88% are glad that they were not permitted to commit suicide.

Dr. Carino: Rousseau once said that man is born free and finds himself forever in chains. But perhaps man is really born in chains and the battle of his life is fought for liberation. I do see the possibility of situations, both social and psychological, where man might be considered irresponsible. But this is rare, especially in the realm of insanity. Psychiatric value judgements are used for the benefit of social control rather than for an individual's contentment. We are doing a great injustice to man by controlling the many thousands that we do under the guise of psychiatric treatment. I do feel that suicide is a personal right, a choice of death over life, many times the only free solution to problems in living. The argument on mental disease is an argument in semantics. For how can moral, political, and ethical problems, human tragedies, be treated as physiological and anatomical abnormalities? The horror lies in the irrational assumption that mental conflict is an illness that must be treated even at the cost of the loss of human rights. We are no longer concerned with what an individual deserves, but only with what will 'cure' him. The qualities of freedom, choice and responsibility should apply to all men—the crazy and the sane.

Prof. Cherry: I have considerable sympathy with the last speaker. 'To be human is to be in a state of dilemma.' All human beings are continually in a state of dilemma: you can never satisfy all your optima. You maximize one thing, at the expense of another. I cannot agree that suicide is a personal affair, nothing is personal. I am a social animal; everything I do impinges on others, there is no such thing as utter altruism or utter selfishness. The next point is that 'all great truth begins as heresy'. All social change is the result of departures from the norm. The average man is the menace to human society; there are simply so many more of them! The other point I wanted to make is that free will is an assumption that all human institutions must make but I do not know any test of the hypothesis of 'free will'. I wonder if anyone can think of such a test? To me it is an act of faith, a necessary assumption.

Prof. Russell Davis: Now I think Dr. Carino could readily attack some things psychiatrists do—there are bad things and good things. It was one of the early psychiatrists—Philippe Pinel—who took the chains off. I suppose psychiatrists are as confused as others are but they have in some sense been champions of freedom. They have also added to tyranny. Ultimately you do have to have people who attempt to understand what is happening when people get into distress and difficulties, and to find ways in which they can be helped. What we are doing at the moment is clearly not very effective, but at least we try.

Prof. O'Doherty: The problem underlying the discussion is not one that can be solved within psychology or psychiatry. It is a problem of values. Weber did not say that there were no values, nor that the study of man and society was independent of values, but that values cannot be established by the empirical or positivistic study of man and society. All you can find out by studying man and society are statements of what happens to be the case, not what ought to be the case and you cannot derive what ought to be the case from what happens to be the case.

There is an enormous difference between the statistical norm and the ideal norm of what man ought to be. To find what he is and find the statistical distributions are very important but they do not tell us anything at all about how he ought to behave. This conference, which is very good indeed, might find itself trapped into thinking that it could determine what man ought to be, ought to do and it cannot do that.

Dr. Scott: Personal irresponsibility, social dangerousness—are you correlating them? Because I think that we may be dealing with a concept of social dangerousness under the fraudulent front of personal irresponsibility, or as if they are gradients on the same scale.

Dr. Carino: We assume that many people are without reason, cannot control themselves, do not know what is for their own good and as physicians we say we must help this man do what he cannot do for himself. In this way it is a means of social control.

Dr. Scott: You are saying control of dangerousness is a social control in human relationships. If a person is socially dangerous, he should be brought under control. I agree with this concept.

Dr. Carino: If a person is socially dangerous, and has committed a crime, he should be punished by the law. If he is socially dangerous and has not committed a crime there is no reason to touch him.

Dr. Masserman: I am sorry—I cannot quite follow. We should not send our children to school if they do not want to go.

I am sorry, I do not agree. There are times, when I did not want to do things and I was very happy when somebody persuaded me to do them. Is the idea that we wait until the crime is committed by the paranoiac or a plane is crashed by an epileptic or social tragedy has to supervene before we try to prevent it? It seems to me a paradox.

Prof. Fox: A good point there, we do have ability to predict but the misuse of predictive knowledge could ultimately lead to repressive control.

Dr. Masserman: Let me cite actual experience. Some twenty years ago I was asked by missionary societies in our country to examine candidates for the missionary field, at a time when one-third of the people they sent out broke down in the field, with dire consequences to himself, his family, his mission and christianity. After I began steering one in six couples to other vocations, the incidence of failures dropped to less than 3% with a fifteen year follow-up. Psychiatric techniques do have some predictive validity. To wait to apply them only therapeutically after some tragedy happens seems to me cruel and contrary to the preventive ideal of modern medicine.

Dr. Lewis: The implication from what Dr. Carino was saying was that psychiatrists were going out and seeking patients. I always understood that one of the basic tenets of psychiatric treatment was that the patient must want to be treated, in other words the patient seeks out the psychiatrist.

Dr. McGrath: As a clinician I think that we are possibly flattering this contribution by dealing with it at a philosophical level. At a clinical level one just has to think of the patient who goes through a depressive cycle. At a certain point in that cycle he is suicidal. One deals with that. One treats him either by ECT or by giving certain anti-depressant drugs and he recovers. Six months or possibly years later he goes through exactly the same cycle. Should one just let him go through with suicide, is one saying that this is not a transient illness? Has it got anything at all to do with individual choice—individual liberties?

Dr. Carino: I think that in that case the person would be depressed and suicidal but he would not be ill.

Prof. Fox: I would like to know what he is doing in that interim three years in the cycle, he might be intensively creative during that time. Many of these drugs may produce a tonic mid-state between the high-low mood oscillation that we all go through. Certainly for the extreme maniac-depression such extreme oscillation should be reduced but perhaps not eliminated by making an emotional plateau. All systems oscillate and therapy should not destroy this normal rhythmicity.

Dr. Kinzel: Many people who are labelled dangerous are labelled dangerous at about the 200th or 300th episode. It is really not a matter of predicting dangerous behaviour, it is a matter of recognizing the presence of it. The problem then becomes what do you do with this man, how do you manage him, how can we help him. I think that your points are well taken if you are talking about the abuses of the law. It is really the abuses of the law that you are talking about and not the abuses of psychiatry.

Dr. Carino: I am stating that the medical model has no place in psychiatry and that all involuntary psychiatric intervention is unjustified.

Dr. Murray: Anyone who visited Kingsley Hall in the East End of London in the 1960s and saw what treatment was like in those days and compared what one sees in the worst psychiatric hospital today to the faecal contamination and smearings at Kingsley Hall would tend to believe that the hospital however bad it may be has more to offer.

Behavioural engineering — reconstruction of responses

The process and practice of participant modelling treatment*

ALBERT BANDURA,
Stanford University

The recent years have witnessed an active growth of treatments based upon learning principles. These approaches differ from conventional interview methods, not only in how they view the causes of human behaviour, but also in what they select as the *content*, the *locus*, and the *agents* of treatment. With regard to content, therapeutic efforts are mainly directed toward the actual problems requiring modification instead of verbal reports. Therapists, therefore, devote the major portion of their time to changing the conditions producing behavioural dysfunctions rather than conversing about them.

To enhance successful results, treatment is typically carried out in the natural settings in which the psychological problems arise. It may be conducted in the home, in the school, in work situations, or in the larger community, depending upon the source of the critical determinants. The third factor is concerned with who implements the corrective practices. Change programmes are generally

*Research by the author discussed in this article was supported by Public Health Research Grant M–5162 from the National Institute of Mental Health.

carried out under professional supervision by persons who have intensive contact with the client and can therefore serve as powerful therapeutic agents. Because of their close association, such persons often exercise considerable control over the very conditions that affect the client's behaviour. By treating the actual problems in the context within which they arise by influential members in those settings, social learning approaches are ideally suited for achieving generalized and enduring changes in psychological functioning. The farther one departs from these optimal conditions, the weaker the results are likely to be.

A full examination of the social learning procedures that have been devised to modify different psychological conditions falls beyond the limits of this paper. This presentation will focus mainly on the treatment of anxiety disorders by participant modelling and the mechanisms through which it achieves its effects.

In the modification of anxiety conditions behaviour therapists tend to direct their attention primarily to emotional arousal. The desensitization procedure devised by Wolpe (1958) is conducted on the principle of minimization of anxiety arousal. Treatment strategies are therefore keyed to this factor. Aversive stimuli are presented in small doses and promptly withdrawn whenever the client experiences anxiety. Should disturbing emotional reactions be evoked, there are essentially two things the therapist can do—relax the client and reduce the threat value of the aversive scenes. As emotional responses to weaker threats are eliminated, more stressful situations are progressively introduced.

More recently, avoidance behaviour has been treated by flooding procedures, which rely upon maximization of anxiety arousal. In this approach, intense anxiety is elicited by prolonged exposure to the most threatening situations. The therapist's main efforts are aimed at inducing and sustaining anxiety at high levels without relief until the reactions are extinguished.

Coupled with the anxiety focus is a heavy reliance upon symbolic renditions of aversive events. In both desensitization and flooding treatments emotional responses are typically extinguished to imaginal representations of anxiety provoking situations. Results of laboratory studies (Bandura, 1969; Paul, 1969) demonstrate that elimination of anxiety to imagined threats produces some degree of improvement in behavioural functioning. However, there is a notable transfer loss of therapeutic effects from symbolic to real-life threats

(Agras, 1967; Barlow, Leitenberg, Agras and Wincze, 1969). It is not at all uncommon for clients to respond fearfuly when confronted with intimidating situations after the imaginal counterparts have been thoroughly neutralized. Such transfer decrements are understandable considering that complete response generalization rarely occurs when treated events differ significantly from the natural ones.

The participant modelling approach favours successful performance as the primary vehicle of change. Persons suffering from intractable inhibitions, of course, are not about to co what they dread. The therapist must, therefore, arrange the enviornment in such a way that, despite himself, the incapcitated client can perform successfully. This is achieved by enlisting a variety of supportive aids and protective controls. To begin with, the threatening *activities are repeatedly modelled* to show the client how they can be effectively performed and that the consequences he fears do not in fact occur. *Joint performance* with the therapist, who offers physical assistance when needed, enables apprehensive clients to engage in threatening activities that they would not consider doing on their own. Highly demanding or intimidating performances are reduced to *graduated subtasks* of increasing difficulty so that at any given step participants are only asked to do what is clearly within their immediate capabilities. Treatment is conducted in this stepwise fashion until eventually the most trying activities are performed skilfully and farlessly.

Another method for overcoming response inhibition is to have the client practice the avoided behaviour over *graduated temporal intervals*. As will be shown later, obsessive-compulsives who spend long hours in cleaning rituals to avoid contamination can initially be led to handle dirty objects without ritualistic washing for manageable short periods, but they would refuse to do so if required, from the outset, to endure distress over a long time. By gradually extending the time interval clients perform with equanimity activities that earlier would have produced intolerable distress.

Arrangement of *protective conditions* that reduce the likelihood of feared consequences is a further effective means of weakening dysfunctional restraints that retard the process of change. Thus, for example, snake phobics are willing to touch snakes, which ordinarily they would not do, provided the model holds the snake securely by the head and tail (Bandura, Blanchard and Ritter, 1969); and acrophobics will climb scarey heights given the security of the therapist's physical support (Ritter, 1969b).

During early phases of treatment, therapists use whatever supplementary aids are necessary to initiate behavioural changes. As treatment progresses, however, the supportive aids and protective controls are gradually removed so that clients come to function effectively without assistance. Although the provisional supports undoubtedly attenuate emotional arousal, performance is not deferred until anxiety reactions have been extinguished. Rather, successful action is considered to be one of the best eradicators of anxiety.

Modelling with guided participation

The therapeutic approach combining modelling with guided participation has yielded impressive results both in eliminating anxiety disorders (Bandura, Blanchard and Ritter, 1969; Ritter, 1969a), and in developing behavioural competencies (Bandura, 1971a). The compound procedure contains the following three major components:

(1) *Modelling*. The desired behaviour is repeatedly modelled, preferably by different models who demonstrate progressively more difficult performances. In competence training, complex patterns of behaviour are broken down into the requisite subskills and organized hierarchically to ensure optimal progress. In producing disinhibitory effects, anxious clients observe models engaging in progressively more threatening activities without experiencing any adverse consequences.

(2) *Guided Practice*. After the demonstrations, clients are provided with necessary guidance and ample opportunities to enact the modelled behaviour at each step in the graduated sequence under favourable conditions. The various supportive and protective aids described earlier are used whenever needed to assist clients through difficult performances.

(3) *Success Experiences*. Modelling and guided performance are ideally suited for inducing psychological changes, but the resultant behaviours are unlikely to endure unless they prove effective when put into practice in everyday life. Clients must therefore experience sufficient success in the use of what they have learned. This is best achieved by a transfer programme in which newly acquired skills

are first tried in natural situations likely to produce favourable results, and then extended to more unpredictable and venturesome circumstances.

In the weakest therapeutic approaches, those relying upon conversational influences, all three components are essentially absent. Therapists favouring such techniques tend to display a limited range of responses, and what they do exemplify most prominently may have little functional value for those seeking their help, who are for the most part, left to devise new modes of behaviour and to try them in their extratherapeutic interactions. Modelling is now increasingly employed, but in many instances its potential is not fully realized because the treatment either fails to provide sufficient practice in the modelled activities or it lacks an adequate transfer programme that helps clients to strengthen their new skills under advantageous conditions. Given appropriate demonstration, guided practice, and success experiences, the multiform method achieves excellent results.

The comparative effectivenss of participant modelling for producing behavioural, affective, and attitudinal changes was initially evaluated in an elaborate design by Bandura, Blanchard, and Ritter (1969). The participants in this project were adolescents and adults who suffered from snake phobias that adversely affected their lives.

One group received the standard form of desensitization involving paired association of relaxation with imaginal representations of snake scenes of increasing aversiveness. A second group participated in a self-administered symbolic modelling treatment in which they observed a film depicting children and adults engaging in progressively more intimidating interactions with a snake. They reviewed aversive scenes repeatedly under self-induced relaxation until the depicted events were thoroughly neutralized.

The third group of phobics received the treatment combining live modelling with guided performance. After observing intimate snake interaction behaviour repeatedly modelled by the therapist, clients were aided through demonstration and protective measures to perform progressively more frightening responses. At each step the therapist himself performed the activities fearlessly and gradually led clients into touching, stroking, and holding the midsection of the snake's body with gloved and then bare hands for increasing periods while the therapist held the snake securely by the head and tail. After clients could touch the snake under these secure conditions, anxieties about contact with the snake's head area and entwining tail were similarly extinguished. The therapist again performed the responses fearlessly and then they both performed them jointly. As clients became more courageous the therapist gradually

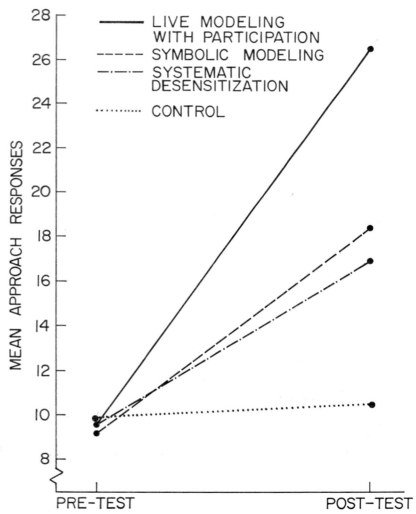

Fig. 1. Mean number of approach responses performed by individuals before and after receiving different forms of treatment and by nontreated controls. Bandura, Blanchard and Ritter, 1969.

reduced his level of participation and control over the snake until eventually clients were able to tolerate the squirming snake in their laps without assistance, to let the snake loose in the room and retrieve it, and to let it crawl freely over their bodies.

As depicted graphically in Fig. 1, nontreated controls remained unalterably fearful. Symbolic modelling and desensitazion produced substantial reductions in phobic behaviour, while participant modelling proved to be unusually powerful, completely eliminating phobias after approximately two hours of treatment.

In order to demonstrate that in cases achieving only partial improvement, the major deficits reside in the method rather than in the client, all subjects who failed to attain maximum performances, including the controls, were subsequently administered the participant modelling treatment. Phobic behaviour was throughly extinguished in all of these cases within a brief period regardless

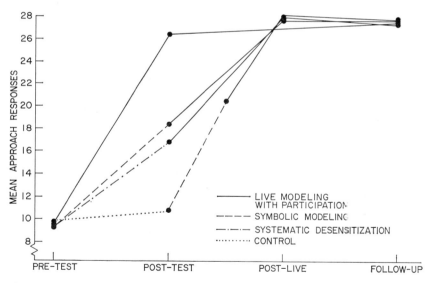

Fig. 2. Mean number of approach responses performed by individuals before and after (post-test) receiving different treatments. Controls were subsequently given symbolic modelling without relaxation. All individuals in the desensitization, symbolic modelling and treated control conditions who failed to perform the terminal tasks then received the treatment combining live modelling with guided participation (post-live). Approach behaviour was measured again in a follow-up study conducted one month later. Bandura, Blanchard and Ritter, 1969.

of their age, sex, anxiety proneness, and severity of avoidance behaviour (Fig. 2).

Hardy (1969) has evolved a highly promising method for treating agoraphobia, a condition that has been highly refractory to change. The disorder typically originates in an experience of overwhelming anxiety. As the person rushes home he experiences immense relief. Sooner or later he suffers similar anxiety, and again the aversive emotional reactions subside in the security of the home. Following several such experiences, the person begins to dread excursions outside the home, which takes on powerful safety value. Avoidance behaviour generalizes to an increasing number of places until the person becomes completely housebound. The disastrous consequences of household confinement now overshadow any original concerns. Less extreme phobics restrict their activities and simply become adept at making excuses for not venturing into perturbing situations.

Hardy employs performance of activities during graduated massive exposure to feared situations until the clients' anxieties and phobic behaviour are eliminated. Clients accompany the therapist into the avoided situations over a period of several days. The longer they are exposed to the aversive events, the more dramatic is the experience that what they dread does not happen. Since a variety of things may assume aversive properties, the specific performance tasks differ from case to case. Transportation phobics ride trains and buses; those who dread automobile travel drive freeways and mountain roads; flying phobics board planes during servicing and then make regular flights with the therapist to neighbouring places; clients who fear bridges repeatedly cross bridges; those who shun supermarkets or department stores accompany the therapist on shopping trips; acrophobics ride elevators and climb scarey heights; claustrophobics visit enclosed places, while those who become apprehensive in crowds walk through busy city streets; clients who dread public speaking deliver simulated talks; and obsequious individuals who invite maltreatment through their passivity are given self-assertive training.

As the clients' anxieties diminish the therapist reduces his support and guided participation. He sends the clients on gradually longer missions alone while he stands by and waits for them. Later, solo excursions are arranged for clients to carry out on their own. They are asked to perform previously threatening activities that bring them to specific locations from which they call after completing their missions. To reinforce and extend therapeutic changes, alumni functions are scheduled. Ex-phobics regularly engage as a group in activities they formerly dreaded. They convene social gatherings, automobile jaunts, mountain excursions, shopping trips, and theatre outings.

Hardy reports that of 100 severe phobics treated by this method, 80% achieve extinction of their phobic behaviour after several days of intensive treatment. Of these cases, approximately half require some supplementary treatment in the form of additional performance assignments or modification of family interactions to ensure continued improvement.

Participant modelling with ritual prevention has been recently applied to chronic obsessive-compulsives who remained incapacitated for many years by their incessant washing and safety checking (Rachman, Hodgson and Marks, 1971; Rachman, Hodgson and Marzillier, 1970). Therapists performed the repugnant behaviour either in graduated stages or at highest level after which clients engaged in the same activities without resorting to their compulsive rituals for increasing periods of time. Assessments based on a variety of measures revealed enduring reductions in compulsive behaviour. Success rates of different versions of the multi-form approach indicate that ritual prevention, a method originally reported by Meyer (1966), plays a vital role in the extinction process (Hodgson, Rachman and Marks, 1972). The authors suggest that supervised home treatment, in which clients perform disturbing activities but refrain from the compulsive rituals, can augment the therapeutic benefits. Since compulsives tend to impose burdensome restrictions on other members of the family, changes are further expedited by withdrawing familial reinforcement of compulsive behaviour and substituting rewarding activities as clients become freed from their time-consuming rituals.

Conditions maintaining defensive behaviour

The notable success accompanying action-oriented treatments raises issues concerning the conditions maintaining defensive behaviour. One possibility is that events become endowed with anxiety-provoking properties through adventitious or genuine but transitory association with aversive experiences. Thereafter, any thoughts about, or tentative approach responses toward, and negatively valenced events arouse anxiety which is promptly reduced by defensive acts that either forestall or avoid the subjective threat. By this process, defensive behaviour becomes self-perpetuating. In effect, the situation that has acquired arousal potential now becomes the cause, even though the historical causes may cease to exist. These are essentially the laboratory conditions under which intractable avoidance behaviour is created and maintained. After a formerly innocuous stimulus acquires threat value by paired association with shock, it can sustain a variety of avoidance responses long after shock has been discontinued.

Conditioned threats not only maintain defensive reactions learned originally to painful stimulation, but they can serve as the vehicle for further acquisition and self-perpetuation of new modes of deviant behaviour. In Miller's (1948) classic study of avoidance, animals that learned to fear a formerly neutral stimulus continued to run from it after the situation was rendered objectively harmless by removing the paired shocks. When running was impeded but the animals could escape the conditioned threat by rotating a wheel, wheel-turning was rapidly learned and perpetuated by fear reduction. When conditions were further changed so that wheel-turning no longer provided escape but bar-passing did, the former defensive response was discarded while the latter became strongly established. A subjective threat thus fostered a succession of defensive activities within a currently benign environment.

Successful avoidance of threats that no longer exist keeps behaviour out of touch with reality. Participant modelling provides a reliable and effective means for securing reality testing. When historical and contemporary determinants differ, as they generally do, defensive behaviour is successfully eliminated by neutralizing current subjective threats, but may be little affected by insight into its origins.

Psychodynamic theories view phobic behaviour as representing internally generated anxieties that are displaced and externally projected. For this perspective, the phobic actually fears his dangerous impulses and tabooed temptations rather than the external events per se. By restricting his activities he presumably protects himself from situations that might arouse menacing impulses. Prolonged interpretative treatments have yielded disappointing results, whereas behaviourally oriented approaches not only eliminate

V

defensive behaviour, but such changes are often accompanied by improvements in other areas of functioning. These findings suggest that either the psychodynamic explanations have limited validity, or action-based therapies provide an unusually effective means of extinguishing internally generated anxieties. It is conceivable that an agoraphobic housewife may remain housebound over fear of sexual entanglements. If this were in fact the case, the question remains whether the problem is best resolved by conversing about it or through dramatic disconfirmation of apprehensions by demonstrating that she can venture outdoors and she neither seduces strangers nor is assaulted sexually.

Not all avoidance necessarily represents aversively motivated behaviour. In some instances, fears have diminished but the behaviour persists because of the benefits it produces. By exhibiting anxiety reactions people can avoid onerous responsibilities and exert some degree of control over others. When avoidance behaviour is maintained by both fear and rewards derived from the inability, clients require a treatment that eliminates fears and fosters more constructive ways of securing positive results. This may necessitate changing the reinforcement practices of others to ensure that anxiety reactions lose their functional value.

Durability of therapeutic changes

If defensive behaviour can be removed by corrective experiences, is it likely to be easily reinstated by a few adverse incidents? Not necessarily. There are several factors that favour persistence of disinhibited behaviour long after treatment has been discontinued. Removal of unwarranted anxieties alleviates distress and enables people to participate in rewarding activities they formerly avoided. A compulsive who spent inordinate amounts of time scrubbing and avoiding contact with 'dirty' objects, for example, was able to hold a job, to go swimming and to walk on grass for the first time in many years after his compulsive rituals were eliminated (Rachman, Hodgson and Marzillier, 1970). Reinstated behaviours are thus likely to be supported by favourable conditions of reinforcement without requiring a special maintenance programme. Moreover, reinforcement of a sense of capability through success often improves functioning in nontreated areas (Bandura, Blanchard and Ritter, 1969). The benefits of restored competencies can counteract the effects of occasional distress.

A second consideration concerns the requisite conditions for re-instating fearful and defensive behaviour. Rescorla (1969) has shown that fear conditioning depends upon the degree of correlation that obtains between events. It would follow from this research that an effective means of reducing a person's vulnerability to mishaps is to have him perform extensively the formerly threatening activities under advantageous conditions after treatment has been terminated. Occasional hapless occurrences in the context of many neutral or rewarding experiences are generally ineffectual in reinstating fearful responding. A dogphobic who, following treatment, has had many benign interactions with a variety of dogs is unlikely to become unduly affected by a few misfortunes. At most, such experiences will establish discriminative avoidance of realistic threats, which has adaptive value. On the other hand, for persons who have had limited contact after treatment with previously feared objects, a few unfavourable experiences may reestablish defensive behaviour that generalizes inappropriately.

If disinhibited behaviour is regularly correlated with punishing consequences in everyday life, then therapeutic changes will be shortlived unless the environmental circumstances are modified. No psychological methods exist that can render an organism insensitive to the consequences of its actions. Nor would imperviousness be desirable, were it possible, because an organism that is unaffected by its response feedback would function in a grossly maladaptive way.

It might also be noted in passing that persons whose fears have been extinguished do not behave recklessly. Elimination of an automobile phobia does not dispose unimpeded clients to saunter heedlessly into onrushing traffic on busy thoroughfares. Rather, stereotyped avoidance is replaced by flexibility and adaptive behaviour that is cognitively controlled by judgments of probable consequences resulting from prospective actions.

Participant modelling and behaviour deficits

Participant modelling figures even more prominently in the modification of problems arising from behavioural deficits. Fears can be overcome without the aid of models, but response learning would be exceedingly laborious, not to mention perilous, if it proceeded solely on the basis of trial-and-error experiences without the response guidance of models who exemplify the appropriate patterns.

For this reason, most competencies, whether they involve social or vocational skills, are acquired and perfected by the combined influence of instructive example and reinforced practice. In the treatment programme devised by Lovaas (1967), behavioural repertoires are established in autistic children who display little functional behaviour, through reinforced modelling. Complex response patterns are gradually elaborated by modelling activities in small steps of increasing difficulty and by rewarding matching performances. Manual prompts and other supplementary aids are used when children fail to respond. The provisional supports are then gradually withdrawn. After the new modes of behaviour are well established, their stimulus determinants are shifted from modelling cues to verbal and appropriate environmental stimuli.

Development of assertiveness provides another illustration of clinical application of participant modelling (Bandura, 1972). People who are unable to behave assertively, a not uncommon problem, are likely to suffer aversive control by others. In teaching people how to behave affirmatively, assertive styles of response must be modelled for them. Depending upon individual needs, these might include such things as complaining about inadequate service, returning purchases, refusing arbitrary or unreasonable demands, responding to unfair criticism, making rightful claims to goods and facilities, defending one's position in the face of opposition, and in other ways standing up for one's rights. Clients practice behaving assertively through role enactments with feedback that rewards their successes and corrects their errors. Fear of revealing one's inadequacies creates initial reluctance to engage in behaviour rehearsals even under simulated conditions. There are several ways in which such resistances can be reduced. First, participant modeling is structured in a nonthreatening manner aimed at fostering new competencies and confidence rather than exposing deficiencies. Concern over poor performance is further decreased by noting that in all successful skill learning initial efforts are awkward; hence, it is progressive improvement with practice rather than instant proficiency that is expected. In an optimistic, forward looking programme clients more readily accept and profit from their mistakes. Prior modelling provides a helpful guide for new styles of behaviour. Participants therefore do not have to grope around for appropriate responses, which reduces needless failure experiences. In addition, assertion tasks are graduated, beginning with relatively easy performances. As apprehensions are extinguished through repeated practice, progressively more difficult encounters demanding more assertive actions are introduced.

In a comprehensive treatment, clients must also learn when and where assertiveness is appropriate. And they need positive reinforcement for asserting themselves in their daily interactions. Transfer of assertiveness from the training situation to the natural environment should be an integral part of the treatment rather than being left to fortuitous circumstances. A transfer programme might proceed as follows: after the client has perfected his social skills and overcome his timidity he accompanies the therapist on excursions into the field where he witnesses further demonstrations of how to handle situations calling for assertive action. The therapist then reduces his level of participation to background support and guidance as the client tries his skills in situations likely to produce favourable results. By careful selection of encounters of increasing difficulty the assertion requirements can be adjusted to the client's momentary capabilities to bolster his sense of confidence. As a final step in the programme, the client would be assigned a series of assertive performance tasks to carry out on his own.

Three-stage research strategy

Development of powerful treatments requires a three-stage strategy of research. First, an *outcome analysis* is carried out to ascertain whether a given approach is sufficiently promising to warrant further examination. Effective methods usually include several component procedures. Given evidence that a composite method achieves good results, *component analyses* are then conducted to determine whether the constituent factors, either singly or in combination, are necessary, facilitative, irrelevant, or serve as impediments to the outcomes produced by the multiple method. After a factor has been established as a significant determinant, *process analyses* serve to identify the mechanisms by which each component achieves its effects. When the modes of influence are understood, the knowledge suggests ways to enhance further the power of an already effective treatment.

Component analysis of participant modelling

The influence of some of the factors contained in participant modelling has been examined singly, especially with respect to defensive behaviour. Observation of both models can, by itself, produce substantial reductions in phobic behaviour both in children and in adults (Bandura, 1971a). Similarly, repeated performance of aversive activities without untoward effects can eventually eliminate fears and inhibitions (Bandura, 1969).

Some efforts have been made to assess the relative contribution of the constituent influences in the multiform procedure. The proportional weights furnished by any given study must be accepted with reservation, however, because only a single value of each component is assessed, whereas other versions of the same factor may have different efficacy. In a study comparing the outcomes associated with various component combinations, Blanchard (1970a) found that modelling accounted for approximately 60% of behaviour change, and 80% of changes in attitude and fear arousal; guided participation contributed the remaining increment. Information influences, on the other hand, had no significant effect on any of the measures.

The guided participation component of the treatment under discussion can be further analyzed into separable elements. When clients are assisted in performing the desired behaviour the protection afforded by the model may facilitate changes by reducing behavioural restraints. As participants enact the feared activities part of the changes are undoubtedly attributable to response feedback experiences. In evaluating the contribution of protective guidance and response performance, Ritter (1969b) reports that modelling accompanied by physically guided performance decreased acrophobic behaviour more effectively than modelling with verbally guided enactment, which, in turn, was superior to a brief demonstration alone.

Numerous studies have also been conducted on the relative contribution of modelling, performance, and reinforcement influences to development of new modes of behaviour or to facilitation of responsiveness that is unencumbered by restraints. Time limitations do not permit detailed examination of the major findings. The evidence generally shows that modelling plays a paramount role in the acquisition of novel and complex patterns of behaviour, whereas differential reinforcement of trial-and-error performances alone is a relatively inefficient way of fostering response learning in humans. On the other hand, modelling influences assume a secondary function in enhancing already established behaviours, while response inducements and reinforcing consequences emerge as prominent determinants. In both cases, modelling supplemented with behavioural enactment and rewarding consequences is the most powerful means of effecting psychological change (Bandura, 1971a).

Process Analysis

Investigations have recently begun into the mechanism by which the constituent influences in participant modelling achieve their effects. With regard to the modelling component, the processes governing observational learning are partially clarified (Bandura, 1971b), but disinhibitory processes remain to be examined. Observing modlled performances can reduce fars and inhibitions in a variety of ways.

Cognitive Processes. According to social learning theory (Bandura, 1969), fearful behaviour is controlled to varying degrees by two stimulus determinants. Responses can be evoked either directly by external aversive stimuli, or through an intermediary self-arousal mechanism. In the latter operation, threatening events activate fear-provoking thoughts which, in turn, motivate defensive behaviour. Extinction of directly evoked responses requires repeated non-reinforced exposure to aversive stimuli, whereas responses arising from symbolic self-stimulation are modifiable by eliminating frightening cognitions.

Several lines of evidence indicate that in many instances emotional responses are largely self-induced rather than automatically evoked. Paired stimulation usually does not produce conditioned reactions in individuals who remain unaware that the innocuous events forebode painful experience. Emotional conditioning can furthermore be attained by substituting thought produced arousal for physically painful stimulation as the source of activation. Not only does cognitive functioning affect acquisition of emotional responsiveness, but conditioned autonomic and avoidance responses decline rapidly when individuals are merely informed that threatening events are no longer accompanied by painful experiences. Fear can thus be reduced informationally without non-reinforced response evocation.

One possible interpretation of observationally induced changes is that modelled performances are a convincing way of informing subjects that what they fear is safe. To the extent that defensive behaviour is influenced by information conveyed in this form, apprehensive individuals may be persuaded to act in accordance with the new factual evidence.

The powerful cognitive control over fearful responding demonstrated under laboratory conditions contrasts with the refractory quality of defensive behaviour in clinical cases. The difference is probably explainable in terms of the severity and predictability of aversive consequences. In experimental situations relatively weak threats are completely removed by an informing agent who exercises full control over the occurrence of painful outcomes. By contrast, the things people fear excessively in everyday life are ordinarily innocuous but can occasionally be seriously hurtful despite assurances to the contrary. Animals do bite, airplanes crash from time to time, and assertiveness is sometimes punished. Laboratory produced fears likewise persist under outcome uncertainty. Hence, the probability of injury, however remote, can negate the potential influence of factual knowledge on action. Moreover, in highly anxious individuals, threats readily evoke frightening thoughts of injurious effects so that they exercise only weak control over their cognitions. For these reasons, intractable fears are rarely eliminated by reassuring information alone. It can, however, reduce fears and inhibitions to some degree.

Motivational Processes. Modelling influences are not only informative; they also have motivational effects (Bandura, 1971c, d). Observed success can function as a motivator by arousing the observers' expectations that they too will eventually succeed if they intensify and persist in their efforts. Variations in observed outcomes determine the speed, the vigour, and the tenacity with which others behave.

Observers may remain frightened at the prospect of performing the modelled activities, but they persuade themselves that if others can do it, they should be able to. Modeled displays could, therefore, facilitate expression of previously inhibited behaviour through motivational increases. In this mode of operation, modelling influences create in observers self-imposed demands for performance and self-critical reactions for faint-heartedness. Reports of adult phobics who watched fearless child performers (Bandura and Barab, 1972), attests to the motivational pressures of courageous displays ('It made me feel foolish that I despise handling these things when the little children in the film looked like they didn't mind doing it. . . . I figured if the little kids had enough moxie to do it, I should be able to.'). Meichenbaum's (1971) finding that phobics acted more boldly after observing a model master fear through perseverance then after watching a facile performance is interpretable in terms of motivational inducements.

Vicarious Extinction Processes. Exposure to threatening performances generates fear arousal in observers. With repeated nonreinforced evocation, even the most alarming modelled responses eventually lose their aversive properties. In a study cited earlier (Bandura, Blanchard and Ritter, 1969) phobics rated the degree

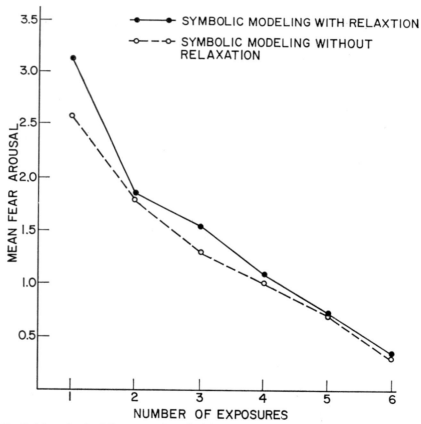

Fig. 3. Mean level of fear arousal evoked by modelled performances initially and by each subsequent exposure to the same filmed scenes in individuals receiving symbolic modelling with relaxation and with symbolic modelling alone. Bandura, Blanchard and Ritter, 1969.

of fear arousal evoked by modelled scenes initially and by each subsequent reexposure to the same scenes. As summarized in Fig. 3, subjects showed a progressive decline in fear arousal with each successive observational trial.

A similar process of vicarious extinction is revealed when emotional responsiveness is measured physiologically (Bandura and Barab, 1972). Adult phobics displayed a high level of autonomic reactivity to filmed scenes of adults or children enacting threatening responses during the initial exposure, but they manifested comparatively low autonomic responsiveness during the second presentation (Fig. 4). Modelling of performances unrelated to the subjects' concerns generated equally weak responses both initially and on reexposure.

Decrements in emotional arousal probably reflect vicarious extinction of both nonmediated fear responses and frightening cognitions. By reducing the aversiveness of threatening activities below the threshold for activating defensive behaviour, modelling influences enable observers to perform responses they previously inhibited. There are some results that lend support to this interpretation. Blanchard (1970b) found that the more thoroughly fear arousal was vicariously extinguished, the greater was the reduction in avoidance behaviour and the more generalized were the behavioural changes. The study by Bandura and Barab (1972), while confirming the relationship between fear extinction and behavioural improvement, indicates that more than one mechanism is responsible for changes achieved by modellig influences. They may operate to varying degrees through informative, motivational, or extinctive processes, depending on their content and mode of presentation.

The performance component in participant modelling most likely relies on similar intervening processes. Several aspects of this therapeutic practice serve to mitigate fear arousal. It has been shown that individuals experience less fear and greater tolerance of aversive stimuli in the company of a familiar person than when alone or in the presence of a stranger. The therapists' mere presence may have sufficient tranquillizing effect to increase clients' willing exposure to threats, if not weaken their behavioural inhibitions. As previously noted, the various protective and supportive aids embolden anxious clients to the point where they engage in activities they would not otherwise attempt.

Performance of frightening responses provide informative feed-

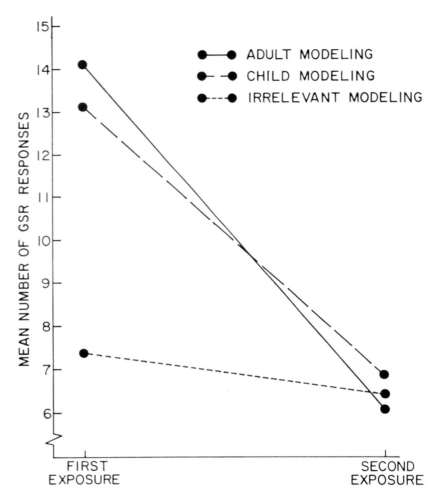

Fig. 4. Mean number of autonomic responses during initial and second exposure to filmed scenes of adults or children enacting threatening responses. Individuals in the irrelevant modelling condition observed modelled performances unrelated to their fears. Bandura and Barab, 1972.

back and reassuring experiences that facilitate extinction of dysfunctional restraints. Finally, apparent progress in a graduated programme serves as a motivating function that enhances the rate of improvement. As the mechanisms governing behaviour change become better understood, hopefully the full power of participant modelling will be realized.

References

1. Agras, W. S. 1967. Transfer during systematic desensitization therapy. *Behaviour Research and Therapy*, 5: 193-99.
2. Bandura, A. 1969. *Principles of behavior modification*. New York: Holt, Rinehart & Winston.
3. Bandura, A. 1971a. Psychotherapy based upon modeling principles. In *Handbook of psychotherapy and behavior change*, eds. A. E. Bergin and S. L. Garfield. 653-708. New York: Wiley.
4. Bandura, A., ed. 1971b. *Psychological modeling: conflicting theories*. Chicago: Aldine-Atherton.
5. Bandura, A. 1971c. *Social learning theory*. New York: General Learning Press.
6. Bandura, A. 1971d. Vicarious and self-reinforcement processes. In *The nature of reinforcement*, ed. R. Glaser, 228-78. New York: Academic Press.
7. Bandura, A. 1972. *Aggression: A social learning analysis*. Englewood Cliffs, N. J.: Prentice-Hall, in press.
8. Bandura, A., and Barab, P. G. 1972. Processes governing disinhibitory effects through symbolic modeling. Unpublished manuscript, Stanford University.
9. Bandura, A.; Blanchard, E. B.; and Ritter, B. 1969. The relative efficacy of desensitization and modeling approaches for inducing behavioral, affective, and attitudinal changes. *Journal of Personality and Social Psychology*, 13: 173-99.
10. Barlow, D. H.; Leitenberg, H.; Agras, W. S.; and Wincze, J. P. 1969. The transfer gap in systematic desensitization: An analogue study. *Behavior Research and Therapy*, 7: 191-96.
11. Blanchard, E. B. 1970a. The relative contributions of modeling, information influences, and physical contact in the extinction of phobic behavior. *Journal of Abnormal Psychology*, 76: 55-61.
12. Blanchard, E. B. 1970b. The generalization of vicarious extinction effects. *Behavior Research and Therapy*, 8: 323-30.
13. Hardy, A. B. 1969. Exposure therapy as a treatment for agoraphobia and anxiety. Unpublished manuscript, Palo Alto, California.
14. Hodgson, R., Rachman, S., and Marks, I. M. 1972. The treatment of chronic obsessive-compulsive neurosis. *Behavior Research and Therapy*, 10: in press.
15. Lovaas, O. I. 1967. A behavior therapy approach to the treatment of childhood schizophrenia. In *Minnesota symposia on child psychology*, ed. J. P. Hill, vol. I. pp. 108-59. Minneapolis: University of Minnesota Press.
16. Meichenbaum, D. 1971. Examination of model characteristics in re-

ducing avoidance behavior. *Journal of Personality and Social Psychology,* 17: 298-307.

17. Meyer, V. 1966. Modification of expectations in cases with obsessional rituals. *Behavior Research and Therapy,* 4: 273-380.

18. Miller, N. E. 1948. Studies of fear as an acquirable drive: I. Fear as motivation and fear-reduction as reinforcement in the learning of new responses. *Journal of Experimental Psychology,* 38: 89-101.

19. Paul, G. L. 1969. Outcome of systematic desensitization. In *Behavior therapy,* ed. C. M. Franks, pp. 63-159. New York: McGraw-Hill.

20. Rachman, S.; Hodgson, R.; and Marks, I. M. 1971. The treatment of chronic obsessive-compulsive neurosis. *Behaviour Research and Therapy,* 9: 237-47.

21. Rachman, S.; Hodgson, R.; and Marzillier, J. 1970. Treatment of an obsessional-compulsive disorder by modelling. *Behaviour Research and Therapy,* 8: 385-92.

22. Rescorla, R. A. 1969. Pavlovian conditioned inhibition. *Psychological Bulletin,* 72: 77-94.

23. Ritter, B. 1969a. Eliminating excessive fears of the environment through contact desensitization. In *Behavioral counseling: Cases and techniques,* eds. J. B. Krumboltz and C. E. Thoresen. New York: Holt, Rinehart & Winston.

24. Ritter, B. 1969b. The use of contact desensitization, demonstration-plus-participation, and demonstration alone in the treatment of acrophobia. *Behaviour Research and Therapy,* 7: 157-64.

25. Wolpe, J. 1958. *Psychotherapy by reciprocal inhibition.* Stanford: Stanford University Press.

Discussion

after paper by BANDURA

Prof. Bandura (replying to comments): I think that the outcome of the types of studies I was describing raise some fascinating issues about modelling processes and I think that there are several alternative interpretations. It may be that in many cases certain disorders arise from I think fortuitous or transitory association of painful experience. Once the situation gets endowed with aversive properties, it now becomes its own cause, even though the historic predeterminants may cease to exist. The situation has acquired threat value. It now generates anxiety. The person avoids it. The avoidance behaviour is reinforced, you have a self perpetuating system. So that in this sense you have a temporary cause and to the extent that you can neutralize the threat value of the situation, you can effect rapid change. Whereas knowledge or conversing about the historical causes may be quite irrelevant. The other interpretation of phobic disorder is that they represent internally generated anxieties which you displace and then project outwards. Now it would seem to me that the results of the experiments raise some interesting challenges for that kind of interpretation and there are several possibilities. One is that the interpretation lacks general validity or it may be that the behavioural approaches are the most powerful ways of extinguishing internally generated anxiety. For example, the standard interpretation of a house-bound housewife is that she fears the loss of impulse control and she fears sexual entanglements. Now if this were in fact the case, the question still remains, can you extirguish that fear more effectively by dramatically reality testing that she can venture outdoors and she neither seduces others nor is she sexually assaulted or can you do it by conversing with her about it. I think these are the kind of fascinating issues that are raised now. It would seem to me that given the kind of evidence that is being produced by these procedures it requires some really thoughtful consideration.

Syndromes resulting from defects in communication—1

Lower animals

GRANT NOBLE,
University of Leicester

Of necessity this presentation is iconic; it attempts to encompass the broadest possible range of experience in the smallest possible frame.

Purpose of paper

In this brief paper the intention is to examine the range and types of animal communication evident in conditions of freedom; to examine the purpose and function of animal communication in relation to concepts of 'normality' in conditions of freedom; and to extrapolate about the relationship between animal communication and human biological communication with regard to the health of the human organism.

Rationale

When talking of animal communication two complementary points must be borne in mind; that the danger of mechanomorphising human behaviour is as great as the danger of anthropomorphising animal behaviour. Namely that it is as dangerous to ignore the animal qualities of the human being as to attribute human qualities to animals. Despite daily experience to the contrary, man flatters himself that he spends his time thinking logical, consecutive thoughts. In reality consecutive thoughts about any one problem occupies a very small proportion of man's waking hours during which the mind is occupied by random thoughts in a state of mental reverie. If, as the Buddha recommends, we become mindful, aware and conscious of our every activity we shall recognize that much of man's communication and behaviour is far from consciously controlled and many thoughts and behaviours percolate into consciousness from the reservoir of man's personal and evolutionary history, which Jung respectively called the personal and collective unconscious. It is this unconscious, and to a large extent uncontrolled, aspect of man's behaviour that is illuminated by studies of animal behaviour. It was after all Freud (1933) who pointed out that our personalities are largely determined by the way the 'animal in man' —was socialized.

While man's communication, because of language, is more highly developed than the lower animal's, humans still communicate at a biological level. By recognizable body movements, called sign stimuli, lower animals communicate emotions probably without the conscious intention of influencing a fellow member of the species. Without necessarily being aware of the fact, man also communicates by means of such body movements. The mysterious apparatus for transmitting and receiving sign stimuli is age old, far older than man himself; it is a part of the history of living things with its roots far back in evolutionary time. Man animal is as much a part of the evolutionary tree as the lower animals. A simple example of such biological communication in man is yawning which induces a ubiquitous response wherever in the world it is seen. The greeting of the Afghan is to put the right hand on the heart and incline the head to expose the area of maximum vulnerability. It is a sign of submission as old as man himself; the weapon hand is displayed in full and harmless view while the vulnerable skull is offered defenceless to the newcomer. It is behaviour made without the conscious intention of influencing fellow man, and yet unconsciously it does have influence.

Range and types of animal communication

It must firstly be noted that animals in captivity do not communicate as do animals in freedom. Huxley (1953) wrote 'Animals do not reveal the higher possibilities of their nature and behaviour, nor the full range of their individual diversity except in conditions of freedom. Captivity cages minds as well as bodies, and rigid experimental procedure limits the range of performance; while freedom liberates the creatures' capacities and permits the observer to study their fullest developments'. Lorenz (1953) wrote 'only by living with animals can one attain a real understanding of their ways'. In the wild, those animals who cannot communicate with others at a biological level, are likely to die.

a. *Communication with the environment.* It is important to understand with whom, or with what, the animal communicates. Recognizing that the word 'communicate' encompasses a broad spectrum of meaning having the word 'common' or 'shared' as its etymological root, it can be argued that animals communicate with the environment or nature. Animal behaviour has been seen to systematically vary in relation to environmental changes, for example cats and dogs 'go wild' in the wind, and it is reliably reported by school teachers that primary school children are similarly affected. Animals respond to the seasons by migration, mating and hibernation. Moreover, shepherds, whose business is to understand animal behaviour, report that Welsh hill sheep, even though they are born in the lowlands, later become attached to their flock's mountain from which they will not stray. Boehme, whose influence on Freud's concept of the unconscious can be directly traced, wrote that animals have a sensual speech: 'that language which is appropriate to a species that is actualizing the true potentialities of its sensuous/sensual nature and as such is in unity with all sensuous nature and all life'. Boehme argues that animals enjoy true self expression and because they achieve unity with nature, are at ease, while the man unaware of his place in the order of the universe remains ill at ease.

b. *Communication between species.* The sick animal, or the young animal, by dint of submissive postures communicates its vulnerability to other species, even to humans, and at an unconscious level. Animals, as Jack London has noted, are able to 'read' men. London finds that husky dogs will not come to their master when he wishes to kill them. Similarly Lorenz tried on many occasions to stage a departure for a parrot, but was never able to elicit the response 'goodbye' until the guest really departed. As he noted 'the animal was tuned into the finest involuntary signs, what these were we could never find out'.

W

c. *Definition of self in terms of the reactions of others.* Animals may communicate with themselves, or better put they may define themselves in terms of the responses of others. The evidence from the vast number of imprinting studies suggests that animals reared by hand regard human beings as their only potential partners. The natural harmony of the design is disturbed so that all those actions not determined by inheritance but by individual experience are unnaturally deflected. It would seem likely that the concept of 'self' in both humans and animals is defined in interaction with others. Data has been presented in this symposium which suggests that young monkeys only establish their 'monkey' identity in interaction with other monkeys. It has been noted that the sick animal adopts submissive postures. Whether it communicates this lack of ease to itself or to the outside world we shall never know, but I have found that such animals can be cured if they can be aroused from their submissive posture to aggressive postures. The sick animal does not appear to understand its lack of ease and often dies from the shock of illness. If a sick dog can be persuaded to raise its ears in aggressiveness, it would seem to be reminded of its normal range of behaviour and recovery is effected.

c. *Communications within a species.* What perhaps is most remarkable is the diversity of animal communication noted between members of the same species in the wild. The following list of animal communications is far from complete: lower animals communicate aggression by means of stereotyped and ritualized behaviours such that a submissive posture is sufficient in the wild to cease the aggressive attack. Lower animals map out their territory to other members of the same species by means of elaborate dances at the territories edge and by being more aggressive on their territory than off it. Amongst the social animals group behaviour can be observed against a common aggressor as is the case with birds, or even against an over-aggressive member of their own flock as is the case with cows. Moreover it has been noted by Lorenz (1953) that social animals, such as jackdaws, communicate knowledge of the aggressor by handing down personally acquired knowledge from one generation to another. Jackdaws do not instinctively recognize their predators, unless it is an animal seen to be holding what could appear to be a young jackdaw, and young jackdaws have to be taught by the parents' warning call note which animals are the aggressors. Social animals also establish colonies on a relatively permanent basis and communicate their rank to other members. If a high ranking jackdaw takes a low ranking female for a mate, the female is afforded the same status as her mate by the other members of the colony. Social animals have also been observed to collectively protect their young. A herd of female elephants with a two year old baby were seen to ring the mother while the youngster was shepherded beneath the legs of the mother, presenting a formidable fortress to the intruder. Similarly social animals communicate the source of likely food supplies and jackdaws have been seen to extricate young members of the colony from flocks of migrating birds thereby showing that they discriminate between members of their own colony and members of other colonies. Lastly, as has been repeatedly noted, animals indulge in a large number of stereotyped behaviours during mating so that copulation only takes place after elaborate biological communication.

Purpose and function of animal communication

a. *Failures in animal communication : a view of abnormality*. While aggressive communications have been seen in the laboratory, few of the social behaviours described above have been seen in captivity. It can be argued that captivity itself results in failures in animal communication—that captivity provides a view of abnormality. Social animals in captivity become lone animals. The wolf unable to find a place in the pack becomes the 'lone' wolf. The control of such lone animals over aggressive impulses seems to be weakened and correspondingly its ability to mate and reproduce is lessened. Animals reared in captivity are often unable to emit the appropriate sign stimuli or to respond to the behaviours of fellow species in the wild. Such animals seem unable to recognize the primary group, nor to find a place therein. Not only is mating difficult for the zoo reared and isolation reared animal, but they often do not seem to recognize the submissive stance of their young which are frequently eaten. Moreover animals kept in close confinement and who are unable to show submission by means of flight are often most gruesomely killed by members of their own species.

b. *Successful animal communication : a view of normality*. Lorenz (1953) writes of the view of normality afforded by nature, 'Like the stones of the mosaic, the inherited and acquired elements of an animal's behaviour are pieced together to produce a perfect pattern'. It is perhaps salutory that this gestalt, this tree of harmonious life, is perceived only by those who study animals in conditions of freedom. The view of normality afforded by nature is of a balance both within and between species which defies human engineering. It is a picture of animals at *ease* with their environment, in the expression of their unity with all life. As Darwin wrote : 'Can we wonder, then, that Nature's productions should be far "truer" in character than man's productions; that they should be infinitely better adapted to the most complex conditions of life, and should plainly bear the stamp of far higher workmanship.'

Nor can it be said that Nature is 'red in tooth and claw'. The view of normality afforded by Nature is that animals rarely indulge in wanton killing, even wolf packs have been observed to take old and crippled moose rather than healthy youngsters. The rule in Nature would appear to be that aggression is ritualized at what might appear to be a play level, rather than allowed to devastate animal species. As further evidence of this Law, Lorenz (1963) observes that the inhibition against killing a member of the same species are proportional to the killing capacity of the animal. Slow kill animals, and that includes non-weapon bearing man, have less fierce inhibitions against killing since flight is the biological communication of submission. On the other hand fast kill animals, those carrying natural weapons, have fierce inhibitions against killing. In submission the defeated canine exposes the jugular vein, and although the victor continues to bite, he is unable to bite the exposed vein and usually exhibits displacement activities. Perhaps most marked in this respect is the way young animals of whatever species manage to communicate their harmlessness to members of all species.

c. *Social behaviour*. Amongst social animals, and the evidence from anthropology is that man is a social animal, there is considerable evidence of communal or primary group behaviour. Social animals exhibit behaviour which may be interpretated as maintaining the cohesion of the primary group. In the jackdaw colony or in the herd of cows, the animals collectively protect the weaker against the intrusions of the stronger, particularly with regard to territory. Older cows, who have been seen placing themselves between combatants, are often put amongst herds of young heifers in order to maintain the cohesion of the herd. Smaller birds collectively combat an external aggressor and even communicate knowledge of aggressors to their young. Although animals have no such purpose in mind, it appears that membership of the primary group ensures that each animal has sufficient space or territory, and that collectively the species will survive against the threat of stronger individual aggressors while maintaining harmony with the outside world. At the risk of anthropomorphising animal behaviour one might ask whether the survival of the fittest means nature red in tooth and claw as Darwin has suggested, or whether fittest means at ease, at harmony with the environment. The word ease has as its etymological root the notion of 'elbow room', not without relevance to the concept of individual territory which is collectively protected by the colony, even when a stronger animal threatens a weaker one. We are reminded that Lamarck maintained that the real force behind evolution results in animal species which best express unity with the sensual force of nature.

Extrapolations and speculations

The theme of this paper has been that by studying the animal world we can learn much about the animal (instinctual) nature of man. If we learn from ethology that animals in freedom are at ease in the world, then it may be time to find a place in the mosaic of nature for man. Instinctually the nature of the healthy animal is at harmony with the greater world. Dis-ease of whatever type is likely when man is led to behave contrary to his animal nature which by definition is unconscious, although man's consciousness is capable of coming to terms with his animal nature. Copernicus reminded man that the human world was neither the purpose nor the centre of the universe. Darwin reminded man that he is one animal among many, with the same roots as the other animals on the evolutionary tree and Freud informs us that the ego is not master in its own house. Indeed, Freud's all important concept of repression would seem to relate to the way conscious man animal contravenes his own animal nature. Ethological studies may help to ascertain the nature of man without repression; the nature of the man whose consciousness does not conflict with his instinctual and unconscious animal component. In these days when we can reconstruct responses by behavioural engineering, we must be absolutely clear of our direction, of our philosophic model of man, before we can employ such techniques in a non-random way. Man is an animal; one base line for comparison of his behaviour is the animal kingdom, without anthropomorphising—but by establishing what of the animal remains part of the human being. Concepts of normality should perhaps not be culture bound, for we have seen mass madness often enough, but recognizing the contribution of Copernicus and Darwin, should be nature bound.

Aggression—conscious man's disease

If Lorenz's observations are the truth, then nature is far from red in tooth and claw. There are in the world of lower animals many inhibitions against killing, both within and between species. There is some evidence that such inhibitions also exist in man. Noble (1972) found that the sight of the victim's pain and suffering in submission is the signal which biologically inhibits aggressive behaviour in children. Children were expected to play less constructively (an index to anxiety) and perhaps more destructively (an index to aggressive drive) after they had seen aggression filmed with sight of victim rather than at a distance and after they had seen realistically rather than stylistically filmed aggression. A two by two design was employed whereby each group of twelve six-year old children was shown a different aggressive film. Observers assessed the constructiveness and destructiveness of post exposure play during which the children played in their classroom with the objects customarily available there. Children played significantly less constructively after seeing aggression filmed with sight of victim rather than at a distance, but sight of victim did not arouse children to destructive play. Children played less constructively after seeing realistically filmed aggression, rather than stylistically filmed aggression, and realistically filmed aggression prompted more destructive play than stylistically filmed aggression. Results suggest that children were so disturbed by the sight of the victim's pain on film, they became so anxious that aggressiveness was inhibited. While realistically filmed aggression made the children anxious it did not stop them from being aggressive. It would seem that the innate inhibitions against killing were activated by sight of victim and that these inhibitions stopped aggression as Lorenz's hypothesis would suggest. There is, therefore, some limited evidence that inherent in man's nature are inhibitions against killing members of the same species. Moreover, it would seem likely that should a man contravene this 'natural' law, he will become ill at ease. If the moral code of man and animal is to cease aggression when the defeated victim submits, we might ask whether we should distance the aggressor from the sight of the defeated victim by means of weapons, whether society can choose at certain times to legitimate war and whether behavioural engineering should be used, as it has in the U.S.A. to reduce anxiety about being drafted to Vietnam?

Social behaviour

A rule amongst social animals is that the young are taught to recognize aggressors by the older members of their primary group. Is seems that such labelling of aggressors is likely in man, perhaps we need look no further than Northern Ireland to see protestants teaching their children that catholics are aggressors and vice-versa. If, as is the case with jackdaws, such labelling is irreversible we might have cause for concern. The Nazis were very successful in their labelling of Jews and Russians as aggressors, so much so that these racial groups were perceived as less than human, with results of which we are well aware. When whole nations engage in amoral behaviour, we must seek out a base line for morality which cannot be so easily perverted.

Another law of nature that may be relevant to man is that normal social animals are brought up in the family within the primary group. As De Tocqueville wrote 'It is man who makes monarchies and establishes republics, but the commune seems to come directly from the hand of God'. Ethological studies may help one to place man in the perspective of his long evolutionary history, rather than in the twentieth century perspective of behavioural engineering. When the young animal is brought up in isolation from the family and the community he exhibits deviant behaviour. We abolish community and family in the man animal at our peril. The evidence is that animals or children brought up without the love of the family group do not seem able to identify with the primary group, and consequently become isolated, exhibiting more 'abnormal' behaviours than those brought up within the group. There is evidence that the animal reared in isolation, whether he is human or not, is unsure of his identity. Identity would seem to be defined in terms of others' reactions, as Cooley (1902) terms it, the looking glass self. Animals unsure of their identity are likely to exhibit divergent behaviour, often they are unable to mate. Similarly, there is evidence that the man animal feels morally right if he is fighting to defend his own territory and his own family against an external aggressor. In the animal kingdom, the animal on its own territory will fight with greater determination than the animal from another territory, and the animal defending his territory will emerge after ritualized aggression as the victor even when he is physically weaker than the other.

Crowd behaviour

Perhaps most convincing of all in demonstrating the animal unconscious communication between men is crowd behaviour, or what Thorpe (1956) calls behavioural contagion. In a crowd the man animal is often swept away by the behaviour of fellow men, almost without desiring it. If in no other sphere of human activity, the unconscious biological communication possible between man animals is convincingly demonstrated in crowd or mob behaviour, when individual responsibility for actions is handed over to the collective whole.

Conclusion

The intent of this paper has been to highlight the similarities between the so-called 'lower animals' and the human animal. We ignore the animal in us at our peril, because our animal (unconscious) behaviour is adaptive to the environment just as is the behaviour of the lower animals. Freud's great contribution to human knowledge was to make us aware that our consciousness does not embrace the totality of human existence, and that disease results when it becomes necessary for man animals to repress knowledge from consciousness. Nor should it be forgotten that man is still in the process of evolution whether the goal is the survival of the fittest or the evolution of the fittest. We should perhaps remember that industrial man is only one century old and is not evenly distributed throughout the globe. The evidence from the anthropologists is that agricultural man does communicate with the environment, he responds to the seasons as do the lower animals. While obvious, it is a point worthy of emphasis that the country man animal seems more at ease with the environment than the city man animal; that both mental and physical illness is less in the country than the city, and perhaps most important of all, that such illnesses are more easily accommodated in the country than in the city. Only as we discover the nature of the animal within us, shall we be able, to quote Huxley 'to undertake the apparently contradictory task of re-establishing our unity with nature while at the same time maintaining our transcendence over nature'. Ethological studies suggest that part of the animal in man is 'moral', and the concept of the unconscious id as a 'chaos, a cauldron of seething excitement' ignores the fact that the animal in man contains both the highest and lowest qualities of mind.

References

Boehme, J. *Mysterium Magnum*.

Cooley, C. H. 1902. *Human Nature and the Social Order*. New York: Scribner.

Darwin, C. 1859. *The Origin of Species*.

De Tocqueville. *Democracy in America*.

Freud, S. 1933. *New Introductory Lectures on Psychoanalysis*. New York: Norton.

Huxley, J. 1953. *Foreword to King Solomon's Ring*. London: Methuen.

London, J. 1969. *To Build a Fire* in The Penguin Book of American Short Stories, London: Penguin Books.

Lorenz, K. 1953. *King Solomon's Ring*. London: Methuen.

Lorenz, K. 1963. *On Aggression*. London: Methuen.

Noble, G. 1972. Effects of different forms of filmed aggression on children's constructive and destructive play. *Journal of Personality and Social Psychology,* in press.

Thorpe, W. H. 1956. *Learning and Instinct in Animals*. London: Methuen.

Syndromes resulting from defects in communication—2

Concordant preferences as a precondition for affective but not for symbolic communication (or how to do Experimental Anthropology)

DAVID PREMACK
University of California, Santa Barbara

Consider two main ways in which you could benefit from my knowledge of the conditions next door. I could return and tell you, 'the apples next door are ripe.' Alternatively, I could come back from next door chipper and smiling. On still another occasion I could return and tell you, 'a tiger is next door'. Alternatively, I could return mute with fright, disclosing an ashen face and quaking limbs. The same dichotomy could be arranged on numerous occasions. I could say, 'the peaches next door are ripe', or say nothing and manifest an intermediate amount of positive affect since I am only moderately fond of peaches. Likewise, I might report, 'a snake is next door', or show an intermediate amount of negative affect since I am less shaken by snakes than by tigers.

For simplicity, consider that everything of interest is next door, making locational information irrelevant. The question to be answered therefore is always, What is it? never, Where is it? Also, for simplicity, assume that everything I tell you is true, even as every affective state I display is genuine and not simulated. These qualifications are not necessary for the simple argument to be made here but they smooth the way.

Information of the first kind consists of explicit properties of the world next door; information of the second kind of affective states that I will assume can be positive or negative, and can vary in degree. Since changes in the affective states are caused by changes in the conditions next door, the two kinds of information are obviously related. In the simplest case, we could arrange that exactly the condition referred to in the symbolic communication be the cause of the affective state. If 'cause' is too simple, then consider that the tiger, apple, snake, etc. is the dominant factor in the affective display; much of what I will say here could be given more sophisticated formulation but without contributing materially to the basic argument.

The use you could make of my statements needs no comment; but the use you could make of my affective states is almost equally obvious. You could go next door when my state was positive, not go when it was negative. The speed and certainty with which you went could be proportional to the intensity of my positive state. The certainty with which you did not go, even perhaps the distance you went to the opposite side of the house or the number of doors you locked behind you, could be proportional to the intensity of my negative state. Or you could go on all occasions but carry a bucket on some occasions, a spear on others. All of this is foretold from a simple fact stated earlier: the two kinds of information are correlated; they are caused by the same factors.

Conveniently locating everything of interest next door is a hypothetical arrangement, of course, but we can see the same affective system operate to good advantage in an actual experimental situation. Menzel (1971) has recently reported some ingenious experiments concerning the social behaviour of a group of young chimpanzees in a one-acre compound. After hiding such objects as food or snakes in the compound, the experimenter took one animal into the compound and showed it the hidden object. He then returned the informed animal to the rest of the group, which was held in a restraining cage on the edge of the compound, and released all animals together (regrettable from the point of view of communication studies but compatible with Menzel's objectives). The animals succeeded in finding the hidden object, snake no less than food, significantly more often than when they were released into the compound without the benefit of an informed animal.

In other experiments, Menzel hid two caches of food, one larger than the other, showed one to animal A the other to animal B, and again released all animals at the same time. Typically they not only found both objects, but found the larger one first. In addition, Menzel noted that the quality and even perhaps quantity of the object hidden could be predicted by an uninformed observer from the exit behaviour of the animals (personal communication). From the moment the animals were released there were detectable differences in posture, gait, and vocalizations.

Why did the knowing animal not simply steal off and enjoy the food to itself? Immature chimps and perhaps even caged adult ones, are apparently afraid to venture too far into the compound alone. Menzel's work shows that they tend not to exceed a certain distance from one another, actually not a distance so much as a time needed to overcome a distance. The informed animal's fears combined nicely with the group's ignorance of the location of the hidden objects, giving rise to a high mutual need for communication. The informed animal was afraid to go alone, while the uninformed animals were unlikely to find the hidden object if they went alone. Each party needed the other.

Man has both affective and symbolic communication. Indeed, conflict between the two—e.g., a father saying to his son through gritted teeth, 'I do agree with you, more than you realize'—has been proposed as a source of mental illness (Mehrabian, 1970). All other species, except when tutored by man (Gardner and Gardner, 1969; Premack, 1970), have only the affective form. Even affective information alone could be of great value in a world where changes in location can be costly in terms of energy, risk or both. As a rule, the individual cannot simply venture forth each time a forager returned in a positive state. Instead he must weigh possible gains against possible losses, taking into account the valence and intensity of the speaker's state on the one hand and his knowledge of predators or distance to be travelled on the other. If predators were abundant a leader's positive state would have to be exceptionally high to induce a positive decision. Conversely, if predators were few a listener could indulge his curiosity, going forth unreservedly to learn what had occasioned a leader's mildly negative state.

In principle, an affective system would permit an animal's choice behaviour to accurately reflect the objective probabilities of his world. This is so despite the fact that a speaker's affective state probably does not distinguish quality from quantity but is proportional to their resultant. For instance, a large amount of a $+ 4$ item would probably occasion the same affective state as a lesser amount of a $+ 7$ item. Yet this need not be seen as a weakness of the affective system. If my preferences are the same as yours, I would be as indifferent as you in a choice between large $+ 4$ and small $+ 7$, and thus would be willing to pay the same price for both commodities in terms of risk and energy.

The affective system could not rely entirely on unconditional factors but for maximum efficiency would seem to require some amount of learning. For example, since all members of a group are not likely to be of the same temperament, listeners should not respond merely to a magnitude of affect but rather to magnitude plus source. Contextual sensitivity of this kind would enable the listener to react in the same way to 0.4 intensity from sluggish Henry as to 0.8 intensity from excitable George. On the other hand, in the field this problem may be reduced if not averted by the fact that a listener would not be guided by the affective state of any one speaker. Instead, the speaker's state would elicit affective states in all his listeners, the intensities of which would vary with their respective temperaments. If each listener more or less integrated over the several affective states, responding, say, to the average intensity of the group, the source of the individual states could be ignored. Only in the laboratory where a listener was restricted to a single speaker would it be necessary to take the source of the affect into account. Yet if one belonged to a group that varied, either through occasionally leaving one group to join another or through changes in membership brought on by the movement of others, the desirability of responding contextually would arise again. Only this time the contextual factor to which a listener should be sensitive would be the group rather than the individual.

Even when helped by learning, the affective system is capable only of answering what-questions and not where-questions. But this does not limit the applicability of the affective system as sharply as it might seem. There are at least three ways in which to circumvent the need for locational information while retaining the value of the what-information. First, everything of interest can be next door, in a department store on 6th street, or across from the fire station, i.e., in some agreed upon location. Second, an informed leader through fear of venturing too far alone or for other reasons can lead his uninformed peers to the hidden objects. Third, the successful forager need not return to the group but can reveal his location by calls, manifesting his affective state on an auditory basis. The latter is undoubtedly the case most often found in the field; nonetheless all three cases share this property: the value of what-information is preserved despite the fact that the affective system does not code for directional information. These examples may help to underscore the uniqueness of the bee's putative communication system (von Frisch, 1967). The proportionality between the rate at which the bee waggles and the quantity, quality or distance of the food is merely another instance of the motivational system now turned to a communication purpose quite like the affective system discussed here. But the coding for direction which the bee's system is said to contain is unique and to my knowledge could not be derived from the classic properties of motivational systems.

We come now to the main point of the paper. Affective communication depends upon a simple precondition: all members of the group must have concordant preference orders for the items about which they communicate. When members of a group are agreed about what is positive and negative, and the order of their magnitudes, then, in effect, any member of the group can use the affective state of any other member to predict his own affective state. But if you and I do not order items comparably then neither of us can use the valence or intensity of the other one's excitement to predict his own.

Suppose, for example, you are very fond of strawberries but I detest them. You return in a high positive state. Knowing nothing of your peculiar tastes I become equally excited in anticipation of a highly positive item. On such an occasion I am especially likely to go next door or to follow you into the compound, only to suffer the disappointment of strawberries. Your excitement has not proved to be a good basis for predicting my excitement.

Is this a problem which learning could resolve? Typically, when owing to some change in circumstances, the unlearned behaviour of a species becomes maladaptive we turn to learning as the most powerful corrective device for restoring adaptive behaviour. Could the affective system be restored by learning in the case of discordant preferences? Only in those special cases where there was a systematic relation between the preferences of several individuals. For example, if the preferences of one party were the perfect inverse of those of another party, the two parties could learn, either swiftly through a rule induced on a few exemplars, or slowly by trial and error, to adjust to this difference. Comparable adjustments could be made in principle for any systematically related preference orders.

But if the relations were not systematic it is not clear that learning could contribute substantively to the problem. Consider a successfully-communicating group in which nonsystematic preferences were introduced. Although the speaker's affective response to snake or food may be largely unlearned, a listener's response to a speaker should have both learned and unlearned components. Thus a listener who had rushed next door on the occasion of a speaker's positive excitement, only to find food that he did not care for, or worse a snake, would learn to inhibit his response to that speaker's positive excitement. But would that solve his problem? On a subsequent occasion he might learn belatedly that the same speaker's positive excitement, which he chose to ignore, was the occasion for an encounter, with bananas, an item which he cared for greatly. He might also discover that some of the speaker's negative states were occasioned by items of which he was quite fond. Yet it would not do simply to respond positively to all of the speaker's negative states since at least some of them would be associated with negative conditions And the listener would have no way of distinguishing 'good' occasions from 'bad' ones. In the long run, when preferences differ nonsystematically, acting on a speaker's positive affective states would lead a listener to negative and positive stimuli with about equal frequency; acting on his negative affective states would have the same outcome. Similarly, the average intensity of the stimuli a listener encountered would be the same for all intensities of the speaker's states.

Could the problem of discordant preferences be resolved by a call system that was not restricted to affective states which were either simply positive or negative? Suppose the species had one call for food, another call for danger, etc. The functional effect of such calls is tantamount to an agreement between members of the species to call the same things food, the same things dangerous, etc. Yet calls of this kind do not differentiate one member of the food class from another member, nor one member of the dangerous class from another member. Thus the call system would protect an anticipation of, say, strawberries against the discovery of a tiger, or vice versa. But it would not protect anticipation of bananas against discovery of strawberries, nor anticipation of snake against discovery of tiger. To avoid within-class, as well as between-class, confusion would require either concordant preferences or calls that were specific not only to classes but to members of the classes.

The disastrous effect upon the affective system of discordant preferences would be comparable to that of a chaotic world the content of which changed before a listener had an opportunity to act upon a speaker's message. Indeed, when first beset by the consequences of discordant preferences, a listener might well conclude that the world had changed, that it was no longer a reliable place. For often before he could get next door apples would have turned into snakes and conversely; or so it might seem to the listener whose companion's preferences had been altered without his knowledge.

Iconic and symbolic communication

Both symbolic and iconic communication escape the simple precondition upon which affective communication depends. Organisms that disagree radically about values can nevertheless guide one another through the world provided they communicate either symbolically or iconically. Communication in this case does not depend upon a unanimity of values but merely upon the consistent application of names or icons to the items in the world. For instance, if you tell me the turnips next door are ready, your possible dislike of them would not detract from the information. If I want to try some I can, your finicky message notwithstanding. Symbolic communication escapes the precondition because the listener is presented not with (only) the speaker's affective response to a condition but with a statement of the condition. In the iconic case he is presented with a piece of the condition. If not a tree full of ripe apples, then an applecore or even a leaf of the tree; or if not a tiger then perhaps a product of the tiger, droppings or claw marks. But the tiger might be constipated, the heroic speaker might die in an attempt to bring home a whisker, or with a more plebeian speaker listeners might die for lack of a warning. Icons are inefficient. Worse, concepts are not equally susceptible to iconic representation; some, such as the logical connectives, could not be represented in that manner at all. Admittedly, symbolic communication is pervaded by iconicity

(Durbin, 1971; Wescott, 1971), but the ultimate unacceptability of the pure iconic approach is incontestable. All this is beside the main point, however, which is simply that organisms agreed about values can guide one another through the world with affective communication alone; whereas organisms disagreed about values can still guide one another through the world provided they communicate symbolically.

Experimental anthropology

The difference in preconditions for affective and symbolic communication can be used to do what might reasonably be called experimental anthropology. Years ago a moratorium was declared on speculating about the origin of language (Hewes, 1972). Learned societies sought to help man resist the temptation of speculating about the unknowable by prohibiting all such publication. Today I think we can go beyond idle speculation, not only about origins of language but of human milestones generally. We can test models concerning the origins of language, agriculture, religion, art, etc., and though perhaps we can never say how in fact they did originate, we can assign weights to the alternatives on an experimental basis.

A model of the origin of language or of any other human activity will have two components. The first will state the cognitive skills that are a prerequisite for the activity. The second will state the selective pressures which, if imposed upon organisms with the prerequisite skills, will lead to the development of the activity in question. The first component deals with the problem solving ability of the species or its information processing capacity generally. The second deals with environmental pressures, problems that are posed a species by changes in the world.

In the rest of this paper, I will take the conclusion from the first half of the paper, and show how it can be utilized as a selective pressure in experiments on the origins of language. In addition, I will make some tentative proposals for a general model of the origin of human activities.

Laboratory-field combination

Consider a joint laboratory-field approach to the origin of language. Even though we cannot yet enumerate the cognitive skills

X

that are prerequisites for language, laboratory studies have already shown that the chimpanzee can be taught some of the principal exemplars of language (Gardner and Gardner, 1969; Premack, 1970). We know, for example, that the chimp is capable of symbolization, of using one event to represent another; of responding differentially to different word orders; of concatenating and rearranging words in ways that are necessary for the production of sentences. A successful comparison of human and animal intelligence requires that we be able to state the cognitive preconditions for these linguistic performances and ultimately all basic human activities. Our progress in achieving this objective could be measured by our ability to predict, for example, that species with certain cognitive skills could be taught language whereas those without these skills could not.

Since we know that the chimp can be taught symbolic communication, it is sensible to apply a selective pressure to this species which may lead it to develop symbolic communication on its own. In the field, using Menzel's procedures, we could induce in a small group of chimps a high need to communicate. As we have seen, the need to communicate which this procedure induces is normally handled nicely on an affective basis. Followers can accurately anticipate both the valence and the intensity of their own future excitement from the current excitement of the informed animal. But we also know that we could undermine the affective system simply by introducing discordances in the preferences, thus leaving an unresolved need to communicate.

In the laboratory we could deprive and satiate the animals on different foods. An animal normally keen on, but now satiated on, bananas would be disappointed to find the bananas to which it was led by a highly excited animal that was not satiated on bananas. Preferences could also be manipulated by contingencies, by arranging that an animal be able to obtain a highly preferred food only by first eating a nonpreferred one. This would increase the animal's preference for a normally nonpreferred food and lead it to bring back 'false' reports (false positive) concerning what was in the compound. With an appropriate combination of these procedures we could arrange that no animal's preference order be a function of the preference order of any other animal, and if this were not enough, we could also change any animal's preference order from time to time by changing the satiation and contingency procedures from time to time. In this way, in animals known to be capable of being taught symbolic communication, we could produce a high need to communicate, while at the same time eliminating the normal mechanism for doing so. Could the chimpanzees then invent iconic or symbolic communication themselves, first when the hints from the experimenter were strong, later when they were made progressively weaker?

Perhaps the first time this experiment is done, the animals should be left entirely to their own resources. If they proved incapable of developing a substitute as seems highly likely or, as is also possible, developed one that we could not decipher, we could attempt to structure their problem solving, not only as an aid to them but also to make certain that we could follow their solution. For instance, we could allow the informed animal to return with a piece of the hidden object. This may duplicate the field situation in which the forager returns not only with its affective state, but also with vestiges of the source of its affective state, for example, with the smell of food on its breath or body. So an observer could use the forager's breath to tell him what was next door and the intensity of the forager's excitement to tell him how much was there. We might sidetrack briefly to explore the chimp's overall ability to use iconic representations. Starting with icons whose relation to the hidden object was that of part-whole, we could progressively weaken the relation, ending up with the cases where the icon was merely an associate of the hidden object. Ultimately we could study metaphors. In addition, by giving the informed animal not one object to return with, but a number of alternatives from which to choose, we could study the informed animal's ability to choose wisely, to pick items that its uninformed companions could use.

When an informed animal returned with icons that were informative as its affective states no longer were, we could observe the possible transition from a reliance on affective states to a reliance on icons. In the course of this transition, we might observe a general degradation of responsivity to emotional cues, since these cues would no longer possess the functional significance they once did.

Words

In quite a different approach we would provide the informed animal not with either icon, metaphor, or a choice among different possible ones, but with words taught both it and the other members of the group in the laboratory. In this case the animal could return to the uninformed group with the word naming the hidden object that it had been shown. Although the proportionality between a speaker's affective state and the hidden object would no longer be an aid to its companions, with words the informed animal could tell the other animals exactly what was there. Possible differences in their evaluations of the hidden object should become irrelevant. Animals with a high preference for the object named by a given word on a particular trial should go forth with the informed leader; those with low preferences for the item should stay home.

Invented words

Once the animals succeeded in using icons or words that had been taught them in the laboratory, we could raise the critical question, Can they devise their own symbols? The invention of symbols would seem to involve a change more difficult than that involved in other kinds of innovation. Changes in food preparation, tool use and the like, well documented in primate groups (Marler, 1965), can be made by one animal and then transmitted by social modelling to other aimals. But a symbol cannot be invented and transmitted in this way. At least two individuals must use a symbol in the same way in order for it to be effective. I may use a blue triangle to represent apple in my private thinking and problem solving while you use a red square for the same purpose, but we could not communicate about apples until we used the same symbol, or found a way to establish the equivalence of our different symbols. Symbols seem, therefore, more likely to be social inventions rather than individual ones. An alternative would be for one inventor to transmit his idea to other animals; an improbable alternative in light of the degree of instruction that would be demanded and the fact that didactic intervention of that kind is apparently totally unknown outside of man. Indeed, instruction is considered to play only a minor role in the child's acquisition of language.

How can we arrange for the kind of joint invention that the symbol seems likely to require? Two animals could be shown a hidden food at the same time and supplied an arbitrary object as the only possible item with which to represent the hidden food. These animals would be in a position to share the same potential symbol. In addition, animals that chanced to follow the first pair into the compound could associate the arbitrary object shown them with the food discovered in the compound. The association is more likely to develop if the interval was short, or perhaps merely if the food were new. In some species (Garcia, Ervin and Koelling, 1966), associations develop between avoidance responses and foods despite long intervals provided the food is new and it results in gastro-intestinal upset. The sickness may be unnecessary, however, and the association between stimuli and food may develop over unusual intervals merely if the food is new.

In another approach to the invention of symbols, words or icons would not be brought back from the compound by the informed animal but would be selected by that animal from alternatives stored in the restraining cage. After being returned to the restraining cage, the informed animal would look over the alternatives available to him there and select the one he considered to best represent the object he had seen in the compound. If the alternatives were con-sistently stored in specific locations, the removal of either the words or icon need not prevent the informed animal from communicating with his peers. He could put his hand in the appropriate place, or merely point in a given direction, and in this way perhaps devise gestures that would substitute for the previous words or icons.

Aesthetics and the discovery of basic causal relations

In the other human milestones—art, religion, agriculture—comparable analyses could be made of cognitive skills on the one hand and selective pressures on the other. Since the logic of these cases is not different from that of language, I will not take them up but will turn to a slightly different problem. One precondition for certain human activities is a knowledge of basic cause-effect rela-tions. In agriculture, for example, the most basic causal relation is that between the seed and the plant. Consider the nature of the circumstance in which relations of this kind are likely to be dis-covered and ultimately used.

Agriculture is considered to have replaced hunting and gathering in areas where population density made earlier forms of provision-ing untenable (Binford, 1971). Population density may have led to agriculture, but is this same pressure likely to have led to the dis-covery of the seed-plant relation? Bushmen of today are reported to know the seed-plant relation yet they continue to hunt and gather nonetheless. Though more efficient than hunting or gathering, agriculture is actually more arduous. People turn to it, I suspect, because they have to and not because they have just discovered the seed-plant relation.

Discoveries of basic cause-effect relations such as the seed-plant relation seem more likely to occur under the aegis of aesthetic or exploratory dispositions than utilitarian ones, and thus to occur in contexts far removed from those in which the knowledge is ultimately used. If this is so and the causal knowledge is often not used directly, some functional respository would seem necessary, a system for preserving knowledge that a group carried but was not yet using. Finally, there is the terminal phase in which appropriate selective pressures operate upon existing knowledge to produce technologies representing solutions to practical problems. This suggests a three state model in which the basic steps in the development of human technologies are discovery, retention, and use.

A principal root of the aesthetic disposition is a preoccupation with the discontinuities of space and with the possibilities of their transformation. We need not go to the human artist in which these dispositions are institutionalized; in a minute way they can be seen even in a rat. Placed in a small box in which a lever projects from a wall, the rat rises onto its hind legs, sniffing and sweeping its vibissae across the wall. In dropping back to the floor, its front legs contact the lever, which gives slightly under the pressure, causing the rat to stiffen and its hair to bristle; there is a momentary excitement. Having discovered this break in the texture of space, the rat is likely to return to reinstate it. The event in the rat is small but it can be magnified in the monkey and still more in the chimp. Consider a monkey that has pressed the same lever hundreds of times, producing no extrinsic consequence. One day the lever sticks before returning to resting position. The visibly excited monkey presses thirty times in the space of a few minutes trying presumably to restore the change in the visual transit of the lever.

There is no end to this kind of event in the chimp; I will offer only one example. Sarah, a ten year old female chimp, who is the subject of a long-term language project, occasionally finds cuts on the hand of her trainer. She squeezes the cut expertly, not by opposing her thumb and forefinger in the human manner, but by placing her index fingers on opposite sides of the cut. The pressure accomplished in this manner can be very finely graded. As she squeezes her attention is rapt; she looks up from the cut only to peer into the eyes of the trainer (who looks back puzzled and a bit frightened, not of Sarah but of the intensity of her preoccupation). The chimp leaves off pressing just as a thin red line appears along the cut, outlining it against the rest of the skin. Presumably she would go on in this manner, raptly attentive, making subtle changes in space— if we had a device that could offer her multiple cuts. But no one has been willing to inflict a series of even small cuts in his hand simply to confirm the obvious.

Rather than elaborate examples from chimp behaviour, I will provide one example from human behaviour, one which, as you will see, applies directly to agriculture. Some months ago in discussing the present thesis with Dr. Barbara Partee (gifted UCLA linguist) she was reminded of an event from her childhood which she has kindly consented to have reported. Walking in the woods in the late fall, she found an unusual clump of small trees. Returning with a small saw, she cut down the trees in the center and stuck them in with the other trees to form 'a fort' as she recalls it. In the spring she rediscovered the clump of trees, finding not only the original trees in bloom but those she had sawed off and transplanted as well. In this way, under the aegis of a disposition to operate upon and 'improve' space, she discovered rooting, one of the oldest forms of horticulture.

Fossilized seeds, recently discovered on the graves of Neanderthal Man, have proved to be the seeds of flowers, suggesting that fifty thousand years ago man was already placing flowers on the graves of his dead. Who can say but that in the context of burial, seed may have fallen in fresh earth, sprouted, and led man to discover the seed-plant relation. The initial discovery of that relation is lost in prehistory; we cannot reasonably hope to recover it. My point is simply to note, first, the urgency of the aesthetic disposition in man and even chimp, and second that the disposition is of a kind to lead man into activities where he is likely to discover basic cause-effect relations.

If knowledge of great utilitarian potential is first discovered in nonutilitarian contexts, it seems reasonable to provide a repository for it, such that it may be preserved for later use. The repository may be ritual, religion, or even art; I have no clear idea. The problem has clear aspects of psychological interest however. What factors make it likely that knowledge acquired in one context will be preserved in some other context; and what factors make it likely that knowledge will be used in contexts different from those in which it was discovered, preserved or both? The literature on problem solving suggests some of the difficulties that can arise in transporting an idea from one domain to another. Also we know the power of metaphor, a power by no means restricted to art but found also in scientific discovery. Can we systematize these matters and show, for example, how causal relations discovered in one context are more likely to be utilized than causal relations discovered or preserved in some other context?

The last assumption in the model is simply that cause-effect relations which may have been a part of group knowledge for years will come to provide the basis of technology when activated by appropriate pressures. These three assumptions provide the tentative basis of a model as to how knowledge may be discovered, carried, and ultimately used. There are psychological issues of considerable interest locked in these assumptions and it is my hope to free them with the help of chimpanzees in a combined laboratory-field approach.

References

1. Binford, L. R. 1971. Post-Pleistocene Adaptations. In *Prehistoric Agriculture,* ed. S. Struever. New York: The Natural History Press.
2. Durbin, M. 1971. Some non-arbitrary aspects of language. Paper presented at the meeting of the American Anthropological Association, New York.
3. Garcia, J.; Ervin, F.; and Koelling, R. 1966. Learning with prolonged delay of reinforcement. *Psychonomic Science,* 5: 121-22.
4. Gardner, R. A., and Gardner, B. T. 1969. Teaching sign language to a chimpanzee. *Science,* 165: 664-72.
5. Hewes, G. W. 1972. An explicit formulation of the relationship between tool-using, tool-making and the emergence of language. Unpublished manuscript. University of Colorado, Boulder.
6. Marler, P. 1965. Communication in monkeys and apes. In *Primate Behavior,* ed. I. De Vere. New York: Holt, Rinehart & Winston. 544-84.
7. Mehrabian, A. 1970. *Tactic of Social Influence.* Englewood Cliffs, N.J.: Prentice-Hall.
8. Menzel, E. W. 1971. Social organization of a group of young chim-

panzees. Paper read at the meeting of the American Anthropological Association, New York.

9. Premack, D. 1970. A functional analysis of language. *Journal of Experimental Analysis of Behavior,* 14: 104-125.

10. von Frisch, K. 1967. *The Dance Language and Orientation of Bees.* Cambridge, Mass.: Harvard University Press.

11. Wescott, R. 1971. Linguistic iconism. *Language,* 47: 416-28.

Syndromes resulting from defects in communication—3

Man

COLIN CHERRY,
Imperial College, London, S.W.7.

I think it quite likely that I may be the only person here who has not been trained formally either as a psychologist or a psychiatrist and I naturally feel rather out of place and apologetic. However, I have been very concerned, during the past twenty and more years, with the nature of human communication, both theoretically and experimentally, and with thinking about the great distinctions between man and the animals, inasmuch as their communicative abilities render their distinction so immense. The immense gap was once expressed by the philosopher Suzanne Langer as being 'one whole day of creation'; she was primarily referring to man's possession of speech and his phenomenal powers of forming concepts

All I am aiming to do then is to outline some of my views upon the nature of human speech and conversation in ways which may highlight certain factors of particular importance, factors which I feel may indicate forms of syndrome where they may have been caused to develop abnormally. It is only that my work has brought me into association with people of several disciplines all related to the field of human communication, in particular certain philosophers, linguists and experimental psychologists.

1. Man is an individual by virtue of being a social creature.

I would accept Emile Durkheim's argument that a person is an individual and a social animal at one and the same time; that the individual and society are two sides of the same coin. When a baby is born it forms first a part of its own mother and has to be taught that it is a separate creature with a separate existence, a name, identity and self-awareness etc. That is we are taught to become self-conscious creatures through the communicative behaviour first of our mothers, of other members of the family, and then of all our associates throughout life. If we accept this then we need continual reminders of our own existence by having verbal exchanges with other members of society; everytime I have a conversation I am reminded of my own existence. Speech, in other words, is *always* a social activity. If anything occurs in the early stages of childhood to prevent a baby's babbling to be conditioned into speech then not only is that child likely to be unable to express itself but it is likely to have a very vague notion of itself as a person.

Normal people, possessing developed spoken language, cannot possibly imagine what animal mental life is like. It is true that we use many other forms of sign and therefore act in ways that are in common with animals but it is the extension of animal signs into developed speech that makes the immense difference and creates us as self-conscious creatures.

The more developed my language the more ways I can distinguish myself from you. I will go so far as to say that I can distinguish myself from any other person in more ways through speech than by any other means whatever.

This self/society duality would imply that the normal individual thinks and so communicates with himself in his language. Thinking, that is to say, is also a social activity. People show intense loyalty towards their language, as we all know from their behaviour when minority languages are threatened with extinction. Language is an essential part of a man's identity. To attack a person's language is then to attack him, and this does not necessarily mean attacking a national language because working-class children may have their language attacked in middle-class schools by being 'taught' literary language as though it were the correct and only way.

2. Language is not one thing but many things

A normal human being can adopt many rôles and he can feel that he is free to choose his rôle. The change of rôle is signified by change of language. That is to say, I do not speak the same kind of English when I am speaking to my students as when I am speaking to my family at home, my pals in the pub etc. In different social groups I am a different kind of person with a different kind of language. It may be that some people have difficulty in making this rôle change perhaps because of difficulties of language form change. Viewed in this way language is part of our adaptive system, it is a biologically adaptive process. At different periods of time we need to identify with specific social groups and to signify this identification by the correct linguistic forms. Can people be frightened of making this change, or for other reasons be unable to make the identification? Suppose a person has been too confined in very early life to one particular form of company; can it be that he will find difficulty in transferring his identity to other groups with corresponding change of language?

3. We speak with our whole bodies not just with our mouths.

It is only too easy for people with normal hearing to think of speech as something acoustic and it is true to say that most studies of speech have been directed towards study of the sound of speech i.e. phonetics etc. But when we speak we use our whole bodies, moving our eyes in glances, gesturing, leaning forward in eagerness for attention, etc. Speech itself really has the nature of gestures, gestures which are normally invisible, apart of course from the movement of the lips. Experiments in our own laboratories have shown that people with normal hearing are mostly unaware of the great extent to which they can lip-read when the circumstances are made difficult for them. (For example, if the environmental noise is raised to a very high level). Deaf people are then handicapped by being unable to 'see' the internal gestures of the vocal organs, movements of the tongue, larynx, epiglottis etc. People of normal hearing learn of these movements through the acoustic evidence that the gestures offer. But I myself am quite convinced of the value of regarding speech as gesture communication and not as acoustic communication. (Incidentally, when you speak on the telephone all the visible evidence of speech is removed from you and it is then found that your speech habits also change to some extent and various forms of vocal ritual are evolved in order to help you with the difficult situation).

4. *Importance of eye movements*

Of all movements of the body, other than those of the vocal organs themselves, eye movements are the most important and they serve the purpose of assisting the whole strategy of human conversation. When two people converse they look at each other relatively little and, even then, their glances meet for only a small fraction of that time. Glances are used for a number of purposes (a) to indicate that your remarks are coming to a close and to give permission for the other person to interrupt, (b) to observe whether the other person is paying attention, (c) to observe a partner's reaction to a remark, (d) to prevent the other person from interrupting, and perhaps for other strategic controls.

Jean-Paul Sartre has made some searching observations concerning the importance of gaze. Like conversation itself, another person's gaze is a regular reminder of our own existence. Sartre observed that we cannot *look at* another person, in a conscious way, and be *looked at* at the same time because, as a looker, we feel as a person scrutinizing the other, whilst we become objects when we are looked at by the other. Sartre was, of course, concerned with the question of embarrassment. In other words, we are conscious scrutineers at one moment, real persons, but we become objects of scrutiny the next. Can it be that some people's early experience may have left them deficient in their ability to use their eyes adequately when engaged in conversation?

Another control of human communication is the distance apart that the partners are seated, or are standing, when conversing. It is possible to arrange seating so that a partner can be put into an inferior position in status and it is possible to arrange seats so that glancing at one another can be made difficult. We ourselves have been concerned with some experiments upon conversation and seating arrangements; television techniques, or half-silvered mirrors and other techniques, have been used partly as a control to the extent of which people can use their visual glances. Incidentally, we are most accurately aware of the direction of a partner's gaze when it meets our own, eye to eye, and we can judge this to an accuracy of the order of two or three degrees.

When we are engaged in conversation, we are then concerned with more than a mere physical phenomenon, speaking and glancing at one another, for we are observing something of our own natures.

5. Human communication is always an act of courage

Conversation is not something that is started lightly or arbitrarily between people. Before I speak to somebody I must select that person to speak to. You cannot approach a stranger and, without any form of ritual or ceremony, start to speak to them upon any subject you wish. If you do you may find yourself in prison. We surround ourselves with ritualistic forms which makes this approach possible and I submit that, to human beings, it takes a positive degree of courage both to start a conversation and to terminate one. Can it be that this courage can be failing in some people, perhaps owing to defects in early training, with the consequence that they withdraw and become non-social, isolated creatures? To approach another person is to lay yourself open to certain risks, of snub, of ridicule, or embarrassment. Both starting and ending conversation are acts of courage, however slight.

6. The many functions of human speech

It is the layman's common view that speech primarily serves to bring individuals together into groups. But it can equally well drive them apart. With language we can not only agree with others but we can disagree. We can converse, dispute, argue, quarrel, negotiate, reason, describe, and do many other things, all with a vocabulary of a few thousand words.

I myself would argue that ability to dispute is more important than ability to agree. All human 'progress', whatever that word means, implies social change and social change could not come about if we lived in a world of agreement only. It would be a world ruled by clichés and platitudes, a tyranny. Children must, it seems to me, be encouraged to dispute with parents and others if they are ever to become separate individual creatures, as part of their social groups. In fact I wonder whether a child could ever become an individual self if it was raised with parents and others who agreed with it on every single issue. On the other hand if a child is regularly and continually contradicted a similar disaster might occur.

7. *Perception as the testing of hypotheses*

Human beings normally have phenomenal power of forming concepts in unlimited numbers. With its earliest babblings a child is beginning to learn to see the world as consisting of separate things or *gestalten,* with names—it begins to see a face as having eyes, a nose, a mouth etc., then to see tables, chairs and other objects around it, all with names. Although the vocabulary of names is limited it can be argued that we can make no perception whatever without perceiving it *as* something. If our attention is drawn to a smudge on the wall it may not look like anything particular except as 'a smudge on the wall' but we cannot make an unidentified perception. We may have feelings from time to time that we have an idea but we do not have that idea as a thought until we can jump on it with both verbal feet. The ability to express feelings into thoughts via language must vary very much among people.

Viewed in this way perception is a process of testing hypotheses. The brain is the means, *par excellence,* for forming and testing hypotheses. The process of perception viewed this way, is then one of inference. To illustrate my point I will quote the famous lines from Macbeth:

'Is this a dagger that I see before me its handle toward my hand . . . ?'
(That is a hypothesis was put up.)
'Come, let me clutch thee . . .'
(The hypothesis is tested.)
'I have thee not and yet I see thee still . . .'.
(The test has led to an unexpected or unpredicted result.)
'Art thou not, fatal vision, sensible to feeling as to sight?'
(Of the evidence of two sense organs leading to contrary predictions.)

It is this process that we go through every time we see or hear or notice something, and the ability to form and test hypotheses may be very varied among people. But the ability to create hypotheses is distinct from the ability to test those hypotheses and to observe whether tests can confirm or deny predictions.

This brings me to my final point concerning human communication which I believe to be a further and important distinction from the animals.

8. *Human prediction—the past, present and future*

The abilities which I have just mentioned, mediated by language, develop in man the sense of time as a kind of ever-flowing stream, past, present, and future. Man can make predictions and be aware of whether his predictions are verified or falsified.

This is possible only because the world appears to man to show regularities or what scientists would call 'law'. Whether the world possesses regularities or not is a philosophical point. I would argue that it is regular only because, if it were not, we could have no knowledge of the world whatsoever. Man has knowledge because of his *assumption* that the world has regularities. This is mediated through the regularities of his own language or what is called 'syntax'. A world without regularity would be unknowable. Man then expects to predict the outcomes of his various actions and, like Macbeth, can sometimes be surprised. But in dreams these regularities seem not to possess regularity and predictability. Is this one reason why dreams are not easily remembered—namely that they are not verbalized and so regularized with language? If a person is unable to conform to the regularities of a language, whether this be spoken language (or other sign languages used by people with sensory defects) is he not then handicapped in his whole view of the world and in his ability to make any kind of prediction about outcomes of his actions? Man has the important concept he calls 'the future'. He looks forward, he hopes, etc.

In this short time at my disposal I have been able to do no more than list some of the characteristics of human communication which I personally feel are most important. I shall be very pleased indeed to be corrected on any points or to learn whether any of these views are relevant to the work of psychiatrists.

References

1. Langer, Suzanne K. 1957. 'Philosophy in a New Key—a Study in the Symbolism of Reason, Rite and Art', 3rd ed., Cambridge, Mass. Harvard Univ. Press.
2. Bierstedt, R., 'Emile Durkheim' Weidenfeld and Nicolson, London 1966 (for bibliography and account of Emile Durkheim's work). See also Ref. 5.

3. Gallie, W. B. 1952. 'Peirce and Pragmatism', Great Britain: Pelican Books, Harmondsworth.
4. Sartre, Jean-Paul, 'Being and Nothingness', Philosophical Library, N.Y. 1956. See Ref. 5 also.
5. Tiryakian, E. A. 1962. 'Sociologism and Existentialism'. New Jersey: Prentice-Hall.
6. Cherry, E. C. 1971. 'World Communication: Threat or Promise?', London: John Wiley & Sons Ltd.
7. Ogden, C. K. and Richards, I. A. 1949. 'The Meaning of Meaning', 1st ed. 1923, London: Routledge and Kegan Paul, Ltd.
8. Popper, K. R. 1953. 'Language and the Body-Mind Problem', Proc. of XIth International Congress on Philosophy, Amsterdam: North Holland Pub. Co.

Discussion

after papers by NOBLE, PREMACK AND CHERRY

Prof. Premack: (replying to comments) The difference between man and other animals is too important to be settled by philosophers. Consider 'displacement', the ability to talk about things that are not present, which has been cited as a design feature of language and as a unique characteristic of man. There is no question that 'displacement' is a design feature of language, but is it unique to man?

Recently we have taught a chimpanzee, Sarah, a number of language exemplars, among them words for such predicates as colour of, shape of, size of (e.g. 'red colour of apple', 'round shape of ball', etc.), and names for a number of objects such as chocolate, apple, etc. The subject's ability to learn such predicates led to the next question. Could she use these predicates productively, i.e. to generate new instances of themselves? As part of the answer to that question, we attempted to teach the animal the word 'brown' with the use of the predicate 'colour of'. We gave the subject the instruction, 'brown colour of chocolate', 'brown' being the new word, 'colour of' and 'chocolate' established words. (The full instructions also included a second positive exemplar, 'green colour of grape', as well as two negative exemplars, 'brown not colour of grape' and 'green not colour of chocolate'). The animal was then asked a series of simple questions, such as '? colour of chocolate' (what is the colour of

Y

chocolate?) etc., which it largely answered correctly, indicating that the instructions had been effective. Finally, the animal was confronted with four wooden discs, only one of which was brown, and told, 'take brown'. The animal performed correctly on this and similar tasks.

Both the initial instructions and the final command were given the animal in the absence of chocolate. Therefore, the animal must have been able to generate or picture the properties (at least the colour) of chocolate on the basis of the word 'chocolate' alone. The ability to generate internal representations of objects in the absence of the objects is what underlies 'displacement'. The chimp's success at tasks of the present kind suggest that it not only has internal representations, which in itself cannot be too surprising, but representations that it can generate on appropriate occasions and use as the basis of problem solving. Man is almost certainly unique, but it is not clear that we are yet able to state in what way, and philosophical pronouncements on the matter have not proved helpful.

Dr. Masserman: 'Anthropomorphism' is one of the most redundant and tautologic words in any language. Anybody who has studied Kant, Hegel, Carnap, Langer or any of the other modern philosophers must wonder what data, what concepts or what inferences are not 'anthropomorphic'. But how far down can we go in 'interpretation'? Do not the bees tell each other by dance and sound the distance, direction and value of a honey source. And with regard to the differences between animal and man, we can certainly 'decondition' an acrophobiac to ascend a high building but if acrophobia is translated to 'reaching heights', 'being prominent' or 'above others' do we also abolish this symbolic concept? Or his desire to have his mother come along with him or his wife take him down town? The question then is how far will some specific behaviour pattern have far deeper connotations?

Prof. Lavelle: Are there animal models for the guilt complex and what happens if you push an animal to aggression in violation of ethological cues of submission?

Dr. Masserman: Have you ever come home to a dog that has taken food that it has been taught does not belong to it and watch it slink to you with its tail between its legs?

Prof. Cherry: I think we use the word 'communication' in several ways, which really ought to be distinguished. We only have the one word in English. We talk about a number of different things using the one term. A bee, for example, communicating with another bee is one thing and what it communicates to us is another thing altogether. When a dog comes up to me and wags its tail it is communicating to me in a certain sense but it is not the same as communicating to another dog. Because I shall hypothesise differently about what it is doing. We do not even have to go as far as animals because in the same way I cannot communicate with a Chinese. I can not be a Chinese. Again someone this morning was talking about 'communicating' with the environment. This is not 'communication' at all, it is observation. Mother nature does not talk to me or use language—I hypothesise about it and test my hypothesis. But this is not communication, it is observation. Communication means 'sharing'.

Dr. Masserman: When an American puts his hand over his heart and bows his head, it is a public display of allegiance to his flag or the playing of God Save America.

Prof. Cherry: Perhaps, but their *significances* differ.

Dr. Masserman: I sometimes infuriate my analytic students, as well as my colleagues by defining so-called insight as that joyous but impermanent state in which both analyst and patient share the same illusions as to what is wrong with either one of them.

Prof. O'Doherty: It seems to me we all object about anthropomorphism, but we are not so ready to protest about zoomorphism. I think that there are valuable analogies which help us understand human behaviour, but we should bear in mind the capacity of man to solve problems in the absence of present stimuli and the concept of language itself. The intervention of man to produce behaviour in an organism, which is very valid, does not guarantee that the use of language in behaviour is the same as the use of language with intentionality. Intentionality as a concept perhaps does not belong to behavioural studies.

Prof. Premack: One can question the appropriateness of the animal as a model of man. We have already considered the question on the cognitive side with regard to language; now consider it on the motivational side with regard to conscience, super-ego or self-control (use whatever idiom you prefer). Since both competences, language and self-control, are considered to represent man at his apogee, they represent vigorous challenges to the animal model. We have only recently begun to explore the possibility of animal analogues in the domain of self-control, so it is not yet possible to answer the question. Basically, we take the same approach we took in the case of language. A list of exemplars defining self-control on the one hand and a corresponding list of training procedures for instilling the exemplars on the other. Briefly, we have more or less arbitrarily divided the behaviour of a species into good and bad, and assigned different contingencies to instances of the two cases. Although we are proceeding somewhat differently, one might punish instances of bad and reward instances of good; the precise motivational procedures applied to the two categories may not be critical. Success will require not merely manipulating the frequencies of the behaviours actually touched by the contingencies but, far more importantly, behaviours that never actually come into contact with the contingencies. The evidence must be of a kind to warrant the inference that the animal has induced certain rules of a basis of its motivational experience. The research is not yet far enough along to say one way or the other; I simply wanted to show the possibility of an animal model in the case of a motivational competence which is typically considered no less unique to man than is language in the cognitive domain.

Prof. O'Doherty: Professor Premack has changed the meaning of the words identifying 'displacement' with 'intentionality'.

Prof. Cherry: So far as I can understand what he has done, I could do the same thing with a computer. The real problems of meaning in human language do not arise so long as we are confined to naming things and their physical properties.

Dr. Masserman: As you have said progress springs from differences of opinion.

Syndromes resulting from defective satisfaction of physical appetites—1

Lower animals

ALASTAIR N. WORDEN AND DAVID E. HATHWAY,
Huntingdon Research Centre, Huntingdon, England

Much of the available material for this paper has already been incorporated in reviews, including one by the senior author on nutritional factors and abnormal behaviour in domestic and laboratory animals and in children (Worden, 1968). As in almost all aspects of comparative medicine, the source material comes from two principal fields—from clinical and anecdotal observations upon wild, captive wild or domestic animals and from planned experimentation, 'hunger strike' in zoological collections exemplifying the former.

It is assumed that the term 'physical appetites' relates to food, water or other physical needs, and not to qualified areas of appetitive or searching behaviour. The nutritional field alone provides a wealth of observations, but any interpretation in terms of resultant syndromes requires careful checking that other factors may not be involved. Hinde (1970) provides examples of inter-relations among different activities, e.g. those related to hunger, thirst, fear and sex, deducing that there is some evidence that motivational variables normally considered relevant to one group of activities can sometimes affect others also. He emphasizes, however, that while the need states or stimuli normally relevant to one type of behaviour can augment others in this way, they do not always do so and that a more sophisticated interpretation is required than that of Hull (1943, 1952), who conceived of all need states or stimuli as contributing towards a general drive, which then influenced all behaviour.

Nevertheless, differentiation between, or association of, components—if more than one is involved—is of importance. In discussing the effects of malnutrition upon the development or integrity of the nervous system Worden (1968) wrote that: 'There are other gross effect apart from nutritional deficiency that may affect behaviour in the physiological sense. Thus growth may be retarded to the degree that limits the social status of the individual or greatly delays sexual and reproductive activity. Even in the already mature animal malnutrition may be sufficient to lower rank or to cause sexual and reproductive failure. Seasonal reproductive patterns may, in part at least, be due to variations in nutritional status'. He quoted Raynaud (1950), who found that in winter the testes of the wood mouse (*Apodemus sylvaticus*) were atrophic if the diet was poor, but could be rendered fully functional on an adequate dietary regimen, and Alexander and Frazer (1952 a, b), who recorded that the substitution of wholemeal flour for a more highly extracted flour in the diet employed counteracted the adverse effect of reducing daily light exposure—from thirteen to nine hours—upon mating performance in male laboratory rats. In captive wild animals, and sometimes in domestic pets, there may not only be an altered climate or micro-climate from that to which the animal was previously accustomed but also solitary confinement, or at least a separation from other members of the same species. This factor contributes to one of the hypotheses relating to the failure of Giant Pandas in Western zoological gardens to exhibit normal mating behaviour.

It may perhaps reduce speculation to suggest that, of syndromes resulting from defective satisfaction of physical appetites, some have clearly an anatomical, or neuro-anatomical, or biochemical basis, whereas others have not—or at least have not yet been shown to have. Although it is tempting to draw a distinction between altered behaviour patterns for which no detectable lesion exists, and the physio pathological consequences of deprivation, there is inadequate information as yet to exclude the possibility of subtle or subcellular changes in the former.

In a short contribution such as this it is not possible to do more than to select almost random examples of the syndromes concerned, and to attempt some general observations. The longer review of one of us has already been referred to, as has Hinde's (1970) standard text on animal behaviour, while another reference source is represented by the Proceedings of the International Conference on Malnutrition, Learning, and Behaviour, edited by Scrimshaw and Gordon (1968), and Widdowson (1966) assessed nutritional deprivation in psychobiological development. Deficiency syndromes are described in standard works on veterinary medicine and animal nutrition.

Barnes, Moore, Reid and Pond (1968), summarizing studies mainly conducted in the rat and pig, concluded that restriction of intake of food of normal composition in early life may have long-lasting effects upon certain behavioural activities, including a heightened attention toward food and a lessened exploratory activity, that an animal can recover from retarded learning behaviour both in complex problem solving and in test situations that are not relevant to drive characteristics resulting from early deprivation, and that there appears to be no relationship between the extent of behavioural change and the degree of stunting in body size of the adult animal nutritionally deprived during early life. Fránková and Barnes (1968 a, b) have since provided further experimental evidence in rats of the adverse influence of malnutrition in early life upon exploratory behaviour and upon avoidance conditioning. The apparent lack of correlation between behaviour and physical stunting would appear to contrast with the observations of Cravioto and De Licardie (1968) upon Mexican and Guatemalan children, although these same children have not of course been tested as adults.

More recent studies with rats have emphasized the importance of a carry-over of maternal nutritional deficiency, be this of protein, calories or a combination thereof. Stewart and Sheppard (1971) found that there was a lower litter weight, a much higher neonatal death rate, and a subsequent failure to catch up in terms of body-weight at least during the suckling period, in the progeny of dams themselves maintained from weaning on a diet having a protein value of $NDpCal\% = 5$, compared with the progeny of controls receiving a diet with a value of NDpCal% = 10. Although some abnormal head and limb movements were recorded, there were not the frank neurological symptoms reported in congenitally mal-nourished dogs (Platt and Stewart, 1967, a, b; 1968). Nevertheless, differences in behaviour, brain size and morphology were observed, the details of which are being published separately.

Widdowson and Cowen (1972) studied protein deficiency and calorie deficiency separately, again using female rats from a few weeks of age, and found delayed puberty, reduced fertility, reduced litter size or interference with lactation. However, a severe depriva-tion of either factor for a limited time (nine weeks) followed by rehabilitation on unlimited amounts of stock diet, appeared not to have elicited any permanent effect upon reproductive performance. In her earlier review, Widdowson (1966) emphasized differences in the behaviour of animals suffering from the two types of deficiency, as follows:

> There is no doubt that undernourished rats and pigs are always ravenously hungry and ready to eat; if food is offered to them they devour it at once. The protein-deficient animals appear hungry too—they come forward as soon as they hear the rattle of the food pots—but when food is offered to them they have no appetite and it is difficult to induce them to take any. Even during the early stages of rehabilitation, when they are offered a first-class diet, they do not go for it as the undernourished animals do, and they eat much less of it in the early stages. The protein-deficient animals are more docile and less easily disturbed. The rats are easy to handle, and the pigs pay little attention when someone comes near the pen. The undernourished rats are more vicious and inclined to bite when they are handled, and they appear more nervous in a strange situation.
>
> Undernourished pigs have subnormal body temperatures and, even when the environmental temperature is kept high, spend most of their time huddled together in an attempt to keep warm. Protein-deficient pigs have normal body temperature and gener-ally lie singly. Their skin seems to be itchy, even if it harbours no parasites, and they spend a considerable amount of their time scratching it. When the undernourished animals are rehabilitated they appear to become normal in behaviour.

Lister and McCance (1967) followed up the earlier studies in their laboratory on deprivation and rehabilitation in various animals, and drew attention to species differences, e.g. those species that can grow only until a certain age, and will not attain full size and stature unless they have already done so by this time, and those in which considerable growth is possible after the age at which it normally occurs. Rats, guinea pigs and pigs stop growing at a fixed chronological age. Cockerels, however, if provided with an opportunity for rehabilitation, grow well at an age when their brood mates have already achieved their full genetic stature and have ceased to grow, although despite this they themselves do not achieve the same stature (Lister, Cowen and McCance, 1966).

Controlled observations on ruminants have been relatively few. Blaxter and Wood (1951) compared findings on adult ruminants with their own observations upon Ayrshire calves. During starvation over a period of four days, urinary N loss by the calves was much greater than in mature ruminants, due entirely to the urea, creatine and uric acid fractions. Urinary inorganic S excretion was increased, the source apparently being body-muscle protein. There was no acidosis or ketonuria during starvation, but a slight ketosis during realimentation. Urinary Ca, Na, K and chloride all increased, due presumably to cellular and not to bone metabolism, but losses of Mg and P were small. The pulse rate fell and the respiratory exchange was characterized by a constant fall in metabolism, some three times greater than the slow fall of metabolism that occurs in man with continued fasting. The fall was at a much greater rate than the weight loss, and was not regarded as a failure to reach a postabsorptive state. The weight loss could be quantitatively accounted for as fat, protein and carbohydrate catabolized and as loss of water from extracellular and intracellular components.

Alexander (1962) demonstrated the fatal effect of a relatively short period of starvation on the newborn lamb, showing the importance of prenatal nutrition on the survival time of the lamb under adverse environmental conditions.

Walker (1967) studied somewhat older lambs that, however, were receiving a milk-diet and were, therefore, at the preruminant stage. The lambs survived a period of four days of complete starvation, showing a loss of weight that was speedily regained during re-alimentation, increased urinary loss of ammonia, creatine, amino acid and purine base but not of creatinine, and an increase total S excretion, mainly in the inorganic sulphate fraction. The ratio of N:S during starvation (27:1) was greater than expected from the catabolism of muscle tissue (N:S ratio, 16.2:1) alone. The titratable acidity and acetone excretion in the urine increased greatly during starvation. The urinary excretion of chloride, K and Na was decreased, that of P increased, and that of Ca and Mg little changed. Pulse rate, respiratory rate and rectal temperature all decreased. Heat production fell during the first day of starvation, but was relatively constant thereafter, while there was little change in the blood urea concentration. There was thus reasonable agreement with the results reported for the calf, except for the marked ketone acidosis and for the high excretion of purine N. By comparison with fasted adult sheep (Morris and Ray, 1939), there was a relatively greater loss of body protein but not a marked change in the purine N distribution (viz. the increase in alantoin N and decrease of uric acid N seen in adult sheep).

The symptomatology of these studies did not indicate any unexpected neurological or behavioural features. but such are observed in the deficiencies encountered in the clinical conditions resulting from fasting or inadequate alimentation of pregnant and lactating ruminants. Pregnancy toxaemia in the ewe (Pugh and Sellers, 1963), known also by a great number of different names such as pregnancy disease and twin-lamb disease, causes a high mortality among both mothers and lambs in many sheep-raising areas of the world. It appears to result from an absolute calorie deficiency, sometimes progressive due to the unmet and increasing demands of pregnancy and sometimes to a sudden and complete deprivation of food, associated for example with a heavy fall of snow. Two broad types may be differentiated on a clinical basis, viz. a nervous form in which clinical signs are pronounced over several days with terminal coma, and a form characterized by a profound lethargy. 'Affected ewes are generally first noticed when they show signs of depression, with refusal of food and usually of water. The main nervous signs include excitability, apparent impairment of vision or blindness, unsteady and erratic gait, convulsions and periods of struggling. The breath smells of acetone, there may be excessive salivation, a frothy discharge from the nose and grinding of teeth and constipation. Emaciation rapidly follows the depression in appetite. As the condition progresses, affected ewes become more and more lethargic and eventually become recumbent in a semi-comatose state progressively becoming deeper; at this stage they may adopt unusual postures. Death occurs in from one to fourteen days although recovery may occur if lambing takes place and the ewe eats and ruminates.'

Biochemically, the condition is associated with hypoglycaemia, hyperketonaemia and abnormally high plasma cortisol levels, and Reid (1960 a, b, c) assumes that the metabolic syndrome is a diabetic one, a view that appears to be supported by haematological evidence and by studies on wool-fibre nutrition.

Ketosis or acetonaemia in cattle (Pearce, 1960; Worden, Sellers and Leahy, 1963), other synonyms for which include ketosis, acetonuria, acidosis, ketonaemia and 'slow fever' bears many resemblances to pregnancy toxaemia of the ewe. Its symptomatology was discussed by Udall (1936), who defined the condition as 'a parturient or non-parturient disease of well-nourished, high-producing cows of all ages characterized by a marked hypoglycaemia, acetonuria and acetonaemia, thought to be due to impaired carbohydrate metabolism'. The symptoms include depression, sometimes motor irritation, paresis, rapid loss of condition and a sweetish acetone-like odour in the breath, urine and milk. There is frequently a sudden and marked fall in milk yield, a loss of appetite especially with regard to concentrated food and sometimes an apparent craving for roughage. Udall recognized at least three clinical types, which overlapped somewhat, viz. a milk fever or paresis syndrome, a digestive type, and a nervous form manifested by excitation, delirium, motor irritation and paraesthesia. Blood (1956), in commenting upon Udall's classification, reported a continuous range from the animal with a simple indigestion-like syndrome to the animal with purely nervous symptoms. There is a very low mortality rate from primary ketosis—a term used to distinguish the condition from that accompanying metritis, pneumonia and foreign-body reticulitis. Spontaneous recovery, heralded by normal dunging and a return of appetite, is the rule. Attempts to find a qualitative deficiency in the diet have not been rewarding, and it would appear that a quantitative deficiency, or a lack of palatability, are to be incriminated, sometimes of a seasonal nature and sometimes coincidental with other metabolic disorders, as at the time of parturition. There was a marked increase in ketosis in Norway during the war years, there being frequently an accompanying hypomagnesaemia: at that time the food offered had commonly a low calorie: normal protein ratio. Although many biochemical investigations have been made, with findings of considerable interest, the disturbance of intermediary metabolism involved has yet to be fully elucidated.

The feeding selectivity of otherwise deprived ruminants, or of ruminants of, e.g. protein or P, has formed the subject of various studies, and the work of Tribe and his colleagues (Gordon and Tribe, 1951; Gordon, Tribe and Graham, 1954) indicates that the dietary preferences of sheep under such conditions is without nutritional significance. Deficiency of Na would appear to be an exception, since sheep are able to correct it accurately by selecting solutions of sodium carbonate or sodium chloride (Denton and Sabine (1961)) or by selecting grasses of high Na content (Arnold, 1964). Wilson (1968) studied the effect of high salt intake or restricted water intake on diet selection by sheep. With a choice of high and low-salt rations, sheep were found able to avoid, or partly avoid, the stress of saline drinking-water or restricted water supply by changing the proportion of each ration eaten.

Hinde (1970) has discussed the behavioural implications of deprivation other than nutritional, and is somewhat adversely critical of many earlier interpretations based upon possibly inadequate allowance for the complex and often baffling associations of genetic and environmental factors. In relation to Lorenz's work on sticklebacks reared in isolation, e.g. he suggests that a general interpretation would be that the so-called deprivation experiment can only tell us that an environmental influence is important, not that it is not. 'For most students of development, the immediate problem is to disentangle a pattern of changes occurring through time. Each stage in the development of an organism depends on preceding stages, and results from interactions between the organism or part of the organism and its environment. The behaviour of the mature organism is thus not the consequence of a series of straightline developmental processes leading from gene to adult pattern, modified in some instances by the environment. Rather, we must think in terms of a web of causal relations such that each part may interact with other parts and with the environment at every stage'.

Hinde (1969, 1970) has summarized the very considerable amount of study and observation upon bird vocalization that has been undertaken during recent years, including the results of experiments involving the rearing of birds in auditory isolation. This deprivation in some instances, e.g. in the chaffinch which has been much studied, but not in others, appears to lead to a situation in which the full adult song pattern is not achieved, although the abnormality may be intensified if the bird cannot hear itself sing, as in the American robin. Hinde suggests that one way of relating the findings from many different observations upon different species is to suppose that the naive bird has a crude 'model', 'template' or sollwert of the species-characteristic song which is improved by experience of that song. The learning process in some of the birds affected by isolation can be understood best as involving first the acquisition of the sollwert in early life, and then an adjustment of the motor output to approximate to this pattern.

References

1. Alexander, D. P., and Frazer, J. F. D. 1952a. Interchangeability of diet and light in rat breeding. *Journal of Physiology,* 116: 50-51.
2. Alexander, D. P., and Frazer, J. F. D. 1952b. The influence of diet on the mating of rats. *Journal of Physiology,* 117: 69.
3. Alexander, G. 1962. Energy metabolism in the starved new born lamb. *Australian Journal of Agricultural Research,* 13: 144-64.
4. Arnold, G. W. 1964. Some principles in the investigation of selective grazing. Proceedings of the *Australian Society of Animal Production,* 5: 258-71.
5. Barnes, R. H.; Moore, A. V.; Reid, I. M.; and Pond, W. G. 1968. Chapter on 'Effect of food deprivation on behavioural patterns', 203-217, in Scrimshaw & Gordon (1968).
6. Blaxter, K. L., and Wood, W. A. 1951. The Nutrition of the young Ayrshire calf. 3. The metabolism of the calf during starvation and subsequent realimentation. *British Journal of Nutrition,* 5: 29-55.
7. Blood, D. C. 1956. Field aspects of acetonaemia of dairy cows. *Australian Veterinary Journal,* 32: 31-39.
8. Cravioto, J., and De Licardie, Elsa R. 1968. Chapter on 'Intersensory development of school-age children', pp. 252-268, in Scrimshaw & Gordon (1968).
9. Denton, D. A., and Sabine, J. R. 1961. The selective appetite for Na+ shown by Na+ deficient sheep. *Journal of Physiology,* London, 157: 97-116.
10. Frânková, S., and Barnes, R. H. 1968a. Influence of malnutrition in early life on exploratory behavior of rats. *Journal of Nutrition,* 96: 477-84.
11. Frânková, S., and Barnes, R. H. 1968b. Effect of malnutrition in early life on avoidance conditioning and behavior of adult rats. *Journal of Nutrition,* 96: 485-93.
12. Gordon, J. G., and Tribe, D. E. 1951. The self selection of diet by pregnant ewes. *Journal of Agricultural Science, Cambridge,* 41: 187-90.

13. Gordon, J. G., Tribe, D. E. and Graham, R. C. 1954. The feeding behaviour of phosphorus-deficient cattle and sheep. *British Journal of Animal Behaviour,* 2: 72-74.
14. Hinde, R. A. 1969. *Bird Vocalization in Relation to Current Problems in Biology.* Cambridge University Press.
15. Hinde, R. A. 1970. *Animal Behaviour: a Synthesis of Ethology and Comparative Psychology,* 2nd ed. New York: McGraw-Hill.
16. Hull, C. L. 1943. *Principles of Behavior.* New York: Appleton-Century-Crofts.
17. Hull, C. L. 1952. *A Behavior System.* New Haven: Yale University Press.
18. Lister, D., Cowen, T. and McCance, R. A. 1966. Severe undernutrition in growing and adult animals. 16. The ultimate results of rehabilitation: Poultry. *British Journal of Nutrition,* 20: 633-39.
19. Lister, D., and McCance, R. A. 1967. Severe undernutrition in growing and adult animals. 17. The ultimate results of rehabilitation: Pigs. *British Journal of Nutrition,* 21: 787-98.
20. Morris, S., and Ray, S. C. 1939. The fasting metabolism of ruminants. *Biochemical Journal,* 33: 1217-30.
21. Pearce, P. J. 1960. Some biochemical aspects of ketosis with particular reference to cattle. *Veterinary Reviews and Annotations* 6: 53-93.
22. Platt, B. S., and Stewart, R. J. C. 1967a. Experimental protein-calorie deficiency: Histopathological changes in the endocrine glands of pigs. *Journal of Endocrinology,* 38: 121-43.
23. Platt, B. S., and Stewart, R. J. C. 1967b. Nutrition and the foetus. *Maternal and Child Care,* 3: 539-44.
24. Platt, B. S., and Stewart, R. J. C. 1968. Effects of protein-calorie deficiency on dogs. 1. Reproduction, growth and behavior. *Developmental Medicine and Child Neurology,* 10: 3-24.
25. Pugh, P. D. S., and Sellers, K. C. 1963. Chapter on 'Pregnancy toxaemia in the ewe' (426-44), in Worden, Sellers & Tribe (1963).
26. Raynaud, M. 1950. Cited by Alexander & Frazer (1952a).
27. Reid, R. L. 1960a. XI. Studies on the carbohydrate metabolism of sheep. The role of the adrenals in ovine pregnancy toxaemia. *Australian Journal of Agricultural Research,* 11: 364-82.
28. Reid, R. L. 1960b. XII. Studies on the carbohydrate metabolism of sheep. Further studies on the diabetic nature of the metabolic abnormalities in ovine pregnancy toxaemia. *Australian Journal of Agricultural Research,* 11: 530-38.
29. Reid, R. L. 1960c. Pregnancy toxaemia in ewes. *Proceedings of the 8th International Grassland Conference,* 657-60. (Section on: Physiological disorders in grazing livestock).
30. Scrimshaw, N. S., and Gordon, J. E. 1968. *Malnutrition, Learning, and Behavior.* Proceedings of an International Conference cosponsored by the Nutrition Foundation and the Massachusetts Institute of Technology, Cambridge, Massachusetts, March 1 to 3, 1967. Cambridge, Massachusetts and London: M.I.T. Press.
31. Stewart, R. J. C., and Sheppard, Hilda G. 1971. Protein-calorie de-

ficiency in rats: growth and reproduction. *British Journal of Nutrition,* 25: 175-80.

32. Udall, D. H. 1936. *The Practice of Veterinary Medicine,* 2nd ed. Ithaca, N.Y.: Udall.

33. Walker, D. M. 1967. Nitrogen balance studies with the milk-fed lamb. 6. Effect of starvation and realimentation. *British Journal of Nutrition,* 21: 289-308.

34. Widdowson, Elsie M., and Cowen, Jean. 1972. The effect of protein deficiency and calorie deficiency on the reproduction of rats. *British Journal of Nutrition,* 27: 85-95.

35. Wilson, A. D. 1968. The effect of high salt intake or restricted water intake on diet selection by sheep. *British Journal of Nutrition,* 22: 583-88.

36. Worden, A. N. 1959. Abnormal behaviour in the dog and rat. *Veterinary Record,* 71: 966-81.

37. Worden, A. N. 1968. Chapter on 'Nutritional Factors and Abnormal Behaviour', 238-260, in *Abnormal Behaviour in Animals,* edited by M. Fox. Philadelphia: W. B. Saunders.

38. Worden, A. N.; Sellers, K. C.; and Leahy, J. S. 1963. Chapter on 'Ketosis in cattle', 409-425, in Worden, Sellers & Tribe (1963).

39. Worden, A. N.; Sellers, K. C.; and Tribe, D. E. 1963. *Animal Health, Production and Pasture.* London: Longmans.

Syndromes resulting from defective satisfaction of physical appetites—2

Primates

ALASTAIR N. WORDEN, RALPH HEYWOOD
AND DAVID E. HATHWAY

Huntingdon Research Centre, Huntingdon, England.

Many of the relevant observations upon infra-human primates have involved neonatal animals, or conditions affected by mother-infant relationships, and belong therefore to other parts of this Symposium. They include in particular many of the findings and summaries of Harlow (e.g. Harlow, 1961, 1963 a, b) and discussions relating to his work (e.g. Foss, 1961, 1963), and an earlier session will have provided Professor Harlow himself with the opportunity of bringing a consideration of these aspects up to date. That same session will have provided Professor Sackett with the opportunity of dealing with the effects of object deprivation, while other sessions will have covered the effects of the social isolation or of the over-rigid or over-lax control of primates. It remains only, therefore, to attempt to deal with defective satisfaction in relation to food and water.

Newberne (1970) has summarized the syndromes of nutritional deficiency disease in non-human primates, dealing with rickets and osteomalacia, scurvy, vitamin A deficiency, potassium deficiency, cardiovascular disease and nutritional liver disease, but not with simple deprivation of food or water. In so far as the conditions are relevant to the present subject, they may be commented upon as follows. Rickets and osteomalacia have long been described in captive primates, often being lumped together and often referred to by, to quote Newberne '. . . the imprecise and nondescript term "cage paralysis" '. Their clinical and pathological features were set out by Fox (1923), and their relationship to the nervous system, or to behavioural patterns, would appear to be secondary. New World monkeys need a sufficient supply of vitamin D_3 as they are unable to utilize vitamin D_2. Scurvy in the monkey appears to resemble closely that in man and in lower animals that require an exogenous source of vitamin C with, as in the case of vitamin D deficiency, only indirect nervous system or behavioural effects. Various cases of vitamin A deficiency have been reported in captive monkeys, probably complicated by other factors and not so far involving nerve damage through bony overgrowth as seen, e.g. in calves. Deficiency of potassium, which accounts for nearly all of the intra-cellular cations, appear to have occurred in two rhesus and one squirrel monkey at the Philadelphia Zoological Gardens, there being typical renal and cardiac lesions in the rhesus and papillary lesions in the squirrel monkey. In all three cases there was a history of prolonged diarrhoea and stress. All three were males, all were emaciated, and one exhibited subcutaneous oedema and petechiation of the small bowel. Microscopically, the adrenal gland showed hyperplasia of the zona glomerulosa, but with a decrease of cell size in this zone. These effects were due to prolonged *enteritis*. The majority of cardiovascular disorders in non-human primates are, according to Gresham and Howard (1969), who themselves have worked mainly with the baboon, caused by infective or traumatic agents: cerebrovascular lesions, hypertension and cerebral aneurysms are rare. Atherosclerosis, with accompanying thrombosis and infarction, have likewise rarely been recorded, but this may well be largely a question of the age-range of animal available for study. Ratcliffe and Cronin (1958), however, reported a frequency of 14.5% of arteriosclerosis in gibbons, orang-utans and chimpanzees at the Philadelphia Zoological Garden, with an overall increase from 3% between 1902-1935 to one of 20% between 1936-58 that was attributed to social pressures and an imbalance in adrenal secretion. Other examples of atherosclerosis from various sources,

Z

are given by Newberne (1970). Nutritional liver disease, in the form of marginal lipotrope deficiency is not infrequently seen in primates, and is described by Newberne (1970) as resulting from a shifting of the balance of lipotrope factor together with a decrease in dietary protein or feeding a plant protein low in the sulphur-containing amino-acids, the liver appearing morphologically and functionally normal until confronted with the additional stress of the toxic agent.

Partial or complete deprivation in the free-living state has been observed in a variety of species. Van Lawick-Goodall (1968) discussed the behaviour of free-living chimpanzees, having published a preliminary report under her maiden name of Goodall (1963). While there was not any apparent shortage of food, in some years some fruits failed, and several failures in any one year seemed capable of affecting health and population. The chimpanzees were mainly vegetarian but took a variety of insects, birds eggs and fledglings, the young but not adult bushbuck and bushpig and, most frequently among animal prey, other primates, including red colobus, redtail and blue monkeys and young baboons. Leaves were chewed with every mouthful of meat. Sometimes a carcase in the possession of an adult dominant male elicited begging for a share of the prey from other members of the group. Some chimpanzees were seen eating soil which was found to contain sodium chloride. When the animals could not reach to drink water collected in the hollow of trees they crumpled or chewed leaves as a sponge to soak up the water. As Dart (1963) has recorded, the baboon practices carnivorous habits to a considerabe degree, sometimes hunting in packs for the purpose and constituting a threat to stock farming in its modern sense in parts of South Africa. Dart was concerned to show that predatory behaviour in this species was consistent with an insectivorous origin of primates, and was motivated by the interest aroused by the predatory habit of the Makapansgat australopithecines and early man. The availability of a new supply of food through the introduction of modern stock farming, would account also for its adoption, especially if it were more easily secured than wild game. There may well, however, be a contributory factor in the case of the carnivorous habit of free-living primates attributable to the temporary lack, or qualitative deficiency, of the vegetation. Kortland and Kooij (1963), in their preliminary communication on protohominid behaviour in primates, reported that complete carnivorous behaviour incidentally occurs in all genera of primates that are regularly kept in zoological gardens with the exception of the orang-utan. Even among orangs, however, there have been reported examples of incipient predatory behaviour, such as catching and killing small vertebrates, and eating dead hen chicks. They do not, however, interpret reported field findings on carnivorous practices as indicative of an everyday activity in wild primates. 'Some respondents with many years of field experience have never seen it, others only a few times; still others report that it is a seasonal and/or local phenomenon, or is caused by prolonged drought and food scarcity, etc. Thus, the field data support our impression, from zoo data, that the potentiality in non-anthropoid primates to exercise predatory activities should be interpreted as an emergency measure for special needs, or under special ecological conditions.' Kortland and Kooij are quite definite that the use of weapons and predatory behaviour have originally emerged and evolved independently of one another and have been combined— probably exclusively in the Hominidae—only in a much later stage of evolution. 'No case has been reported to us of a chimpanzee, or any other ape or monkey, demonstrating true armed hunting. . . . It is only the early hominids that have integrated the use of weapons with the procurement of proteins. From this point of view the consummation of human evolution would seem to be the achievement of cannibalism!'

Hall (1963) was able, during July 1961, to study the effects of near-starvation in baboons on an island with an area of about ten square miles formed in Lake Kariba. He pointed out that the existence of baboons in groups is so characteristic of them that the strength of the cohesive force may well be proof against any but very severe disintegrative ecological factors. The island, cut off from the mainland, had a vegetation consisting chiefly of *Mopane* and *Terminalia* trees, growing amongst grasses varying in height from a few inches up to about six feet in patches, with a few thorn-acacia and baobabs, but no riverine vegetation. From comparison with the mainland habitats of baboons in what was then Southern Rhodesia it seemed as though the island provided an inadequate selection of vegetation food-items and that the baboon population on it was living under highly abronmal conditions.

Even had the island been adequate in food resources, its baboon population in relation to its actual area would not have been expected to exceed the order of from fifteen to thirty animals.

'Repeated counts, chiefly on the northern part of the island, suggested that the baboons surviving on the island were not, with two exceptions, living in integrated groups, but were wandering about foraging singly or in very small parties of between two and nine animals. The only parties larger than this were one of thirty-one and one of seventeen, seen successfully on the same afternoon. On twenty-five occasions, one, two, or three baboons were apparently the only ones in foraging parties, on seventeen occasions four to six were observed, on nine occasions seven to nine.' Hall conceded that there might have been several different explanations for this apparent lack of normal organization, one being the actual history of the island's formation and cutting off from the mainland, in the course of which several groups may have been gradually isolated. If this had been the case, the straggler parties seen might have been the survivors of different groups which did not show any tendency to re-group into larger units. He felt, however, that from the position of the island relative to the mainland it was likely that three or four groups at most would have been involved, and that a likely explanation was that one or more groups had gradually split up, under the prevailing conditions of food shortage, into small parties or individuals. Not a single female in part- or full-oestrus was observed, and it is tempting to compare this with the amenorrhoea recorded in women in Japanese P.O.W. camps during World War II. Only one carried infant was seen for certain, and not a single occurrence of mating, mounting or presenting was observed. 'The squealing of young animals, and the occasional squabbles amongst them and older ones, so characteristic of the day's routine of groups in the Cape and on the mainland, did not occur. The cohesive tendencies of mating, of mother-infant relations and the 'attractiveness' of them to others in a group, and of other social gestures of greeting, vocalization and so on, together with the aggressive dominance (also cohesive) of the adult males . . . were never evident in the undisturbed behaviour of the small parties, and one may suppose that social responsiveness is altogether reduced in these animals as a result of malnutrition—all activity being directed at seeking for food. Although the amount of observation time spent on the island is insufficient to justify any conclusions, it is at least plausible to suppose that disintegration, and some numerical reduction, may have taken place without any inter-group or inter-individual fighting. Certainly, there was no visual

or auditory evidence of any fighting or even squabbling.' Hall did
not mention the availability of any animal prey or potential prey
on the island, although he referred in other areas to the consumption of shell-fish, sand-hoppers, sea-lice, bird's eggs and fledglings.
He could not add to the observations of others upon the taking
of lambs or other relatively large animal prey, and although con-
ceding that such predation occurred he considered that much
further observation was required to establish the dependence or
otherwise of this form of feeding upon drought and scarcity of
preferred vegetation foods, and the extent to which baboons seek
out the lambs rather than simply come across them in the course
of day-ranging.

It would be expected that, in natural or semi-natural environments, deprivation might occur not only from severe food or water
shortage as such but also from the added effects of dominance.
In his observations on squirrel monkeys (*Saimiri*) in a Columbian
forest, Thorington (1968) noted they had very active feeding
patterns, starting in the morning with fruit eating and later tending
to forage for insects. Frequently they would eat fruit where it was
gathered, but when a more dominant animal moved nearby, they
would carry it elsewhere to eat. Efficient foraging for insects was
found to require each animal to take a different path through the
forest, and appeared to be the basis of the fragmentation of the
subgroups during the day. The high humidity of the forest was
correlated with a high respiratory water loss.

DuMond (1968), who studied *Saimiri* in a semi-natural environment found that the normal seasonal cycle of spermatogenesis was
paralled by the appearance of 'fatted' males in the colony. These
fatted males had significantly greater amounts of subcutaneous fat
and fluffier fur, and their bodyweight averaged 937 g. compared
with 715 g. in the non-fatted state. This weight gain was found
to be associated with the establishment of a dominance hierarchy.

The food habits of four species of New World monkeys have
been studied in the field by Hladik and his colleagues in Panama
(Hladik, Hladik, Bousset, Valdebouze, Viroben and Delort-Laval,
1971), who have reported an apparent balancing of amino-acid and
soluble carbohydrate intake by means of the detection of food-
stuffs spread, in some instances, over wide home ranges.

Mukherjee and Gupta (1965) studied the food habits of the
rhesus macaque in low mangrove forests in West Bengal. Typical

troops numbered from twenty to thirty, but solitary individuals were observed. The mainly arboreal vegetarian diet was seen to be supplemented by the consumption of crabs and mushrooms, although the monkeys avoided swimming in the saline black water. Water was obtained by licking dew from leaves or by eating succulent leathery leaves.

These habits are presumably all liable to exaggeration or variation under conditions of stress or shortage, and to the influence of dominance. Bernstein (1970), has, however, pointed out the several changes in meaning of the word 'dominance' since the concept of 'peck order' first published by Schjelderup-Ebbe in 1913, leading to 'priorities and incentives' as the basic expression and measure. Boelkins (1967), in his study of dominance in rhesus, used water deprivation and drinking scores with apparent success, but found less than satisfactory results on re-test, which he felt reflected the fluidity of the relationships. Bernstein has reviewed the earlier studies of Carpenter, Crawford, Jay, Zuckerman and others, all of whom have stressed priority to incentives as the key criterion, whether the incentive be food or some other activity such as access to sexual partners or entry into the cage of another animal. Hall (1964) expressed the view that animals may use aggression to obtain priority to incentives, that spacing and other mechanisms serve to limit the form and scope of aggression within the social unit, that a social code is apparently established, and that most aggression within a social group is directed at punishing nonconformist behaviour. It would seem that, in the wild, shortage of food or water may lead to a breakdown, or breaking up, of the social unit, with the possible consequences in terms of redirection of aggressive or other aspects of dominance relationships, although the observations of Hall (1963) on the Chacma baboon, already referred to, would suggest that in this species, at least, near-starvation was not accompanied by fighting or squabbling, perhaps—in part at least—because of the dispersion that had occurred.

The stresses resulting from the retention of primates within a laboratory environment ought to be mentioned. In particular, such animals are housed in individual cages and are fed commercially available, semi-purified diets. Although the diets are nutritionally balanced, they represent a deprivation of choice to the animals; this deprivation may be disturbing. The diets themselves are uniformly monotonous and unappetising, but primates, fed on them consistently thrive physically for many years. In other words, monkeys adapt to the stresses of confinement and isolation, and appear to eat diets devoid of a strong appeal to them. Confronted with no alternative, the acceptance of such food results from the animals' 'will to survive'. If the animals are maintained in captivity under more tolerable conditions, with other animals of the same species, and with opportunities for exploration and investigation, they are then less likely to accept standardized diets. However, some animals reject food from the start, and they develop an inability for food retention. This is reminiscent of *anorexia nervosa* in human subjects, and death eventually results. This phenomenon is much more common in New World monkeys than in Old World monkeys. If standardized food, and supplementary fruits and vegetables are available without restriction, then boredom plus a strong preference for the fruits and vegetables would be likely to lead ultimately to a state fo dietary imbalance and malnutrition. Stress situations in conjunction with monotonous diets do, in fact, produce a disease syndrome, characterized by gastric dilation.

Although feeding order and the acquisition of presumed incentives have formed a popular measure of dominance and social relationships between pairs of animals in laboratory studies, the correlation of this measure with others, e.g. the direction of agonistic episodes, has not been good (Bernstein, 1970). Thus Warren and Maroney (1958) recorded a correlation of 0.77 between priority to access to food and agonistic dominance, while Bernstein (1969) obtained similar results with larger social groups. Hall (1968) concluded in fact that food tests correlated so poorly with social rank that they were not a useful measure even in approximating the dominance relationship in a group.

In his review of abnormal behaviour in primates, Mitchell (1970) includes a note on coprophagy, which Hill (1966) has stated to be one of the most difficult problems to deal with in primates in zoological gardens. Mitchell, in earlier joint studies, had found that coprophagy occurred often in animals raised in isolation, and was more pronounced the longer the period of isolation, but seldom if ever in control rhesus. Coprophagy has never been observed in the Huntingdon Research Centre colony of over five hundred Old World primates. Mitchell states that whereas coprophagy is common among captive gorillas, it was not recorded by Schaller (1963) in the latter's observations on the gorilla in the wild. The higher the primate, the more likely is coprophagy to occur under conditions of abnormal environment.

Poirier (1970), in his report on the Nilgiri langur of South India, recorded geophagy or dirt eating on several occasions. There was no evidence that the sites, which were on soil of clay-humic origin with a high aluminium (alkaline) content, were being searched for insects. The water requirements of different langur species were said to vary widely, a phenomenon apparently related to regional differences in rainfall and abundance of succulent vegetation.

Studies on captive primate populations appear to support findings in the field on the relationship of feeding activity to social structure, but do not provide much information on marked physical deprivation. Ploog, Blitz and Ploog (1963) in their observations on a group of six squirrel monkeys, found that by all other criteria one male remained dominant throughout, whereas in feeding studies— whether based upon food won or food stolen—a second male was more or less his equal. 'In stealing behaviour individual characteristics and relationships were decisive'. Draper and Menzel (1966) found that young orang-utans responded to the cut properties of food, readily discriminating between differences in both size and distance, and adjusted their reactions accordingly, and that there was essentially no change in performance with time. Fitz-Gerald, Barfield and Grubbs (1970) established an order of preference for a dozen individual foods by a group of nine female and five male wild-born gorillas. Tree shrews are of interest to primatologists, in view of their possible protosimian taxonomy—although Sorenson (1970) has recently concluded that they are—and will remain—a transitional group in the eyes of most taxonomists. Their feeding behaviour has been well described (Kaufmann, 1965; Sorenson, 1970), and shows them to be omnivorous, feeding even upon newborn and upon dead adults of their own species. Again however, there is little to demonstrate the effects of deprivation.

Apologies must be offered for the paucity of data relevant to the pre-selected title of this contribution, but much work remains to be done, if syndromes of this origin are to be described with any degree of adequacy.

References

Bernstein, I. S. 1969. Stability of the status hierarchy in a pigtail monkey (*Macaca nemestrina*) group. *Animal Behaviour*, 17: 452-58.

Bernstein, I. S. 1970. Chapter on 'Primate status hierarchies' 71-109, in Rosenblum (1970).

Boelkins, C. R. 1967. Determination of dominance hierarchies in monkeys. *Psychonomic Science*, 7: 317-18.

Dart, R. A. 1963. Contribution on 'The carnivorous propensity of baboons' pp. 49-56, in Napier & Barnicot (1963). (vid. infra).

Draper, W. A., and Menzel, E. W., Jr. 1966. Size and distance of food: cues influencing the choice behaviour of orangutans (*Pongo pygmaeus*). *Folia Primatologica*, 4: 186-90.

DuMond, F. V. 1968. Chapter on 'The squirrel monkey in a seminatural environment' pp. 87-145, in Rosenblum & Cooker (1968).

Fitz-Gerald, F. L.; Barfield, M. A.; and Grubbs, P. A. 1970. Food preferences in lowland gorillas. *Folia Primatologica*, 12: 209-11.

Foss, B. M. 1963, ed. *Determinants of Infant Behaviour: Proceedings of a Tavistock Study Group on Mother-Infant Interaction*. London: Methuen.

Foss, B. M. 1961, ed. *Determinants of Infant Behaviour: Proceedings of the Second Tavistock Seminar on Mother-Infant Interaction*. London: Methuen.

Fox, H. 1923. *Disease in Captive Wild Animals and Birds*. Philadelphia: Lippincott.

Goodall, Jane. 1963. Contribution 'Feeding behaviour of wild chimpanzees: a preliminary report', 39-47, in Napier & Barnicot (1963).

Gresham, G. A., and Howard, A. N. 1969. Chapter on 'Cardiovascular Diseases' pp. 1-7; discussion, pp. 7-8, in *Using Primates in Medical Research, Part II. Recent Comparative Research*, ed. W. I. B. Beveridge. Basel and New York: S. Karger.

Hall, K. R. L. 1963. Contribution on 'Variations in the ecology of the Chacma baboon. *Papio ursinus*' pp. 1-28, in Napier & Barnicot (1963).

Hall, K. R. L. 1964. Chapter on 'Aggression in monkey and ape societies' (51-64) in *The Natural History of Aggression*, ed. Carthy & F. J. Ebling. New York and London: Academic Press.

Hall, K. R. L. 1968. Chapter on 'Social learning in monkeys' pp. 383-97, in *Primates*, ed. P. C. Jay. New York: Holt, Rinehart & Winston.

Harlow, H. F. 1961. Chapter on 'The development of affectional patterns in infant monkeys' 75-88; discussion, 89-97, in Foss (1961).

Harlow, H. F. 1963a. Chapter on 'The maternal affectional system' 3-29; discussion, 29-33, in Foss (1963).

Harlow, H. F. 1963b. Chapter on 'Basic social capacity of primates' 174-185, in *Primate Social Behavior*, ed. C. F. Southwick. Princeton, N.J.: Van Nostrand.

Hill, C. A. 1966. Coprophagy in apes. *International Zoo Yearbook*, 6: 251-57.

Hladik, C. M.; Hladik, A.; Bousset, J.; Waldebouze, P.; Viroben, G.; and Delort-Laval, J. 1971. Le régime alimentaire des Primates de l'île de Barro-Colorado (Panama). *Folia Primatologica*, 16: 85-122.

Kaufman, J. H. 1965. Studies on the behavior of captive tree shrews (*Tupaia glis*). *Folia Primatologica*, 3: 50-74.

Kortland, A. and Kooij, M. 1963. Contribution on 'Protohominid behaviour in primates (preliminary communication)' 61-88, in Napier & Barnicot (1963).

Mitchell, G. 1970. Chapter on 'Abnormal behavior in primates' 195-249, in Rosenblum (1970).

Mukherjee, A. K., and Gupta, S. 1965. Habits of the rhesus macaque *Macaca mulatta* (Zimmermann) in the Sunderbans, 24 Parganas, West Bengal. *Journal of the Bombay Natural History Society*, 62: 145-46.

Napier, J., and Barnicot, N. A. 1963, eds. *The Primates. Symposia of the Zoological Society of London*, No. 10.

Newberne, P. M. 1970. Chapter on 'Syndromes of nutritional deficiency disease in nonhuman primates' 205-32, in *Feeding and Nutrition of Nonhuman Primates*, ed. R. S. Harris. New York and London: Academic Press.

Ploog, D. W.; Blitz, Jean; and Ploog, Franke. 1963. Studies on social and sexual behaviour of the squirrel monkey (*Saimiri sciurens*). *Folia Primatologica*, 1: 29-66.

Poirier, F. E. 1970. Chapter on 'The Nilgiri langur (*Presbytis* johnii) of South India', 251-383, in Rosenblum (1970).

Ratcliffe, H. L., and Cronin, M. T. I. 1958. Changing frequency of arterio-sclerosis in mammals and birds at the Philadelphia Zoological Gardens. Review of autopsy records. *Circulation*, 18: 41-52.

Rosenblum, L. A. 1970, ed. *Primate Behavior: Developments in Field and Laboratory Research*, Vol. 1. New York and London: Academic Press.

Rosenblum, L. A., and Cooper, R. W. 1968, eds. *The Squirrel Monkey* New York and London: Academic Press.

Powell, Thelma E. 1963. Chapter on 'The social development of some rhesus monkeys' 35-45; discussion, 45-49, in Foss (1963).

Schaller, G. B. 1963. *The Mountain Gorilla: Ecology and Behavior*. Chicago: University of Chicago Press.

Schjelderap-Ebbe, T. 1913. Honsenes stemme. Bidvag til hönsenes psykologi. *Naturen*, 37: 262-76.

Sorenson, M. W. 1970. Chapter on 'Behavior of tree shrews' pp. 141-93, in Rosenblum (1970).

Thorington, R. W., Jr. 1968. Chapter on 'Observations of squirrel monkeys in a Columbian forest' 69-85, in Rosenblum & Cooper (1968).

Van Lawick-Goodall, Jane, 1968. The Gombe Stream Reserve. *Animal Behaviour Monographs*, 1: 161-311.

Warren, J. M., and Maroney, R. J. 1958. Competitive social interaction between monkeys. *Journal of Social Psychology*, 48: 223-33.

Syndromes resulting from defective satisfaction of physical appetites—3

Death, survival and the continuity of life

ROBERT JAY LIFTON
Yale University

Though I think the work I will talk about today has connections with ethological perspectives and a general biological evolutionary point of view I should say—in light of the orientation of this conference—that the birds I draw in my avocation as a bird cartoonist are the only animals with which I work. In one of the more existential of these cartoons a small bird is looking up hopefully, even euphorically, and saying, 'All of a sudden I had this wonderful feeling: I am me!' The other bird—appearing more jaundiced, experienced and cynical—looks down and says, 'You were wrong.'

That comment reflects much of what we do in psychiatry, despite ourselves. But the profession of psychiatry, like almost all the professions now, is in crisis and is beginning to change. My own work in the field of psychohistory is an effort in which I and others are trying to confront psychological theory with issues and events surrounding historical change. I have been asked about the psychohistorical or psychoformative approach and I would like to talk first about that, then about the psychology of the survivor, and finally about an evolving theoretical position oriented around the paradigm of death and the continuity of life. This grows out of work I did with atomic bomb survivors in Hiroshima ten years ago and relates to recent work with veterans of the Vietnam war.

The term 'psychohistory' means simply an application of a systematic psychological approach to historical events, in my own work on-going contemporary historical events. This is a post-Freudian development in which a small group of Americans have been active. There are four models along which psychohistorical research has proceeded, two Freudian ones which are necessary for our own developing post-Freudian models but which are misleading when taken too literally and used exclusively. Such a paradoxical situation is often the case when one tries to learn from a classical system of thought and yet be free enough in relation to that system to be creative and innovative.

The first Freudian model is based on Freud's famous description of the primeval encounter between the father and the rebelling sons. Freud explained this *pre*-historic encounter along the lines of the Oedipus complex and used it as a model for the original creation of civilization and religion and for recurrent social change. This principle of the rebellious sons remains important for psychological theory, but it is disastrous when used to interpret specific historical events. It is a very convenient principle for those who wish, for example, to put down student rebellion as nothing more than the expression of the Oedipus complex; it is especially handy because the fathers happen to be the ones making the interpretations.

The second Freudian paradigm is the psychopathological one—the study of the great man and his psychopathology as exemplified by the infamous Freud-Bullitt study of Woodrow Wilson. Bullitt did most of the writing of this but Freud bears some of the responsibility because the approach taken is essentially Freudian: the whole Versailles tragedy is interpreted around Wilson's early psychopathological difficulties with masculinity. Obviously such an approach eliminates history in the name of studying it.

Erik Erikson is responsible for the third paradigm, that of the great man in history. Erikson takes the historical dimension very seriously and in his psychobiographies of Luther and Ghandi he sees the great man as solving a personal conflict in a way that is significant for a whole culture and historical era.

The fourth paradigm, the one with which I have worked, involves the study of groups of people. Often the great man is inaccessible and if he is accessible perhaps not great. But in either case it is difficult for one man to exemplify a whole culture or a whole ethic, and so I have evolved what I call the study of shared psychohistorical themes. In this I have tried to be empirical in studying a particular group of people through intensive interviews. These are people who have experienced a certain moment of history together. This is true of the Hiroshima survivors who survived a tragic moment of history, and also of American and Japanese youth and anti-war Vietnam veterans.

In connection with discussing the psychology of the survivor I want to explain the psychoformative, as opposed to psychoanalytic, approach. Psychoanalysis derives in terminology and spirit from the nineteenth-century principle of breaking things down into their component parts, analyzing them and finding in them the source and causation of what one is studying. I think a more contemporary principle of causation and change has to do with an evolving chain of causes. I see this psychologically in a series of inner images and inner forms which move from images toward symbolization. The essential mental function of creating and re-creating images and forms I call the psychoformative process. My approach here is strongly influenced by the symbolic philosophy of Cassirer and Langer.

In addition to a stress on shared themes and reliance on a psychoformative understanding of psychic life, a third principle in psychohistorical work is that of advocacy. This is very important to emphasize. I think the hiding of the subjectivity of the self, the pretence that it is not there, is the most unscientific approach to this kind of work because it results in a distortion of the process in the name of objectivity. Of course in relation to the kinds of things I have studied—Hiroshima survivors or Vietnam veterans—value neutrality would be spurious. So I go further than the notion of disciplined subjectivity, a phrase used by Margaret Mead and Erik Erikson, and talk of specific advocacy. In this I try to combine a rigorous intellectual commitment to my tradition and my own position in relation to that tradition on the one hand with a kind of out-front advocacy on the other. I try to make this advocacy clear to the groups with which I am working. This has been true of my relationship with anti-war Vietnam veterans; I was called in and asked to work with them partly because of ethical and political statements I had made. My relationship with the veterans has continued to be based both on my sense of myself as a psychological investigator and on my shared advocacy with these men in the political struggles in which they are engaged.

Finally, my psychohistorical work has been death-centred. It is extraordinary the degree to which psychological theory has ignored the element of death. There are strong historical influences on the research we do both in the methods we use and in the subjects we choose to study. In Freud's time in the late Victorian era there was a hypocritical attitude and morality about sexuality which created an overwhelming problem for man and threatened to do him in. The problems caused by sexual repression have not been solved by any means, but now a more overwhelming problem is that which I referred to at the end of my Hiroshima book as massive techno-logical violence and absurd death.

Our age—characterized by absurd and premature death—has made of us all psychological survivors. We speak of ourselves as post-modern, post-Freudian, post-historical, post-everything: we do not quite know what we are but we know that we exist after some-thing that we have survived. In writing my book on the Hiroshima survivors I compared the records of those who had survived Nazi death camps and the plagues of the Middle Ages. I found strong similarities in all these experiences and also in more humble sur-vivals of an everyday kind, the work psychiatrists have done with dying patients and the relatives of the dying patient. All these experiences—both personal and cultural survival—come together around a general theme of the survivor, if one defines the survivor as one who has come into contact with death in a bodily or psychic form and has himself remained alive. Thus survival can be psychic, symbolic or even cultural. For many reasons there is a strong sense of cultural survival now.

In the Hiroshima experience, the first use of a nuclear weapon on a human population, the individual survivor became subject to what I came to think of as a permanent encounter with death. This encounter came in four distinct stages. At the time the bomb fell there was overwhelming exposure to the dead and near dead around him. The next stage, weeks and sometimes only days after exposure to acute irradiation effects, involved mysterious, grotesque and terri-fying symptoms including vascular bleeding into the skin and out of all the bodily orifices as well as loss of hair, severe diarrhoea, weakness, often resulting in death. I spoke of this syndrome as an epidemic of invisible contamination, and that was the way it was perceived. The third stage occurred years later with the increase of leukaemia and other forms of cancer as well as other less malignant conditions all understood by the survivors under the general rubric 'A-bomb disease'. Even though the actual increase in incidence of these conditions was relatively slight, A-bomb disease was infused with imagery of death and this made the psychological effect enormous. It made the survivors feel that the contamination process was endless. This suggests the fourth stage: a lifelong identity of atom bomb survivorship, what I came to think of as an identity of the dead; one became so bound to the dead and to death imagery that one was entrapped in it and found it hard to escape.

This particular four-stage sequence was peculiar to atomic bomb survivors, but there are parallels in it with themes of survivorship in general. The first is a simple and basic one, the death imprint. This is an indelible image of death all around one and occurs in combination with an equally indelible image of one's own psychic breakdown and disintegration in response to that perception of all engulfing death. But it is the image of being engulfed in death that remains and from which subsequent death anxiety derives, the sense that one has lost one's invulnerability to death, and that the whole world has 'died' in massive holocaust. The sometimes compensatory feeling of invulnerability renewed—the feeling that one has traversed an ultimate boundary and is now untouchable—sometimes occurs, and lends to the survivor a kind of elite status. But this feeling tends to be fragile, hiding more basic underlying anxiety and profound vulnerability.

Also related to the death imprint are retaliatory images having to do with a wished-for destruction of the world. This occurred as a kind of underground theme in Hiroshima survivors as well as in some anti-war Vietnam veterans. But it is important to recognize that the death which the survivor has seen in both these examples is grotesque, absurd and premature. We never speak of death as being timely; we always say it is untimely. But some death is more untimely than other death and is then considered premature. I think man's basic fear is of premature death and of unfulfilled life, rather than of death itself.

All of this is part of the death imprint, a concept I think has clinical applicability beyond what I can describe here. It would be interesting, incidentally, to see broader studies of survival patterns in animals as has been done in a beginning way with the process of mourning.

A second survivor theme is that of death guilt. It is a profound theme, central to the experience of all survivors, centring on the question: Why did I survive while he or she or they died? Accompanying that question is an inner image of organic social balance which, however irrational it may seem, the survivor feels in this logic: Others died, I lived; because they died I lived; f I had died they could have lived. This kind of reasoning is the source of profound guilt.

Some survivors live a life of grief. This has been true for anti-war veterans in whom the mourning process cannot be fully completed. This impaired mourning derives from an image I have found to be present in the people in Hiroshima and again in Vietnam veterans. This is an image unique to each survivor but found in some form in almost all, an image in which is condensed all the pity and horror and guilt felt by a particular survivor. It is an image of ultimate horror. It is interesting that American G.I.'s are both the ones doing most of the killing and are also survivors. I have tried to understand them as both victims and executioners, as indeed they see themselves. These men have profound images of ultimate horror or ultimate transgression that are part of their continuing death guilt. This guilt can be focused either on deaths of other G.I.'s or on deaths of Vietnamese.

Death guilt can take the form of identification guilt when, as in the case of the Hiroshima survivors, one identifies with specific people known to the survivor or even with the anonymous dead. This identification process in guilt has important value, I think, for the survival of the species. When this kind of guilt is lost a necessary transforming relationship to holocaust can also be lost.

In the rap group programme in which I have participated during the last year and a half with anti-war veterans we have found that psychological recovery for these men after their profoundly disturbing and guilt-infused experiences depends upon discovering the humanity of the Vietnamese whom they have so brutalized Becoming human again depends, paradoxically, upon seeing one's victims as human, in this case seeing the Vietnamese not as 'gooks' but as men. This is a process of recovering identification guilt.

A third survivor pattern is psychic numbing, an extreme form of psychic desensitization and the loss of the symbolizing or formative process. This is a kind of psychological impairment which I see as more important at this historical moment than the repression of which Freud spoke. Repression refers to ideas that are held out of consciousness; psychic numbing refers to an impairment in one's capacity to relate symbolically to the world. One is unable to inwardly recreate one's experience; thus one becomes incapable of experiencing and of feeling. Psychic numbing was a necessary psychological defence for the people of Hiroshima but it has been a contributing factor in the atrocities committed by American G.I.'s. The Americans involved in the My Lai atrocity were at an advanced stage of numbing.

I learned about psychic numbing partly from my own experience, and this is an example of how one's own subjectivity itself becomes an instrument in the research process. During my first week in Hiroshima I was overwhelmed by the grotesque stories that I heard. The things I was told were so disturbing that I thought I might be unable to continue with the work. But then, after a week or ten days, I was suddenly less disturbed by the stories and felt more able to move into my professional function as an investigator. I came to see this process as a partial professional numbing necessary for my task as an investigator, but as having malignant potential when over developed as it is in most of our culture. We live in an age of numbing, numbing being most necessary for those who make and use the technological weaponry which our culture produces.

Another psychological pattern found in survivors has to do with response to help and support. Though one feels wounded and in need of help and nurturance, one is at the same time suspicious of all help and reluctant to accept it because that help is itself a reminder of one's personal weakness. This becomes what I call suspicion of counterfeit nurturance and it characterizes, I think, what we see in the response of minority groups—people who have been victimized and are in a sense survivors—to offers of aid.

The final task of the survivor is what I call formulation: giving inner form and significance to one's immersion in death in order to find significance in one's subsequent life. This is the whole struggle of anti-war veterans. Hiroshima survivors tried to do it through aligning themselves with peace movements. There was the feeling that if the world could be made to understand what the survivors had been through then the experience itself would assume significance. That process had only small success. Survivors of Nazi death camps tried in their own way to achieve formulation of their experiences in creating the state of Israel, but that too has had its difficulties. The anti-war veterans are doing something unique in coming

A1

together as a veterans group and finding their sense of significance not in identifying themselves as chauvinistic veterans' groups, as is the habit of most veterans in most wars, but rather in speaking out against the war. They adopt as their survival mission the telling of the truth about the war to the American public and ask the American public to share their own guilt about the war.

From this work on the psychology of the survivor my evolving theory of death imagery takes two directions, one a theory of symbolic immortality and the other a theory of evolving images of mortality over the course of the life cycle. Freud thought that all ideation about immortality was mere denial of death and as such was delusional. My point, in contrast, is that man has need for a sense of symbolic connectedness or continuity with the past and the imagined future. He needs a sense of continuity with other human beings and the creations of other human beings. This can be seen as a need for a sense of symbolic immortality in a biological or biosocial mode: I live on in family, in my children and their children. Through the mode of works man lives on through his achievements —whether great scientific or artistic ones or more humble ones as a teacher or therapist. Through the idea of the conquest of death through spiritual attainments man lives on in the traditional religious mode. Through an identification with the process of eternal nature man feels himself to live on in the on-going life of the natural world. And through intense psychic experience man conquers death in the psychic state of experiential transcendence. This last mode is different from the others because it refers to purely psychic experience. But I think it is basic to the other four because it lends both intensity and a feeling of unity to experiences in the other modes.

The imagery of mortality over the life cycle and the eventual formation of an idea of death takes place around three polarities which are present as inchoate images from earliest infancy. The first is an image of connection and separation (my thinking here is influenced by the work of John Bowlby), the second an image of integrity and disintegration (and here I am influenced by the ideas of Melanie Klein), and the third a rather neglected polarity of movement and stasis. Experience of each of these polarities begins in infancy as a kind of inchoate image or direction of the organism and later taes on symbolic and ultimately ethical qualities. The separation, disintegration and stasis experiences lend to the developing conceptual idea of death a negative quality, as a young child between three and five begins to think consciously about death.

I wish to close with several quotations. A man called Yeats, whose name is sometimes heard around here, said, 'Man has created death'. Man did not create death; I am sure Yeats meant that man created the *idea* of death and above all the idea of absurd death. Joseph Campbell, a leading American student of mythology, has emphasized that 'The mythical hero is the champion not of things become but of things becoming; the dragon to be slain by him is precisely the monster of the status quo, of existing forms.' My final quotation is from Stanley Milgrim, an American psychologist who did the famous 'Eichman' experiments in which he discovered that naive experimental subjects would go to a very disturbing extreme in shocking or seeming to shock instructed subjects whom they thought they were harming. They continued to give electric shocks to these subjects even when told the shock might endanger the lives of those receiving them. Milgrim was rather appalled when he observed the willingness to follow these instructions when given by people in apparent authority. He concluded: 'Man is doomed if he acts only on the alternatives handed down to him.'

I think these principles of Yeats, Campbell and Milgrim have some applicability at this moment in Irish psychiatry, and for the rest of us as well.

Syndromes resulting from defective satisfaction of physical appetites—4

Loss of sleep and mental illness

STUART A. LEWIS,
Department of Psychiatry, University of Edinburgh

Everyone goes without sleep at some time. As students at least we went to all-night parties and still managed to function to our satisfaction the next day. There would be little subjective effect other than weariness and sleepiness. It is unlikely that any of you were aware of gross alteration of affect. However, Wilkinson (1968) has demonstrated that behaviourally we are impaired with as little sleep loss as four hours. To demonstrate this it is necessary to use prolonged, boring vigilance tasks. The impairment is failing to detect infrequent events. More detailed analysis, using signal detection techniques, indicates that the change with sleep loss is one of loss of sensitivity and not increased caution in deciding that a given event is a signal (Deaton et al. 1971). This effect cannot in any way be considered mental illness even though such effects may have important implications in industry and for brain physiology.

Freud (1953) and many before and since have suggested explicitly or implicitly that going without our dreams results in psychological disturbance. Before looking at recent studies pertinent to this hypothesis I would remind you of the non-unitary nature of sleep. There are two kinds of sleep, each with its own characteristics. On the one hand there is paradoxical, rapid eye movement (REM) or active sleep in which there is loss of muscle tone, penile erections or increased clitoral blood flow, a low voltage desynchronised EEG and of course characteristic eye movements as well as many other features. The other type of sleep which is subdivided into four distinct stages depending on the EEG, does not contain eye movements, the muscle tone is not lost and the EEG contains sleep spindles and a varying abundance of delta and theta activity. This type of sleep is variously known as orthodox, non-rapid eye movement (NREM) or passive sleep, and it alternates throughout the night with paradoxical sleep which accounts for about 20-25% of the total sleep time and has a mean periodicity of about ninety minutes. The mental life of the two types of sleep is different. In paradoxical sleep there is dreaming while in orthodox sleep the mentation is much less vivid, less distorted and less elaborate (Foulkes, 1966).

Selective deprivation of stage 3 + 4 of orthodox sleep can, in the present context, be dismissed since it leads to no observable behavioural changes either in mood or performance (Naitoh, 1969). However, in passing, it is worth commenting that these stages of sleep are associated with increased output of growth hormone (Sassin et al. 1969). Deprivation of stage 3 + 4 sleep leads to incomplete suppression of HGH (Karacan et al. 1970) so presumably there is some detrimental physical consequence.

Deprivation of paradoxical sleep, or, as some would have it, deprivation of dreaming, has bearing on the theme of this meeting. The early study by Dement (1960) indicated that paradoxical sleep deprivation results not only in a compensatory increase in this type of sleep on subsequent recovery nights but there was also an increase in the number of attempts to enter this type of sleep during the deprivation night. Psychic changes were also reported. These results led Dement to postulate a 'need to dream'. Although subsequent studies (Clements and Dement, 1967) have reported 'distinct unhealthy changes in the personality profile', it seems that to obtain these major psychic alterations it is necessary to use prolonged paradoxical sleep deprivation. Of course, the prior personality of the subject cannot be ignored. Indeed, Dement himself subsequently (1965) retracted his 'need to dream' interpretation and substituted a 'need for paradoxical sleep' hypothesis.

The current favourite among the myriad hypotheses for the behavioural function of paradoxical sleep is that it is concerned with learning and memory (Empson and Clarke, 1970). The majority of the evidence for this comes from animal studies. There are many methodological problems such as the stress induced by the deprivation technique and the probable involvement of stated dependency in the learning and recall (Stern, 1970). If we are now saying that for some reason there is a 'need for paradoxical sleep' rather than that there is a 'need for dreams' then dreaming becomes an epiphenomenon of paradoxical sleep. This does not, however, absolve us from the necessity of considering the function of dreams.

These inconsistently reported psychotic symptoms brought on by paradoxical sleep deprivation are also found with total sleep deprivation. The symptomatology includes visual misperception, ranging from frank hallucinations to misperceptions of an illusionary nature. The arguments as to why these symptoms do not occur in all sleep deprived subjects are roughly the same as those advanced for paradoxical sleep deprivation; that is they occur only after very prolonged sleeplessness and the subjects in whom florid psychotic phenomena appeared seem to have atypical personalities and personal histories. However, it is worth noting that in the subject described by West and his colleagues (1962) the psychotic phenomena appeared at roughly ninety minute intervals. You will recall that when I was describing the general characteristics of paradoxical sleep I mentioned that the mean periodicity of paradoxical sleep is ninety minutes. On the same line, Oswald (1970) described oral behaviour as having a ninety minute rhythm confirming a study by Friedman and Fisher (1967). There is one other relationship which may be worth comment. Grey Walter has described the contingent negative variation (CNV) in schizophrenics as being positive rather than negative. In studies of the CNV in sleep deprivation (Johnson, 1972) it was found that the CNV also tended to be positive going. While this may obviously be a mere coincidence rather than a direct link between the brain physiology of schizophrenia and sleep deprivation, it should perhaps be considered as one small brush stroke in the total picture to attempt to link disorders of sleep and psychotic phenomena.

Even in the face of these results we still have an intuitive feeling that sleep should influence our waking mood. There have been studies which do link sleep and mood though these too are inconclusive. The best relationships between mood and sleep have been found when considering the change in mood between going to bed and getting up. For example, using a subjective measure of 'a good night's sleep' Hauri (1970) found a positive relationship between the evening and morning mood difference and subjective quantity of sleep. Similarly, Roehls and his colleagues, in some recent unpublished work, used the Clyde Mood Scale and found the 'strongest' correlations were between the cognitive rather than the affective scales and total sleep time.

But what about changes in sleep in psychiatrically ill patients? Mendels and Hawkins (1967, 1968) described the sleep of a group of patients with depression. It was found that in particular, these patients had very disturbed sleep. This resulted in a decrease in total sleep time coupled with decreases in paradoxical sleep and stage 3 + 4 sleep. As soon as patients are studied there are problems concerning the drug status of the patients. The importance of this has been emphasized by many but in particular by my colleague Dr. Oswald (1968). The treatment of depression raises very large questions as to the relationship between paradoxical sleep and mental state because it is found that both the monoamine oxidase inhibitors (Akindele et al., 1970) abolish paradoxical sleep and this change is coincident with clinical improvement. The tricyclic anti-depressants also reduce paradoxical sleep (Dunleavy et al. 1972) though the association between this effect and clinical improvement is not as neat as with the MAOIs. Electroconvulsive shock therapy has effects on sleep and depression similar to those of the tricyclics (Zacone, et al. 1967). Perhaps I should add at this point that a reduction in paradoxical sleep is accompanied by a reduction in bizarreness and vividness in the dream content (Carroll et al. 1968).

With the Freudian implications for the function of dreaming it was inevitable that studies using schizophrenics, both acute and chronic, should have been undertaken. The question of drug status is just as pertinent here as it is when considering depression. However, the general finding has been that in schizophrenia there is a reduction in the amount of paradoxical sleep. This of course is contrary to prediction from Freudian theory. However, as Feinberg (1969) has suggested, it may be that what is important is not the absolute amount of paradoxical sleep, but the proportion of paradoxical to stages 3+4 sleep.

An awareness of partial sleep loss may be important to the clinician as Daly (1970) has shown. In looking at reported sleep in a group of patients on home dialysis, he noted that on the dialysis nights not only was the patient's sleep time reduced, so was the spouses. There is in this situation increased irritability and lowered tolerance of frustration both of which, on top of the stress of human dialysis, may contribute to marital disharmony and breakdown.

In summary I feel that although mental illness undoubtedly leads to disorders of sleep, the study of total, partial or selective sleep deprivation contributes little to the understanding of the aetiology of psychiatric illness and has only very tenuous connection with the understanding of the brain mechanisms underlying mental disorder.

References

Akindale, M. O.; Evans, J. I.; and Oswald, I. 1970. Monoamine oxidase inhibitors, sleep and mood. *Electroenceph. clin. Neurophysiol.,* 29: 47-56.

Carroll, D.; Lewis, S. A.; Oswald, I. 1968. Effect of barbiturates on dream content. *Nature,* 223: 865-66.

Clements, S., and Dement, W. C. 1967. Effect of REM deprivation on psychological functions. *J. nerv. ment. Dis.,* 144: 485-91.

Daly, R. J., and Hassell, C. 1970. Reported sleep on maintenance haemodialysis. Brit. Med. J. 2: 508-9.

Deaton, M.; Tobias, J. S. and Wilkinson, R. T. 1971. Effect of sleep deprivation on signal detection parameters. *Quart. J. Exper. Psychol.,* 23: 449-52.

Dement, W. C. 1960. The effect of dream deprivation. *Science,* 31: 1705-7.

Dement, W. C. 1965. Studies on the function of rapid eye movement (paradoxical) sleep in human subjects. In *Aspects anatomo-functionels de la physiologie du sommeil,* ed. M. Jouvet. Paris: C.N.R.S.

Dunleavy, D. L. F.; Brezinova, V.; Oswald, I.; Maclean, A. W.; and Tinker, M. 1972. Changes during weeks in effects of tricyclic drugs on the human sleeping brain. *Brit. J. Psychiat,* in press.

Empson, J. A. C., and Clarke, P. R. F. 1970. Rapid eye movements and remembering. *Nature,* 227: 287-88.

Feinberg, I. 1969. Recent sleep research: findings in schizophrenia and some possible implications for the mechanism of action of chlorpromazine and for the neurophysiology of delirium. In *Schizophrenia: an appraisal,* ed. D. V. Siva Sanker. New York: P.J.D. Publications.

Foulkes, D. 1966. *The Psychology of Sleep.* Scribner.

Freud, S. 1953. *The Interpretation of Dreams (1900).* In The Standard Edition of the Complete Psychological Works of Sigmund Freud, eds. J. Strachey et al. London: Hogarth, Vol. IV-V.

Friedman, S., and Fisher, C. 1967. On the presence of a rhythmic, diurnal, oral instinctual drive cycle in man. *Amer. J. Psychoanal,* 15: 317-43.

Hauri, P. 1970. What is good sleep? In *Sleep and dreaming,* E. Hartmann. Internat. Psychiat. Clinics, Vol. 7. Boston: Little, Brown & Co.

Johnson, L. C. 1972. In *Aspects of Human Efficiency,* ed. W. P. Colquhoun. London: English Universities Press.

Karacan, I.; Rosenbloom, A. L.; Williams, R. L.; Finley, W. W.; and Hursch, C. J. 1970. Slow wave sleep deprivation in relation to plasma growth hormone concentration. *P.D.M.,* 2: 104-6.

Mendels, J., and Hawkins, D. R. 1967. Sleep and depression: a controlled E.E.G. study. *Arch. gen. Psychiat.,* 16: 344-54.

Mendels, J., and Hawkins, D. R. 1968. Sleep and depression: further considerations. *Arch. gen. Psychiat.,* 19: 445-52.

Naitoh, P. August 1969. Sleep loss and its effects on performance. Report No. 68-3, Naval Medical Neuropsychiatric Research Unit, San Diego.

Oswald, I. 1968. Drugs and sleep. *Pharmacol. Rev.* 20: 273-303.

Oswald, I.; Merrington, J.; and Lewis, H. M. 1970. Cyclic 'on demand' oral intake by adults. *Nature,* 225: 959-60.

Sassin, J. F.; Parker, D. C.; Mace, J. W.; Gotlin, R. W.; Johnson, L. C.; and Rossman, L. G. 1969. Human growth hormone release: relation to slow wave sleep and sleep-waking cycles. *Science,* 165: 513.

Stern, W. 1970. The relationship between REM sleep and learning. In *Sleep & dreaming,* E. Hartmann. Internat. Psychiat. Clinics. Vol. 7. Boston: Little, Brown & Co.

West, L. J.; Janszen, H. H.; Lester, B. L.; and Cornelisoon, F. S. 1962. The psychosis of sleep deprivation. *Ann. N.Y. Acad. Sci.,* 96: 66-70.

Wilkinson, R. T. 1968. Sleep deprivation: performance tests for partial and selective sleep deprivation. In *Progress in Clinical Psychology,* eds. L. A. Abt and B. F. Reiss. Vol. 7. New York: Grune & Stratton.

Zacone, V.; Gulevich, G.; and Derwent, W. C. 1967. Sleep and electro-convulsive therapy. *Arch. gen. Psychiat.,* 16: 567-73.

Discussion

after papers by HATHWAY, LIFTON AND LEWIS

Dr. Kinzel: Were the dreams of the survivors like the dreams of those with traumatic neuroses; did their dreams show any kind of paralysis of problem solving?

Dr. Lifton: The survivors of Hiroshima had their experience seventeen years before I interviewed them. I interviewed them in 1962 and they sometimes recalled those dreams but it was not a very reliable process. The survivors of Vietnam, the American Vietnam veterans, have dreams—very vividly all through the experience—and reported them regularly. The dreams show many experiences. Many resemble a traumatic neurosis which I tend to see as a sort of problem solving process, from which issue expressions of anxiety, death and death guilt full of vivid recollections of what may be called ultimate horror, ultimate transgression. We also in the Vietnam veterans have indications specific to a bad war, a sense of being tainted and in the mud and filth. This comes out in the dreams.

Prof. Forrest: Can Dr. Lewis explain why drugs which have an amelioration effect, in some illnesses reduce REM sleep and why on the other hand if you deprive schizophrenics of REM sleep their symptoms get worse?

Dr. Lewis: It seems to be a general phenomenon that all drugs of this type reduce REM sleep. This may mean that we are looking at two completely different processes. I do not think that there is necessarily any link between these two.

Prof. Cherry: Has Dr. Lewis anything to say about lucid dreams? For many years I have been a lucid dreamer and the experience is utterly different from normal dreams when I can talk about it to myself and argue and make scientific observations.

Dr. Lewis: There is an excellent book by Greene.

Prof. Cherry: Yes, and the details he gives conform exactly to what I have but I do not have body experiences which he does.

Dr. McKenna: Freud explained dreams as a regression to primary process. The notion of primary and secondary process is akin to Pavlov's first and second signal system. Primary processes were those mental processes which occurred in a pre-verbal thought stage. Now if you give drugs that act on the sub-cortical system and drive through into the cortex thus minimizing REM sleep, these cases may become more rational, with the kinds of drugs you give relieving them of the thought processes which were regressing to the level of first signal systems or Freud's primary process.

Dr. Lewis: A variety of studies have been done looking at drug effects and in that you get a marked increase in the amount of REM sleep. Feinberg suggested that what is important is the relative proportion of REM sleep to three and four sleep. He has got a fair amount of evidence for this. The other hypothesis of the function of dreams is related to this memory and learning process. The idea is that events taken in during the day are kept in a buffer store and that during sleep you flick through this lot and see what you are going to remember. Those you lay down in the long term memory store, the rest you throw out. The majority of dream content is in fact day-related or situation related. Dreams in the laboratory are very laboratory oriented, dreams at home are home oriented, things that happen during the day. This may well be the sort of things that are going on in dreams.

Dr. Kagan: I understand that REM dreams are not remembered unless the subject wakes up during them and writes them down, but dreams in other kind of sleep can be remembered more easily.

Dr. Lewis: Yes, basically you do not remember your dreams. It seems as though provided you wake up briefly at the end of a dream period, you will remember that dream. Somebody has calculated that if you allow people to sleep and wake spontaneously then they awakened spontaneously about 25% of the time from REM sleep. From all studies it looks as though about 80% of all wakenings produce dream reports and therefore you would be assuming that one third of your population should normally remember a dream in the morning, but then there are all the other little bits of wakening after a REM sleep as well, and this does seem to be terminated by a period of very brief arousal.

Prof. Levine: I have two comments—first I would like to indicate to Dr. Hathway that the fatting response that is seen in the squirrel monkeys is not due to dominance but to seasonal breeding. The squirrel monkey is a seasonal breeder and the fatting develops as a result of increase in testosterone during the season and has nothing to do with dominance or overeating. Its diet does not change very much at all. I do not remember Dr. Lewis talking much about dreaming. He specifically said that it was the loss of paradoxical sleep and not dreaming that he thought relevant. He focused predominantly on learning and memory. You do not normally see permanent changes with REM sleep in humans, yet a number of animal studies clearly show that even after a recovery period there are changes in certain characteristics of behaviour with loss of REM sleep.

Dr. Lewis: It has something to do with brain recovery processes during the night, like repairing the wear and tear of what has happened during the day; it must involve protein metabolism in some way. If you look at the amount of REM sleep regained during recovery, it is only 50 to 60% of that which was lost, so that there is a permanent loss of whatever that function is, be it live state, protein synthesis, be it the signals system and so on. This may very well persist for a very long time. The recovery process in REM sleep after drug deprivation of REM's gives an excess of about 150%. This goes on for weeks after the patients become behaviourly normal.

Prof. Browne: I have been working clinically or in research with patients with LSD for more than ten years now and a minority of these have reproduced experience of grief or traumatic events that they seemed to be experiencing emotionally for the first time. Up to then the experience had been registered in some way, recorded but not experienced. I wonder if Dr. Lifton found this in the survival cases. Can a person really inhibit an intense experience so that it does not really happen for them?

Prof. Lifton: The process you describe is parallel to that we see in the anti-war veterans. We speak of it as learning to feel, especially their guilt which is very much there. I did not have time to distinguish kinds of guilt which is very germane to that kind of recovery of the mourning or the grief experience in patients. There is a negative kind of guilt, in Freud's terms a repressed guilt, which one does not really know one feels. Or there is a static sort of guilt which is a classical neurosis guilt—I am evil. As opposed to that, it may be of significance where LSD has positive usage clinically for related processes of recovery of feelings and animated guilt, the opposite kind of guilt, is an enormously useful energizing stimulus towards a new world view, new energy in life and all sorts of recovery processes making you become a larger person than before. So in my experience that kind of process is first seen, when the men do not have access to their guilt, when they start dreaming about it. It is revealed and they talk about it and gradually come to feel it. Then they will seek their guilt so to speak, learning that it has its useful attributes.

Dr. Masserman: Dr. Lifton, if we define guilt as literally fear of punishment here on earth or somewhere else, how about the veterans who have very few conscientious reactions?

Prof. Lifton: Perhaps the more basic aspect of guilt is at two levels —some sense of transgression which is related to fear of punishment on the one hand or some sense of self dissatisfaction on a more broad level, where guilt and shame converge. They are still struggling with the same emotions and there is a study by Murray —a young historian who did a series of interviews with veterans from all kinds of backgrounds and political views—in which he found that all of them who were dissatisfied with the war in any conscious way have a strong sense that there was something wrong about what they were asked to do.

Prof. O'Doherty: In your Korean studies, you found significant factors common to the pre-Korean personalities of the subjects and related to the subsequent data on distress. Do you find from the personal backgrounds of your present subjects common factors which would account for this excessive guilt?

Prof. Lifton: I do not find the guilt excessive. These are not veterans who are psychiatrically disturbed. They were kind of troubled by the whole thing and thought that they needed help from people who understood these things, but they did not seek formal psychotherapy. So the interesting thing about guilt is the difficulty a veteran gets into where he does not have access to this guilt. Given what the men did, the human condition seems to be so universal there is some guilt there, this is not excessive in the way the veterans seek and need even more than they find. Now the question which I try to ask about the pre-Vietnam personality is what is there that enables a man to say, as one man in the middle of a group said after he had described how he had killed a soldier with a knife and he said: 'I felt sorry, but I do not know why I felt sorry—John Wayne never felt sorry!' He is in a sense a stereotype of a T.V. notion which is called in the group a John Wayne thing—which has a whole lot of meanings—masculinity, falseness, American pride and everything; while some men have access to that larger morality, which is around their guilt, the animated guilt, others do not. There are interesting and many reasons but there is no single reason. They vary enormously, those who did not fire at My Lai. I asked one man very systematically in interview why he had this extraordinary capacity to hold his fire, which only two or three others did from the entire unit. I came up with three reasons which I could see were important.

1. He had a very intense Catholic background in which he had been instilled with ideas of right and wrong.

2. He had always been a loner and had not been very active in group processes, had engaged in individual sports.

3. This is the most paradoxical—he had been profoundly identified with the military—he had wanted to follow the military as his career and had come out first in all of his military training groups prior to Vietnam and was appalled by what had happened there because it had violated military honour.

So there are many issues involving many senses of integrity in a broad sense that seem to come from pre-Vietnam personalities.

Prof. O'Doherty: For too long we have taught people the facts of life and we should begin to teach them the facts of death. A vast population now never see a dead organism not even a dead mouse and I wonder how this would be related to the general phenomenon of your study?

Prof. Lifton: It is very much related to death becoming more central for me and others in psychological and other social investigations of various kinds. It seems as though our American culture most so, but all cultures in some degree, can no longer manage with this degree of denial. I find that, again opposed to Freud's view, denial is at maximum where what I call symbolic immortality is impaired. It cannot be connected to something larger than oneself. You have need to deny the idea of death because it becomes more unacceptable. Our capacity for accepting death seems to be always limited never full, but it is maximized by the symbolic form immortality.

Dr. Masserman: There is no culture without some concept of life after death.

Prof. Fox: In Gestalt therapy groups where people are trying to encounter their guilt, if you start peeling off the onion skin, there is resentment, and under that there are intense feelings of aggression which have been bottled up. I wonder if in some of your veterans you get this?

Prof. Lifton: Actually each man is full of rage and part of the experience is a struggle to deal with the rage and violence in these anti-war veterans. They are committed to something like non-violence but barely so in their feelings and their rage is on many levels, it has to do, in a way, with the sense of being betrayed by the whole culture and by the military and by society which is the essential image of their feeling about their country. The strongest rage seems to come when they go all out to bring the truth to the American public and to get them to care and they reject it. Then they come back enraged and they talk for the first time about planting bombs. The feeling of that is that they have been thrown back on their own guilt, and this stimulates their rage more.

General discussion

Prof. Levine: For years now people have been training animals on unpredictable schedules of food and shock and so on and there is no severe aberration of behaviour that anybody can attribute to unpredictability if the animal is trained on an unpredictable schedule.

Dr. Masserman: We have a certain tolerance for unpredictability and have to live with it. If we are accustomed to predictability a disturbance may follow unpredictability that has an import for our safety.

Prof. Levine: That is the critical thing. If you train an animal in an unpredictable schedule, then shift it to a predictable schedule, nothing very much happens to its gluco-corticoids. If you train the animal on a fixed-interval schedule and change it to a variable interval schedule, it gets the same number of reinforcements, its corticoids elevate rapidly.

Dr. Masserman: I accept that. The animal is expecting a routine life which then becomes unpredictable. If, however, we are accustomed to a great deal of tolerance, it is predictable unpredictability.

Prof. Browne: As we are getting to the end of the conference and our ultimate purpose is a deeper understanding of human behaviour, perhaps you could emphasize the clinical aspects in so far as they can apply to human behaviour.

Prof. Harlow: Well, unpredictability is no doubt of variable importance in producing psychopathic behaviour in animals. We will have to have an unpredictability that will produce profound and prolonged psychopathic behaviour. I can see no sign of either profound or prolonged psychopathic behaviour in the monkeys and, therefore, it is unpredictability about what?

416

Dr. Masserman: One must see the monkeys. Certainly the cats that are not treated stay pretty sick for the rest of their lives unless you use some techniques to bring them out of it.

Dr. Mitchell: As long as the animal is in that situation?

Dr. Masserman: Oh, no, if it were only in the situation I would not consider it very significant. It generalizes outside the situation, like a human does.

Dr. Kinzel: What made you pick unpredictability other than any other stimuli that might cause symptoms?

Dr. Masserman: If I may review my previous experiments in which the monkey was taught to feed in a certain place after various manipulations. A snake was presented. If you presented the snake predictably it had far less effect in disturbing the animal than if it never knew when the snake was coming.

Dr. Kinzel: Was there anything in your clinical experience that supported this?

Dr. Masserman: In almost any respect, the unpredictability of any important issue in our lives is rather disconcerting.

Dr. Mitchell: These animals, it looked to me, were apprehensive, showing anxiety, but I did not see any very abnormal behaviour as shown by an isolate. Did they ever bite themselves, show bizarre movements—is the difference between neurosis and psychosis here?

Dr. Masserman: They do show self destructive behaviour and starve themselves. One monkey almost killed itself after these experiences.

Prof. Fox: Was their social behaviour affected?

Dr. Masserman : They almost immediately fall from dominance to quite a sub-dominant position, and may be persecuted by the other animals.

Dr. McQuaid: The monkeys were adult—I was wondering if you did work with the younger monkeys too.

Dr. Masserman: Not in this experiment—in others, yes.

Dr. McQuaid: Dr. Mitchell, would you regard the copying behaviour of the infant lying down and looking at the isolate, as regression or disturbed behaviour?

Dr. Mitchell: This is one thing I am very concerned about. If we can call this pairing a type of therapy, will the therapist pick up abnormal behaviour as readily as the patient picks up normal behaviour through imitation. I don't know.

B1

Dr. Harlow: The answer is no. There are occasions when over a period of six months a normal animal will show some increase in semi-normal behaviour.

Dr. Mitchell: They pick up a little bit of abnormal behaviour. It goes in the direction of normal behaviour. I have seen laboratory animals pick up a bizarre movement by being close to a disturbed animal that performs it.

Dr. McQuaid: If the monkeys are left with each other, do they both continue to show what you describe as deviant behaviour?

Dr. Mitchell: The infants were normal to begin with and they still are. They are not showing extreme abnormality. The isolate is still showing some, but not self-directed aggression. They had only been together for three weeks.

Dr. Masserman: I never saw neurotic behaviour transferred to normal animals. I have seen it the other way around, if you put a neurotic cat in with a normal group it will gradually recover, but the normal animals will not copy the neurotic.

Rev. Prof. O'Doherty: I agree with Dr. Massermann of course that unpredictability generates anxiety. During the German bombing of London, by the V-bomb, massive services were laid on to cope with the expected increase in neurosis. The interesting thing was that there was a massive decrease in the incidence. The same thing has happened in Belfast. Psychiatric research there in the last few years has shown, with the exception of young mothers, a decrease in overall incidence of neurotic process. It could be that unpredictability within short time intervals generates conflicts of anxiety but unpredictability on massive scales when resources have been mobilized to cope with it does not seem to have this consequence.

Prof. Russell Davis: I think Professor O'Doherty is making this out far too easy. There were not any figures for the war. The prevalence of neurotic disturbances is extremely difficult to know. The evidence refers simply to referral patterns. Now one would expect that in the wartime situations in Belfast there would be a marked change in the referral patterns. One of our difficulties is that we use words like 'neurosis'. If one could stick to some description of the actual behaviour, I think it would be much easier to discuss when it occurs and when it does not.

Prof. Latane: A very interesting book that has just been published by David Glass and Gerard Singer called 'Urban Stress', which contains a series of laboratory studies on the effects of unpredictable stimuli. Their general finding is that unpredictability has very few negative effects during the course of the unpredictability distress itself. There are some deleterious effects afterwards. People can argue but it may have some later cost.

Dr. McKenna: It is reckoned that a good number of industrial workers have to be retrained about three times in the course of their work. Do you think there is any evidence that you can train animals, condition animals for unpredictable futures like that?

Dr. Masserman: If you raise an animal on the schedule that is predictably unpredictable, then it can accommodate. With regard to the word 'neurosis' you will notice that I said these are phenomena that in any human would be called neurotic. I had a psychoanalyst friend come down to the laboratory once. He observed one of these animals crouching in a corner that had developed all sorts of psychosomatic symptoms and was away down in the social hierarchy. He said, 'Jules, I can prove to you this animal is not neurotic.' Since I am always looking for a proof of some sort, I said, 'Please do so.' He said, 'Does this animal know its own father?' I had to think about that one, for very few of us can be absolutely sure of our own fathers. I had to admit it did not. Then he said, 'If it doesn't know its own father, it doesn't have an Oedipus complex. Therefore it cannot be neurotic.'

Prof. Sackett: I'd like to talk about some experiments that addressed themselves to some of the major issues for which we are here, psychiatrists, applicators and animal behaviourists. One is the issue of the so-called free environment.

Singh captured rhesus monkeys in India, in urban areas and in rural areas. He studied them on standard rhesus monkey tests for exploratory behaviour, motor activity, sociability and learning. There is not any natural environment for rhesus monkeys any more than for man; they live everywhere. The rural monkeys were more sociable and affiliative, and much less aggressive than urban raised monkeys. Urban monkeys were more curious, explored more, preferred more complex stimuli but he found no difference whatsoever between the two on standard tests of learning ability. Just about the basic pattern that you find as a function of rearing in different conditions in a laboratory.

The second experiment is a cautionary study. Rosenblum worked with pigtail monkeys and bonnet monkeys. Mothers and infant bonnet monkeys group together and infants move freely between mothers. Pigtail mother-infant pairs stay away from other pairs. In the pigtail monkey, if we take the mother away, the baby goes into the separation stages that Dr. Harlow described —agitated, depressed or some combination. There is an extreme reaction. If you take a bonnet monkey's mother out of there, nothing very much happens. If we cross foster and take a pigtail baby and put it into a bonnet group, instead of being very rigidly kept away from anybody except its mother, it is passed around and has a lot of contact. The pigtail usually shows an extreme response to separation. But in a bonnet group, when separated from the foster mother, it does not show the usual depressive reaction. It looks like this has something to do with the kind of early experience that the baby has. What happens if you take a bonnet monkey baby and put it in a pigtail room where the room mother keeps it away from everybody else. The prediction is, of course, that it will show depressive reactions on subsequent separation. Unfortunately it doesn't. The bonnet baby acts about the same regardless of the environment, the pigtail baby shows dependence on the environment. Now here are two very closely related species, yet their reaction to separation is tremendously different and the effect that the environment has on them is quite different. We have to be even more careful about how we generalize effects between humans and animals. On the question of the natural environment, and the abnormal individual, we can apply a Darwinian kind of test to this. If an individual imported into a situation can't survive when other members of its species can survive, then something is wrong. Whether you call it neurotic or psychotic or abnormal doesn't matter. Animals raised in a laboratory with mothers and peers are laboratory normative animals. Animals who were raised in a partial isolation, total isolates and feral-born monkeys are not. If we take animals like this and put them out into a free ranging environment, on an island in Puerto Rico, where there are troupes of what we would call natural monkeys, free ranging monkeys, what happens if we take and introduce animals like this with their competencies; isolates which are incompetent in the laboratory, although at the peak of maturity; partial isolates—they are not very competent, in the laboratory, mother-peer raised animals are quite competent, and ferals are pretty competent in the laboratory too. If we put them out in nature, who lives? The ferals live. Some of these live. These all die. Some of these isolates, the most incompetent animals, survive. The feral animals integrate themselves into the troupes that are there within a few days. One of the feral females had a baby almost exactly five and a half months after she was introduced into the troupe. After a year one of the mother-peer raised animals, the dominant male of all the animals that were released here, disappeared for a year. Three months ago it reappeared, killed the dominant animal of the biggest troupe and is now the dominant animal on the island. This is a laboratory born and cage reared monkey. When it became dominant a whole bunch of the other monkeys swam over to another island. What criterion do you apply to say what is the competence level in this animal? Talk about neurotic, psychotic, they are words. Take a behavioural situation and see what is the competency of the behavioural repertoire and how well can the animal cope.

Dr. Murray: About ten to fifteen years ago the description of schizophrenia in the text books was so much different to what it is now that we assume it was due to institutionalization and so on. We are now seeing in Ireland children who have gone through a true autistic phase, have not been to some of the therapy units which deal with these and have come out of it fairly well. How do we know that the descriptions of, let us say, neurosis/psychosis/abnormal behaviour that we see here are not a manifestation of a laboratory rather than a free range environment? In other words, what happens when an animal, be it primate or otherwise, becomes neurotic or psychotic in the free range?

Prof. Sackett: There is bizarre behaviour in nature. If you do not fairly well understand something about the social and natural history of the particular species you would not know that this deviated from a norm. It is an arbitrary term because it does not behave like something that we have arbitrarily called the norm.

Dr. Levine: If you watch the behaviour of chimpanzees eating meat you would say that this was extremely abnormal behaviour on the background of everything you have ever seen of the animal before. For up to four hours you get the most incredible level of activity, far above any background noise you have heard—howling, screeching, footstamping of sub-dominant animals, animals who would not normally display under these circumstances. You only see it every three or four months.

Dr. Kinzel: I am fairly concerned about how we are going to get from the animals to the man. Most of the time I think it is separation anxiety and not the effects of actual separation that matters. Separation anxiety can occur without actual separation. Some of the things that have been mentioned are potentially productive of symptoms, be they neurotic symptoms or psychotic symptoms. We can get together on a definition of symptoms. I was hoping Dr. Massermann would say that the mothering of a psychotic mother is often characterised by unpredictable behaviour and this is not an uncommon finding in patients. We can use some of these models as a mirror. But the difficulty is that we are not talking about the most human difficulties—the severe actual deprivations—so much as we are talking about anxiety.

Dr. Browne: We have not heard much about the possibility of separation anxiety coming out of an ultra stable environment, being the lack of preparation for facing the unpredictable life.

Dr. P. Cullen: I wanted to ask whether the behaviour of isolates is very much different from the behaviour of a brain damaged animal?

Prof. Harlow: Totally.

Dr. Mitchell: These isolates are abnormal because they are the ends of some sort of distribution. Evolution takes place because of this sort of thing, cultural evolution also, and if a normal animal—statistically speaking a normal animal—does not at some time copy an abnormal animal we are not going to have cultural evolution.

Dr. Harlow: The history of the Wisconsin laboratory is that without even trying we have produced abnormal animals in abundance. John Bowlby once went to my laboratory and said, 'Why do you try to produce abnormal animals? All your animals are abnormal,' and he was dead right. The tough thing is not to produce abnormal animals but to produce normal animals. One of the things is to raise them with mothers and with peers and probably some other variables which would make them totally normal in terms of unusual behaviour.

Dr. Lewis: In a lot of the comments that have been made to-day, it is the human observer that is saying what is abnormal or normal. Now in man as I see it, what defines normality and abnormality is the society that one is living in and not the outside observer.

Prof. Sackett: I think that needs an experimental response not a philosophy. If you give monkeys a preference test, for monkeys reared like they were or monkeys reared differently, they prefer monkeys reared like they were in normal or in isolate conditions. That is a social definition of the discrimination that you are making.

Prof. Levine: This story is appropriate to this gathering. When they set out the bids for the tunnel connecting the English coast with the French coast, the bids came in at the usual billions of pounds except from a Mr. O'Flannery, which was for £10,000. So they called O'Flannery and they said, 'Mr. O'Flannery, how do you expect to build the tunnel under the English channel for £10,000?' He said, 'It is very simple. I will start at one end and my brother will start at the other end and we will meet in the middle.' After a little thought the man asked, 'Mr. O'Flannery, what happens if you do not meet?' Mr. O'Flannery thought for a minute and then he said, 'You will have two tunnels.'

Workshop session —
areas for research

The workshop sessions were arranged so that a focus might be provided for the participation of those attending in a more intensive debate of problem areas for the clinician than could be allowed in the discussion periods after the formal presentation of papers, throughout the preceding week. Groups, each of which represented a cross-section of the disciplines, were assigned to consider one of the periods in the life-cycle. These were denoted under the following topic areas : —

Problems of infancy
Problems of school and family
Problems of adolescence
Problems of work
Problems of marriage
Problems of ageing

and summary reports of these workshop sessions are reported here under the appropriate headings.

PROBLEMS OF INFANCY

The group recognized the important questions that animal behaviour research raises for the study of early human development. It is clear the early infancy period is of critical importance for the healthy development of the human being.

The group proposed the following topics for consideration.

1. The need to disseminate information on behavioural development particularly to para-medical personnel (e.g. nurses, midwives, and orphanage staff) as well to staff in other agencies in contact with the pre-school child. It was felt that as much attention should

be paid to the social adjustment as to the physical well being of the child at visits to child welfare clinics.

2. The need for adequate social support for young families was emphasized. The adverse effects of kinship disruption arising from social mobility demanded by urbanization and industrialization were thought to be important research areas, especially with regard to attachment anxieties. In the Irish context study might be made of the problems arising from the flight from the country to the city, e.g. emigration (especially the absence of fathers), and the increasing tendency for women to go out to work, rehousing, tinkers and high rise flats. The group felt that it was undesirable that undue emphasis be given to formal schooling for the under fives—social training and contact with peers was felt to be more important.

3. Considerable importance should be attached to the way the child's self concept develops and to the conditions under which he achieves a degree of independence in the pre-school years. Healthy development in these respects is threatened by the failure of the mother's attachments to the child during the puerperium (e.g. when the infant is cared for in an incubator). We wish to stress that generous facilities should be provided for visiting and mothering of the hospitalized pre-school child so that mother and child could remain together and the nursing staff could give help and support to the role of the mother.

4. Research might be conducted into the differences between rural and urban children as regards the child's integration into the community and that a developmental study to establish the validity of predictions about 'at risk' children made at the antenatal period in terms of family history might be useful.

PROBLEMS OF SCHOOL AND FAMILY

Problems within these systems should be conceived in terms of resolution modalities and not in terms of analysis or 'working through' of conflicts in individual, family or group therapy. Such therapeutic (helping, interventionist, etc.) modes have value if there is emphasis on role modelling with experimental and innovative behaviour designed to alleviate or eliminate the problem behaviour.

Inadequate model availability was postulated as a significant cause of childhood disorder manifesting itself in behavioural, emotional or educational deviance, and the matriarchal nature of

cl

society was noted as eliminating, in part or totally, the availability of male models in early childhood and school-going age.

Family Problem Resolution Techniques were examined and four main factors were identified as contributing to the functioning of the 'Family System'. These were the quality of relationships between

(1) Parent and Child
(2) Sibling and Sibling
(3) Family and environment
(4) Media and family

all of which significantly modify behaviour. Discussion and behaviour modelling with parent involvement permits parents to operate as therapists. Orientation of therapist or helping agent to the family's problem, as defined by the family, permits therapy sessions to focus on changing behaviour most prejudicial to growth and fulfilment.

Various ways of looking at classifications and typologies were examined including factor analysis of data on children describing problem behaviour. It was agreed that 'relationship pathology' and operational problem classification were the most relevant for research planning.

Early life experience, the relevance of brain damage and the importance of nutrition and stimulation in 'growing a brain' were recognized. Early and continuing deprivation was seen as a significant feature in Irish society and it was agreed that what was 'in the *child's* best interests' should guide intervention techniques. The child has basic civil rights.

Models for change in communities designated as 'problems' by other elements in the general social system were examined and the changes that are taking place at community level, such as in Ballyfermot, were accepted as having relevance as models for extension to other areas with problems far greater in number and type than could be helped by traditional 'outside' middle-class agencies. The problem areas have to change themselves. 'Outside' agencies operating within such areas have to be held accountable by those they serve. This extends to the administration of such agencies right to top levels of central government.

Research should focus on innovative and imaginative techniques with, for example, regulation of the behaviour of individuals and individual sections of society by those 'reinforcers' most immediately contingent and humanly relevant. Learning theory and reinforcement techniques provide models that would quickly permit wide and sweeping positive and progressive social change. Professionals should be available to advise on experimental design at various social levels.

PROBLEMS OF ADOLESCENCE

1. It was noted that among primates there are distinct patterns of behaviour based upon sex. Males are more adventuresome in the juvenile period, these young males are often at the edge of the troop and they are more likely to be taken by predators than are females. These young males are disciplined by adults more often than females.

2. The traditional Irish rural attitude towards adolescents is that the boys are kept close to home for work on the land, whereas the girls tend to be pushed in the direction of secondary education and marriage to a partner who is unlikely to keep them tied to the land. The mother makes these decisions.

3. The end of adolescence in primates involves either a period of solitary life away from the troop, succeeded by a return, challenge and a fight for a position in the hierarchy; or gradual acceptance of a sub-dominant role.

4. In Ireland the pattern involves 'bachelor' groups of young men who go to activities such as horse races or football matches together. Individuals stick to these groups even after marriage.

5. And in Ireland there are strong ties to a locality, a village, a town or a county, e.g. a football team. This is reminiscent of the phenomena of the 'placer' lambs!

6. Social observations in Ireland include low marriage rates and late age of marriage, many more single men than women in the high migrant areas, and a high reported rate of schizophrenia.

7. There is reported to be in Ireland both a higher hospitalized rate for major mental illness, and a higher community tolerance of such illness.

Research recommendations

1. A trial of a scheme in which delinquent adolescent males would be used as caring persons, to 'treat', take care of, or help in

the upbringing of deprived children, such as orphans, illegitimate children or possibly mildly or moderately mentally handicapped children (cf. Skeel's Iowa study, and the study at Henley-on-Thames).

2. An epidemiological study to investigate whether it is in fact true that the major mental illnesses (schizophrenia and depression), are higher in the Western areas of high celibacy, migration, etc. Is community tolerance higher? In this study attention should be paid to statistics from the North of Ireland.

3. An attempt to identify adult models who are accepted by adolescents, and adult models who are rejected.

4. Further study of the initiation of drinking practices by adolescents. The use of ex-addicts as educators in this area was endorsed by all of the group with one exception.

5. There should be more workers trained with special skills in the treatment of adolescents.

6. More investment should be made in applied research in this field.

THE PROBLEMS OF WORK

Work was accepted as an activity with overtones of compulsion. However, it can come to be seen as pleasurable when there is self-actualization.

The problems identified can be listed as:

1. Boredom or over-complexity in the task (e.g. production-line work and air traffic controllers).

2. Minor problems of work and living become exaggerated out of all proportion in boring work situations. This results in paranoid reactions.

3. Poor job satisfaction including finding appropriate job-personality match, lack of credit for work done which is not just monetary, and the need to feel useful.

4. In areas of high unemployment the opportunity to work may be an incentive in itself while in more affluent areas there is a need for personal achievement. This carries long term dangers.

5. The personality of management whether executive, foreman or shop steward.

6. Interpersonal relations i.e. between management and workers and between workers and workers.

7. The need to see and be in avenues of promotion.

8. Redundancy and retirement (loss of identity).

9. Group dynamics including communication channels, and the pressures on the work-group *isolate* (who may become the scape-goat for grievances).

It was recognized that these factors could not only aggravate but could be utilized in alleviation of dis-ease. Identification of areas of problem naturally points to areas of research. The workshop would like to see research in all the areas mentioned along the lines of

    (i) Epidemiology of illness in the industrial setting
    (ii) Vocational guidance, rehabilitation and retraining
    (iii) Acceptance of the psychiatric patient by the work force and management
    (iv) Manipulation of the environment and consideration of environment—personality interaction in morbidity
    (v) Effects of sudden loss of job security
    (vi) Work therapy (including token economics).

The group considered the strategy for this kind of research in Ireland with its limited resources.

PROBLEMS OF MARRIAGE

The group began by acknowledging the possibility that marriage may not, in fact, be an ideal social institution, recognizing that the single state, polygamy, polyandry, and even the Californian 'eighteen year old marriage' all had their merits, but was more in agreement than disagreement that there is probably a strong tendency toward and value derived from marriage analogues, even if not identical to the drive toward pair bonding in many other animal species.

In defining factors in marriage that are important in predisposing to mental disease, the group acknowledged the conclusion inherent in determining whether marital disorder was more productive of mental disorder or whether mental disorder was more productive of marital disorder. In addition, the numerous external stresses on marriage such as divorce, permissiveness, overcrowding, late age marriage customs, family size, excessive demands made by work, and effects of third party intrusion, all effect the marital equilibrium making the degree of isolation of variables necessary for research extremely difficult.

Nevertheless it was felt that certain syndromes might have a particular association to marriage. For example, the relationship of alcoholism, murder, delusional jealousy, psychosomatic disease and sexual discontent to marriage should be surveyed in systematic fashion to better relate specific conditions to descriptions of stresses in the marital bond.

It was noted, furthermore, that marriage appears to have a specific effectiveness in the prevention of ill health—both emotional and physical. Research might be directed toward defining more precisely the nature of the 'good' marriage, e.g. those qualities that best fulfil the security and welfare needs of both partners. In this regard, it would be valuable to learn which models of marriage have more weight in effecting the formation of marital style, types of parental marriage, television models of marriage, etc.

Disappointment of expectations in marriage was felt to be a potent force toward the production of emotional disorders. Two hypotheses are worth testing in this regard. Are those who are disappointed in their expectations as the marriage evolves, more prone to marital disorder, and, are those who are mismatched in expectations more prone to marital disorder?

How much proximity is required to maintain the marital bond? The effect of the absence of one partner on the mutual health of both partners would be a valuable area of research. In particular the kind of absence, predictable or unpredictable, short or prolonged, etc. should be investigated.

There may be a tendency for some kinds of anxiety to be generated more than others by the intimacy unique to marriage. In this regard, investigations could be carried out to determine if, for example, 'castration anxiety' was more often generated than guilty fear or 'separation anxiety' in the normal course of marital stresses and strains.

Finally, the group discussion suffered from the lack of knowledge or basic science of normal development of marriage. This lack could be related to the failure to study marriage as a biological phenomenon. In the fear that Lorenz may know more about 'marital' patterns in geese than we know about human marriage, it was suggested that couples with and couples without the marital bond might be compared, in a laboratory apartment setting, for their responses to stresses such as the introduction of children, alcohol, female and male strangers, and even cardboard versus real mother-in-laws to determine the cues, and releasers to which the condition of the marital attachment makes each partner uniquely sensitive.

THE PROBLEMS OF AGEING

The group considered the nature of multidisciplinary study concerning behavioural and physiological characteristics, and the social roles of aged individuals.

It was suggested that the study of ageing problems can be approached by an adaptation-level theory. That is the effect of discrepancies from previously developed norms on the present condition of aged individuals. It was suggested that this could be done in the following ways:

1. Expose the individual organism to stimuli of varying complexity, and record EEG and physiological responses at different age levels.

2. The study of basic abilities in young people, and comparing them to the basic abilities of elderly individuals.

3. The study of the responses and behaviour of aged animals, e.g. rats, to different stimuli.

In all of these it should be borne in mind that the process of ageing may in fact be influenced by environmental factors, for example, humans and insects mature faster in warm climates.

Research areas

1. Analysis at the animal level of the process of ageing by manipulation of diet and other early environmental enrichments.

2. Cross sectional developmental and prospective studies could be done on human subjects particularly in Ireland with its small and relatively stable population.

3. The clinician and the researcher may in this country be able to work together on research projects on ageing.

4. Prospective study, where environmental influences are manipulated. At a later date the effects of these earlier influences could be reviewed and their influence on the ageing process assessed.

This could be confined to a specific psychological variable e.g. reaction-time, or methods could be used for assessing endocrine responses to stress, and apply the test to a population of different age groups, or populations of similar age, or special types of population such as institutional populations.

In this way the characteristics of individual differences within the population could be established.

6. As there is a considerable body of research on the effects of ageing, it is suggested that in a research programme, the establishing of a goal or target should be emphasized and that, data already available should be used in achieving the goal.

In the examination of the problems of ageing our concern should be to study:

    (i) The feelings and preferences of the aged population—what do they really want?
    (ii) The attitude and needs of the general population towards the aged.
    (iii) The special skills and characteristics (behavioural and physiological) of the aged.
    (iv) How these skills relate to the needs of society.
    (v) What happens when these needs and skills are discrepant.

The implication of these points is, that the aim of research or therapeutic measures directed towards the aged should be the resolution of these discrepancies.

Summary of discussion on the workshop

Chairman: AUBREY KAGAN

Dr. Kagan: I wonder if we can now turn off the clock and open the discussion on these reports particularly in the light of the last item on the Agenda which is 'Psychiatric Research and Utilization of its Results'. I think that these reports which have come before us are dealing with chronological ranges which of course overlap very considerably.

I would hope that we can leave that overlapping for the organizers to deal with it. I think that there is also some indication that the mechanisms for research which might be set up could very well overlap, for example, it seemed to me that the ageing group were setting up, talking of setting up a system for examining people, old people in several ways which might be very applicable to the problems of people in the other age groups. It seemed to me we are talking about research at different levels, for example, there were suggestions that present knowledge should be applied more vigorously. Now I would expect that when this is done some sort of evaluation system would be put in to see that it is doing what it is expected to do, some feedback to see that it is the right thing to do. There was clearly evidence from what people said that new knowledge is required and this is a question of making observations, seeing, for example, what people are doing during the course of their marriage or of testing hypotheses. I would hope that these sort of things can be done in such a way that they can help families. I think there was a theme going through, not of all of the reports but of many of them, a theme that the things one ought to research upon were the themes the community felt it needed. Then there was brought up in the report on ageing another notion, some way or other one would have to have some sort of system of balancing conflicting demands. All of this is research, all of this is action oriented and all of this costs money. So somewhere along our discussions you might like to consider funding for this kind of thing. I will throw out a suggestion that any Health Act deserves to have spent on it, to decide whether it is a good Act or not, at least 1% of the cost of the Act. If you are buying a house,

you send in a surveyor, you are quite prepared to pay 5 or 10%
for that, if you build a bridge you pay at least 5% to determine
whether it is going to be a good bridge. If you pay for a
health action you usually don't spend any research money at all.
You never know whether you are wasting resources or not. The
discussion is open—these were just a few suggestions.

Dr. Lewis: Following on from those remarks, Professor Jessop
I gathered is the secretary of the Medical Research Council of
Ireland. Presumably they are one of the major funding bodies
for research in Ireland in relation to health coverance. Perhaps
for those of us from outside Ireland it might well be useful in
relation to this discussion to hear from him what sort of resources
are available at this current time because it is very nice to be
optimistic and to make plans for research and for health management and all the rest of it but we have got to be realistic. And
the only way we can be realistic, I think, is to hear from someone
like Professor Jessop what sort of funds are available.

Prof. Jessop: The question that Dr. Lewis asks really cannot be
answered properly. There are two research bodies that would
have an interest in research into mental illness in all its aspects,
The Medical Research Council and The Medico-Social Research
Board. The Medical Research Council receives applications from
research workers and people who want to do research specifying
the project that they would like to work on, stating the scope
of this, the possible cost of it. Now, The Medical Research Council's budget is only about £120,000 a year. It has to apportion
that amongst all the various applications that it receives throughout the whole area of medical research and you take your chance
depending on the merit of your project as we see it or as we are
advised about it by the special committees. The Medico-Social
Research Board on the other hand carries out research itself.
It has a budget of about £100,000 a year and it appoints people
to do research on projects that the Board has agreed are worthwhile and which the Department of Health thinks it would like
to support. So in total there is about £250,00 a year for these
two Boards. There are other specific foundations of course—for
heart disease, cancer and so on, but if we confine ourselves to
the bodies that have general funds to distribute in these two
separate kinds of ways, then you have a total of about a £¼ million to distribute. The point of being specific in our recommenda-

tions as to the research areas that are worthwhile is that I think it is true of almost every research funding body that it will not give or will give with great reluctance money for a project if that project is not properly defined and of some direct interest in the general context of the country's needs. He will find it very hard to get money for something like a general research into the effects of ageing, documenting the characteristics of old people in a general sort of way without any particular reference to some benefit or some result that might be drawn out of that. This is work that should be done of course but it has to be put into the context of a particular defined objective, if you want to get a grant for it.

Dr. Murray: I would like to ask Professor Jessop one question and follow it up with a comment. The question is of the total amount of money available for research, approximately how much of it goes into the mental health need compared to the other facilities? The point I would like to make is this, if we, for instance, set up a programme to attempt to reduce the incidence of mental handicap or total morbidity in childhood or, e.g. reduce autism, we can save State moneys. At this moment in time this State's total capital commitment to one mentally handicapped child who is never going to be productive is approximately £20,000. Now if you set up a programme which at the end of a year will save three children from being non-productive, you are saving the State £60,000 in capital expenditure but it is very difficult to put this across to economists or people in the Department of Health and other such Departments because they will tell you that money saved is not money realizable.

Prof. Jessop: What percentage of our funds are spent on the mental health field?—almost nothing. The Medico-Social Research Board has a project for a study of mental health which is costing perhaps one-fifth of its total funds. The Medical Research Council supports a relatively small project in the mental health field. I think it probably costs of the order of £2,000-£2,500 per year which is perhaps 5% of our total funds. The reason for this is that in the past we have not had in the Medical Research Council any good project put forward to us by people who want funds for research. This is true. This is to a certain extent why we are here. The Medical Research Council has been conscious that with this considerable problem in the country we could be accused of not doing anything about it. The reason we are not doing anything about it is that we have not enough funds to start a big project of our own and we have not been receiving applications from people for funds to investigate specific themes that they want to study. I think that second factor is to be traced back to the fact that it is only recently that wholetime departments of psychiatry have been started in the medical schools, these are the places where we must expect research to be fostered.

Prof. Russell Davis: It does seem to me at the present time that young people are getting themselves extremely interested and involved in mental health problems in the community. In secondary schools pupils are beginning to do projects where they are involved in identifying family problems, the location of invalids or the location of specific health problems. It seems to me that since we are evidently going to be extremely short in research money we have to think of how we can mobilize this kind of voluntary effort to do a good deal of data collection for us. Now in the mental health field, particularly, there are important social factors where the actual techniques of data collection are relatively easy. They don't involve pieces of apparatus. They don't involve expensive capital on building or laboratories or anything else of this kind. It simply needs the provision of guidance for young people, voluntary groups and so on, to do systematic or reasonably systematic studies of, for instance, family structure in relation to particular kinds of problems. So one's hope is that if money is going to be spent, it can be done by having one or two people who are concerned in organizing this kind of research. I don't know very much about the existing examples of this type of project but what I have heard about them struck me that this was the kind of enterprise that could well be drafted without much additional expenditure. If you could do that you would be doing two things, you would greatly disseminate information about these kinds of problems amongst the community which I think is absolutely of vital importance. The other is you could get quite large quantities of data on the cheap and it could be quite reasonably good quality data.

Prof. Browne: I am involved in planning services for the aged this year for the eastern area of Ireland and I have already found some of the suggestions here of real practical value. I am not saying that I can get finance to implement them but I would certainly put forward this point of view to the Department of Health, because the reinforcing of what Dr. Murray has said is particularly found in ageing also, that it is going to cost this country millions of pounds in clogging our health services if we don't invest in research. That now may not be the best reason but it certainly is a very cogent practical reason because our general hospitals are becoming full of old people, it is causing housing problems and so on and we are going to be spending a lot of money on it anyway. I think it would be far more productive to spend a relatively small amount of money along the sort of lines suggested here, which could have quite vast implications over a number of years in improving the health services.

Rev. Prof. O'Doherty: To clarify a little on the same topic of funding research, I think it is quite clear that priorities have to be established among all the suggestions and I thought that the assembly might like to know one or two items. Because of the lack of communication between research people we have seen a good deal of overlap already in this country and there will be a great deal more unless we are careful. For example, Economic and Social Research Institute has a budget of about £$\frac{1}{2}$ million a year and they have a large team of research people working on the family relationships, family lateral displacement and so on; the Human Sciences Committee of the Department of Industry and Commerce spends between £20,000 and £30,000 a year on the mental health problems of the work situation and the Educational Research Centre under the Minister of Education disposes of a figure which I do not know but it is certainly of the order of £30,000-£40,000 a year and they are concerned very much at this time with home and school climate, developmental problems and mental health problems in the school. I thought I would mention all this because if priorities have to be chosen, and I think they should be, this would simplify the cost considerably.

Dr. Hathway: As a researcher always searching for funds, what other sources of money are there? Surely there are other charitable bodies that you can tackle. Are there any world bodies— what about WHO, for example, would you like to sponsor a project in this area and failing all this what about the pharmaceutical industry which, after all, sells millions of pounds worth of drugs to the mentally disordered. Following up on what

Professor Russell Davis was saying, children do quite a lot in England especially in the public schools with regard to helping mentally disabled and geriatric people. This is an alternative to sort of combat training. One of our children used to fly aeroplanes but the other used to help the mentally disordered in this way.

Prof. Daly: I would like to preface my question with a little comment and that is to say that I'm sure that most of the invited people here feel that this has been a marvellously run conference by the organizers and also a most enjoyable series of papers in terms of both information and entertainment. It has been particularly an interesting one for me personally because being short of staff in Cork we have to teach our own Behavioural Science Course and this has been very instructional and provided for a great deal of revision as well. But the question I have for the organizers is regarding the nature of the theme of the conference. I feel that in a country like ours our first priority obviously is going to be the need of the country and the second priority is going to be the resources—the need I think is information, very basic information of an epidemiological kind.

In terms of resources one must think of the actual researchers, trained researchers we have here; people trained in epidemiology are amongst the trained researchers we have. We don't unfortunately have any ethologists in the country to my knowledge. We have a visiting anthropologist, we don't have a sleep laboratory. I don't think we are likely to set up a primate laboratory. A sleep laboratory as I understand it is immensely expensive. Having lived next door to Dr. Lewis and his laboratory for some years I am very well acquainted with the cost of it. So I'd like some information about the theme of the conference and its relatedness both to the problems of the country and the opportunities here for research.

Dr. Cullen: Our enterprise if you like was one in which we hoped to bring the sorts of people to this country who would not normally come here. As Professor Daly has said, we have no ethologists here and we have few people working with animals, particularly primates in this sort of way and I think it is unlikely that we will see this developed for some time in any case. So, therefore, I feel the first purpose of our conference was to bring to this country workers in these fields which are beginning to be seen to ask questions, at least, which are basic about behaviour. We felt that we ought to start from this sort of base before we undertook any other conference of the scientific kind in the mental health field.

Dr. Kagan: This word primate is a curious one. When Zuckermann first started to publish his book on 'The Sex of the Monkeys at the Zoo' he wanted to call it 'The Sex Life of the Primate' but, of course, in England the primate is the Archbishop of Canterbury.

I think the point Professor Daly was trying to bring out is that this is a rather peculiar meeting and I am very grateful for its peculiarities because it is when you have stones up that you find things underneath. I think they will be extremely useful to the people who are planning research in Ireland in this field. I'd hate to decide on which way they would go about things, indeed how to lever up some cash. I think that there are always bonuses. These sort of meetings make people think. That is always a good thing. People are going to go away and think about something in the next week or month or year, that is due to their having been at this meeting, not every one of us, but even if one does, it may turn out to be well worth while. I would like to thank the organizers of this meeting for, on behalf of all of us, the excellent organization and friendliness with which it has been done. I would like to thank then also in particular the backroom boys and girls, who have worked extremely hard, efficiently and looked pleasant about it.

Prof. Jessop: I would like to say one thing, I am the only actual member of The Medical Research Council who has been able to attend all of these sessions of the conference. While I started off about a year and a half or two years ago by being terribly sceptical about how this thing would work out and that scepticism and doubt loomed larger in my mind for the first six months with all the various complications, but it wasn't resolved until I found that the people meeting here were really people, that I had been writing to people that existed and I saw what they looked like. The proceedings have gone extremely well and the Medical Research Council will be extremely gratified to hear this when they meet next week.

But getting a little bit nearer the bone as it were, we did feel we have failed in stimulating interest in mental health because we have not had any projects worthwhile over a great number of years, no applications and we were not able to ask the Minister for funds especially for this particular area of research.

In due course we hope the Irish people, psychologists and scientists, who have come here will be able to produce projects, good sound projects for the Medical Research Council or the Medico-Social Research Board—I happen also to be a member of that body—which they will be able to put to the Minister and be able to get more funds. I am quite certain there are funds in the Department of Health if we got proper good projects to put up to them. I am very sympathetic towards the views expressed by Dr. Hathway and Professor Russell Davis about the ways and means of getting funds from other places and getting things done on the cheap. I have been an epidemiologist now for some time and my experience of getting epidemiological work done on the cheap is that it is much easier in theory than it is in practice. You can get a whole lot of girls, give them questionnaires or instructions of other kinds and that goes very well for perhaps a few weeks or a few months. Then they get something else to do, they get near the end of their course or they get married or something, then you train new ones and before you know where you are, you are in a shocking mess. Unless you have a really good core of research workers who have to be paid and therefore can be expected to keep their noses to the grindstone, you really don't get solid work done. So I think we have to envisage a situation in which we are supported in our demands to the Minister for Health for more funds by a solid body of good standard projects put up to us. I am not going to say that the first good project is going to get all the money that is required. We have to have a load of pressure on this Department before we even have the first trickle of financial results. But we will get nothing at all if we go on the way we have been going. The Medical Research Council is founded since 1937 and in all those years we have nothing to spend on mental health. So with that addressed more especially to all our Irish colleagues, I thank you, Sir, particularly for taking Chair at this meeting and for your contributions earlier and everybody else who came here. I have nothing more to say.

Dr. Kagan: Thank you very much. The meeting adjourns.